PENGUIN BOOKS

THE PENGUIN HISTORY OF ECONOMICS

Roger Backhouse is Emeritus Professor of the History and Philosophy of Economics in the Department of Economics at Birmingham Business School.

ROGER E. BACKHOUSE

The Penguin History of Economics

New and Revised

PENGUIN BOOKS

PENGUIN BOOKS

UK | USA | Canada | Ireland | Australia
India | New Zealand | South Africa

Penguin Books is part of the Penguin Random House group of companies
whose addresses can be found at global.penguinrandomhouse.com.

First published by Penguin Books 2002
Revised and updated edition published in Penguin Books 2023

006

Copyright © Roger E. Backhouse, 2002, 2023

The moral right of the author has been asserted

Set in 9.25/12.5pt Sabon LT Std
Typeset by Jouve (UK) Milton Keynes
Printed and bound in Great Britain by Clays Ltd, Elcograf S.p.A.

A CIP catalogue record for this book is available from the British Library

The authorized representative in the EEA is Penguin Random House Ireland,
Morrison Chambers, 32 Nassau Street, Dublin D02 YH68

ISBN: 978-1-802-06301-1

www.greenpenguin.co.uk

Contents

Preface to the First Edition   vii

Preface to the Second Edition   ix

Prologue   1

1 The Ancient World   13

2 The Middle Ages   31

3 The Emergence of the Modern World View – the Sixteenth Century   53

4 Science, Politics and Trade in Seventeenth-century England   67

5 Absolutism and Enlightenment in Eighteenth-century France   93

6 The Scottish Enlightenment of the Eighteenth Century   119

7 The Emergence of Political Economy   143

8 Mid-Victorian Political Economy   165

9 The Split between History and Theory in Europe, 1870–1914   185

10 The Rise of American Economics, 1870–1939   207

11 Money and the Business Cycle, 1898–1945   235

12 Quantitative Economics   265

13 From Marshall to Mathematical Economics   281

14 Welfare Economics and Socialism, 1870–1945   301

15 The Second World War and After   321

16 Markets and the State since 1945   347

CONTENTS

17 Macroeconomics and Policy, 1939–2008   369

18 Economics in the Twenty-first Century   391

Epilogue   413

A Note on the Literature   421

Notes   447

Index   459

Preface to the First Edition

Most of this book was written during my tenure of a British Academy Research Readership from 1998 to 2000. I am grateful to the British Academy for its support, and to several colleagues who read various drafts of the manuscript and whose detailed comments have helped me remove many errors and improve the argument. These are Mark Blaug, Anthony Brewer, Bob Coats, Mary Morgan, Denis O'Brien, Mark Perlman, Geert Reuten and Robert Swanson. I also wish to thank those subscribers to the History of Economics Society's email list who answered my requests for bits of information (usually dates) that I could not find myself (Bob Dimand proved a mine of information). I am also very grateful to Fatima Brandao and Antonio Amoldovar for inviting me to teach a course at the University of Oporto, which helped me to sort out my ideas on how to organize the material in the second half of the book. Stefan McGrath, at Penguin Books, encouraged me to embark on this project, and was patient when I overshot the initial deadline by a long time. He also provided helpful suggestions, as did Bob Davenport, whose editing of the final draft was exemplary and saved me from many mistakes. None of these people, of course, bears responsibility for any errors that may remain. Last, but definitely not least, I would like to thank my family: Alison, Robert and Ann.

Preface to the Second Edition

The new edition of this book reflects the enormous increase in the literature in the twenty years since it was first published. Mark Blaug, an early inspiration, once expressed the view that after the millennium there would be a sharp increase in interest in what had happened to economics since the Second World War. His prediction turned out to be correct. Although the book's basic structure and many of its assessments have held up well, the first edition therefore no longer reflects the latest scholarship. Not only has the history of economics increasingly been brought much nearer to the present day, often by young scholars, but the way in which the subject is approached has changed, often for the better. There has been much greater engagement between economists studying the history of their field and other historians who have developed an increased interest in the discipline, reflecting the increased prominence of economic arguments in society. The list of scholars from whom I have learned is too long for it to be possible to acknowledge them all. I would like, however, to pick out a few who were particularly important but who are no longer with us: Mark Blaug, mentioned earlier; Denis O'Brien, from whose vast knowledge of economics I learned much, Donald Winch, who did more than anyone else to persuade me that, especially in earlier periods, the history of economics should not be considered in isolation from the societies in which economists worked; Craufurd Goodwin, with his interest in policy and the unconventional aspects of economics; Tony Brewer, a former teacher who remained a continual source of encouragement; and Antonio Amoldovar, with whom I had long conversations on my repeated visits to Portugal to teach the course he oversaw.

The bulk of the revisions relate to the twentieth and twenty-first centuries, though there are changes throughout the book. For example, economic thinking is now related to eighteenth-century debates on luxury and the incredibly widely read *Telemachus* by Fénélon. More attention is paid than in the first edition to the way Adam Smith was interpreted (arguably misinterpreted) in the early nineteenth century. The coverage of the twentieth century has been reorganized and expanded, emphasizing the application of economics to policy, including ideas of market failure and government failure, as well as the development of economic theory. There is a new chapter on economics in the twenty-first century, something obviously not possible in the first edition, published in 2002. As well as discussing how economists' methods have changed, it focuses on a sample of topics widely considered to be of great importance, namely globalization and inequality, the financial crisis and the environment. Throughout the book I have tried to be more alert to women who have made significant contributions to the discipline, from Jane Marcet to Esther Duflo. There is an entire section on Joan Robinson, whom I inexplicably overlooked in the first edition.

As with the first edition, I am indebted to friends and colleagues who have read draft material, providing advice and helping me to avoid errors that I would otherwise have made. The revisions also reflect many of the things I have learned from co-authors with whom I have worked since the first edition. Though only some of them have seen the revisions, the list of people to whom I am indebted includes Bradley Bateman, Antoinette Baujard, Mauro Boianovsky, Ivan Boldyrev, Beatrice Cherrier, Philippe Fontaine, Verena Halsmayer, Lars Jonung, Steven Medema, Tamotsu Nishizawa and Keith Tribe. I list them purely in alphabetical order, but two people need to receive particular thanks: Keith Tribe, with whom I taught a course for several years and wrote a textbook, and whose ideas changed the way I thought about several topics; and Steven Medema, who has offered advice on virtually everything I have written over the past few years, including the revisions to this book.

Prologue

THE HISTORY OF ECONOMICS

This book is about the history of attempts to understand economic phenomena. It is about what has variously been described as the history of economic thought, the history of economic ideas, the history of economic analysis and the history of economic doctrines. It is not, except incidentally, concerned with the economic phenomena themselves but with the ways in which people have tried to make sense of them. Like the history of philosophy or the history of science, this is a branch of intellectual history. To illustrate the point, the subject of the book is not the Industrial Revolution, the rise of big business or the Great Depression – it is how people such as Adam Smith, Karl Marx, John Maynard Keynes and many lesser-known figures have perceived and analysed the economic world.

The story told here is largely a story of Western economics – of ideas developed in Europe and North America. There are several reasons for this, in addition to my lack of knowledge of non-Western economics. The main one is that the economic ideas that are dominant today, due above all to the economic, political and cultural dominance of the United States, stem from that tradition. There was economic thinking in China, India, Iran and other societies with rich cultural traditions, but they have not had the same worldwide impact that Western ideas have achieved. Thus the book starts with ancient Greek thought, not because it was superior to ideas being developed at the same time (or earlier) in other parts of the world, but because that is where the roots of the economics discussed in the book lie. A book such as this has, of necessity, to be selective in its coverage, and developments outside the Western world have been discussed only where they feed into that story.

Writing the history of economic ideas involves weaving together many different stories. It is clearly necessary to tell the story of the people who were doing the thinking – the economists themselves. It is also necessary to cover economic history. Natural scientists can assume, for example, that the structure of the atom and the molecular structure of DNA are the same now as in the time of Aristotle. Economists cannot make comparable assumptions. The world confronting economists has changed radically, even over the past century. Maybe there is a sense in which 'human nature' has always been the same, but the precise meaning and significance of this are not clear. Political history matters too, for political and economic events are inextricably linked, and economists have, as often as not, been involved in politics, either directly or indirectly. They have sought to influence policy, and political concerns have influenced them. Finally, it is necessary to consider changes in related disciplines and in the underlying intellectual climate. Economists' preconceptions and ways of thinking are inevitably formed by the culture in which they are writing. The history of economics has therefore to touch on the histories of religion, theology, philosophy, mathematics and science, as well as economics and politics.

What makes the problem difficult is that the relationships between these various histories are not simple. There is no justification for claiming, for example, that connections run solely from economic or political history to economic ideas. Economic ideas feed into politics and influence what happens in the economy (not necessarily in the way that their inventors intended); the three types of history are interdependent. The same is true of the relationship between the history of economics and intellectual history more generally. Economists have sought to apply to their own discipline lessons learned from science – whether the science of Aristotle, Newton or Darwin. They are influenced by philosophical movements such as those of the Enlightenment, positivism or postmodernism, as well as by influences of which we are completely unconscious. However, links also run the other way. Darwin's theory of natural selection, for example, was strongly influenced by the economic ideas of Malthus. In short, economic ideas are an integral component of culture.

One factor that contributes to the interdependence of economics and other disciplines and intellectual life in general is that, at least until recently, economics was not an activity carried out by a group of specialists called 'economists'. Modern disciplinary boundaries simply did not exist; also, the role of universities in society has changed almost beyond recognition. The people responsible for developing economic ideas included theologians, lawyers, philosophers, merchants and government officials. Some of these held academic positions, but many did not. For example, Adam Smith had an academic position, but only for a small part of his career, his main work being done later in life. Moreover, he was not primarily an economist: he was a moral philosopher, and his economic ideas formed part of a much broader analysis of society, rooted in moral philosophy. Furthermore, the people who wrote the conventional canon of economic literature occupied various positions in the societies in which they lived, which means that comparisons across time have to be made with great care. When Thomas of Chobham wrote about trade and finance in the early thirteenth century, he was offering guidance for priests taking confession. Perhaps the present-day counterpart to his work should be sought not in modern academic economics but in papal encyclicals. Gerard de Malynes and Thomas Mun, both of whom wrote in seventeenth-century England and are considered to have contributed to our understanding of foreign trade and exchange rates, were respectively a government official and a merchant. Perhaps they should be considered the forerunners of people like the late Dutch economist Jacques Polak at the International Monetary Fund, or the businesspeople and financiers who contribute to the *Economist* or the *Wall Street Journal*. This book is based on the assumption that we should not treat past writers as though they were modern academic economists but should try to understand what they thought they were doing.

3

WHAT IS ECONOMICS?

The discussion so far has rested on the assumption that we know what economics and economic phenomena are. But economics is notoriously difficult to define. Perhaps the most widely used definition of the subject is the one offered by Lionel Robbins: 'Economics is the science which studies human behaviour as a relationship between ends and scarce means which have alternative uses.'[1] According to this view, the phenomena we associate with economics (prices, money, production, markets, bargaining) can be viewed either as consequences of scarcity or as ways in which people try to overcome the problem of scarcity. Robbins's definition goes a long way towards capturing features common to all economic problems, but it represents a very specific, limited view of the nature of such problems. Why, for example, should the operations of multinational corporations in developing countries, or the design of policy to reduce mass unemployment, be seen as involving choices about how to use scarce resources? It is perhaps ironic that Robbins's definition dates from 1932, during the depths of the Great Depression, when the world's major economic problem was that vast resources of capital and labour were lying idle.

A different type of definition is that of the great Victorian economist Alfred Marshall, who defined economics as the study of mankind in the ordinary business of life.[2] We know what he means by this, and it is hard to disagree, though his definition is very imprecise. It could be made more precise by saying that economics deals with the production, distribution and consumption of wealth or, even more precisely, is about how production is organized in order to satisfy human wants. Other definitions include ones that define economics as the logic of choice or as the study of markets or the business system.

Perhaps as important as what these definitions say is what they do not say. The subject matter of economics can include more than the buying and selling of goods, markets, the organization of firms, the stock exchange or even money. These are all economic phenomena, but there are societies in which they do not occur. It is possible, for example, to have societies in which money does not exist or performs only a ceremonial function, in which production is not undertaken by firms, or in which transactions are undertaken without markets. Such societies face economic problems – how to produce goods, how to distribute them, and so on – even though the phenomena we normally associate with economic life are missing. Phenomena such as firms, the stock exchange, money, and so on can better be seen as institutions that have arisen to solve more fundamental economic problems common to all societies. It is better, therefore, to define economics in relation to these more fundamental problems, rather than in relation to institutions that exist in some societies but not in others.

Anyone writing a systematic 'principles of economics' has to decide on a specific definition of the subject and work within it. This is, however, a dangerous approach for the historian because, even if we can settle on a precise definition that fits today's economics (and even that may be difficult), such a definition may not fit the thinking of previous generations. If we are to take past ideas seriously, we must make some effort to understand how they were understood at the time. Even the term 'economics' may be inappropriate. Faced with this problem, given that our aim is to understand how economics got where it is today, a good strategy is to take a more pragmatic approach.

When asked to define economics, the eminent economist and intellectual historian Jacob Viner is reputed to have quipped, 'Economics is what economists do.' This suggests that we should start with the ideas that make up contemporary economics – ideas that are found in economics curricula and are being developed by people recognized as economists. These, however, do not provide a precise definition, for the boundaries of the discipline are indistinct. Academics, journalists, civil servants, politicians and other writers (even novelists) all develop and work with economic ideas. The boundaries of what constitutes economics are further blurred by the fact that economic issues are analysed not only by 'economists' but also by historians, geographers, ecologists, management scientists and engineers. Such writing may not be what professional economists would consider 'good' or 'serious' economics, and it may be riven with fallacious arguments, but that is a different matter – it is still economics. Approaching the subject in this very pragmatic way might seem less desirable than defining economics in terms of its subject matter. In practice, however, it is a workable approach and probably corresponds with what most historians actually do, even if they profess to work within a tight analytical definition of the subject.

Having decided on what constitutes contemporary economics, it is possible to work backwards, tracing the roots of the ideas that are found there, as far as it is decided to go. Some of these roots will clearly lead outside the subject (for example, to Newtonian mechanics or the Reformation), and the historian of economics will not pursue these further. Others will lead to ideas that we see as antecedents of modern economics, even though their presentation and content may be very different from those of modern economics, and these will be included in the history. The result of such choices is that the further we go back into history, the more debatable it becomes whether or not certain ideas count as 'economics'. This means that the book will not be concerned with 'When did economics begin?' because there is no reason to think that economics began at a specific moment. Our choice of where to begin is essentially arbitrary and to see the subject as beginning with a particular individual or group is to misunderstand the process through which it emerged.

The significance of this approach is best seen by thinking about where economics might have begun. Some scholars would argue that economics does not begin until we enter the modern world (say the fifteenth or sixteenth century, though this is a controversial claim), or even until the eighteenth century, when Adam Smith systematized so much of the work of his predecessors. Economics, the argument runs, is about analysing human behaviour and the way people interact through markets and respond to changes in their economic environment. Early writers, it is claimed, had quite different concerns, such as moral and theological issues about the justice of market exchange or lending at interest, and their work should not be classified as economics.

There is, however, a big problem with this argument: it is simply not possible to draw a clear dividing line between what constitutes economic analysis and what does not, or between what constitutes 'proper' or 'real' economics and what does not. For example, the moral and theological arguments of medieval theologians about the justice of commercial activities presuppose an understanding of how the economy operates. The economic content of such writing may, to our eyes, be half hidden or obscure, but it is there. The view underlying this book is that economic ideas were present even in antiquity, and that those ancient ideas are relevant in trying to locate the origins of modern economics. Furthermore, even today, economics deals with normative questions (questions about what ought to be done), some of which parallel those tackled by the ancients. Economists are forever arguing that this policy or that will improve the welfare of society. It may be unfashionable to think of this as involving ethics, or morality; nonetheless, ethical presuppositions underlie modern economics just as much as they underlay Aristotle's thinking about the market. The Old Testament contains many economic ideas, as does the poetry of Homer. In a general history of economics, it may not be necessary to dwell long on these texts, but they are part of the story.

The book starts with ancient Greece and the world of the Old Testament, not because this is where economics began, but because this is as far back as the written records out of which modern (Western) economics emerged can be taken.

UNDERSTANDING THE PAST

The approach outlined above, focusing on what has been termed 'the filiation of economic ideas', is now unfashionable. In a postmodern world, the fashion is to stress the historical relativity of ideas and to decry any attempt to view past ideas from the perspective of the present. However, anyone who writes a history of economic thought necessarily views the past, to some extent, from the perspective of the present. Simply to focus on 'economic' ideas is to select past ideas according to a modern category. However much we try to do so, we can never completely escape from our preconceptions attached to the questions we are trying to answer. It is better to state these preconceptions as explicitly as possible rather than to pretend that they do not exist.

7

A common approach is to write a history that covers the accepted canon of 'important' writings on economics. However, to do this is to rely on judgements that others have made in the past. It does not avoid the problem of one's choice of material being influenced by one's interests. What usually happens is that historians start with a conventional canon – a list of the works, figures or movements that are considered to represent the economics of the past. They then modify this, increasing the emphasis in some places, reducing it in others in response to the questions that interest them and the evidence they find. As economics has changed, so too have views about what constitutes the appropriate canon.

Writing the history as a story of progress from crude beginnings to the 'truth' reached by the historian's friends, contemporaries or other heroes results in what has come to be called 'Whig history', after the nineteenth-century Whigs who told the story of Britain in this way. This is the approach favoured by many economists, including some who write histories of economics. For example, the eminent mid-twentieth-century economist Paul Samuelson once gave an address titled, 'Out of the closet: a program for the Whig history of economic science'.[3] The main reason for this attitude is that an economist typically finds it hard to accept that their own generation's theories and techniques (to which they may have contributed) are not necessarily superior to those of earlier generations. However, such an approach is likely to misrepresent the views of past economists whose assumptions and purposes may have been different from those of modern economists. Reading past ideas as crude versions of modern economics may result in the creation of caricatures, and readers are right to be suspicious of such histories.

At the other pole, the history can be told as a story of retrogression – as an account of how important ideas were lost – perhaps because they were thought politically inconvenient or because they did not fit conventional ideas about how to do science. Thus Marxists and some Keynesians claim that contemporary economics has lost sight of key insights that are to be found in the writings of Marx and Keynes. Such accounts recognize that history does not necessarily involve progress, but, like Whig history, it involves letting present-day concerns shape our view of the past. Like Whig history, such accounts can be enlightening, but they need to be treated with great caution.

However, examining the past in order to understand the present need not mean telling the story as one of progress or retrogression. The reasons why ideas evolved as they did will include historical accidents, vested interests, prejudices, misunderstandings, mistakes and all sorts of things that do not fit into such accounts. The story may involve certain lines of inquiry dying out, or moving away from what is currently considered economics. We may discover, when we look back, that earlier generations were asking different questions – perhaps even questions we find it hard to understand – with the result that notions of progress and retrogression become problematic.

THE STORY TOLD HERE

The story told in this book clearly reflects certain conventional views about what constitutes economics – certain topics are included because it is 'obvious' that they should be there. The publisher (not to mention many readers) would have been unhappy if it said nothing about Adam Smith, David Ricardo, Karl Marx or John Maynard Keynes. It is recognizably a history of economics, as the term is commonly understood. However, it departs from the conventional canon both in the relative importance attached to different figures and in many of the topics that are included. It also tries to place people in an appropriate historical context – hopefully one that the figures discussed would have recognized.

The book is not organized around the 'great figures' of the past, as was once common practice. Chapters typically start with a discussion of the historical context and proceed from there to the economic ideas that emerged. The emphasis on economic, political and broader intellectual history varies throughout the book, and these dimensions of the story generally become less prominent as the story unfolds. The most important reason for this is that when we are discussing periods when economics was less clearly distinguished from other disciplines it is more important to discuss ideas outside economics. Indeed, it may not even be clear whether certain ideas should be seen as economics, theology, political theory or philosophy, for academic disciplines as we now understand them emerged only towards the end of the nineteenth century.

The task of distinguishing economics from other types of knowledge becomes easier as we approach the twentieth century because, by then, economics was developing into an academic subject and an economist was increasingly someone who had been trained and had a qualification in the subject. The problems economists tackled were increasingly ones that arose within the discipline, even if they were often motivated by problems in society at large. Throughout the book, there is an emphasis on the communities and circumstances out of which economic ideas emerged, rather than simply on individuals: on what could loosely be called the sociology of the economics profession. Alongside the development of economics as an academic discipline, there have been changes in the position of economists (or, more accurately, the position of people reflecting on economic matters) in society, and this has influenced the way in which ideas have developed. The result is that chapters dealing with early material contain much general history but, as the story develops, there is a narrower focus on economic ideas and general history plays a smaller part, though it is not entirely absent.

So although the book covers the conventional canon, it seeks to go beyond it in many ways. The Islamic world enters the medieval story. Political philosophy and the Hobbesian challenge are an important element in the chapter on seventeenth-century England. Smith is viewed as a moral philosopher and is set in the context of the Scottish Enlightenment and eighteenth-century debates over commerce and luxury consumption. Malthus is portrayed not just as a pure economist, or demographer, but as someone who contributed to contemporary political debates. Theoretical contributions of early-nineteenth-century French and German writers are placed alongside those of their English counterparts. Chamberlin is discussed in the context of US industrial economics, not that of the British cost controversy. A distinction is drawn between the Keynesian revolutions in Britain and the United States. The list could be continued.

The most significant change, however, is that whereas the traditional canon focuses on the eighteenth and nineteenth centuries, here, the twentieth century is a major part of the story and there is a chapter on the twenty-first century. In covering this period, I have attempted to give as broad a picture of the subject as possible, albeit through discussing some case studies that illustrate what has happened. Given that my main aim is to explain how the discipline reached its present state, developments within its theoretical 'core' (the traditional domain of the history of economic thought) are clearly important. However, they are not the whole story, for a crucial characteristic of modern economics is the collection and analysis of data, especially statistical data. Advising policymakers is, of course, as important as it has always been.

Readers who are familiar with more traditional histories of economics may expect to find discussion centred on 'schools of thought' such as scholasticism, mercantilism, classical and neoclassical economics. However, I have largely avoided such terms. It is useful to use the term 'scholastic' as shorthand for the theologians who, from the thirteenth to the sixteenth centuries, worked in European universities, but the term 'scholasticism' is not used because it might be taken to imply that they all thought in the same way. They did not. In so far as there are common themes in their writings, these can be brought out without artificially packaging them into a school of thought.

The term 'mercantilism' is even more problematic. It is derived from 'the mercantile system', a term used by Adam Smith as a label for policies he believed were misconceived. He was anything but fair to his predecessors and the term fails to do justice to the rich variety of thinking about economic problems that can be found in the literature it is usually used to denote. It is true that arguments during the two to three hundred years before Smith's magnum opus often focused on the government policy, that there was widespread concern with money and trade, and that it was widely believed that economic activity needed to be regulated to ensure prosperity (all features of 'mercantilism'), but this is very little on which to hang a coherent school of thought. Describing several centuries' thinking about economic questions as 'mercantilist' distracts from the many debates that took place and the fundamental differences between, for example, English merchants responding to the commercial crisis of the 1620s and Colbert's attempts to use economic policy to underpin the political ambitions of the 'Sun king', Louis XIV.

'Classical economics' is the term used by Karl Marx as a label for the ideas of his predecessors and contemporaries. Again, although he drew on these ideas, he was a critic, believing himself to be proposing a deeper way of thinking. Like 'mercantilism', the term suggests greater homogeneity in the period's economic thinking than was the case. The same is true of 'neoclassical' economics, a term invented by Thorstein Veblen to lambast an economics that, in his view, failed to deal with key aspects of the real world.

An issue of which historians of economics have become much more conscious in the twenty years since the first edition of the book is the role played by women. Saying more about the role of women presents a challenge, as even some female historians recognize. Women were important but, for obvious reasons, until recently, they were unable to have the same influence on economic thinking as were men. To pay the same attention to Adam Smith as to his female contemporaries would therefore distort the history. Notwithstanding that, some women were significant figures and so, in revising the book, I have tried to be alert to places where, in the first edition, I failed to acknowledge the role of women, often as co-authors, and sometimes in the background. I make no claim that the resulting treatment is enough, but I hope it is a significant move in the right direction.

In telling this story, I have inevitably drawn on accounts written by specialists in the various periods the book covers. Any 'innovations' in the book draw on such works. The number of places where I have been able to depart from the conventional story reflects the range of recent work on the history of economic thought. My main debts are acknowledged in the suggestions for further reading at the end of the book.

I

The Ancient World

HOMER AND HESIOD

Plato suggested that Homer educated Greece, his epic poems providing the values by which life should be lived. In the literary papyri found in Egypt, Homeric scrolls outnumber those by all other authors put together. Even today, stories of Hector, Achilles, Troy and the journeys of Odysseus form part of Western culture. It is not clear whether the *Iliad* and the *Odyssey* should be regarded as the work of a single individual or as compilations of the work of many poets, but in either case they represent the writing down, somewhere around 750–725 BCE, of a long oral tradition. The Homeric epics, together with the poems of Hesiod (*c.* 700 BCE), are as far back as the written record takes us in Europe.

The society described in the *Iliad* and the *Odyssey* probably reflects, in part, the Mycenaean (Bronze Age) world of Troy around 1400–1100 BCE, and in part Homer's own time. It was ordered and hierarchical, based not on market relationships but on the distribution of wealth through gifts, theft, prizes for winning competitions, plunder received in war, and tribute paid by defeated cities to their conquerors. Troy might have fallen earlier, it has been suggested, if the Greek army had not been so intent on pillaging. Trade was viewed by Homer as a secondary and inferior way of acquiring wealth. Heroes were aristocratic warriors, rewarded strictly according to their rank. Gifts were governed by a code of reciprocity, in which it was important that, when gifts were exchanged, those involved should hold the same rank after the exchange as before. Hosts were obliged to provide hospitality and gifts for their guests, who in turn had an obligation to provide gifts, perhaps to the hosts' families, at a later date in return.

The basis for this economy was the household, understood as the landowner, his family and all the slaves working on an estate. Owners and slaves would work alongside each other. Prosperity was seen by Homer as the result of being in a well-ordered, rich household. On the other hand, there was suspicion of excessive wealth – households should be rich, but not too rich. There were, of course, traders and craftsmen (we read of Greek soldiers exchanging their plunder for provisions, and craftsmen were brought in to do certain tasks on landed estates), but they were less important than landed estates. Even if he gained his freedom, a slave who lost his place on a landed estate might lose his security. The acquisition of wealth through trade was regarded as distinctly inferior to obtaining it through agriculture or military exploits.

Of the two poems attributed to Hesiod, the one that is seen as having the most substantial economic content is *Works and Days*. He starts with two creation stories. One is the well-known story of Pandora's box. The other, undoubtedly influenced by Mesopotamian creation stories, tells of a descent from the golden age of the immortals, 'remote from ills, without harsh toil',[1] to a race of iron – those living in his own time – for whom toil and misery are everyday realities. Hesiod offers his readers much advice about coping with life under these conditions. *Works and Days* is a poem within an Eastern tradition of wisdom literature, moving seamlessly between advice that would nowadays be seen as ritualistic or astrological and practical advice on agriculture and on when to set sail in order to avoid being lost at sea. Though they fall within the same tradition, however, when compared with the Babylonian and Hebrew creation stories, Hesiod's stories (like those of Homer) are comparatively secular. It is Zeus who provides prosperity, and Hesiod regards morality and pleasing Zeus as the main challenges that men have to deal with, but the stories are the product of the author's own curiosity, not the work of priests.

Hesiod can be read as having realized that the basic economic problem is one of scarce resources. The reason men have to work is that 'the gods keep men's food concealed: otherwise you would easily work even in a day enough to provide you for the whole year without working'.[2] Choices have to be made between work (which leads to wealth) and leisure. Hesiod even suggests that competition can stimulate production, for it will cause craftsmen to emulate each other. However, though these ideas are clearly present in *Works and Days*, they are not expressed in anything like such abstract terms. Hesiod describes himself as a farmer, and says that his father was forced to emigrate owing to poverty. The virtues he sees as leading to prosperity are thus – not surprisingly – hard work, honesty and peace. His ideal is agricultural self-sufficiency, without war to destroy the farmer's produce. This is far from the aristocratic disparagement of work and support for martial virtues that can be found in Homer, but the two poets share the idea that security is bound up with land.

Hesiod's poetry provides a good illustration of the earliest writings on economic questions. Economic insights are there, but nothing is developed very far and it is difficult to know how much significance to attach to them.

ESTATE MANAGEMENT – XENOPHON'S *OIKONOMIKOS*

The period from the seventh to the fourth centuries BCE saw great literary, scientific and philosophical achievements. Thales (*c.*624–*c.*546 BCE) proposed the idea that water was the primal substance underlying all forms of life, and the notion that the earth was a disc floating on water. Anaximander (*c.*610–*c.*546 BCE) drew the first map of the known world and composed what is believed to be the first treatise written in prose. We know little of their reasoning, for very little of what they wrote has survived, but the important point is that they were trying to reason about the nature of the world, liberating themselves from mythology. Towards the end of the sixth century Pythagoras (*c.*570–*c.*490 BCE) used theory and contemplation as means of purifying the soul. Though he was engaged in what we would now see as a form of number mysticism, in which numbers and ratios have mystical properties, he and his followers made enduring contributions to philosophy and mathematics. The fifth century saw the emergence of playwrights, Aeschylus (c.525–456 BCE), Sophocles (c.495–406 BCE) and Euripides (c.480–406 BCE), and historians such as Herodotus (c.485–c.425 BCE) and Thucydides (c.460–c.400 BCE).

These developments form the background to the world of Xenophon (c.430–354 BCE) and Plato (c. 429–347 BCE). For this period there is virtually no economic data. Our knowledge of it therefore comes solely from political history. But we do know that the economy of this period was, like that of Homer's day, still based on agriculture, with landed estates as the main source of wealth. There had, however, been enormous political and economic changes in the intervening centuries. Among the most important of these were the reforms introduced in Athens by Solon, appointed archon, or civilian head of state, in 594 BCE. These curtailed the power of the aristocracy and laid the basis for democratic rule based on the election, by the property-owning classes, of a council of 400 members. Land was redistributed, laws were codified, and a silver currency was established. The Athenian merchant fleet was enlarged, and there was an expansion of trade. Specialized agriculture developed as Athens exported goods – notably olive oil – in return for grain. The old ideal of self-sufficiency began to break down.

Though intended to bring stability, Solon's reforms resulted in class divisions and political upheaval. Athens and the other Greek cities also became involved in a series of wars with the Persians. In 480 BCE Athens itself fell to the Persians, but the Persian fleet was defeated at Salamis. The following year the Persian army was defeated by the Spartans at Plataea and hostilities came to an end. The legacy of the Greek naval victory was that Athens became the leader of a maritime alliance of Greek states, exacting tribute from them. In effect, Athens was the centre of an empire, her great rival being Sparta. The strengths of Athens were trade and sea power; Sparta's position was based on agriculture and its army. War eventually broke out between the two states in 431 BCE – the start of the Peloponnesian War that ended with the defeat of Athens, in 404 BCE, and the dissolution of the naval league.

For the fifty years from the end of the Persian Wars until the start of the Peloponnesian War, Athens was essentially at peace. The result was a period of great prosperity known as the Periclean Age, after Pericles, who led the more democratic party from 461 to 430 BCE. Piracy was removed from the eastern Mediterranean, trade flourished, and commercial agriculture and manufacturing developed, along with many of the activities now associated with a commercial society: banking, credit, money-changing, commodity speculation and monopoly trading. One historian has written of Athens being 'a commercial centre with a complex of economic activities that was to remain unsurpassed until post-Renaissance Europe'.[3] The resulting prosperity was the basis for great building projects, such as the Parthenon.

Athenian democracy was direct, involving all the citizens, i.e. adult males of Athenian parentage. Even juries could involve hundreds of citizens, and the fondness of Athenians for litigation – in which plaintiffs and defendants had to speak for themselves – meant that it was important for people to be able to defend their own interests, and argue their case. There was thus a demand for training in rhetoric, which was provided by the Sophists. The Sophists were itinerant, travelling from one city to another, and, though the main requirement was for skills in public speaking, many of them believed that their pupils needed to know the latest discoveries in all fields. The Sophists were thus the first professional intellectuals in Greece – professors before there were universities.[4] The first and greatest of the Sophists was Protagoras (c.490–420 BCE), who taught successfully for forty years before being banished for his scepticism about the gods.

Socrates (469–399 BCE) emerged against this background of 'professional intellectuals'. Because they travelled, they could stand back from the laws and customs of individual cities. They engaged in abstract thought, and, though many paid respect to the gods, they looked for non-religious explanations of the phenomena they saw around them. What stands out about Socrates is his method: relentlessly asking questions. It was this that attracted to him pupils as able as Plato and Xenophon. He was, however, the butt of Aristophanes' satire in The Clouds, in which his questioning of the gods' responsibility for rain and thunder is ridiculed. As he wrote nothing himself, our knowledge of Socrates stems only from Aristophanes and, above all, from the dialogues of Plato and Xenophon. We can be confident about much in their accounts; however, it is often hard to know precisely which ideas should be attributed to Socrates himself and which come from Xenophon or Plato using him as a mouthpiece.

Xenophon came from the Athenian upper classes and, like all Socrates' pupils, was well off. For some reason (maybe linked to his association with Socrates, who was tried and executed in 399 BCE), he left Athens, and in 401 BCE he joined a military expedition to Persia, in an attempt to help Cyrus the Younger take the throne from his brother. The attempt failed, and Xenophon, if we are to believe his account of the event, was responsible for leading the troops back to Greece. From 399 to 394 BCE he fought for Sparta, after which he lived, under Spartan protection, on a country estate, until he returned to Athens in 365 BCE. Most of his writing was done in this more settled period of his life.

Oikonomikos, the title of Xenophon's work, is the origin of the words 'economist' and 'economics'. It is, however, better translated as 'the estate manager' or 'estate management'. Taken literally, it means 'household management', *oikos* being the Greek word for 'household', but by extension the word was used to refer to an estate, and Xenophon's *Oikonomikos* is in fact a treatise on managing an agricultural estate. Familiar Socratic themes such as an emphasis on self-discipline and training people to wield authority are found in the book, but its main theme is efficient organization. Given the Greeks' emphasis on the human element in production (perhaps a feature of a slave society), efficient management translated into effective leadership.

The prime requirement of an effective leader was to be knowledgeable in the relevant field, whether this was warfare or agriculture. Men would follow the man they saw as the superior leader, Xenophon claimed, and willing obedience was worth far more than forced obedience. Though he illustrated this with examples taken from war, Xenophon saw the same principles as applying in any activity. The other requirement for efficiency was order. Xenophon used the example of a Phoenician trireme (a ship propelled by three banks of oars) in which everything was so well stowed that the man in charge knew where everything was, even when he was not present. This was how an efficient estate should be run – with stores efficiently organized and accounted for. It was commonly believed that good organization could double productivity.

Seen from this perspective, Xenophon's emphasis on efficiency seems simply an exercise in management, applied to an agricultural estate rather than to a modern firm. His conception of the 'administrative art',[5] however, was much broader than this, extending to the allocation of resources in the state as a whole. He makes this clear when he discusses the way in which Cyrus the Great organized his empire, with one official in charge of protecting the population from attack and another in charge of improving the land. If either failed to do his job efficiently, the other would notice, for neither could perform his task properly if the other was not doing so. Without defence, the fruits of agriculture would be lost; and without enough agricultural output the country could not be defended. Though officials were given the right incentives, it was still necessary that the ruler took an interest in all the affairs of the state – agriculture as well as defence. Administrative authority, not the market mechanism, was the method by which resources would be efficiently allocated and productivity maximized.

It is also important to mention Xenophon's account of the division of labour, with which later writers including Plato, Aristotle and Adam Smith were probably familiar. He observed that in a small town the same workman may have to make chairs, doors, ploughs and tables, but he cannot be skilled in all these activities. In large cities, however, demand is so large that men can specialize in each of these tasks, becoming more efficient. Turning back to the estate, Xenophon argued that division of labour could be practised in the kitchen, anything prepared in such a kitchen being superior to food prepared in a smaller kitchen where one person has to perform all tasks.

Xenophon's model is of men interacting with nature – not with each other through markets. Productive efficiency involves managing the use of natural resources so as to get the most from them. His is a static world in which it is taken for granted that nature is known and understood. Trade and markets are peripheral. Given the development of trade and commerce in Athens by this time, it is perhaps surprising that agricultural estates are as central to Xenophon's view of economic activity as they were for Homer's. This can be explained by his position as a soldier and, for thirty years, a landowner under Spartan protection. For some of his contemporaries, such explanations are harder to defend.

PLATO'S IDEAL STATE

The background to Plato's *Republic*, which attempts to provide a blueprint for the ideal state, is the political turmoil that engulfed Athens and the other Greek city states in the fifth and fourth centuries BCE. Experience had taught Plato that neither democracy nor tyranny could provide a stable society. Leaders in a democracy would not do what was just but would use their office to gain support. Tyrants, on the other hand, would use their power to further their own interests, not those of the state as a whole. But without any leadership there would be chaos. Plato's solution to this dilemma was to create a class of philosopher-kings – the 'guardians' – who would rule the state in the interests of the whole society. These would be self-appointed, for they would be the only ones capable of understanding how society should be organized. In the ideal state their whole upbringing and way of life would be designed to train them for their role and to ensure that they fulfilled it properly. To ensure that the guardians would not become corrupt, pursuing their own interests, they would be forbidden to own property or even to handle gold and silver. They would receive what they needed to live as a wage from the rest of the community. Unlike tyrants, they would have to put the interests of the state first.

Plato's vision was concerned with the efficient organization of society – with a just society organized on rational principles. Like other Greek writers, he saw efficiency as involving the human element in production. Men should specialize in those activities for which they were naturally suited and should be trained accordingly. Indeed, the origins of cities (states) lay in specialization and the dependence of people on one another. He took the physical endowment of resources and technology for granted. His was a static world, in which everyone had a fixed place, maintained by efficient administration undertaken by disinterested rulers. Though he saw a role for trade, the role for markets in his ideal state was very limited. Consumer goods might be bought and sold, but property was to be allocated appropriately (on mathematical principles) between citizens. There would be no profits or payment of interest.

This view of the state presumed that cities would remain small. In a later work, Plato argued that the optimum number of households in a city was 5,040. The reason for this number was that it was divisible by the first ten integers, and so allowed division into an optimal number of administrative units. The idea that cities should remain small was consistent with the experience of Greek cities, constrained by the availability of agricultural land and resources. When populations rose, a city would organize an expedition to establish a colony. This colony would become a new city in which the Greek way of life would be maintained. Such colonies, which often became independent of the cities from which they stemmed, were to be found throughout the Mediterranean, notably in southern Italy, Sicily and North Africa.

Plato was an aristocrat, involved in Athenian public affairs, who fought several military campaigns. In his early life he had travelled widely, visiting the Pythagorean communities in Italy, from which he probably acquired his interest in mathematics. While in Sicily, he became involved with the ruler of Syracuse, unsuccessfully trying to train Dionysius II for leadership after the death of his father, Dionysius I, in 367 BCE. In around 375 BCE he founded his Academy (in the grove sacred to the hero Academus just outside Athens) in order to train statesmen to become philosophers. Unlike the school founded a few years earlier by Isocrates, which emphasized the teaching of rhetoric, Plato believed that it was more important to teach principles of good government. Several of his students became rulers (tyrants), and Plato saw the task of his Academy as offering advice to such people. In at least one case, a tyrant is believed to have moderated his rule in response to Plato's teaching.

ARISTOTLE ON JUSTICE
AND EXCHANGE

Aristotle (384–322 BCE) was a son of a physician and a student of Plato. He joined the Academy at the age of seventeen, and remained there until Plato's death twenty years later. The influence of Aristotle on subsequent generations was such that, for many, he was simply 'the philosopher'. His writing encompassed philosophy, politics, ethics, natural science, medicine and virtually all other fields of inquiry, and it dominated thinking in these areas for nearly 2,000 years. His contributions to what are now thought of as economic issues are found in two places: Book V of the *Nichomachean Ethics* and Book I of the *Politics*. In the former, he analysed the concept of justice; in the latter he was concerned with the nature of the household and the state.

In the Athenian legal system, men who were in dispute with each other had to go first to an arbitrator, who would try to reach a fair or equitable settlement. Only if the arbitrator's decision was unacceptable to one of the parties would the dispute go to court, in which case the court would have to decide on a settlement in between the limits set by the two parties' claims, or in between that set by the arbitrator and that claimed by the aggrieved party. In Book V of the *Nichomachean Ethics* Aristotle was considering the principles of justice that ought to apply in such disputes. This perspective is important, because it immediately establishes that he was thinking of principles that should apply in judicial decisions, and that he was dealing with cases of isolated exchange (in which individual buyers and sellers negotiate with each other about specific goods). He was not dealing with exchange in organized, competitive markets. Indeed, it is likely that, though trade was well developed in Athens by the fourth century BCE, competitive markets were few and far between. There is much evidence that prices of standard commodities were regulated (even the price of singers; if demand for the services of particular singers was too high, they would be allocated by a ballot), and the quality of manufactured goods was probably sufficiently variable that the price of each item would have had to be negotiated individually, as in isolated exchange.

When dealing with exchange and the distribution of goods, Aristotle distinguished between three types of justice. The first is distributive justice. This requires that goods (or honours, or whatever is being distributed) are distributed to people in proportion to their merit. This was a common problem in Aristotle's day, for much was distributed by the state – booty from war, silver from the mines at Laurium, and many other goods. Aristotle's concept of distributive justice was a very elastic notion, for merit can be defined in different ways in different settings. After a battle, merit might be measured by the contribution of soldiers to the victory. Within a partnership, justice would require that goods be distributed in proportion to the capital that each person had invested. Furthermore, different criteria may be used to assess merit: in a democracy it might be assumed that all citizens should receive an equal share, whereas in an oligarchy the oligarchs would be thought to merit larger shares than other citizens. The second type of justice is rectificatory justice – putting right previous injustices by compensating those who have lost out. Rectificatory justice restores equality. Finally comes reciprocal (or commutative) justice, or justice in exchange.

If two people exchange goods, how do we assess whether the transaction is just? One way, commonly understood in ancient Greece, is to argue that if exchange is voluntary, it must be just. Xenophon cited the example of two boys – one tall and with a short tunic, the other short and with a long tunic – who exchanged tunics. The conventional view was that this was a just exchange, for both boys gained from it. Aristotle recognized, however, that in such exchanges justice does not determine a unique price, but merely a range of possible prices in between the lowest price the seller is prepared to accept and the highest price the buyer is prepared to pay. There is therefore still scope for a rule to determine the just price within this range. His answer was the harmonic mean of the two extreme prices. The harmonic mean has the property that if the just price is, say, 40 per cent above the lowest price, the seller will accept; it is also 40 per cent below the highest price the buyer is prepared to pay. Justice involves finding a mean between extremes, neither of which is just.

The principle that justice involves finding a suitable mean also applies to the two other forms of justice. Distributive justice involves proportionality, or geometric proportion, and is associated with the geometric mean. (The geometric mean of two quantities is found by multiplying them together and taking the square root of the result.) Rectificatory justice involves arithmetic proportion (compensation should equal what has been lost). We thus find that Aristotle has related the three types of justice to the three types of mean that were known to him: the geometric, arithmetic and harmonic means. This was far from accidental. Aristotle, like Plato, was strongly influenced by the Pythagoreans, who worked out the mathematical relationship between musical notes. It was believed that similar harmonies and ratios could explain other phenomena, and it is therefore not surprising that there were close parallels between Aristotle's theory of justice and the mathematics of ratios and harmonies.

The influence of Pythagorean mathematics on Aristotle's account of exchange extends even further. By Aristotle's time it was widely accepted that all things were built up from common units (atomism). Geometry was based on points, arithmetic on the number 1, and so on to the physical world. It was believed that this meant that different phenomena were commensurable in the sense that they could similarly be expressed as ratios of whole numbers. This was why it had been a great blow to the Pythagoreans to discover that there were irrational numbers like π or $\sqrt{2}$ that could not be expressed as ratios. Exchange of one good for another was important because it made the goods commensurable – shoes could be measured in terms of wheat. But if the shoemaker did not want wheat, or the farmer did not want shoes, exchange would not take place, making it impossible to compare the two goods. How was this problem to be resolved? Aristotle's answer was money. The shoemaker and the farmer might not want each other's produce, but they would both sell it for money, which meant that shoes and wheat could be compared through taking the ratio of their money prices. It is demand that makes goods commensurable, and money acts as a representative of demand.

ARISTOTLE AND THE ACQUISITION
OF WEALTH

However, although money was fundamental to Aristotle's thinking, he believed that there were clear limits to the legitimate role of commercial activity. His argument was based on a distinction between two types of wealth-getting. The first was a part of estate management. People should know things such as which type of livestock would be most profitable, or whether to engage in planting wheat or bee keeping. These were natural ways in which to acquire wealth. In contrast, the second type – getting wealth through exchange – was unnatural, for this involved making a gain at someone else's expense. Unnatural ways to acquire wealth included commerce and usury (lending money at interest). Somewhere in between came activities such as mining.

The Socratic philosophers, including Xenophon, Plato and Aristotle, held that citizens should aim at a good life. This was the life of the polis, or independent city state in which citizens played an active part in civic life. To do this they needed material resources, provided by their estate. Natural ways of acquiring wealth were ones that increased the stock of goods needed to live the good life. Though estate management was fundamental, trading to obtain goods that could not be produced at home and exchanging one's surplus produce for something of which one had greater need were perfectly natural. But an important part of such a life was that wants were limited, and that once a man had enough wealth to live in the right manner he would have no need for further accumulation of wealth. High levels of consumption were not part of the good life. There was therefore a limit to the natural acquisition of wealth.

What disturbed Aristotle about commerce was that it offered the prospect of an unlimited accumulation of wealth. This was something of which Athenians were well aware, for, although the self-sufficient city state was the ideal, there had been several crises when the city had been forced to raise money from traders. Typically, merchants were not citizens, so raising money in this way meant going outside the polis. The puzzle was that, even though they did not do anything useful, traders and speculators managed to create so much wealth that they could help out cities in times of crisis. How was this possible? Aristotle's answer was that goods can be either used or exchanged. Of these, the former is a proper, natural procedure, as is exchange between people who need goods different from those they currently possess. On the other hand, exchange simply for the purposes of making money is unnatural, for goods are not being used for their proper purpose. If wealth could be created by exchange, then it could be accumulated without limit, something Aristotle considered impossible. If followed that such activities must be unnatural. Men might be rich in coin, he argued, yet starve through lack of food.

The view that there are limits to the proper acquisition of wealth and the use of exchange simply in order to make money fits in with Aristotle's theory of justice. The essence of natural acquisition of property is that it enables men to live a good life in the polis. It has a clear objective and is not being pursued for its own sake. Similarly, when he turned to the question of justice in the *Nichomachean Ethics*, Aristotle was dealing with the injustice that arises 'not from any particular kind of wickedness, such as self-indulgence, cowardice, anger, bad temper or meanness, but simply from activities for which the motive is the pleasure that arises from gain'.[6] In making this distinction, one can see Aristotle separating out one sphere of life – one that it is tempting to describe as 'economic' – money-making. What is significant, however, is that Aristotle did not see this sphere as covering the major part of those activities that we now think of as economic, for production and the most important types of trade were excluded. Even more significant, he did not see markets and money-making activities as providing a mechanism that could regulate society. Order was produced not through individuals pursuing their own ends, but through efficient administration.

Like Plato, Aristotle was a teacher. In 342 BCE he was appointed tutor to Alexander the Great, and in 335 BCE he returned to Athens to establish his own school, the Lyceum. It was Alexander who finally destroyed the independence of the Greek city states, so weakened by the Peloponnesian War, as he expanded his Macedonian empire to include not only the rest of Greece, but also Egypt and much of the

Persian empire, right across to India. Though Alexander's empire was relatively short-lived, disintegrating after his death in 323 BCE, its major effect was to spread Greek culture throughout the ancient world. The age of independent city states was over, and the empire's administration was run along lines taken over from the Persian and Egyptian empires that preceded it. Greek became the official language and was widely spoken in the towns (though not in the countryside), and Greek mathematics, science, medicine and philosophy flourished in cities such as Alexandria in Egypt. The writings of the Greek philosophers, though rooted in the Greek city state, reached a far wider audience.

ROME

At the time of Alexander's death, the Roman republic controlled no more than a small area on the west coast of the Italian peninsula. During the following three centuries this grew into an empire that covered most of Europe and North Africa. On the death of Augustus (CE 14) the Roman empire stretched from Spain to Syria, and from the Rhineland to Egypt. It reached its greatest extent in the reign of Trajan (98–117), and, though it lost territories, notably to the Frankish tribes in the north, it retained much the same boundaries until the end of the fourth century. Roads, cities and other major public works were built on an unprecedented scale. Rome was without any doubt the greatest civilization the Western world had seen.

Rome produced armies that conquered this world, and architecture that produced a sense of awe in those who later looked upon its ruins. Latin became the language of the educated classes in Europe. Yet the centre of the empire was always in the East. Rome relied on Egypt for its supplies of grain. The empire's largest cities and much of its population were in the eastern provinces in Asia Minor. In contrast, the Western empire remained largely rural. The cultural centre of the empire was also in the Eastern empire – in Hellenized cities such as Antioch and Alexandria, in which Greeks continued to make advances in science and philosophy. Roman writers readily acknowledged their debts to the Greeks, with the result that the Romans themselves are widely believed to have contributed little to economics. They are said to have been doers, rather than thinkers; engineers, rather than scientists. However, while there may not have been contributions comparable with those of Plato or Aristotle, this view is far from justified. Roman writers made a different type of contribution, the explanation for which is to be found in the structure of Roman society.

The Roman constitution linked political power to the ownership of land and to military service. War and conquest were a major source of wealth, and soldiers were rewarded with grants of land, associated with political power. Romans were expected to be willing to endure the hardships and risks of war in order to preserve their wealth. It followed that the rich, who had more wealth to preserve, should face the greatest risks. The poor man gained little from war and should therefore neither pay taxes nor be required to fight. Trade offered a route to wealth, but this wealth had to be converted into land if it were to bring political power. Land, therefore, was the pre-eminent form of wealth.

The philosophies that gained most adherents in Rome, especially among the upper classes, both originated in Greece: Cynicism, founded by Diogenes of Sinope (c.410–c.320 BCE), and its offshoot, Stoicism, founded by Zeno of Citium (c.335–263 BCE). The last great exponent of Stoicism was Marcus Aurelius, Roman emperor from CE 161 to 180. Cynicism, like the later teaching of Epicurus (c.341–270 BCE) emphasized the here and now. Freedom from want was to be achieved through reducing one's needs to the barest minimum, living in what ordinary men would consider poverty. The Stoics believed that happiness resulted not from material possessions, but from virtue. Moral virtue was the only good, which meant that a man who had done the best he could had nothing to regret. For both the Cynics and the Stoics, virtue involved following nature. They were thus responsible for the idea of natural law, by which human laws and institutions could be judged.

The concept of natural laws, applying to the whole of humanity, provided the foundation for the field where the Romans made perhaps their greatest contribution to social thought – jurisprudence.

Roman law has exerted a major influence over subsequent legal systems. More important, many significant economic ideas were articulated in Roman commercial law. The Romans had great respect for property, and the law contained many provisions to safeguard ownership. The idea of the corporation having an existence independent of the individuals involved in it goes back to Roman law. The law on contracts permitted trade, and guaranteed property and allowed it to be transferred. However, though trade was allowed, wealth acquired from trade remained more controversial than wealth from landed estates. There was always a sense that wealth from trade, which appeared almost to arise out of nowhere, was tainted in a way that wealth derived from the land was not. Stoic ideas were the origin of the concept of reasonableness as it later appeared in much commercial law.

Of particular importance was the idea, going back to Aristotle, that if all parties had agreed to a contract voluntarily, that contract must be just. For a contract to be valid, all that was necessary was that the parties had consented to it, not that a particular ritual or formula had been followed. This focused attention on the circumstances under which an action was voluntary – on the point at which coercion rendered an action involuntary. If someone could show that he had entered into a contract under threat, he might be able to have it annulled on the grounds that he had not entered into it voluntarily. In general, however, a threat was held to invalidate a contract only if it were sufficient to scare a man of firm character. It would normally, if not always, have had to involve a threat of physical violence. The need for consent was the reason why wilful fraud rendered a contract invalid. For example, someone did not truly consent to a contract if he was misled about the quality of the goods being offered. Normal bargaining over a contract, however, was allowed.

CONCLUSIONS

The world of ancient Greece and even Rome can seem very remote. However, the ideas developed there are more important than their remoteness might suggest. Greek philosophy has exerted a profound influence on Western thought, and the economic thought discussed in this book forms part of that broader tradition. Our way of reasoning goes back to Plato and Aristotle. Plato argued for the existence of universals – ideal, pure forms that could be understood only through abstract reasoning. Aristotle, in contrast, saw concrete facts as fundamental, and general principles had to be derived from these through a process of induction. These two different attitudes still beset modern economics. Roman law has been similarly influential. In addition, the Classics, both Greek and Latin and including many works not mentioned here, formed an important part of many economists' education, at least until the twentieth century, with the result that many of the writers discussed in the following chapters will have been directly influenced by them.

The ancient world was dominated by self-sufficiency and isolated exchange. As the terms of such exchanges were clearly something over which men had control, it was natural that great attention should be paid to whether they were just. However, although there was no market economy in the modern sense, commercial activity was sufficiently developed and sufficiently prominent to provide a significant challenge. On the whole, the thinkers whose views are known to us (we have less evidence of how merchants themselves viewed things) were suspicious of commerce. These two normative themes – justice and the morality of commerce – dominated discussions of economic issues right up to the seventeenth century, by which time the existence of a market economy and a commercial mentality had come to be much more widely accepted.

2

The Middle Ages

THE DECLINE OF ROME

The ancient world is conventionally said to have ended with the fall of Rome and the Roman empire. This was a long-drawn-out process, with its end commonly dated to the fall of the Western empire in 476, though the Empire continued in the East, based on Constantinople (Byzantium), for almost another 1,000 years. The modern world is often said to have begun in the fifteenth century. This was the century of the Renaissance, when Europe rediscovered classical humanism and Portuguese explorers discovered the New World and sea routes to the Far East. An important symbolic date was that of the fall of Constantinople to the Turks, in 1453. In between we have the so-called Middle Ages.

Dated in this way, the Middle Ages span nearly a millennium of European history during which profound economic, social and political changes occurred. The way in which men made sense of these changes cannot be understood separately from religion. The key event here was the adoption of Christianity as the religion of the Roman empire. The emperor Constantine (c.272/3–337) was converted to Christianity in 312, and under Theodosius (c.346–95) Christianity became the official religion, with non-Christians and heretics being persecuted. Religion and politics remained entangled for centuries, with outsiders to the ruling elite often favouring non-orthodox versions of Christianity. For example, Arian Christianity (heretical in relation to the official religion of the empire) was widespread in the countryside. After Rome fell and Islam had come into being, the conflict between Christianity and Islam overshadowed the many disputes within Christianity.

Economic problems played an important role in the fall of the Roman empire, even though attacks by waves of barbarian invaders provide the popular explanation of what happened. A critical period for the empire was the third century. Population fell by a third, partly due to plague brought in by eastern invaders. The supply of gold fell, possibly because there were no longer new imperial conquests, a major source of gold in the past. Alternatively, the reason for economic decline may simply be that commerce was failing. With the fall in the supply of gold, trade to the East collapsed. Furthermore, given that the empire was held together only by the army and that there were many people in the cities who needed to be pacified with distributions of food, taxation rose. At times, the authorities had to requisition food directly to feed the army and the poor. Some of the money needed was raised by debasing the coinage. In the time of Augustus coins were pure silver, but by 250 the silver content had fallen to 40 per cent, and by 270 to 4 per cent. Despite attempts at financial reform by a series of emperors, culminating in Diocletian's famous edict of 301 in which he sought to fix prices and wages, inflation continued.

An important economic and social change during the last years of the empire that became even more marked during the Middle Ages was the decline of the towns. Cities in the Western empire were essentially colonial towns, whereas those in the Eastern empire were larger and generated much wealth. As trade declined, so did the position of towns in the Western empire. There was a general retreat from them, symbolized by the fact that for Christian ascetics such as St Jerome (c.347–420) abandoning worldly possessions meant retreating into the desert.

To understand the economic thought of the Middle Ages, it is necessary to understand not simply the Greek and Roman ideas discussed in the previous chapter but also two other strands of thought: Judaism and early Christianity. This involves going back to the time of the Old Testament.

JUDAISM

The economic thinking of the early Christian Church owed much to Judaism. In the Old Testament tradition, it was thought that restricting one's wants was an important way to cope with the problem of scarcity. As in ancient Greece, there was also great suspicion of trade, and hostility to lending money at interest. There were, however, some distinctive features in the biblical teaching on economics. People were seen as stewards, with a responsibility to make the best possible use of what God had entrusted to them. Work was seen as good – as part of the divine plan for mankind. Adam was told to multiply and fill the earth and, even in the Garden of Eden, he was to work the soil and to look after it.[1] Abraham was amply rewarded for his faith. These texts can be read as favouring economic growth – those who follow the Lord accumulate wealth.

The Old Testament also contains many laws that regulated economic activity. Charging interest on loans to fellow Israelites was forbidden. After working for six years, slaves were to be set free and given enough capital to make a new start. Even more radical, all debts were to be cancelled every seventh year (the sabbatical), and in every fiftieth year (the jubilee) ownership of all land was to revert to its original owner. There is no evidence that the jubilee was ever enforced, and certainly by the time of the monarchy (c.1000–900 BCE) there was considerable inequality. This was partly due to the king's imposition of taxes, requisitioning of goods, and forced labour. (The state of the poor was a major theme in the writings of the prophets.) The provisions of the law nonetheless helped keep alive the view that men were only stewards, not outright owners, of their lands.

Though wealth was the reward given to the righteous man, the pursuit of individual wealth was criticized as leading people away from God. For Moses, worship of the Golden Calf was incompatible with the worship of God. Similarly, when Isaiah wrote of Israel being crowded with foreigners and traders, and (presumably as a result) being filled with gold and silver, he observed that the land was also filled with idols and that people bowed down in front of the work of their own hands.[2]

Throughout the Old Testament, seeking to increase one's own wealth is associated with dishonest business practices and the exploitation of the poor. This attitude was clearly expressed by the prophet Amos (eighth century BCE):

> Listen to this, you who grind the destitute and plunder the humble, you who say, 'When will the new moon be past so that we may sell our corn? When will the sabbath be past so that we may open our wheat again, giving short measure in the bushel and taking overweight in the silver, tilting the scales fraudulently, and selling the dust of the wheat; that we may buy the poor for silver and the destitute for a pair of shoes?'[3]

In the same way, moneylenders were seen, along with traders and retailers, as behaving unjustly – exacting interest in advance and depriving people of essentials such as the cloak under which they needed to sleep.[4]

There was thus a clear distinction between the pursuit of wealth, which was castigated, and the wealth that arose through following God's commands. As obeying God's commands involved working and acting as a responsible steward, this was far from a condemnation of all economic activity. The objection was to bad practices, not to the acquisition of wealth itself. Pursuing wealth was wrong because it encouraged such practices. Thus, so long as they looked after their own people and behaved justly, the Israelites were encouraged in their business activity. The book of Ecclesiastes even encourages people to engage in foreign trade and gives advice on taking (and hedging) risks: 'Send your grain across the seas, and in time you will get a return. Divide your merchandise among seven ventures, eight maybe, since you do not know what disasters may occur on earth.'[5] The Old Testament is not about withdrawing from the world. Money corrupts only when it becomes people's sole motive.

EARLY CHRISTIANITY

In the New Testament the emphasis is different. Jesus was steeped in the Old Testament, and much of his teaching followed the laws of Judaism very closely. In the parable of the talents, he spoke of stewardship and risk-taking, and he taught that the righteous would be rewarded. But he was a working man, many of whose followers came from the poorest parts of Jewish society and had no hope of bringing about major economic, social or political change. Thus he required his followers to give up their possessions, warned that the rich might find it impossible to obtain salvation, and taught that rewards for righteousness would be found in heaven rather than on earth.

For the earliest Christians, notably St Paul, who was responsible for transforming Christianity from a Jewish heresy into a religion open to all races, Christ's Second Coming, and with it the end of the present world, was imminent. This meant that the idea of economic progress found in the Old Testament was pushed aside. Even the importance of good stewardship of resources was played down. Paul wrote that those who have wealth should not count on keeping it, or even on having time to use it to the full. His advice was that people should carry on as they were, the imminence of the end of the world meaning that there was no point in starting anything new. This was an environment in which economic thought was clearly not going to develop. However, when it became apparent that the end of the world would not happen within the lifetime of the original Apostles (Peter is believed to have died in Nero's persecutions in AD 65), the Church began to think again about economic development. There are some hints of this in the later books of the New Testament, notably the Revelation of St John.

The early Fathers of the Church were therefore confronted with a tension between the views of the Old and New Testaments. On the whole they opted for retreating from the world, possibly influenced by their Cynic and Stoic contemporaries. Poverty and detachment from worldly possessions were encouraged, and we have the examples of hermits and saints who gave up everything, retreating to a life of poverty. The Old Testament injunction to work was explained away by arguing that the problem had been that idleness would lead to corruption. Work was desirable because it prevented people from being idle, but if one could resist temptation this was even better.

The outstanding figure of this period was St Augustine, Bishop of Hippo, in North Africa (354–430). His City of God was written to rebut the charge that the fall of Rome to Alaric and the Goths in 410 was retribution for the empire's having adopted Christianity. The book is significant because it looks forward to the possibility of creating a new society, rather than simply looking back to preserve, or re-create, the past. Unlike Plato, Augustine did not seek to establish a blueprint for a new society, for it is impossible to create a perfect society on earth. Instead he saw progress as trying to get closer and closer to a perfect society.

Wealth, Augustine argued, was a gift from God; but, though it was good, it was not the highest good. It should be regarded as a means, not an end. Though he considered it best not to own property at all, he recognized that not everyone could do this. Private property was, for Augustine, entirely legitimate, but it was important for people to abstain from the love of property (which would cause it to be misused). In the same way, Augustine distinguished between the trader and his trade: there was nothing wrong with trade in itself, for it might benefit people through making goods available to those who otherwise would not have them, but it was open to misuse. Sin was in the trader, not in trade. There was, however, an unresolved conflict between this teaching about the legitimacy of private property and the natural-law doctrine of communal property. Private property was the creation of the state, which therefore had the right to take it away.

Augustine took many ideas from Greek thought, but his horizons were incomparably broader. Whereas Xenophon and even Aristotle were concerned with the polis or city state, Augustine dealt with a people defined not by birth or locality, but by agreement on a common interest. Depending on the nature of this shared interest, the community might progress or regress. He broadened out the Old Testament notion of development to make it relevant to Christendom, not simply Israel, and provided a perspective on history that proved influential in the emerging societies of western Europe.

ISLAM

The Western empire ceased to exist in 476. Though this event was of great symbolic importance, little changed. The barbarian kingdoms that emerged in western Europe sought not to overthrow the Roman empire but to become part of it. They still looked up to the Roman emperor, even though that emperor was now in Constantinople, not Rome. The significant event marking the end of the ancient world was not the fall of Rome, but the rise of Islam and the Muslim conquest of Arabia, the Persian empire, North Africa and much of Spain. The Muslim advance across Europe was stopped only in 732, by Charles Martel at Poitiers. It was at this time that European society was cut off from the Mediterranean and had to reorganize itself. For example, this was when Syrian traders disappeared from western Europe. In contrast, trade flourished in the Muslim lands and a great civilization was established, absorbing Persian culture in addition to the Hellenistic culture brought by Alexander. Centres of learning were established in cities such as Baghdad, Alexandria and Córdoba, and there the legacy of Greece was preserved at a time when it was lost in the rest of Europe. Plato and Aristotle first entered the Latin West through translations from Syriac and Arabic.

The Islamic economic literature of this period falls into two categories: the literature of the 'golden age' of Islamic dominance (750–1250) and that of the crisis years which followed (1250–1500), by the end of which the Moors had been driven out of Spain and the European nations were embarking on voyages of discovery. The background to this literature was the Koran. Like the Old and New Testaments, this contained no systematic exploration of economics, but it did discuss isolated, practical economic issues. It said that income and property should be taxed in order to support the poor. The taking of interest on loans was prohibited. Inheritance was regulated, so that estates had to be broken up instead of being passed on to a single beneficiary. Beyond this there was little. While these rules presented a challenge, given the highly developed urban civilization that Islam had taken over, Islamic society was very traditional, and the role for economics was rather limited.

In the Islamic golden age, two main types of literature can be found. One is the so-called 'mirror for princes' literature. The mirror books were open letters, usually written by scholars and viziers, which presented rulers with an image of efficient and just government and advised on how commerce and public administration might best be organized. One of the most economically developed examples was by al-Dimashqi (in the ninth century), who explained how the merchant could contribute to the good of the community by linking parties who have surpluses or shortages of particular products. He argued, however, that for the merchant to benefit society he must refrain from speculation and the desire to accumulate wealth. He might take a normal profit, but no more. Another type of writing concerned the organization of either the city or the household. It was written by lawyers and civil servants – sometimes by the sheriffs responsible for ensuring that markets functioned in an orderly manner. They analysed the conflict between free markets (supported in the Koran) and the desire for administrative control of markets and prices – something for which there was great pressure when shortages threatened to make goods too expensive for the urban poor to survive. Such writing frequently discusses economic problems such as pricing, factors influencing consumption, and the supply of goods.

The potential conflict between the Greek heritage and Islamic thought is illustrated by Averroes (Ibn Rushd, 1126–98), writing near the end of the golden age, the last in a line of outstanding Muslim philosophers. His father and grandfather had held the position of chief judge in Córdoba, and in 1169 he was appointed to the same position in Seville. Part of his life was spent in Marrakesh, including a spell late in life as chief physician to the emir. His commentaries on Aristotle were probably written in Córdoba in the 1170s, and are particularly important because it was through these, translated from Arabic into Latin, that Aristotle came to be known in the Christian West.

Though he had sympathies with Plato's ideal of a strong ruler, Averroes followed Aristotle in seeking to establish ethical principles through reasoned argument. This brought him into conflict with religious traditionalists, who were not happy with the way in which he sought to reconcile ethics based on reason with the revealed ethics of the Koran. At one point the emir banished him from Marrakesh, and his many books on Greek philosophy were burned.

Perhaps the point where Averroes departed furthest from Aristotle was in his treatment of money. Aristotle had recognized three functions of money: means of exchange, measure of value, and a store of value for future transactions. To these, Averroes added that of being a reserve of purchasing power: unlike other goods that could also serve as a store of value, money could be spent at any time without having first to be sold. He also took a different view from Aristotle on the question of whether money is a commodity like any other. Writing in the twelfth century, Averroes took monetary transactions for granted in a way that Aristotle did not: the economy could not function without it. Money was thus unique. Furthermore, the value of money had to be unchangeable, for two reasons. One was that money is used to measure all things. Like Allah, also the measure of all things, it must be unchangeable. The other was that, if money is used as a store of value, changes in its value are unfair. The money a ruler makes by reducing the amount of precious metal contained in coins is pure profit that he has done nothing to earn, similar to interest on a loan, and is as such unjustifiable. Averroes thus broke with Aristotle's view that the value of money is a convention that the ruler might alter at will.

In the thirteenth century the situation changed. Following the Mongol advance into Europe, much of Persia and Asia Minor fell to the Seljuk Turks. The Catholic princes of Aragon, Castile, Navarre and Asturias managed to reclaim much of Spain from the Moors. This was the background to the writings of Ibn Khaldun (1332–1406), who came from a Moorish-Andalusian family but who migrated to North Africa after the fall of Seville to the Catholics. He pursued a varied career as a civil servant, jurist and historian – at one point he accompanied the Sultan of Egypt to negotiate a peace treaty with the Mongol conqueror, Tamerlane. He was well educated in the science and philosophy of his day. But though he was a member of the ruling class, with close connections to emirs and sultans, his Spanish upbringing gave him the attitude of an outsider to North African civilization.

Ibn Khaldun's major work is a history of civilization in which he wove together economic, political and social changes. It was a work in social science, or the science of culture, in which his aim was not to derive moral precepts, but to explain the organization of society. He was familiar with Greek philosophy, but became sceptical about very abstract theorizing, on the grounds that it could lead to speculation and a failure to learn lessons from past experience. Inquiries had to be exhaustive if their results were not to be misleading.

Civilization, according to Ibn Khaldun, went through a series of cycles. His theory has been summarized by one historian as follows:

> A new dynasty comes into being and as it acquires strength, it extends the area within which order prevails and urban settlement and civilization can flourish. Crafts increase in number and there is greater division of labor, in part because aggregate income rises, swelled by increase in population and in output per worker, and provides an expanding market, a very important segment of which is that supported by governmental expenditure. Growth is not halted by a dearth of effort or by a shortage of demand; for tastes change and demand rises as income grows, with the result that demand keeps pace with supply. Luxurious consumption and easy living serve, however, to soften both dynasty and population and to dissipate hardier qualities and virtues. Growth is halted by the inevitable weakening and collapse of the ruling dynasty, usually after three or four generations, a process that is accompanied by deterioration of economic conditions, decline of the economy in complexity, and the return of more primitive conditions.[6]

Though this might be seen as a political theory, explaining the rise and decline of dynasties, and though sociological factors (such as the contrast between the values acquired in Bedouin 'desert' life and 'sedentary' city life) are in the forefront of the story, economic factors are nonetheless equally important. Though not discussed separately, concepts such as the effect of division of labour on productivity, the influence of tastes on demand, the choice between consumption and capital accumulation, and the impact of profits (and hence taxation) on production are all analysed as part of the story.

Ibn Khaldun's account of the process of economic development is a remarkable achievement. When taken together with the other Muslim literature of this period, it shows how great an understanding of economic phenomena existed among certain circles of Islamic society in the fourteenth century. Trade and science both flourished in the Islamic world, and men such as Ibn Khaldun, involved in the legal and administrative systems, were able to use their own experience and the traditions handed down to them to amass a large stock of economic knowledge. Ibn Khaldun's work had little lasting influence in the Islamic world, however. It was in western Europe, not North Africa, that the next major developments in economic thought were to arise.

FROM CHARLES MARTEL TO THE BLACK DEATH

The golden age of Islam was the dark age of Christian Europe. In the south, Muslims controlled most of Spain and were at the gates of Constantinople, while in the ninth century Vikings dominated the north. Flows of gold into much of Europe ceased, and there was a lapse into rural self-sufficiency. Yet Christian Europe survived, primarily through the development of two institutions. One was the monastic cell, in which Christianity was kept alive. By 700, Benedictine monasteries in the rest of Europe had fallen to invaders, but Christian learning, including knowledge of Latin and Greek classics, was kept alive in monasteries in Ireland and Northumberland. By the time these were sacked by the Vikings, Christianity had spread back to France and Germany.

The second vital institution was the system, sometimes referred to as 'feudalism', by which grants of land were linked to military service. ('Feudalism' is a term invented many years later, and meant different things in different parts of Europe, so it has to be used with great care.) The invaders threatening Europe were horsemen. To defeat them it was necessary to follow the Persian and Byzantine example and use heavily armoured men on horses specially bred for their strength. The problem of how to support such horsemen, which had imposed a serious economic drain on the Persian and Byzantine empires, was solved by Charles Martel (ruler of the Franks in 719–41), who used lands confiscated from the Church to endow a new class of warriors. These received rights over land in return for an obligation to put a knight (or a certain number of knights) into the field when called upon to do so by the king. Around this grew up an entire social and economic system based on relationships between land-holding and military service. At the same time, Charles Martel brought monks from England and Ireland to reorganize the Frankish church. Monasteries were established, along more puritan lines than the old Benedictine foundations. An alliance at all levels of society was formed between state and Church, the most notable sign of which was the concordat between the ruler and the Pope, and the coronation of Charlemagne (742–814) as emperor in Rome.

The combination of military power and highly disciplined religious orders provided the basis for a period of European expansion. Norman knights conquered England (1066) and southern Italy (1057–85) and were, together with the monks of Cluny (in Burgundy), instrumental in organizing the 'reconquest' of Spain from the Moors (1085–1340). Between 1096 and 1291 the Crusades (inspired by the Church, but undertaken by Frankish knights and their followers) established Christian states in Palestine. The twelfth and thirteenth centuries saw the colonization of the plains of northern Europe. This involved both knights (the Teutonic Knights – the order of St Mary's Hospital in Jerusalem) and religious orders. The Cistercians were particularly active: monasteries set up colonies, usually further east, bringing wasteland under cultivation. In the same way, towns set up new towns further east. Other towns were established by kings. Long-distance trade was revived by the Crusades, Venice and other Italian trading cities providing much of the finance and transport, and gold began to be coined again in Europe. Expansion of trade with the Far East was made possible by the Mongol conquests in Asia, which established a unified, tolerant and peaceful empire stretching from eastern Europe to China.

In the fourteenth century, however, this expansion halted. Jerusalem and the other conquests in Palestine were lost by the West, advance in the East was halted, and the Moors managed to halt the reconquest of Spain for two centuries. The eastern Mediterranean was ruled not by knights organized on the Frankish model but by Italian trading cities. Archers (including those of the English at Crécy) began to defeat armoured knights. Trade began to fall, bringing about the collapse of many of the great banking houses of Europe. Then in 1347–51 the Black Death spread throughout Europe. Population fell by a third, and in some areas by a half. Labour became scarce, and conflicts between labourers and landlords became endemic, with peasant rebellions, legislation to control labour, and attempts by the Church to recover lands it had lost. Feudal society, once the means of expansion, became conservative and inflexible.

THE TWELFTH-CENTURY RENAISSANCE AND ECONOMICS IN THE UNIVERSITIES

But before this, in the midst of the process of expansion, there took place what has been called the twelfth-century renaissance. Perhaps linked to rising prosperity, conflicts between emerging powers (notably Church and state), the loosening of the feudal system and the emergence of an urban middle class, there arose a demand for learning. Peripatetic teachers, not unlike the Sophists of ancient Greece, emerged. In the first half of the twelfth century, Peter Abelard (1079–1142) argued for the use of reason and against censorship. Conquests of parts of Europe previously controlled by the Moors made Arabic learning available, and via this route Europeans rediscovered the Greek classics. The commentaries of Averroes were enthusiastically taken up, and through them Western scholars were introduced to Aristotle. This ferment led to the establishment of a new institution, the university: Bologna, Paris and Oxford were the first, and by 1400 there were a further fifty-three.

It was from these universities that the period's economic writing emerged. The scholars involved formed a mobile, international community centred on one university: Paris. The economics they produced – usually referred to as 'scholastic' economics – was concerned primarily with ethics. Ethical questions, however, inevitably required people to think about the way in which economic activities actually worked.

The earliest scholastic writings on economics are found in manuals for confessors – books on how priests should advise people who came to them for confession. Economics figured prominently because many priests were unfamiliar with the business practices on which people sought spiritual guidance. An example of such a manual is the *Summa Confessorum*, by Thomas of Chobham (*c.*1163–1235), written around 1215 – the year in which it became compulsory for all adults to go to confession at least annually. Economics comes into the book when Thomas reviews the moral hazards of various professions, including that of the merchant. His list of capital sins includes both usury and avarice. However, he provides a strong defence of commerce, missing from many earlier writings:

> Commerce is to buy something cheaper for the purpose of selling it dearer. And this is all right for laymen to do, even if they do not add any improvement of the goods which they bought earlier and later sell. For otherwise there would have been great need in many regions, since merchants carry that which is plentiful in one place to another place where the same thing is scarce. Therefore merchants may well charge the value of their labour and transport and expenses in addition to the capital laid out in purchasing the goods. And also if they have added some improvement to the merchandise they may charge the value of this.[7]

He goes on to place merchants alongside craftsmen (a favoured occupation, since Joseph was a carpenter). Thomas warned, however, that it was sinful to deceive the buyer or to charge more than the just price.

Thomas brought several arguments to bear on the question of usury. (1) When money is lent, ownership of the money passes from lender to borrower, so usury involves the lender profiting from property which belongs to someone else. (2) The usurer sells time, which belongs to God. (3) Lending for a share of profits is sinful unless the lender also shares expenses and losses in the same proportion. Thomas did not allow interest to be paid as compensation for opportunities lost by the lender during the period of the loan, but it was acceptable to seek compensation for losses incurred through a borrower's failure to repay a loan on time.

A significant advance in such thinking was made by William of Auxerre (c.1140–1231) – the theologian who, in 1230, is thought to have played a part in persuading Pope Gregory IX not to ban Aristotle's work. William based ethics on natural law, in the sense of 'that which natural reason dictates to be done either without any deliberation or without much deliberation'.[8] A modern scholar has written:

> The importance to social philosophy of a concept like this is hard to overestimate. It provides a set of more or less self-evident rational postulates on which further arguments are based. The conclusions reached via such arguments (provided they are logically correct) are rationally valid, but they are also normative since they are based on law.[9]

William paid much attention to private property, concluding that it was a necessary evil, subject to the qualification that, in times of need, those with property were obliged to share it with those who had none. In a similar vein, he argued that the use of coercion, including the bargaining power that might result from a borrower needing a loan, rendered a contract invalid. It could not be argued that payment of interest was morally acceptable because the borrower had entered into the contract voluntarily.

The major figures in scholastic economics, however, are usually considered to be Albert the Great (Albertus Magnus, c.1200–1280) and Thomas Aquinas (c.1225–74), both Dominican friars. By the time of their work, economic thought was found not just in confessional manuals but also in commentaries on Peter Lombard's *Sentences* and on Aristotle, both of which were very common literary forms.

Aristotle (*Nicomachean Ethics*, V.5) argued that justice was served if the ratio of shoes to food equalled that of shoemaker to farmer, or if the ratio of houses to shoes was that of builder to shoemaker. This passage has provoked enormous controversy, because the meaning of 'shoemaker to farmer' and 'builder to shoemaker' is far from clear. Albert, in his commentaries on this passage, suggested that it should be read as meaning that the value of one good in terms of another should be in proportion both to the relative need for the two goods and to the labour involved:

> As the farmer is to the shoemaker in labour and expenses, thus the product of the shoemaker is to the farmer's product ... [It is] with regard to communal toil and trouble, they are sufficiently measured.
>
> Exchange is to be made ... according to a proportion between the value of one thing and the value of the other thing, this proportion being taken with regard to need, which is the cause of exchange.[10]

In the first of these sentences, Albert is saying that the values of shoes and food should be proportional to the labour and expenses of the shoemaker and the farmer. In the second he brings in need as what should determine relative values. When taken together, these passages can be read as explaining why labour should be rewarded: if the bed-maker does not receive enough to cover his expenses, no more beds will be produced. Values should thus be related both to the need for goods and to the costs of producing them. Albert starts with an ethical question, and on the basis of an obscure passage from Aristotle he reaches a conclusion about what prices must obtain if society is to be supplied with the goods it requires.

Thomas Aquinas was a pupil of Albert the Great, and in much of his work he sought to simplify and clarify his teacher's writings. Like Albert, he brought together ideas from Aristotle and leading theologians, such as Augustine. This is well illustrated by his teaching on property. This contains all the major arguments used by the scholastics, many of which originated in Aristotle. These include the need for private property if people are to be in a position to exercise liberality, the argument that people will take more care over their own property than the property of others, and the argument that private property leads to order. But it is in the argument from peace that Aquinas's skill in bringing together ideas from Christian theologians and Aristotle is perhaps best illustrated. The argument is Aristotelian, but Aquinas christianizes it by arguing that private property is necessary for peace only because of the corrupt state of man following the Fall. However, though Aquinas recognizes that property must of necessity be private, the fruits of that property are common and must be shared, either through giving one's surplus goods to those in need or through buying and selling.

To understand their attitudes towards property and wealth, it is important to remember that many of the scholastic writers were mendicant friars who were committed to a life of poverty. They did not consider wealth to raise the quality of life, let alone to be an end in itself. On the other hand, they recognized that most poor people had not chosen to live in poverty. They also recognized that if everyone were poor there would be no one who could support them. This explains why Aquinas, for example, warned against an excess both of poverty and of wealth. Wealth was beneficial only if used in a way that was consistent with the demands of justice and charity.

One demand of justice was that, where goods were used for exchange, buying and selling must take place at the just price – that there must be commutative justice, or justice in exchange. Here the scholastics took over from Roman law the idea that something is worth as much as it can be sold for without fraud. They were, however, unwilling to draw from this the conclusion that it was just to sell a good for the highest price that could be obtained for it. It was agreed that wilful misrepresentation of a good or its quality was unjust. However, this argument from Roman law presumed that both parties consented to the terms on which the goods were being exchanged, which raised the question of how much information about a good the seller had to provide. Aquinas allowed that a seller could hide some information. If there were an obvious defect, it was enough to charge a suitable price, and the seller did not have to tell everyone about the defect (which might result in the good selling for less than the just price). It was accepted that haggling took place – that buyers and sellers would always try to outwit each other. There was also no requirement for a seller to tell a buyer about factors that might lower the price in future. For example, the owner of a ship full of grain did not have to tell buyers about other ships that would shortly be arriving. The just price was the price that was appropriate in the present, not the one that would prevail in future.

The main idea underlying scholastic discussion of the just price was that the market offered protection against economic compulsion.

If the value of a good to its seller were more than its normal value, it could be sold for this higher value; otherwise the seller would experience a loss. However, it was unjust for a seller to take advantage of circumstances affecting the buyer. (Indeed, there was a long tradition in natural law that said that in cases of severe need, such as famine, taking what one needed did not constitute theft – that property became communal.) Competition between sellers, as occurs in public markets, was recognized as protecting buyers.

What the scholastic writers were doing in their discussions of issues such as property and the just price was providing arguments based on natural law to support and interpret (or qualify) the teaching of the Church on economic matters. Their focus was continually on injustice arising from people being under compulsion, and the need for the victims of compulsion to be compensated. In discussing these problems, they developed and clarified many economic concepts. Nowhere is this more obvious than in their teaching on usury. The injunction in the Sermon on the Mount to 'Lend without expecting any return' was widely cited,[11] as was St Ambrose's claim that 'If someone receives usury, he commits robbery',[12] but they also tried to find rational arguments to support their case.

The fundamental idea underlying all discussions of usury was that money is sterile. Making money from money is unnatural. Thus, if a borrower makes a profit using money they have borrowed, this is because of their efforts, not because the money itself is productive. This idea of the sterility of money was reinforced by the legal concept of a loan. In law, most loans took the form of a mutuum, in which ownership of the thing lent passes to the borrower, who subsequently repays in kind. The original goods are not returned to the lender. This can apply only to fungible goods, such as gold, silver, wine, oil or grain, of which one unit is interchangeable with another and can be measured or counted. Because ownership passed to the borrower, it followed that any profit made using the goods belonged to the borrower, and that the lender was not entitled to a share.

The main qualification to the prohibition of any payment by the borrower was that the lender could seek compensation if they suffered a loss because the borrower failed to repay on time. Thomas of

Chobham, for instance, gave the example of a lender who needed the money to trade at the fair, to pay their rent, or to provide their daughter with a dowry. Compensation for an actual loss was widely accepted. Controversy began when the idea was extended to cover an expected loss caused by default (*damnum emergens*), or to cover the loss incurred by the lender within the period of the loan (*lucrum cessans*). Aquinas, for example, rejected the argument for *lucrum cessans* on the grounds that, as ownership passed to the borrower, the lender who took money was effectively selling something that was not his to sell. One problem with these qualifications was that, if they were allowed, they could be used systematically to get around the prohibition on usury. A penalty clause could be included in a loan contract on the understanding that the borrower would default and that the penalty would be paid.

NICOLE ORESME AND THE
THEORY OF MONEY

The scholastic economic tradition was an evolving one, and, though Aquinas provided what was in many ways its definitive statement, it continued to evolve in the centuries that followed. The framework laid down by the theologians of the early Church and, from the twelfth century, by Aristotle was all pervasive but it still left room for change and the exploration of new lines of inquiry. Nowhere is this more evident than in fourteenth- and fifteenth-century writings on money. Aristotelian ideas provided the analytical framework, but new ideas were developed in response to new problems.

The fourteenth century was a time of economic, political and social upheaval. For example, feudal institutions such as the links between military service and rights over land were declining, and commerce was expanding. New forms of credit and banking were being developed. In the middle of the century the Black Death produced a chronic shortage of labour, substantially changing the relations between the different classes of society. Kings found themselves short of income and made increasing resort to measures such as debasement (reducing the gold and silver content of the coinage) to increase their revenues. Questions of money and its role in the economy therefore became much more prominent.

The way in which the Aristotelian tradition could be developed to deal with these new problems is well illustrated by Nicole Oresme's *Treatise on the Origin, Nature, Law and Alterations of Money*. This was written in Latin in the mid-fourteenth century by a Frenchman born around 1320 who studied in Paris, served as adviser to Charles V of France, and died as Bishop of Lisieux in 1382. It was unusual in being written as a short tract on the evils of altering the currency, but it drew heavily on Aristotle and probably reflects ideas that, by this time, were widely accepted by scholastic writers. In the *Treatise*, Oresme puts forward the Aristotelian arguments about the origin of money (in exchange) and condemns 'unnatural' uses of money. There are, however, emphases not present in writing a century earlier. Debasement is condemned as undermining trust in the currency (Oresme regards it as worse than usury, which in turn is worse than making money through exchange). Clipping of coins (in order to melt down and sell the metal clipped off) is also harmful, because the clipped coins circulate as if they are of full weight. In both cases, Oresme's argument is that the action leads to confusion about the value of the currency, and that this is harmful. He cites Aristotle's contention that the thing that should be most stable in character is money.

Another issue to which Oresme pays attention is the ratio of gold to silver in the currency. This, he argues, should reflect the natural scarcity of the two metals – because gold is scarcer, it should be valued more highly than silver. Implicit in this is the idea that scarce commodities are more valuable than those that are more abundant. When the relative scarcity of metals changes, the ratio of gold to silver in the coinage will have to change too. However, such changes, Oresme believes, are rare, and most attempts by rulers to change the currency are arbitrary and designed solely to raise revenue. He likens attempts to raise the value of a scarce metal to a monopolist charging a high price for his product and condemns it accordingly.

Oresme's main argument, however, is that money is intended for the community, to be used at a price set by the ruler. In the same way that people may own property but the community has a right to the fruits of that property, the ruler has the right to coin money and to set its price, but is required to exercise this right in the interests of the community. Thus, although it is wrong for a ruler to alter the value of money for his own ends, it is legitimate for him to do so on behalf of the community:

> Since money belongs to the community ... it would seem that the community may control it as it wills ... And if the community has great need of a large sum of money for a war or for the ransom of its prince from captivity, or for some other emergency, then it might raise it by altering the money, and this would not be contrary to nature or usurious, since it would not be the act of the prince alone, but of the community to whom the money belongs.[13]

The significance of this passage is explained by an event that happened in 1356. The King of France, Jean le Bon, was captured by the English at Poitiers, and the dauphin was faced with a demand for 4 million crowns as his ransom. This sum was so large that to pay it threatened the stability of the French currency. The dauphin (who became Charles V) turned to Oresme for economic advice.

There is, in Oresme's work, a tension between different ways of thinking about economic activity. The first idea is that it is the prerogative of the ruler to determine the value of money. This implies that people should accept clipped coins at full value and not value them according to their intrinsic value (as natural riches). Against this, Oresme recognizes that men do what they find profitable: they ignore the price set by the ruler and sell money 'as if it were natural riches'. This practice leads to precious metal being transported abroad, when it is lost to its proper purpose – to finance trade in the country where it was minted. Oresme thus glimpses the power of the market, for he sees that undervalued money will be exported, causing economic difficulties at home. He also sees that it is important for a ruler to retain the public's trust in a currency, for by this time money had ceased to depend solely on the value of the silver it contained. In other words, money had become more than a piece of precious metal marked with a stamp to save people the trouble of weighing and testing it. However, when Oresme challenges the way in which rulers alter the value of money, his objection is the moral/political one that the interests of the community must be placed above those of the ruler himself. It is thus moral or political constraints, not economic forces, that constrain what the ruler should do. Although the context is much more modern, the underlying argument is thoroughly Aristotelian.

CONCLUSIONS

The idea that the Middle Ages produced no significant economic thought is far from the truth. The underlying framework remained an ethical one, informed by theology and law. However, the scholastic writers tried to find rational arguments for their moral judgements – to develop ideas based on natural law. In order to do this, they had to develop and analyse economic concepts.

Underlying much of their thinking was the notion that a transaction must be just if all the parties involved enter into it voluntarily and that coercion implies injustice. This way of thinking led scholars to explore what was and was not coercive in the different situations that confronted them. For example, under what circumstances did monopoly imply coercion on the part of the seller? In order to answer this question it was necessary to think about what determined the value of a commodity and the role of competition in regulating prices. They also considered the nature of money and paid attention to the development of new commercial institutions, and lending at interest. Clearly most people who borrowed money did so because they needed it, but under what circumstances did the ability of lenders to withhold loans amount to coercing borrowers into paying interest? In addition to paying attention to the difference between a person who and needs food to avoid starvation, and a merchant who is borrowing in order to engage in trade, scholars used concepts of expected profit or loss and opportunity cost in order to make sense of the problem. Thus, although the scholastics' focus, like that of their predecessors in the ancient world, was on morality, and hence on normative questions, they ended up, consciously or not, trying to understand how the economic world worked.

3
The Emergence of the Modern World View – the Sixteenth Century

THE RENAISSANCE AND THE EMERGENCE OF MODERN SCIENCE

Medieval society did not suddenly disappear. In parts of Europe, feudal institutions continued into the eighteenth and nineteenth centuries. Serfdom, for example, was not abolished in Russia until 1861. Medieval views of the world, in which religion, science and mysticism exist alongside one another, have lasted even longer. In many respects, however, the fifteenth century marks the beginning of the modern world. This is symbolized by the fall of Constantinople to the Turks, which marked the end of the Roman empire in the East. In the second half of the century the Portuguese explored the African coastline and arrived in India in 1498. The West Indies were reached in 1492, and within a few years Europeans discovered the continents of North and South America: they no longer saw the world as centred on the Mediterranean.

Dramatic as the new discoveries were, they were only a part of an even more extensive transformation of European society that took place between the fifteenth and seventeenth centuries. Central to this process was the artistic, literary and cultural flowering centred on Italy known as the Renaissance. This would never have been possible without the rediscovery of the Greek and Latin classics. In the fourteenth century, Petrarch (1304–74) had looked back on the preceding thousand years as a 'dark age' in comparison with the highly developed cultures of Greece and Rome and had started the process of rediscovering ancient literature. The scholastics of the Middle Ages had, of course, rediscovered much ancient writing, but, whereas they had been interested primarily in philosophy, and above all in Aristotle, Petrarch sought to learn from the entire corpus of classical writing – poetry, history and biography as well as philosophy and science. Classical scholarship (*literae humaniores*) provided an alternative source of moral inspiration to that provided by the Church.

Even in artistic works commissioned by the Church – which were extensive (work on St Peter's Basilica in Rome was started in 1506) – there was an increased interest in humanity. Less and less did major works of art have a religious theme, and, when such themes were treated, the impact of the rediscovery of the classics and the new humanism was clear. To illustrate this, it is enough to cite the names of Leonardo da Vinci (1452–1519), Michelangelo (1475–1564) and Raphael (1483–1520). The same was true of music. Art and music were no longer being used solely in support of religion.

As people rediscovered classical literature, they discovered new perspectives on science, many deriving from Plato rather than Aristotle. It was a view of the world where science, astrology and pagan gods all had a place. A significant part of this was the Neoplatonic association of the sun with divinity, from which it was a short step towards seeing the world as going round the sun rather than vice versa.

The man who took this step, Copernicus (1473–1543), was driven by a Pythagorean search for a simple, mathematical formula that would explain the motion of the planets. What he objected to in the geocentric cosmology he inherited from Aristotle and Ptolemy was its inelegance as much as its inaccuracy – though deriving a more accurate system was of crucial importance because of the urgent, practical problem of reforming the calendar. (Because the calendar year was not exactly the same length as the solar year, the seasons were moving away from their traditional places in the calendar.) Copernicus turned to classical writers other than Aristotle and Ptolemy and found there the idea of a sun-centred universe whose implications he worked out. Though the predictions of such a system were still far from satisfactory, Copernicus was nonetheless able to produce results that were superior to those derived from the old system. However, although displacing the Earth from its position at the centre of the universe involved a radical break with tradition, the rest of his cosmology was medieval. Heavenly bodies still travelled in circles, at constant speed, moved by crystalline spheres. Postulating a moving Earth was anomalous in that Copernicus could not answer obvious objections, such as why, if the Earth was moving, objects on its surface did not fall off.

Further movement away from the medieval world view towards that of modern science occurred during the following two centuries. Kepler (1571–1630), working with the more accurate astronomical observations provided by Tycho Brahe (1546–1601), discovered that elliptical orbits, with the sun at one of the foci, fitted the data far better. He too was inspired by the Neoplatonic search for harmony and pattern in the universe. However, he still did not answer the main objections to the idea of a moving Earth, nor provide any theoretical explanation of why the Earth should move. It was left to Galileo (1564–1642) to develop new methods of inquiry (such as turning a telescope on the stars) and to postulate a uniformity between the motion of bodies on the Earth and in the heavens. Descartes (1596–1650), again developing ideas from classical writers, took the step of seeing heavenly bodies as particles moving freely in an infinite space. Taking his lead from Galileo, he provided the first statement of the law of inertia. The system was then completed by Isaac Newton (1642–1727), who added the law of gravity. Newton was able to use his laws of motion to explain not only the movement of the planets but also that of bodies on the Earth's surface. For the first time, there was a coherent and complete alternative to medieval cosmology. The universe was seen no longer as being kept in motion by God but as governed by mechanical laws. God might play a role in setting it in motion (a divine clock-maker), but thereafter his role was at an end.

Such a brief account of the rise of modern science is necessarily oversimplified, but it is enough to make several important points. The Scientific Revolution involved a profound transformation in how the world was viewed, with implications not only for the way in which natural phenomena were thought of but also for thinking about religion and society. A change of this magnitude was a long-drawn-out process. At its beginning, anticipations of the Scientific Revolution can be found in the *via moderna* ('modern way') stemming from the work of William of Ockham (*c*.1285–*c*.1349), with its separation of the spheres of human reason and divine revelation. Towards the end of the transformation, even Newton retained a belief in astrology that cannot be separated from his astronomy.

THE REFORMATION

The sixteenth century was also the time of the Reformation, when the Protestant Church separated from the Roman Catholic Church. This event, or series of events, had profound political and social consequences. Although this has been disputed, it may even have been an important factor underlying the economic growth in England and the Netherlands, two Protestant countries, during the seventeenth and eighteenth centuries. However, there was only a limited break with traditional economic thinking, for it was essentially a conservative movement – a reaffirmation of Judaeo-Christian morality and theology against the humanistic-pagan influences of the Renaissance. The event that provoked Luther's publication of his *Ninety-five Theses* in 1517 was the arrival of a friar selling indulgences to pay for the building of St Peter's Basilica.

One of the factors that made Luther's stand against the Church hierarchy more far-reaching than the many similar protests that had been made in earlier centuries was the invention of printing. The Gutenberg Bible was printed in 1455, and by the end of the fifteenth century the number of books printed probably exceeded the number written by scribes in the previous thousand years. Printing meant that Protestant ideas could spread rapidly within Europe. Luther's protest thus became much more than a single monk's quarrel with the Church. The other factor underlying the success of the Reformation was the emerging nationalism within Europe. In the German states, Luther found protectors against both the papacy and the Habsburg empire. Religious differences could be used as weapons in political battles.

The major figures in the Reformation – Martin Luther (1483–1546), Jean Calvin (1509–64) and Ulrich Zwingli (1484–1531) – were conservative on economic questions. Luther strictly upheld the prohibition of usury and the doctrine of the just price, even rejecting some of the exceptions that had come to be accepted. However, instead of basing such arguments on Aristotelian notions of natural law, his condemnation of usury was based on Christ's teachings about loving one's neighbour as oneself. It was greed, and the appearance of greed, that he condemned. In general, however, Luther had little interest in economic questions and certainly no real curiosity about economic matters. This could explain why in some passages he appears to endorse the argument that money was sterile, even though elsewhere he rejected such reasoning. Similarly, although Calvin relaxed the teaching on usury, he too held strongly to the idea of the just price. Merchants were expected to make only moderate profits, and were not to seek all they could get. Even on usury, however, his thinking was, in practice, close to scholastic doctrine. While he accepted that the payment of interest was legitimate, he hedged it with qualifications: people should not be professional moneylenders, they should not take advantage of the poor, and they should obey legal restrictions on interest rates. The theology might have changed but in practice the implications in relation to economic activity were not dramatically different.

The Reformation had a very direct impact on political thought. In the medieval world view, good laws were judged by their conformity with God's law. Sovereignty derived from God. Thus it was on the authority of the Pope, Christ's vicar on earth, that Charlemagne was crowned Holy Roman Emperor in 800. Though there were continual disputes between secular and ecclesiastical authorities, neither side sought to dispense completely with the other. Conflict between the two jurisdictions was a defining feature of medieval politics, not something that could be eliminated. On the other hand, given the need to resolve such conflicts, a large literature grew up on the claims that secular and ecclesiastical authorities might rightly make. Radicals entertained the notion that sovereignty might come from the people, though at the same time seeking to reconcile this with the idea that God was sovereign over all.

This situation was transformed with the Reformation. There was no longer any single ecclesiastical authority to which everyone owed allegiance. If a ruler became Protestant, there was a problem for those of his subjects who remained loyal to the Catholic Church. Individual Protestants living under a Catholic ruler were in a similar situation. It was possible to conceive how subjects might find themselves in a situation in which religious scruple called for disobedience to their ruler. In short, there was now a problem of political obligation. A new basis for political structures was required. One way to obtain this was to appeal to the idea of natural law. Though stemming from Stoic and Roman thought, and developed by the scholastics, the idea of natural law was taken up by Protestant lawyers and philosophers. However, before discussing this, we need to take account of an equally fundamental political configuration of Europe.

POLITICAL CHANGE

Medieval society was one where a variety of powers competed for supremacy. This was most clearly represented in the long struggle between the emperors (first the Roman emperor, later the Holy Roman Emperor) and the papacy. Alongside these, numerous local princes also claimed allegiance. There had, of course, been monarchies for centuries, but they rarely ruled over lands that had any strong national identity, and their power was frequently limited by the power of nobles living within their realms: kings had no monopoly over military force. However, from the fifteenth century, this began slowly to change. European politics remained dominated by the Hapsburg and Bourbon dynasties, but in some places, power over a particular territory became more centralized. These emerging states included England and the United Provinces of the Netherlands (the Dutch Republic). A key dimension of these changes was the Reformation and the resulting split between Protestant and Catholic Christianity in an age when religious diversity was generally believed to weaken a state. Political competition between states was therefore frequently linked to religious differences, notably between the Protestantism of England, the United Provinces and several German states, and the Catholicism of France and the Hapsburg empire.

These competing states had meagre resources available to them. They had to raise armies and maintain navies, but their administrative apparatus and tax powers were very limited. Rulers, even of the most prosperous parts of Europe, were chronically short of money. Thus not only did people increasingly think in national terms, they also started to consider ways in which the economic power of nations could be increased. There were changes in the economic environment too.

The geographic discoveries made by the Portuguese and Spanish changed trade patterns. The opening of long-distance maritime trade routes had an enormous effect and arguably marked a turning point in western European economic history. Spanish conquests in America brought large quantities of gold and silver to Europe. Prices, which had fallen steadily through the fourteenth and fifteenth centuries, began to rise in the sixteenth. The changing role of the Church in society meant that the state had to take on new responsibilities. The Poor Law, introduced by Elizabeth I of England in 1597–1601, to provide support for the destitute, was something that had not been needed a century earlier, when much of this activity had been undertaken by the religious institutions that Henry VIII abolished.

These changes were associated with two significant shifts in the economic balance of Europe. The first was the decline of independent city states. The cities that grew most rapidly during the sixteenth century were capital cities. For example, the population of London rose from less than 50,000 in 1500 to around 575,000 in 1700. Other cities did not grow to the same extent. Venice, for example, declined in importance relative to London, Paris and Amsterdam. The second shift was the increased prosperity of the countries bordering on the North Sea and the decline of the Mediterranean.

There was therefore a change to the context in which people thought about economic problems. Although nation states as we now understand them had not emerged, there was increased concern with state policy. There were natural law philosophers who continued to work in the scholastic tradition, but there was also a large literature written by lawyers, government officials, merchants, speculators and adventurers. They almost always focused on practical problems of policy relating to the state. Government officials were concerned with developing the societies in which they lived, typically to increase the resources available to the state. Policies might include regulating trade or the promotion of industries they believed to be important. The continental European literature in this vein is sometimes known as Cameralism, on account of its connection with the science of state administration. In contrast, English merchants generally argued for policies that would promote their own interests, or the interests of the companies with which they were associated, even if they framed their proposals as being in the national interest. Sometimes this involved regulating trade in ways they considered advantageous; sometimes it involved freeing them from regulations they believed were harmful.

THE SCHOOL OF SALAMANCA AND AMERICAN TREASURE

Scholastic thought continued through the sixteenth and seventeenth centuries, though its content changed in response to new circumstances. One place where it remained strong was Spain, where the pre-eminent school was at Salamanca. Here, theologians and jurists continued to write in the traditional scholastic style – full of questions, objections, distinctions, solutions and conclusions, quoting extensively from Aristotle and Aquinas. Their economic analysis began with Aristotle, but, despite this, they were responsive to the new problems posed by the growth of commerce and the influx of vast quantities of treasure from the New World into what was a backward part of Europe. The main problems facing the School of Salamanca were usury, prices and money, where it was necessary to bring Thomistic doctrines into line with contemporary business practices, and to explain the dramatic changes that American treasure was having.

An important figure in the line of Salamancan writers was Martín de Azpilcueta Navarro, or Navarrus (d.1586), a Dominican who had taught law at Toulouse and Cahors before moving to Spain. Navarrus's account of the value of money is contained in 'Comentario resolutorio de usuras', an appendix to a theological manual published in 1556. He began from Aristotle's observation that the purpose of money is to facilitate trade. However, where earlier writers had condemned other uses of money as unnatural, Navarrus argued that changing it for profit was an important secondary use of money. In the same way that it was just for merchants to make moderate profits from buying and selling goods, money-changing was lawful if done to obtain a moderate living. He also took a more relaxed view of usury, allowing a greater range of compensation for loss.

However, how could someone make a profit at the same time as always dealing in money at its just price? Navarrus's answer was that the value of money was not constant, determined simply by its tale (the stamp on it) or the quantity of precious metal it contained. The value also depended on money's scarcity and the need for it, as well as on factors such as uncertainty about whether it would be raised or lowered in value, or even repudiated. Though it was wrong for money-changers to create artificial shortages in order to make a large profit, it was legitimate to take advantage of normal variations in the value of money, buying monies where or when they were cheap, and selling where or when they were dear.

These moral assertions rested on a supply-and-demand theory that was applied to money as well as to other commodities: that

> all merchandise becomes dearer when it is in great demand and short supply, and that money, in so far as it may be sold, bartered, or exchanged by some other form of contract, is merchandise and therefore becomes dearer when it is in great demand and short supply.[1]

This, Navarrus contended, was why prices rose 'after the discovery of the Indies, which flooded the country with gold and silver'.[2] Though it might look as though all other goods had become more expensive, this was because money had fallen in value. He went on to explain changes in the relative price of gold and silver in a similar way.

One of the problems faced by Spain was that, though it received vast quantities of treasure from America, little of it remained in the country. Money flowed out to the rest of Europe: it was most abundant in cities such as Genoa, Rome, Antwerp and Venice. One response to this was to impose laws forbidding its export. Thomas de Mercado (*d*.1585), another member of the School of Salamanca, used exactly the same arguments as Navarrus to claim that such laws would fail to keep money in. If money was being exported it was because it was more highly valued abroad than at home – in Antwerp rather than Seville, say – and so the only way to stop it leaving the country was to increase its domestic value relative to other commodities. Like Navarrus, Mercado argued that these natural variations in the value of money in different places justified making profit through engaging in foreign-exchange transactions.

The idea that scarcity makes goods dear and plenty makes them cheap has a history going back to ancient times, so it is not surprising that the Salamancans were not alone in seeing a link between American treasure and rising prices. Another to do so was Jean Bodin (1530–96), a lawyer and official in the French government. Bodin noted that prices of all goods had risen along with the price of land. He claimed that the principal reason for this was neither scarcity nor monopoly (two reasons often given for high prices), but the abundance of gold and silver resulting from the inflow of bullion from America. Bodin cited historical examples, from biblical and ancient times, to support this claim. One way in which his *Response to the Paradoxes of Malestroit Concerning the Rising Prices of All Things and the Means to Remedy the Situation* (1568) stands out from the Salamancan works is in its detailed factual discussion of monetary conditions in different parts of Europe, which enabled him to discuss with some authority how trade caused money to flow from one country to another.

ENGLAND UNDER THE TUDORS

The end of the Middle Ages in England is usually dated to the accession to the throne of Henry Tudor in 1485. Though the Tudor monarchy confronted many of the problems facing other European rulers of the period, such as inflation and a chronic shortage of revenue, defining national boundaries was not one of them. The most interesting economic work from the Tudor period is *A Discourse of the Common Weal of This Realm of England*, probably written by Sir Thomas Smith (1513–77), a Cambridge don, lawyer and government official, in 1549 and revised in 1581.[3] It takes the form of a conversation between a doctor (the leading figure), a knight, a merchant, a craftsman and a husbandman (farmer), in which many of the social and economic problems of the day are discussed – the major ones being inflation and the enclosure of common land so that it can be used for grazing sheep.

Rising prices were, as in the rest of Europe, considered a serious problem in sixteenth-century England. In earlier centuries prices had fluctuated, but there had been no long-term tendency for prices to rise, whereas by the end of the sixteenth century wheat prices were between four and five times higher than they were at its beginning. The author of the *Discourse* clearly sees the difference between real and money incomes, for he points out that rising prices harm only those people on fixed incomes: landlords whose rents are fixed by pre-existing contracts, and workers who work for fixed wages. Those who buy and sell gain from rising prices. He also points out that it does not make sense to complain about foreign goods being more expensive if the goods that are exported to buy them have also risen in price.

People were very familiar with the idea that scarcity, or 'dearth', could cause high prices, but the problem now was that prices were rising even when goods were plentiful. The explanation offered by Smith was debasement of the currency – hardly surprising, given that the first version of the *Discourse* was written in the middle of the so-called 'Great Debasement' of 1542–51, during which the silver content of the shilling was reduced to a sixth of its previous amount. Such changes in the value of the currency were roundly condemned. In 1581, perhaps because Smith had by now read Bodin, a new explanation of inflation was introduced: an increase in the quantity of money caused by imports of gold and silver from the Indies and other countries.

Enclosure of common land was associated with the expansion of sheep farming, to satisfy the growing demand for wool for export. Wealthy landlords were seen to be fencing off common land to graze sheep, causing a dearth of food and depriving poor people of their livelihoods. Not surprisingly, enclosure was bitterly controversial and was the major issue discussed in the *Discourse*. Smith's explanation was that enclosure was the result of the price of wool being high relative to the price of grain. He argued that men would not engage in difficult or dangerous work unless they received an appropriate reward.

> Take these rewards from them ... [and] what man will plow or dig the ground or exercise any manual art wherein there is any pain? ... [I]f all these rewards were taken from them all these faculties must decay, so if part of the reward be diminished the use of those faculties shall diminish ... and so they shall be the less occupied, the less they be rewarded and esteemed.[4]

Smith argued that it was necessary for 'the profit of the plow to be as good, rate for rate, as the profit of the grazier and sheepmaster', otherwise 'pasture shall ever encroach on tillage for all the laws that ever can be made to the contrary'.[5] The way to stop the expansion of sheep farming, therefore, was not to legislate against it, but to make it less profitable. The way to do this was to remove the tariffs that made it so profitable to export wool.

Smith saw the importance of the balance of trade, and frowned upon importing unnecessary luxuries, or goods manufactured from English raw materials. He encouraged the introduction of new industries that would create work and bring treasure into the country. However, despite advocating such measures, he showed a keen awareness of the price mechanism, assuming that men were motivated by self-interest. In this, his work marks a major break with scholastic economics.

ECONOMICS IN THE SIXTEENTH CENTURY

The changing religious and political configuration of Europe had an enormous impact on economic thinking. Economic strength was vital to national power, and much thought was given to designing policies that would achieve this. There was a change in the focus of economic thinking. It was also important to tackle the new problems thrown up by the Spanish conquests in America and the expansion of commerce and finance. In the longer term, the Renaissance and the Scientific Revolution were to have a major impact on economic thinking, but in the sixteenth century their influence was much less. The movement away from earlier ways of thinking was gradual – there was no sudden revolution in economic thought.

This slow change in ways of thinking is illustrated by the School of Salamanca, which ended up with an attitude towards commercial activities that was very different from that of Aristotle or Aquinas: its methods lay squarely within the scholastic tradition. Men of affairs such as Jean Bodin and Sir Thomas Smith (both of them lawyers cum government officials) moved even further from the medieval view. To a still greater extent, moral questions were pushed aside in favour of analysing what was actually going on in the world and what could be done. Instead of disputing the morality of profit, such writers were beginning to take profit-seeking behaviour for granted and attempted to work out its implications.

4

Science, Politics and Trade in Seventeenth-century England

BACKGROUND

The seventeenth century was also an age when people began to think differently about how the world was to be understood: about what we would now describe as scientific method. Two figures were crucial. The first was Francis Bacon (1561–1626), whose *Novum organum* (1620) provided a manifesto for experimental, empirical, science. He called for a reconstruction of knowledge on the basis of two principles: natural history (the detailed, systematic collection of facts about nature) and induction (deriving laws of nature from these facts). Scientists were to be servants and interpreters of nature. Bacon was critical of Aristotle and other ancient authorities for creating elaborate arguments founded on premises that were not based on careful observation and that were frequently contrary to nature. He was far from being the first to make these complaints, but his views were widely discussed.

The second dominant figure was René Descartes (see also Chapter 3). Like Bacon, Descartes challenged scholastic philosophy and sought to establish firm foundations on which knowledge could rest. He is most famous for his phrase *Cogito ergo sum* ('I think, therefore I am') – the only thing that cannot be doubted is that I am doubting. However, in the scientific context, the most significant aspect of his thought is the importance he attached to reason. Whereas Bacon sought to base knowledge on experimental science, Descartes sought, in the manner of mathematics, to base it on a set of simple, self-evident truths. Using deductive logic, more complex truths could then be derived from these. The result would be a body of knowledge that was certain and free of internal contradictions.

In that Bacon emphasized induction and Descartes deduction, the methods they offered were radically different. However, there were important similarities. Both challenged traditional authority and offered methods that they believed would provide secure foundations for knowledge. Where Bacon advocated experimental science, Descartes believed in measurement. He argued that the simplest, most comprehensible view of the world was to see it not as a single organism but as made up of various parts. It was to be understood in terms of the way those parts moved and interacted – as a mechanical system. The scientist should rely not on subjective judgements about the world but on qualities that could be measured. They were united in rejecting authority as the basis for knowledge.

However, although these new conceptions of science were important in the longer term, the immediate stimulus to economic analysis came not from ideas about science, but from immediate practical problems. In England, where censorship was less than in France, there was an explosion of pamphlets dealing with economic questions. This vast literature was directly related to the economic problems facing the country and to a political system that gave people the incentive to provide rational arguments for the policies they wanted to see adopted. Underlying it was an increasingly secular outlook, reflected in new attitudes to both science and politics, which had profound effects on the way in which people thought about economic questions. In most of these writings, merchants and businessmen sought to defend their own interests and to argue for policies that were to their own advantage. Much trade was organized through trading companies (such as the Merchant Adventurers and the East India Company) which regulated trade to parts of the world in which they were given monopoly privileges. Each of these companies had its own interests, as did outsiders who were opposed to the companies' privileges. However, the fact that most writers were motivated by self-interest did not preclude careful and subtle analysis.

THE CRISIS OF THE 1620S AND DUTCH COMMERCIAL POWER

In the fifteenth and sixteenth centuries the economic heart of Europe was northern Italy. The city state of Venice dominated trade in the Mediterranean and was a thriving manufacturing centre. Trade across the Atlantic was dominated by Seville. In the seventeenth century, however, economic power shifted decisively from the Mediterranean to north-west Europe. During the seventeenth century the population of northern and western Europe (Britain, Ireland, the Low Countries and Scandinavia) rose by a third, while that of the Mediterranean countries (Italy, Spain and Portugal) fell by 4 per cent. After 1600, Venice entered a period of decline. The Dutch acquired the spice trade, the Counter-Reformation in Italy created difficulties for book publishing, and the Thirty Years War (1618–48) in Germany took away important markets. Currency debasement in Turkey raised the cost of cotton and silk, two vital raw materials for the textile industry. In Spain, the inflow of American silver declined and the government of Castile faced a series of financial crises. The previous century's prosperity had not been accompanied by any sustainable industrial growth. In contrast, though they experienced severe economic crises, the economies of northern and western Europe did experience a period of growth.

In Northern Europe, the most successful economy was the Netherlands. The *fluitschip*, first launched in 1595, whose long flat hull and simplified rigging made it much cheaper to build and run than comparable ships elsewhere, was perhaps the main symbol of this success. Like England, the Netherlands was very dependent on overseas trade, and the two countries were widely seen as rivals. Naval wars, in which trade was the main bone of contention, were fought in 1652–4, 1665–7, 1672–4 and 1680–84. People sought to understand why the Dutch were so prosperous. In particular, were the low interest rates on loans in Amsterdam the cause or the result of Dutch prosperity? If they were the cause, then this could be used to support measures to lower interest rates (such as usury laws); but if they were the result, then such measures might be harmful.

However, under the first Stuart kings, James I and Charles I, the main stimulus to economic analysis came not from these longer-term problems but from the commercial crisis of 1620 to 1624. Its immediate cause was a decline in sales of cloth to Europe following the outbreak of the Thirty Years War which caused a loss of markets, first in Germany and the Baltic States and later in the Netherlands. The number of cloths exported from London by English merchants fell from 102,300 in 1618 to 85,700 in 1620. Two years later, sales had fallen to 75,600, and it was not until 1628 that they returned to their 1618 level. Unemployment was widespread. However, the problem was widely seen as a particularly acute scarcity of coins. The context in which these issues were discussed was a growing disquiet over James's attempt to govern through creating networks of patronage, bypassing Parliament, whose members generally saw royal spending as lavish. When Parliament eventually met in 1621, MPs, who had up to then been comparatively isolated, realized the extent of the crisis, and there was intensive debate over what was seen as a major public issue. The crisis was also a major subject of discussion in the Privy Council (a body of advisers to the king).

By the seventeenth century, printed pamphlets had emerged as a cheap means of communication, and so the crisis also provoked a large number of pamphlets arguing about its causes and proposing remedies, with different groups seeking to defend their own interests and to blame people other than themselves. Some located the cause of the crisis within the cloth industry itself – the growth of foreign competition and a fall in the quality of English cloth. Others blamed merchants, criticizing the monopoly privileges of the Society of Merchant Adventurers, which accounted for over half of England's cloth exports. The most significant discussions, however, were to do with money. There was a widespread view that 'shortage of money' was a major problem, and that this was related to instability in the foreign exchanges. Currency upheavals in Germany, linked to the outbreak of the Thirty Years War, could plausibly be seen as the reason why exports fell so rapidly from 1618 to 1620. However, there was no agreement that the two problems – trade and money – were connected.

THE BALANCE-OF-TRADE DOCTRINE

When Parliament debated the problems, trying to reconcile the trade crisis with the shortage of money, two views emerged. One was that the root cause was problems with money and the foreign exchanges; the other that the problem lay in an adverse balance of trade (imports exceeding exports) which was causing the shortage of money. As the controversy developed, opinions polarized.

The former explanation of the crisis was put forward by, among others, Gerard de Malynes (1586–1641), a merchant during the reign of Elizabeth I, connected with the Merchant Adventurers, who had also served the king on several occasions. He claimed that silver had left England because the English coin was undervalued, not reflecting recent currency changes on the continent. Foreign-exchange dealers could force the value of English coin below its par value, the value set by the Mint. If the par value reflected the world price of gold and silver, this would cause English coin to be exported, for it would be worth more as precious metal than as coin. This would account for the shortage of money in England. The low exchange rate explained both why English goods were sold cheaply and why imports were dear. The remedy, he argued, was to restore the Royal Exchange and to regulate foreign-exchange transactions in order to restore the exchange rate to its proper level.

Against this were ranged the arguments of the so-called balance-of-trade theorists, notably Edward Misselden (fl.1608–54, a member of the Merchant Adventurers) and Thomas Mun (1571–1641, a member of the East India Company). In June 1622, Misselden started the pamphlet controversy with *Free Trade, or the Meanes to Make Trade Flourisheth* (1622), with the motive of justifying his company's practices in the face of Parliamentary and Privy Council scrutiny.[1] The next year he followed this with *The Circle of Commerce, or the Balance of Trade* (1623), in which, like Mun, he argued that it was flows of goods that governed the exchange rate and flows of bullion, not the other way round. To stem the outflow of treasure it was necessary to increase the balance of trade – to reduce imports, especially of unnecessary items, and to increase exports. This required a low exchange rate, not a high one. More significantly, it was the 'balance of trade' that determined flows of money, not the other way round.

It can be shown that if exports and imports do not respond at all to prices, Malynes was right in wanting a higher exchange rate; but that if exports and imports are very responsive to prices, Misselden and Mun were right. However, their differences involved more than different assumptions about the responsiveness of trade flows to prices. They agreed that money was the 'soul' of commerce and that England's losses of money abroad had to be stopped, but behind this agreement lay two different views as to how the economy worked. In Malynes's world view, coins had an intrinsic value, dependent on their gold or silver content, and it was the sovereign's prerogative to establish this value. The Royal Exchange was thus necessary to provide merchants with information on the true value of the coinage, so that exchange transactions could reflect this value. In contrast, for Misselden and Mun, the buying and selling of goods was fundamental: supply and demand, not the sovereign, determined values, including the value of the currency.

The work of the balance-of-trade theorists was important in establishing a link between money and economic activity. They viewed money not as wealth to be accumulated but as working capital. For Mun, the clearest exponent of this view, money was needed to drive trade. The way to accumulate treasure was to allow it to be used in trade. In a chapter entitled 'The exportation of our moneys in trade of merchandize is a means to encrease our Treasure', Mun argued that the purpose of exporting money is

> to enlarge our trade by enabling us to bring in more forraign wares, which being sent out again will in due time much encrease our Treasure. For although in this manner wee do yearly multiply our importations to the maintenance of more Shipping and Mariners, improvment of His Majesties Customs and other benefits: yet our consumption of those forraign wares is no more than it was before; so that all the said encrease of commodities ... doth in the end become an exportation unto us of a far greater value.[2]

Mun's pamphlet *England's Treasure by Forraign Trade* was published only posthumously, in 1664, probably because by the time he wrote it he was able to influence the relevant committees directly, with the result that he could make his views known without publishing it. His theory of the balance of trade was important for several reasons. Though not conceived in these terms, it was a theory of growth centred on foreign trade: as such, it embodied a particular conception of economic activity, increasingly challenged in the seventeenth century, in which production was fundamental. In the passage just quoted, Mun states explicitly that consumption of foreign commodities will not increase. England's entrepôt trade will grow. In addition, Mun's theory provided a justification for the East India Company, of which he was a director, being allowed to export bullion to India. This was necessary because the company could not find suitable goods for export.

POLITICAL FERMENT

England was in a state of political turmoil for much of the seventeenth century. The early Stuart kings, James I (r.1603–25) and Charles I (r.1625–49), were obliged to turn to Parliament when they needed more funds than they could raise from the royal estates and from established forms of taxation such as customs duties. For a time (the 'eleven years' tyranny', 1629–40) Charles tried to rule without Parliament altogether. The country then experienced a period of civil war (1642–9), which was eventually followed by the Protectorate under Oliver Cromwell. The Stuarts were restored in 1660 and, though it was now clear that they could not revert to the absolutism of their forebears, constitutional conflict persisted. This came to a head when Charles II (r.1660–85) was succeeded by James II (r.1685–8), a Catholic. James was forced to flee England in 1688 after William of Orange (r.1689–1702) landed at Torbay with a large army. William took the crown as a strictly constitutional monarch. All this political turmoil raised fundamental questions about the basis on which society was organized.

Lying behind such questioning was a deeper change in attitudes towards what were, at the time, known as the passions: greed, envy, lust and so on. By the seventeenth century it had become accepted that such destructive passions could not be contained by religious or moral teaching, and that it was necessary to look for an alternative explanation of how society might be held together. One possibility was that one passion might be used to keep others under control. Bacon had argued that, just as a hunter uses one animal to catch another, or rulers use one faction to control another, so one 'affection' could be used to master another, an approach that has been traced back to Niccolò Machiavelli (1469–1527). He had argued, in *The Prince* (1513), that the ruler of a state should work on the assumption that people around him will behave in a self-interested way not because he believed that men had no moral principles, but because this was the safest and most reliable assumption to make. People might behave morally or altruistically, but it was foolish for rulers to rely on this. Like Machiavelli, Thomas Hobbes (1588–1679) drew conclusions from general assumptions about human nature, arguing that the destructive passions (the desire for riches, glory and domination) could be checked by countervailing passions (the fear of death, the desire to live comfortably, and the hope of achieving this through work). These countervailing passions came to be known as 'interests'.

However, at the same time as people started thinking that society was held together by interest, there was a profound shift in the way in which the term was understood. In the late sixteenth century 'interest' was synonymous with 'reasons of state' and was seen as lying in between passion and rationality. In England, during the Civil War, the concept of interest began to be applied not simply to the national interest but to individuals and groups within the nation. At this time, the term covered all human aspirations (glory, security and honour as well as material comfort) and implied an element of reflection and calculation about how these were to be achieved. By the end of the seventeenth century, however, interest had begun to take on a more narrowly economic interpretation. The same changes happened in France. In 1661 Cardinal Richelieu's secretary could write, 'the name of interest has remained attached exclusively, I do not know how, to the interest of wealth'.[3] By the eighteenth century we find writers regularly assuming that people are motivated by, as it was put by David Hume (see pp. 122–5), 'avidity of acquiring goods and possessions' or, more simply, the 'love of gain'.[4]

One of the most widely debated contributions to this process was Hobbes's *Leviathan* (1651). This book was influential not because people agreed with it but because, although his conclusions were intensely disliked, Hobbes's arguments seemed so compelling that they could not be ignored. *Leviathan* offended all sides: royalists by arguing against the divine right of kings, and the opponents of monarchy by arguing that sovereignty must of necessity be absolute.

Hobbes's argument was that civil society is possible only if there is a government to make and enforce laws. Without government, society would revert to a state of nature in which every man had to look after himself. Hobbes went so far as to describe such a state of nature as a state of war. Every man would be free to do as he liked, there being no government to stop him. Furthermore, every man would be aggressive towards his neighbours, in order to defend himself. Human behaviour would be unpredictable, and the result would be universal fear and insecurity. Property would be insecure, contracts would be unenforceable, and economic life would be impossible. Hobbes worked on *Leviathan* during a decade (1641–51) spent in France after fleeing England to avoid the Civil War. While England's descent into civil war after Parliament had challenged the king's sovereignty may have influenced his views, it seems likely that Hobbes was influenced as much by what happened in Germany. During the Thirty Years War Germany descended into economic as well as political chaos as competing rulers fought each other while seeking to establish their own claims to sovereignty.

The way out of such a situation, Hobbes argued, was for men to choose a sovereign (either an individual or a group) who would become both lawgiver and law-enforcer. If they did this, civil society would become possible. In itself, this is a standard social contract theory of sovereignty. What distinguishes Hobbes's theory from other social contract theories is his argument that sovereignty must be absolute – that it cannot be divided or limited. To impose limitations on sovereignty, Hobbes argued, would create conflict, ultimately resolvable only by war. The sovereign therefore must have the right to administer justice, to appoint and reward his servants (for it is physically impossible for one person to rule alone), and to censor political and religious opinions. The last of these was inevitable given that religious divisions were one of the major sources of conflict in both the Thirty Years War and seventeenth-century England.

Hobbes's argument about sovereignty is important in the history of economic thought because in *Leviathan* he was tackling the fundamental question of what it is that holds society together. He saw this as a purely political question, not addressing how politics and sovereignty might be related to issues such as commerce and wealth. Almost as important is Hobbes's method. His conclusion that civil society requires an absolute sovereign is based not on theological arguments but on rational deductions from assumptions about human nature – that, in the absence of restraints, people will be aggressive towards their neighbours in pursuing their own security. This is a resolutely secular outlook on society. It resembles Machiavelli's approach to politics, but it goes a step further. Whereas Machiavelli argued that it was prudent for rulers to base their actions on the assumption that men might behave in this way, Hobbes works out his whole theory of sovereignty on the assumption that they will do so.

A thinker who developed Hobbes's arguments was Samuel Pufendorf (1632–94), a German jurist and political philosopher who worked in German and Swedish universities from the 1660s to the 1690s. Where Hobbes had portrayed people as solitary beings, Pufendorf allowed that they could be sociable, not because of any innate sociability, but because they had to satisfy basic human needs. Without cooperation, children could not live at all, and adults could not live well. Commerce thus provided a utilitarian basis for sociability, independently of any motivations such as friendship, love or altruism. The state of nature was therefore less brutish than Hobbes had claimed. This was a significant move away from Hobbes, implying that political thought needed to take account of society and raising the possibility that moral arguments might play a role in social relations. However, for many of his critics his invocation of commercial sociability was insufficient: whereas some saw him as a Christian critic of Hobbes, others saw his utilitarian sociability as no more than a facade, disguising a fundamentally Hobbesian position. As will be seen in Chapter 5, Pufendorf's extension of Hobbes's arguments was one of the starting points for important eighteenth-century debates.

POLITICAL ARITHMETICK

Bacon's programme was taken up by the Royal Society, which received its charter in 1662 and included most of the leading scientists of the period, such as Robert Boyle (1627–91, the leading figure), Isaac Newton, Robert Hooke (1635–1703), John Locke and Samuel Pepys (1633–1703). Its motto, *Nullius in verba* ('On no man's word'), echoed Bacon's rejection of arguments from authority, and the society laid down procedures about how experiments were to be conducted and reported on whether their results were to be accepted. There were serious difficulties with the inductive part of the programme (even the concept of induction was ambiguous). The society's critics, among them Thomas Hobbes, raised justifiable questions about its experimental procedures; some of the fact-gathering was pointless, and some of the experiments performed by the 'virtuosi' merited the scorn poured on them by writers such as Jonathan Swift (1667–1745). However, despite these problems, the Royal Society was extremely successful. The achievements of Boyle and Newton alone are enough to establish that.

From the start, economic questions formed part of the society's programme. Bacon had called for natural histories of different trades – of 'nature altered or wrought'. The major figure here was William Petty (1623–87). Petty studied medicine in the Netherlands and France, served for a short time as an assistant to Hobbes (who himself may at one time have been an assistant to Bacon), and then returned, in 1646, to Oxford. There he met Boyle and became involved in the circle from which the Royal Society developed. However, having become established as professor of anatomy at Oxford, and professor of music at Gresham College in London, he took leave of absence in order to go to Ireland as physician to Cromwell's army. Cromwell was faced with the task of dividing Irish lands to reward his soldiers and financiers. In 1655–8 Petty undertook the task of surveying, and produced some of the best maps of any country at the time. Through buying land from soldiers who wanted to sell the land they had been given, he established himself as a major landowner, though he had to spend much time defending his titles.

Petty's thoroughly Baconian approach to economics is stated clearly in the preface to his *Political Arithmetick*, written in the 1670s though not published until 1690, after his death: 'Instead of using only comparative and superlative words, and intellectual arguments, I have taken the course ... to express my self in terms of number, weight or measure; to use only arguments of sense, and to consider only such causes, as have visible foundations in nature.'[5] His objective in writing the book was to show that, contrary to much popular belief, England was richer than ever before. He tried to achieve this by providing arguments based on numbers and arithmetic calculations.

Central to Petty's claim about England's wealth was an argument about the value of labour. Wealth comprised people as well as land (of which France clearly had more than England) and capital. Starting from the observation that people each spent £7 per annum and assuming a population of 6 million, he calculated that national income must be £42 million. Deducting £8 million for rents and a further £8 million for profits on 'personal estate' (housing, ships, cattle, coins and stocks of goods), this left £26 million which had to be produced by labour. This gave the following national accounts:

Expenditure		Income	
Personal spending	£42 million	Wages	£26 million
		Profits	£8 million
		Rents	£8 million
Total	£42 million	Total	£42 million

Petty went on to compute the value of the population itself. He made the assumption that the rate of return for labour was the same as that for land. He further assumed that its value was twenty times the annual revenue that could be derived from it (implying a rate of interest of 5 per cent per annum), and deduced that, if labour contributed £26 million a year, its value must be twenty times that – namely £520 million. Dividing by the population, this gave him a value for the population of £80 per head. This could then be used to calculate such things as the value of the population lost in the Great Plague.

In his other works, Petty produced more detailed national accounts. In *Verbum sapienti* (1665) he derived his figures for average annual spending from assumptions about the distribution of spending (that one sixth of the population spent 2d. per day, another sixth spent 4d. per day, and so on), the number of days worked in a year (287), and the proportion of the population that worked (50 per cent). He also derived his figure for rents by assuming that England had 24 million acres of land yielding rents of 6s. 8d. per acre. Even more detailed accounts were prepared in *The Political Anatomy of Ireland* (1672), in which he analysed the distribution of landholdings, house sizes and occupations.

Simple as these national accounts were, they involved major conceptual advances. Expressing these in modern terminology, these included the following ideas. (1) National expenditure (or output) and national income are equivalent. (2) National income is the sum of payments received by all factors of production (land, labour and capital). (3) The values of all assets are linked by a common discount rate to the incomes received (i.e. the ratio of rent to the value of land is the same as the ratio of profits to the value of capital). This was clearly a major achievement. However, the accuracy of the numbers involved in these calculations was, to say the least, highly dubious. Petty estimated population from bills of mortality (parish records of deaths from different causes) without discussing the assumptions he had to make in order to do his calculations or the reliability of the underlying data. Even worse, many of his figures were pure guesswork. He admitted as much in the preface to *Political Arithmetick*, where he wrote that many of his observations were 'either true, or not apparently false ... and if they are false, not so false as to destroy the argument they are brought for; but at worst are suppositions to shew the way to that knowledge I aim at'.[6] In short, by modern standards he was cavalier about his figures. The reason for this may have been that he was not interested in completely precise figures. His aim was just to establish magnitudes sufficiently precisely to make the points he wished to make.

Petty believed that a nation benefited from accumulating treasure, and that taxes on imports might help to achieve this (the view Adam

Smith later argued was central to what he called 'the mercantile system'). However, he did not confuse treasure and wealth. He recognized that foodstuffs were riches too, but he had a theory about why money was particularly important. What was different about silver, gold and jewels was that they were not perishable and thus were wealth 'at all times and all places'. Furthermore, money was needed to drive trade. This is why it might benefit a country for plate to be melted down and coined. The amount of money that was needed depended on how quickly it circulated. Here again Petty turned to a numerical example. If 6 million people spend £7 per annum each, their total spending amounts to some £800,000 per week. If 'every man did pay his expence weekly', money would circulate within the week and £1 million would be enough. On top of this, however, rents of land (amounting to £8 million) are paid half-yearly, requiring a further £4 million, and the rent of housing (another £4 million a year) is paid quarterly, which requires a further £1 million. In total, therefore, £6 million is required by the nation. Petty also argued that increases in the quantity of money led to falls in the rate of interest. Over the previous forty years, he claimed, the interest rate had fallen from 10 per cent to 6 per cent per annum, this being 'the effect of the increase of mony'.[7]

It is easy to look at Petty's data and conclude that he failed to match the achievements of his contemporaries in the Royal Society, such as Boyle and Hooke. His arguments were mercilessly satirized by Jonathan Swift in *A Modest Proposal, for Preventing the Children of Poor People in Ireland from being a Burden to their Parents or Country* (1729). It is possible to argue that Petty failed to live up to his Baconian methodology – that his deductions were not about causes that had 'visible foundations in nature', that they were no less speculative than those of his predecessors, and that his use of arithmetic was no more than a rhetorical device. This, however, is to miss the point that his methodology did lead him to ask new questions. Merely to ask about the size of labour's contribution to national wealth, the amount of money needed to drive trade, or the effects of different taxes was to view economic phenomena in a new way. In asking these questions Petty was indeed being faithful to the methods of Bacon and the Royal Society. His involvement in surveying Ireland provided him with some data and stimulated much of his work. However, given the extreme paucity of information available to him and the complexity of the problems he was trying to tackle, it was inevitable that his statistics were unreliable.

Though historians of economics usually associate the term 'Political Arithmetick' with Petty, he was not alone in applying such methods. John Graunt (1620–74), a close friend of Petty, was elected a fellow of the Royal Society in 1662 on the basis of his book *Natural and Political Observations ... made upon the Bills of Mortality* (1662). He studied data on births and deaths to estimate the population of London and to construct the first survival table (showing how many people lived to various ages). Towards the end of the century, his work and Petty's were followed up by Gregory King (1648–1712). Having more data available, King produced improved estimates of population and much more detailed national accounts than Petty had been able to construct. He calculated national savings, dividing the population into those classes that saved and those with expenses in excess of their incomes. He also produced comparative accounts of income, population and income per head for England, France and the Netherlands, for 1688 and 1695. These and several of his other calculations were motivated by his interest in understanding the potential of these countries to continue in their then state of war. For the case of England, he estimated the sources of war finance, calculating the amounts met from increased production, reduced consumption and disinvestment. He calculated, in 1695, that war could not be sustained beyond 1698. (Peace was negotiated in the summer of 1697.) Finally, mention should be made of Charles Davenant (1656–1714), who studied the distribution of taxes across different regions and was responsible for publishing King's work after the latter's death.

The twentieth-century creators of national-income accounts saw Graunt, Petty, Davenant and King as pioneers. However, interest in their work fluctuated greatly. Adam Smith, like many eighteenth- and nineteenth-century economists, was sceptical about the value of *Political Arithmetick*, with the result that it had little influence on the discipline. It was only when the resources of the modern twentieth-century state were applied to the task that it became possible to construct systematic, reasonably reliable national accounts.

THE RATE OF INTEREST AND THE
CASE FOR FREE TRADE

From the restoration of Charles II to the end of the seventeenth century a recurring question was whether or not legislation should be passed to lower the rate of interest. In 1668 a bill was introduced into Parliament to lower the maximum legal interest rate from 6 to 4 per cent per annum. The most influential advocate of the proposal was Sir Josiah Child (1630–99), a merchant who had made money through supplying the Royal Navy and who was one of the chief defenders of the East India Company. Child was in many respects a representative of what one scholar has called the 'old style' of doing economics: 'he looks like an advocate rather than theorist, a purveyor of patent remedies, an interested party asserting his objectivity, an imperfect copyist rather than a vigorous innovator, and only an occasional liberal'.[8] (The new style was that of the objective scientist.) His *Brief Observations Concerning Trade and Interest of Money* (1668) opened by asking why the Dutch were so much more successful than the English. He offered fifteen explanations, but claimed that the last, a low rate of interest, was the most important, being the cause of the other reasons for Dutch wealth. Child supported his case with two types of evidence. The first was that previous reductions in the legal maximum interest rate (from 10 to 8 per cent in the 1620s, and from 8 to 6 per cent in the 1640s) were followed by increases in both the number of merchants and their individual wealth. The second was evidence from comparing different countries. Parts of Italy paid 3 per cent interest and were prosperous; Spain paid between 10 and 12 per cent and was desperately short of money; France, with 7 per cent, was in the middle. According to Child, countries were 'richer or poorer in exact proportion to what they pay, and have usually paid, for the interest of money'.[9] This rule, he claimed, never failed.

Child recognized that such evidence did not establish that a low interest rate was the cause rather than the effect of prosperity. However, he offered almost no arguments to support his claim that it was. He claimed that reducing the interest rate from 6 per cent to 4 per cent or 3 per cent would double the nation's capital stock, but he did not explore this and turned instead to answering other people's objections to lowering the interest rate. In response to the absence of usury laws in the Netherlands, he argued that other Dutch institutions had the same effect: high-quality securities, banks, the use of bills of exchange, and low public spending.

The opposite case was argued by John Locke (1632–1704), secretary to Lord Ashley, then Chancellor of the Exchequer, in a pamphlet entitled *Some Consequences That are Like to Follow upon Lessening of Interest to 4 per cent* (1668). Although Locke is not completely consistent (perhaps not surprising, since it was his first venture into economics), his pamphlet differs from Child's in that its method is to construct tight logical arguments.

Restricting the rate of interest to 4 per cent would, Locke argued, reduce the supply of funds available for lending. Going beyond this, he argued that there was a 'natural' rate of interest determined by the quantity of money in a country relative to the volume of that country's trade: 'By natural use [interest] I mean that rate of money which the present scarcity makes it naturally at.'[10] Unlike Child, who focused exclusively on the rate of interest, Locke saw that if a lower rate of interest was produced by increasing the supply of funds (by banks, the use of bills and so on) its effects were very different from the effects of imposing a statutory maximum interest rate.

If interest depended on the amount of money needed for trade, how much money was required by a nation? Petty's calculations, discussed above, could be seen as an attempt to provide a definite answer to this question. Locke's answer introduced the idea of 'quickness of circulation':

> Because it depends, not barely on the quantity of money, but the quickness of its circulation – which since it cannot easily be traced [observed] . . . to make some probable guess we are to consider how much money it is necessary to suppose must rest constantly in each man's hands as requisite to the carrying on of trade.[11]

Such arguments took Locke away from the rate of interest into the broader questions of monetary economics, such as the relationship between the money supply and the price level. Echoing sixteenth-century writers such as Navarrus and Bodin, he argued that the value of money (or equivalently the value of commodities) depended on the quantity of money in relation to trade. Plenty of money would mean that money would be cheap and commodities dear. If the economy were isolated, this would mean that the quantity of money would not matter: if the quantity of money were lower, prices would be lower and more trade could take place.

On the other hand, in a country open to world trade and that used the same money as its neighbours, there must be a particular ratio of money to trade. The reason is that, if a country has less money (relative to trade) than its neighbours, then either prices must be lower or else goods must remain unsold, there being insufficient money to buy them at the prices prevailing abroad. If home prices were lower than foreign prices, the country would lose through paying more for its imports than it received for its exports. In addition, the country would risk having workers migrate to countries with higher wages.

Locke was not alone in insisting that low interest was the result of wealth, not its cause. Another writer to argue this was Dudley North (1641–91), who made a fortune trading with Turkey, before returning to England to become a Commissioner of the Customs and then the Treasury. His *Discourses upon Trade* (1691) was stimulated by renewed moves to lower the legal maximum rate of interest. It was published with a preface in which his brother Roger North (1653–1734), an accomplished political writer, emphasized the importance of abstraction and of reasoning being based on 'clear and evident truths'. Knowledge arrived at in this way had become 'mechanical'. This Cartesian method of reasoning, Roger North argued, was characteristic of his brother Dudley's work: 'He begins at the quick, from principles indisputably true; and so proceeding with great care, comes to a judgement of the nicest disputes concerning trade ... he reduceth things to their extreams, wherein all discriminations are most gross and sensible, and then shows them.'[12]

Dudley North's starting point was that trade was 'a commutation of superfluities'.[13] Those men who are most diligent, grow the most crops or produce the most goods will be wealthy even if no one has any gold or silver. However, in order to get the goods they require, such people have to exchange their surplus produce for goods that other people have produced. It is differences between people that lead to trade.

North then applied this argument to interest. Some men, he argued, will have much stock (capital) but lack the skill to use it; while others will have the required skills but no stock. Those who have too much stock will lend it to those who have too little, in return for interest. It is exactly the same as with land. Those with too much land allow others to use it in return for rent. Interest and rent are essentially the same. It follows, North continued, that if stock and land are plentiful, interest and rent will be low; if they are scarce, interest and rent will be high. Dutch interest rates were, he claimed, low because stock was plentiful, not the other way round.

If interest were lowered by legislation, North continued, the supply of loans would be reduced. Many lenders would be unwilling to accept a lower rate of interest, for it would not compensate them for the risk involved. They would prefer to hoard their wealth or turn it into plate. Alternatively, people might resort to 'underhand bargains' to avoid the law. A notable feature of North's argument here, consistent with his underlying premisses, is that not all borrowers and lenders are the same, so the same interest rate will not be appropriate for all transactions. Lenders and borrowers should be free to make their own bargains. Take away interest, North contended, and you take away borrowing and lending.

North's analysis of money followed the same lines. It rested on the premiss that wealth arises not from having money but from 'land at farm, money at interest, or goods in trade'.[14] Gold and silver are 'nothing but the weights and measures, by which traffick is more conveniently carried on than could be done without them; and also a proper fund for a surplusage of stock to be deposited in'.[15] Thus, if someone cannot sell their goods, the reason must be that too much is being offered for sale, overseas sales are wanting, or poverty is keeping down domestic sales. The reason could not be a shortage of coin, for a rich nation could obtain the money it needed through trade.

A consequence of this view was a favourable attitude towards luxury spending. The opposing view was that luxury spending should be curbed by restrictions on imports or by sumptuary laws. Imported luxuries, it was argued, caused money to leave the kingdom unnecessarily; luxury spending was also opposed on moral and political grounds (see pp. 95–7). North, on the other hand, saw that spending was necessary if goods were to be sold and if people were to be employed. Perhaps equally important, luxury consumption provided an incentive to work: 'The main spur to trade, or rather to industry and ingenuity, is the exorbitant appetites of men, which they will take pains to gratifie, and so be disposed to work, when nothing else will incline them to it; for did men content themselves with bare necessaries, we should have a poor world.'[16]

Though Dudley North did not take his arguments so far, in his preface Roger North argued that any trade that profited individuals was beneficial to the public, and that regulations on trade were always harmful:

> That there can be no trade unprofitable to the publick; for if any prove so, men leave it off; and wherever the traders thrive, the publick, of which they are a part, thrives also ... That no laws can set prices in trade, the rates of which, must and will make themselves: but when such laws do happen to lay any hold, it is so much impediment to trade, and therefore prejudicial ... That all favour to one trade or interest against another, is an abuse, and cuts so much of profit from the public.[17]

THE RECOINAGE
CRISIS OF THE 1690S

North's pamphlet and Locke's writing on interest illustrate the great change that had taken place in economic thinking since the early seventeenth century. The reason for most writing was still to influence policy, and pamphlets were still written by men actively engaged in trade or with interests to defend. There had, however, been an enormous change in the arguments used. In the writing of Mun and most of his contemporaries, economic thinking was mixed together with advice on how to be a successful merchant: *England's Treasure by Forraign Trade* was primarily a manual on good business practice. In contrast, though Locke and North certainly had interests to defend, they were attempting to stand back – to distance themselves from their material and to analyse it in what they understood to be a scientific way. The influence of thinkers such as Bacon, Descartes and even Hobbes is evident.

Equally important was a profound change that had taken place in attitudes towards economic growth. At the beginning of the seventeenth century the idea that the role of government was to maintain a stable, established order was still strong. Malynes's advocacy of the Royal Exchange followed naturally from such a perspective. This view was challenged by merchants who used the doctrine of the balance of trade as an argument in favour of greater freedom. They promoted a view of the economy in which the objective was growth, fuelled by the money brought in by a balance-of-trade surplus. Resources were to be developed in order to promote exports, and government policy was to be subordinated to this end. Economic growth was seen purely from the producers' and merchants' point of view – it was not based on the goal of increasing consumption.

The merchants' perspective on growth was radically different from the Tudor and early Stuart emphasis on the importance of preserving an established social order. It was, however, unable to explain England's increasing wealth after the Restoration in 1660 – something remarked on by numerous writers, including Petty. London was magnificently rebuilt after the Great Fire of 1666, and the city's prosperity attracted comment from both critics and admirers. There was also, especially from the 1670s, controversy over Indian cottons and silks, imports of which had increased dramatically since the freeing of trade in bullion in 1663. English clothiers began to use the balance-of-trade doctrine to criticize the activities of the East India Company in promoting Indian manufacturing and trade.

The response to this was the emergence, in the works of many writers, including Dudley North, of new ways of thinking about wealth and economic growth. Instead of seeing trade through the eyes of producers, they focused on the role of trade in satisfying consumers' demands. Consumption rather than production came to be seen as the aim of economic activity. It was linked to growth because the only way in which people could satisfy their desires was by increasing their purchasing power. They could do this only by selling more goods in impersonal markets where supply and demand ruled, which meant that producers had to lower their costs and become more competitive. The outcome was a literature in which self-interest was assumed to rule human affairs. This challenged long-established conceptions of society (one reason why Hobbes's ideas were thought so scandalous was his assumption that men formed governments solely because of self-interest) and had potentially radical political implications in its view that the market provided a way of holding society together.

However, not everyone accepted this new view of the market. As trade expanded and commercial relations increasingly dominated economic life, some sectors fell behind. Clothiers and landowners found their incomes rising less rapidly than those of merchants, and they also faced the burden of the rising taxes (levied locally) needed to support those without any means of supporting themselves. Pointing to the problems faced by the poor, such men denied that individual and public interests coincided. Indian manufactures, with which English woollens could not hope to compete, were seen as wrecking businesses, causing unemployment and producing poverty. The solutions offered were to encourage investment and to restrict imports. Whereas in the 1620s the balance-of-trade doctrine had been used as an argument against traditional regulation of the economy, in the 1690s it came to be used to defend manufacturing and landed interests against the threat presented by free trade and commercial expansion.

This conflict came to a head in the recoinage crisis of the 1690s. Since the Restoration, English silver coins had fallen significantly in weight, owing to their edges being clipped as well as to normal wear and tear. It was widely accepted that a recoinage was essential, especially now that milled edges could be used to prevent further clipping. The controversial issue was how much silver should be in the new shillings (the main silver coin in England). If their original silver content were restored, there would be fewer coins in circulation and the result would be deflation. So men who emphasized the importance of expanding demand wanted the recoinage to reflect the decline in the shilling's silver content that had taken place during the preceding decades. In contrast, creditors wanted deflation and the restoration of the currency's original silver content. Unlike men in the City of London, where the subject was widely debated, many landowners probably failed to grasp the issues involved in the recoinage crisis, even though they may have understood the balance-of-trade doctrine and the link between trade and employment.

The scheme adopted by the government (and advocated by Locke) involved recoining shillings at their full value. Not only was this in itself deflationary, but the government agreed to accept old shillings at their face value for the first six months. The result was that Gresham's Law went into effect. This law – named after the Elizabethan financier Sir Thomas Gresham (1519–79), though it was known to medieval writers – is usually summarized as 'Bad money drives out good.' If someone has a coin containing the full weight of silver and also a badly worn, clipped coin with the same face value, they will choose to spend the bad one and keep the good one. Good coins will therefore be hoarded and bad ones will circulate. In the 1690s this meant that, as old shillings went into the Mint for recoining, the new full-weight coins were largely melted down and exported. Estimates suggest that the value of silver coins in circulation may have fallen from £12 million in December 1695 to only £4.2 million in June 1696. Though there was no corresponding fall in the circulation of either gold coins or banknotes (usable only for large transactions), there was a sharp deflation. Prices fell, and landlords and creditors reaped the benefit. The long-term effect was that England went on to a de facto gold standard, as silver, now overvalued, began to disappear from circulation. The theory underlying this transition was Locke's. This held that it was gold and silver that were the instruments of commerce. They had an intrinsic value, determined by common consent. The only thing that was different about money was that it contained a stamp confirming its weight and fineness.

Against this, men such as Nicholas Barbon (*d*.1698) claimed that it was money (coins), not the silver in them, that drove trade. This meant that when the government coined more (or fewer) shillings from a certain weight of silver, it raised (or lowered) the money supply. It was money, not silver, to which people attached value. However, it was Locke's natural-law theory, supported by the self-interest of land-owners and creditors, that triumphed. The price of gold established by Isaac Newton in 1717 – £3 17s. 10½d. per ounce – came to be regarded as an almost magical figure, and was not finally abandoned until 1931. The arguments of the free-traders such as North were able to explain England's prosperity since the Restoration. However, the balance-of-trade doctrine proved better able to serve the needs of the dominant political class.

ECONOMICS IN SEVENTEENTH-CENTURY ENGLAND

Seventeenth-century England produced the balance-of-trade doctrine, and the book, Mun's *England's Treasure by Forraign Trade*, that Adam Smith was later to take as representative of what he called 'the mercantile system.' However, although Smith's interpretation gained wide currency among scholars under the label 'mercantilism', it is clear that such a simple characterization of this period's economic thought is grossly misleading. Even the balance-of-trade doctrine, used to justify protection late in the century, was used by its inventors, Misselden and Mun, to argue against restrictions on trade.

During the seventeenth century, England experienced numerous economic problems that provided merchants and government advis-ers with an incentive to advocate policies that were in their own interests. In an environment largely free of censorship, and a polit-ical system where reasoned argument might influence policy, they did this in an unprecedented number of pamphlets on economic questions. The manner in which they argued their case was strongly influenced by new thinking about science, a subject in which men were also passionately interested. At the same time, the century's political turmoil raised fundamental questions about what held society together. Though Hobbes's work fell squarely in the realm of political philosophy, the challenge he posed related to the whole of society and was taken up, especially in the eighteenth century, by many writers who, following Pufendorf, took economic factors into account.

5
Absolutism and Enlightenment in Eighteenth-century France

PROBLEMS OF THE ABSOLUTE STATE

The conditions that led to the proliferation of writing on economic questions in seventeenth-century England had no parallel in France. Many more feudal institutions remained than in England (although some feudal obligations had effectively become marketable commodities), and the king possessed absolute power. Throughout the seventeenth and eighteenth centuries it was frequently dangerous to express opinions that the state might view as subversive. Of the writers discussed in this chapter, Boisguilbert suffered exile and Mirabeau imprisonment for their economic opinions. In private, however, radical opinions were expressed even in salons patronized by the royal family. Political and social criticism could also be left implicit by formulating it as general principles or by directing it against practices found in other countries. Thus, while French writing on economic questions was sparse during the seventeenth century, it grew substantially during the eighteenth, and by the 1750s and 1760s Paris had become the centre of European economic thinking, to which most of the leading figures came.

The structure of French government policy was laid down in the seventeenth century by Jean Baptiste Colbert (1619–83), finance minister under Louis XIV (r.1643–1715) from 1661. He is important because of the policies for which he was responsible. His primary aim was not to raise the living standards of the population but to increase the power of the king. Internally, he wanted to unify the country, economically as well as politically, so that, for example, famine in one

93

region could not coexist with plenty in another. Externally, his belief was that the volume of world trade was fixed, meaning that one country's gain had to be matched by a corresponding loss elsewhere. If France were to gain, it could only be at the expense of England or the Netherlands, the two dominant commercial powers.

Colbert's policies followed logically from these beliefs. He sought to increase exports and reduce imports, thereby both achieving national self-sufficiency and accumulating the treasure which would drive trade. Attempts were made to increase the population and to keep wages low, thus forcing people to work hard. Immigration of skilled workers was encouraged through subsidies, and Colbert tried to stop emigration. Trade was carefully regulated, and new industries were set up, sometimes with foreign workers. It was a comprehensive programme of economic development.

France had long faced severe financial and economic problems, and Colbert's policies failed to solve them. It was not until much later that death from famine became a thing of the past. Throughout the century, shortages of food, sometimes occurring alongside surpluses in other parts of the country, were common. Such shortages were particularly acute in towns, for these were beginning to outgrow the resources of their traditional hinterlands. The government resorted to numerous measures in order to deal with the problem, including price-fixing, prohibiting speculation in grain, and direct coercion of producers. However, it did not remove the taxes and barriers to the internal movement of food that lay at the problem's heart.

The government also faced chronic financial difficulties, these being due in large part to military expenditures incurred by both Louis XIV and his successors. The state was continually on the verge of bankruptcy. The clergy and the nobility, who owned most of the nation's wealth, were largely exempt from direct taxation, and among those who were liable the burden of such taxes was very uneven. Collection of taxes was arbitrary and inequitable. A major reason for this was that the state did not have the administrative apparatus to collect them itself but farmed the job out to private companies. These would pay an agreed sum to the exchequer in return for the right to collect certain levies. This process was inefficient, and unjust methods of collection were often used. On top of this, in 1738 the *corvée*, or system of forced labour, was extended from specific regions to the whole country.

ABSOLUTISM AND LUXURY

Debates over the significance of luxury spending have a much longer history, being traceable to antiquity and religious teaching about the dangers of wealth, but they were given added significance by the extravagance of the court of Louis XIV and much of the French aristocracy. Many of Colbert's industrial policies were aimed at the production of luxury goods that ordinary people could never afford. This contrasted with the apparent simplicity of the rulers of the Dutch republic. This posed the question of whether there was a link between absolutism and luxury.

A very widely discussed author who tackled this problem was François Fénélon, Archbishop of Cambrai (1651–1715), who became tutor to the king's grandson. In 1693–4, he wrote *The Adventures of Telemachus*, published anonymously in 1699. This is a travelogue about the journey of the son of Ulysses to find his father, accompanied by his tutor, Mentor, who teaches him about being a king. The story centred on Salentum, which had been corrupted by despotism and luxury, and laid out a programme of reform that would prevent the outbreak of a violent revolution.

The book was a thinly veiled attack on Louis XIV, and as a result Fénélon was excluded from the court. It challenged Colbert's view that the luxury spending of the rich both maintained the poor and made civilization possible, claiming that state support for industry undermined the social order and caused agriculture to decline and, with it, the monarch's ability to raise taxes. This would eventually lead to military defeat and undermine the monarchy. Instead, Salentum should be reformed, abolishing luxury, distributing land to workers so that they could support themselves, and confining manufacturing to essential goods such as the tools needed to cultivate the land. So that this new order could be sustained indefinitely, it would also be necessary to create a new public spirit. Commerce would not be abolished, but would be confined to a port, 'an immensely rich maritime beehive, whose citizens were "industrious, patient, laborious, clean, sober and frugal" as well as "constantly employed" ... isolated from the rest of the economy' and subjected to draconian financial regulation.[1] Revenues from the port would be used to finance an armament industry, but this would not be used for conquest, just to maintain the European balance of power. Such a system would produce growth without luxury. The book was extraordinarily successful, becoming a bestseller that was still cited a century later.

In debates over luxury, Fénelon represented one pole, opposing luxury. At the other pole was a Dutch physician, Bernard Mandeville (1670?–1733). He moved to England and was a supporter of William of Orange and his wars against France. He feared that the Tories, who were attacking the regime of debt and luxury created by the recent financial revolution (which included the founding of the Bank of England) would make peace with France, initiate a counter-revolution and create an England modelled on the reformed Salentum. He argued against such a counter-revolution in *The Grumbling Hive: or Knaves Turned Honest* (1705), a twenty-six-page poem that was later expanded into *The Fable of the Bees: or Private Vices Turned Public Benefits* (1714).

The Grumbling Hive began with a large, prosperous hive, well stocked with bees. Vice abounded, in that all the bees were driven by lust and vanity. Wealth was unequally distributed, but all the bees, even the poorest, were better off than they would otherwise have been. The reason was that high consumption created employment. Every bee was kept busy attempting to satisfy another's demands. Even crime and fraud provided opportunities for honest employment – burglars provided employment for locksmiths. This was England under the House of Orange, ruled not by 'wild democracy' but by kings whose 'power was circumscribed by laws'. However, despite prosperity and economic growth, the bees felt insecure and allowed themselves to be persuaded that the land would sink under the weight of fraud, and that everyone should become honest. In this reformed Salentum, crime and military spending ceased, and luxury was spurned. The result was unemployment and the collapse of entire industries. Many bees fled the hive. The moral of the tale was clear.

Despite being an attack on the Jacobites, some believing that the ruler of Fénélon's Salentum was modelled on the exiled James II, Mandeville's poem aroused a public outcry, for it was perceived to be an attack on Christian morality, praising luxury and arguing against frugality and self-denial. Industriousness, pride, envy and striving for gain were crucial to prosperity. An honest economy, such as Fénélon's reformed Salentum, would not work because it would undermine the psychological factors that created prosperity. The poem resonated because it engaged not only with Fénélon but with the series of debates that had raged since Hobbes over the foundations on which society rested. Were humans innately sociable or purely naturally selfish? Mandeville argued for the latter, claiming that, in a well-ordered society, people would be induced voluntarily to do what is best. Private vices produce public benefits. Vices should not be encouraged, but they should be recognized and turned to good effect. Mandeville did not advocate pure laissez-faire, however. The market could be allowed to coordinate much economic activity, but he still favoured regulation of foreign trade in order to create employment and to stock the nation with money. There were also many projects that the government could undertake to provide employment for the poor.

THE CIRCULATION OF MONEY AND THE STATE

Another critic of Louis XIV's economic policies was Pierre de Bois-guilbert (1646–1714). In *La Détail de la France* (published in 1695, but possibly written some years earlier), and in a series of other publications during the following two decades, Boisguilbert sought to explain what he saw as the disastrous decline in the French economy under Louis XIV. Income had, he claimed, halved during the previous thirty years. The starting point of his analysis was the necessity of exchange. As economic development took place, exchange became more and more complex, making it necessary to use money. However, money did not in itself create wealth. It had to circulate actively if it were to be effective. If money could circulate rapidly – perhaps being augmented by money substitutes such as bills of exchange – this would be as efficient as having a larger money supply. Paper money could perform the functions of metallic money and had the advantage of costing nothing to produce.

What kept money circulating, Boisguilbert argued, was consumption, for one man's spending is another man's income. Consumption and income were therefore equivalent. This meant that the decline in French income could be attributed to a decline in consumption. What had caused this? Boisguilbert's answers included the burden of taxation; the distribution of income away from the poor, who spent money quickly, to the rich, who were more likely to hoard it; and the uncertainty that made the propertied class less willing to invest. More fundamentally, however, Boisguilbert linked prosperity to the price system: prosperity requires that there be a balance or equilibrium between different goods and that 'prices are kept in proportion with one another and with the costs necessary for creating the goods'.[2]

This perspective led Boisguilbert to conclude that nature alone, not the state, can maintain order and peace – *laissez faire la nature*. Though buyers and sellers are both motivated by profit, the balance between the needs to buy and to sell forces both sides to listen to reason. Thus, although individuals are concerned only with their own interests, provided the state does not interfere they will contribute to the general good. The state's role is to establish security and justice.

However, although Boisguilbert saw markets as establishing order, they would sometimes fail. Uncertainty and incorrect expectations meant that output prices would fluctuate. This was particularly noticeable in the market for grain, where price fluctuations were particularly violent. High prices would mean that even the worst land could profitably be cultivated, leading to a glut that pushed prices so low that all farmers made a loss. Boisguilbert thus proposed an exception to his rule of laissez-faire: the government should intervene to stabilize the price of grain, holding stocks that could be bought and sold to achieve this.

The idea proposed by Boisguilbert that paper money could fulfil the functions of gold and silver at lower cost was taken even further by a Scotsman, John Law (1671–1729), in *Money and Trade Considered: A Proposal for Supplying the Nation with Money* (1705). Like Boisguilbert, Law started from the premises that the value of goods depended not on the quantity of money but on the ratio of the quantity of goods to the demand for them, and that the role of money was to facilitate trade. An increase in the quantity of money would therefore raise employment, cause more land to be cultivated, and increase output and trade. Law worked on the assumption that there were normally unemployed resources that could be brought into use when activity increased. However, where others proposed measures to accumulate bullion, Law argued for an expansion of paper currency. Apart from being cheaper, a paper currency would have the advantage that its supply could be regulated so as to stabilize its value and the level of economic activity. Security would be provided by the titles to land against which loans would be issued. By being linked to the value of land, which Law claimed was more stable than the value of silver, the value of the currency could be assured.

Law's proposal was designed to revive the Scottish economy, and he submitted it, unsuccessfully, to the Scottish parliament in 1705. In 1706, however, he was forced to flee Scotland to avoid being arrested for murder. The reason was that in 1694 he had killed a man in a duel and, after being arrested, had escaped from prison with the connivance (and possibly the assistance) of the authorities. Union with England in 1707 raised the prospect that he would be rearrested. He settled in France, where he persuaded the regent under Louis XV to put some of his ideas into effect as a way of solving France's financial problems.

In 1716, in Paris, Law formed the Banque Genérale, which in 1718 was nationalized as the Banque Royale. Notes issued by the bank were to be accepted in payment of taxes. In return Law offered to put the French finances, severely weakened by Louis XIV's wars, in order through reducing the rate of interest to 2 per cent. However, the bank's capital was only 825,000 livres, in comparison with a total government debt of around 450 million livres. The result was that the bank had little control over interest rates. As a result, Law became drawn into debt management. He also became involved in other ventures when the Compagnie d'Occident (Company of the West) that he established in 1717 was given exclusive trading rights in Louisiana in return for taking over a large quantity of government debt, and tax farms were also centralized within the company. To pay for the government debt, shares were issued. Law used numerous marketing devices to sell shares in the Compagnie d'Occident, and through 1719 they rose in value, supported by lending from the Banque Royale. In May 1719 shares were selling for less than their nominal value of 500 livres, but by December they sold for as much as 10,025 livres per share. In January 1720 Law was appointed Controller-General of Finances, the highest administrative post in France, and from January to March plans were made for the demonetization of gold and silver.

In May 1720, however, Law realized that the financial situation still needed to be brought under control and he proposed a plan gradually to reduce the price of shares from their unsustainable value of 9,000 livres per share to 5,000 livres per share by the end of the year. This outraged the public, who had counted on shares rising in value (there was a highly developed forward market, with some trades taking place on the basis that shares would rise as high as 15,000 livres), and by September the price had fallen to only 4,367 livres per share. This conceals the extent of the collapse, for during this period overissue of banknotes had reduced the shares' value substantially. Valued in sterling, which was tied to gold, the price of a share had fallen from £302 to £47. Much of the public's financial wealth had been destroyed, though the government benefited through having its debts substantially reduced. Despite the collapse in the company's share price, Law persisted in believing that it could have survived had it not been for the arrival of plague in Marseilles in 1720. This caused people to demand coins instead of banknotes and created a liquidity crisis for the bank.

CANTILLON ON THE NATURE OF COMMERCE IN GENERAL

One of those who saw the flaws in Law's scheme and got out in time to save his fortune was Richard Cantillon (*c.*1680–1734?). Cantillon was an Irish merchant banker who spent most of his life in France. He is surrounded in mystery. His home burned down, and for a long time it was assumed either that he was killed in the fire or that the fire was started by an aggrieved servant to cover up his murder. A year later, some of his papers were taken by an unknown traveller to Surinam, leading to the idea that the fire might have been a ruse by Cantillon to cover his disappearance. The motive may have been to escape the law-suits against which he still had to defend the fortune he had acquired through his activities with Law in the 1720s. The fire, however, had destroyed most of his papers. A book that did survive was *An Essay on the Nature of Commerce in General*, probably written in 1730, but not published until 1755. It appeared in French, purporting to be a transla-tion from English in order to get round the French censorship laws. Some scholars have seen this book as so significant as to mark the birth of the subject of economics. Cantillon's *Essay* opens with the statement that land is the source of wealth: 'The land is the source or matter from whence all wealth is produced. The labour of man is the form which produces it: and wealth is nothing but the maintenance, conveniences and superfluities of life.'[3] Labour, regarded by many economists as the source of wealth, simply adjusts to demand. If there are too many labourers in a country, they will emigrate or become poor and starve. In an implicit criticism of Colbert's policy, Cantillon argues that it is impossible to raise wealth by training more craftsmen. He likens this to training more seamen without building more ships. It is land that deter-mines wealth, and the number of labourers will adjust automatically.

Cantillon attaches particular importance, however, to one type of labour – that of the entrepreneur. Entrepreneurs are people who buy goods either to engage in production or to trade them, without any assurance that they will profit from their activities. For example, the farmer, who is an agricultural entrepreneur employing people to work for him, cultivates land without knowing whether corn will be cheap or dear, or whether the harvest will be good or bad. Merchants buy goods in bulk without knowing whether demand from consumers will be high or low, or how many sales will be lost to competitors. However, although entrepreneurs perform an important function in undertaking risky activities, they are still, like labourers who work for a wage, dependent on the proprietors of land.

Two implications follow from this view of land as the source of wealth. The first is that land is the source of value. Cantillon's analysis is based on the concept of 'intrinsic value'. This is not the same as market price. It is the amount of land and labour that enters into the production of a commodity. If labour is valued according to the amount of land needed to maintain the labourers, this reduces to a land theory of value. To produce corn, for example, requires land on which to grow it plus the land necessary to produce the labourers' subsistence. In contrast, market price depends on supply and demand and may fluctuate above or below the intrinsic value of a commodity.

The second implication that Cantillon draws from his view of land as the source of wealth is that all other classes are maintained at the expense of the landowners. Only the landowners are 'naturally independent', for it is their spending that determines how resources are allocated between different uses and, as a result, the values of different goods. To quote one of Cantillon's chapter titles, 'The fancies, the fashions, and the modes of living of the prince, and especially of the landowners, determine the use to which land is put in a state and cause the variations in the market price of all things'.[4] He gives the example of a large self-sufficient estate that is initially cultivated by the owner himself, who directs overseers to manage it so as to produce the goods that he requires. The division of the estate into pasture, arable, parkland, orchards, gardens and so on will be determined entirely by the owner's tastes (though he will of course have to allocate sufficient land to produce the goods that his labourers consume). Cantillon then considers what would happen if the owner decentralized decision-making, setting up his overseers as independent producers equipped with the relevant amounts of land, and linked to the owner and to each other through markets. His conclusion is that everyone on the estate would live in exactly the same way as before. Only if the owner changes his consumption pattern will economic activity change:

> For if some of the farmers sowed more corn than usual they must feed fewer sheep, and have less wool and mutton to sell. Then there will be too much corn and too little wool for the consumption of the inhabitants. Wool will therefore be dear, which will force the inhabitants to wear their clothes longer than usual, and there will be too much corn and a surplus for the next year. And as we suppose that the landowner has stipulated for the payment in silver of the third of the produce of the farm to be paid to him, the farmers who have too much corn and too little wool, will not be able to pay him rent . . . So a farmer who has arrived at about the proportion of consumption will have part of his farm in grass, for hay, another for corn, wool and so on, and he will not change his plan unless he sees some considerable change in the demand; but in this example we have supposed that all the people live in the same way as when the landowner cultivated the land for himself, and consequently the farmers will employ the land for the same purposes as before.[5]

If the landowner were, for example, to dismiss some of his domestic servants and to increase the number of horses on his estate, corn would become cheap (for demand would be less) and hay dear (demand having increased). Farmers would then turn corn fields into grassland.

Throughout this discussion, as in his discussion of value, Cantillon makes it clear that he is dealing only with long-run equilibrium: 'I do not consider here the variation in market prices which may arise from the good or bad harvest of the year, or the extraordinary consumption which may occur from foreign troops or other accidents, so as not to complicate my subject, considering only a state in its natural and uniform condition.'[6]

After considering production and wealth, Cantillon turns to money. Here his ideas owe much to Locke, for he focuses on the circulation of money, accepting the link between the price level and the money supply. However, he criticizes Locke on the grounds that, while 'he has clearly seen that the abundance of money makes everything dear, . . .

he has not considered how it does so'.[7] To resolve this, Cantillon considers the way in which money enters the economy and the channels through which it flows. He considers three main sources from which an increase in the money supply might arise: gold and silver mines, the balance of trade, and subsidies paid by foreign powers.

If money comes from mines, the first people to be affected will be the mine owners and workers in the mining industry. Their incomes will rise and they will spend more, which will raise the prices of the goods they buy. This will increase the incomes of the farmers and manufacturers from whom the goods are bought, who will in turn increase their spending, raising other prices and incomes. Money will gradually spread out throughout the country, raising prices as it goes. Classes on fixed incomes, such as landowners whose rents are fixed by long-term agreements, will be worse off until their leases can be renegotiated. As prices rise, producers will find that their costs have risen, forcing them to raise prices further. As prices continue to rise, people will be encouraged to buy abroad, where goods are still cheap. This will ruin manufacturers. When the inflow of new money ceases – perhaps because the mines are exhausted – incomes will fall and people will have to cut back their spending. Money will become scarce, and poverty and misery will follow. Because much of the gold and silver will have gone abroad to pay for the increased imports, the state will not end up with any more money than its neighbours. This, Cantillon argued, was roughly what had happened in Spain after the discovery of America.

In contrast, if the inflow of money arises from a favourable balance of trade, it will first accrue to merchants. This will in turn raise the incomes of those who produce the goods being exported. The prices of land and labour will in turn also be raised. However, because the money will accrue to industrious people who are keen to acquire property, they will not raise their consumption but will save money until they have sufficient to invest it at interest or to buy land. Only then will they raise their consumption. The rise in prices will cause goods to be imported, but such a situation, Cantillon argues, can continue for many years. The effects will be different from those of an increase in money from mines, because the money will be received by different classes of people, whose spending behaviour will be different.

The effects of subsidies from foreign powers will depend on whether the monies are hoarded or spent. Only in the latter case will they have any effect, raising prices.

Cantillon recognized what has come to be termed the price–specie-flow mechanism – the notion that a rise in the money supply will raise prices, resulting in a trade deficit that causes money to flow out of the country. In its pure form, this mechanism implies that attempts to increase the money supply are self-defeating. Cantillon could thus write that when a state's money supply, and hence its wealth, is at its greatest, the state 'will inevitably fall into poverty by the ordinary course of things'.[8] This would appear to undermine the so-called 'mercantilist' notion that increases in the money supply bring prosperity. However, Cantillon could also write that 'It is clear that every state which has more money in circulation than its neighbours has an advantage over them so long as it maintains an abundance of money.'[9] Higher domestic prices will mean that the same quantity of goods exported will purchase more imports. In addition, plenty of money makes it easier for the ruler to raise taxes. For prices to rise in this way it is necessary that the money be retained within the state. This is more likely if it were obtained from trade than if it were obtained from mines, for the incomes would be received by those more likely to invest it rather than engage in luxury consumption.

Having discussed money, Cantillon could move on to finance. The issues he covered included foreign exchange, variations in the relative values of different metals used as money, debasement of the currency, and, finally, banks. Like Law, he saw that banks could be of value to a nation, this value being measured by the paper currency that entered into circulation. He estimated that the Bank of England kept reserves equal to around 1 million ounces of silver, but its notes amounted, on average, to 4 million ounces of silver. When the circulation of money needed to be speeded up, this situation was, he claimed, of great bene-fit to England. Banks were of particular benefit to small states where silver was scarce. However, given the experiences of the early 1720s, when both England and France had experienced major speculative bubbles which had burst dramatically, Cantillon pointed out the dan-gers of insolvency should a bank increase its note issue too far. The example of Law's scheme, from which he had managed to get out in time, was one that he could never have forgotten.

THE ENLIGHTENMENT

Some of the most important ideas underlying the Enlightenment can be traced to seventeenth-century England – to Locke and to the scientific revolution associated above all with Bacon and Newton. The Enlightenment involved a belief in reason, progress, liberty and toleration. Reason was believed to be man's central capacity, which enabled him to think and act correctly. Because all men were equal by virtue of their having reason, it followed that everyone should be free to act and think as his reason directed. The Enlightenment was therefore a revolt against the alleged unreason of earlier ages – reason was to replace religious authorities, sacred texts and traditions as the criterion by which all things were to be judged. Above all, however, the Enlightenment was characterized by a belief in progress. Replacing superstition by reason would enable man to progress without any divine assistance. Newton had shown that the physical world could be understood in terms of a system of laws, comprehensible through reason, and Locke had shown that the human mind could build complex ideas from the basic data of sensory experience. Innate or externally supplied ideas were not needed: reason was sufficient. In the same spirit, Locke had also offered a utilitarian framework for morality, and provided a theoretical basis for representative government.

Such challenges to traditional ideas were suppressed in France under Louis XIV. Censorship still persisted under his successor, Louis XV (r.1715–74), though less rigorously. Printing was still controlled for many years, with the result that unorthodox ideas, circulating only in manuscript form, could not spread as rapidly as if they were printed. However, the relaxation was sufficient to release a pent-up flood of criticism of established ideas and institutions. In the mid-1740s censorship was significantly decreased, and the following decade saw a profusion of new ideas from men such as Diderot (1713–84), on the relativity of knowledge and morals, Montesquieu

(1689–1755), on the rule of law, and Condillac (1715–80), who developed Locke's psychology. The optimism of the movement was captured by Diderot and d'Alembert (1717–83), who edited an encyclopedia that would bring together all human knowledge and serve to propagate the new ideas. Between 1751 and 1772, despite periodic attempts by the authorities to suppress it, twenty-eight volumes were published. Covering practical as well as theoretical knowledge, the *Encyclopédie* included articles on economic questions.

PHYSIOCRACY

Among the many writers on economic questions in mid-eighteenth-century France, the physiocrats were an organized group of economists. The name 'physiocrat' emerged because of their belief that nature should be allowed to rule. Their ideas were developed between 1756 and 1763, primarily by two men, François Quesnay (1694–1774) and Victor Riqueti, Marquis de Mirabeau (1715–89), at a time when the Seven Years War with England was putting great strain on French finances. They held regular meetings to discuss their ideas, they had a journal, *Ephemerides*, that published their work between 1767 and 1772, and their *La Philosophie rurale* (1763) could be regarded as a textbook in physiocratic economics. Physiocracy attracted devoted followers, including Du Pont de Nemours (1739–1817) and Mercier de la Rivière (1720–93). There were also economists such as Turgot (see pp. 112–117) who were sympathetic towards physiocracy, though not in complete agreement with its ideas. Physiocratic ideas underlay some of Turgot's reforms during his term as Controller-General of Finances from 1774 to 1776.

By the time Quesnay turned to economics, he had acquired a considerable reputation as a doctor, first as a surgeon and then as a physician (at the time regarded as having significantly higher status, in England as well as in France). His position in the French court was as the private physician to Madame de Pompadour, mistress of Louis XV, and it was for his medical services that he received a title and considerable wealth. His position was important in that, because he had little control over his schedule, he needed to rely on collaborators to undertake research and to write up his ideas. His circle during this period has been described as 'a writing workshop'. Also, as someone who relied on royal patronage until de Pompadour's death in 1764, he had to be careful, which accounts for why he published so few works under his own name. After 1764, he moved to the salons in Paris, in an intellectual environment no longer tied to the court.

Quesnay's medical background is important, as it influenced his perspective on economics. In turning to economics, he sought to analyse the pathology of society and to propose remedies. Influenced strongly by Boisguilbert and Cantillon (on whose work Mirabeau drew heavily), he focused on the circulation of money – a clear analogy with the circulation of blood within the body, discovered over a century earlier. It is tempting to suggest that the term 'physiocracy' reflected the attitude of an experienced physician who knew the importance of working with nature in effecting a cure. Equally significant, the physiocratic system rested on a clear analysis of the structure of French society.

To understand a society, Quesnay and Mirabeau claimed in *La Philosophie rurale*, it is necessary to understand the means by which it obtains its subsistence, on which both politics and law rest. They outlined the evolution of society, culminating in the commercial societies that had grown up alongside agricultural ones. Trade was essential, which meant that it afforded a secure means of obtaining subsistence, but agriculture remained fundamental. The main reason for this was that it alone, the physiocrats argued, yielded net revenue – a surplus over the necessary costs of production. They expressed this by describing agriculture as productive and other sectors (trade and manufacturing) as sterile.

The physiocrats' assumptions about different classes were developed from Quesnay's observations on agriculture, first published in an article in Diderot's *Encyclopédie*. Most land was cultivated by sharecroppers, who paid a fraction (usually one half) of their produce to the landowner in return for the use of the land and the loan of seed and livestock. Their methods were hardly more productive than those employed by peasant proprietors who cultivated their lands with minimal capital. In contrast, there had developed in parts of northern

France, as in England, a new class of farmers – agricultural entrepreneurs. These were able to improve the lands they rented from their proprietors (usually the nobility or the Church) and produce large surpluses. The crucial difference between them and the sharecroppers was that they had access to capital, for it was this that made it possible for them to employ more productive techniques. In contrast, though it was essential for producing the goods that people needed, industry produced no surplus. It simply covered its costs. Agricultural capital was therefore the key to economic growth.

The relationship between agricultural capital and economic growth was explained by Quesnay in several versions of his *Tableau économique*, the first of which was published in 1758. A version produced in 1767 is shown in Fig. 1. This was a diagram that depicted the circulation of money and goods between the three classes in society (proprietors, farmers, and artisans who produce manufactured goods) on the assumption that policies were ideal for agricultural development. In different versions of the *Tableau*, Quesnay listed up to twenty-four conditions that had to be satisfied for the economy to operate in the way he outlined. These included the following. (1) The entire revenue enters into circulation. (2) People are not led by insecurity to hoard money. (3) Taxes do not destroy the nation's revenue. (4) Farmers have sufficient capital to achieve a net revenue (surplus) of at least 100 per cent. (5) There is free external trade in raw produce. (6) The needs of the state are met only through the prosperity of the nation, not through raising credit from financiers. (7) People are free to cultivate their land as they think best. Given that none of these conditions was satisfied, obtaining them would amount to a very substantial policy agenda.

The starting point for the *Tableau* is a situation in which farmers have capital, or an 'annual advance', say £2,000 (in corn) and proprietors have a stock of money of £2,000. Agriculture produces a surplus of 100 per cent, which accrues to the proprietors as rent. Consider first the circulation of money. Proprietors spend half their revenue (£2,000) on food and half on manufactured goods, so £1,000 flows to each sector. This generates incomes, which are spent, again half on food and half on manufactures. Each sector thus gains a further £500

Tableau Économique

Objets à considérer. 1°. Trois sortes de dépenses; 2°. leur source; 3°. leurs avances; 4°. leur distribution; 5°. leurs effets; 6°. leur reproduction; 7°. leurs rapports entr'elles; 8°. leurs rapports avec la population; 9°. avec l'Agriculture; 10°. avec l'industrie; 11°. avec le commerce; 12°. avec la masse des richesses d'une Nation.

DÉPENSES PRODUCTIVES relatives à l'Agriculture, &c.	DÉPENSES DU REVENU, l'Impôt prélevé, se partagent aux Dépenses productives et aux Dépenses stériles.	DÉPENSES STÉRILES relatives à l'industrie, &c.
Avances annuelles pour produire un revenu de 600ll sont 600ll	*Revenu annuel de*	*Avances annuelles pour les Ouvrages des Dépenses stériles, sont*
600ll produisent net	600ll	300ll

Productions — *moitié passe ici* — *Ouvrages, &c.*

300ll reproduisent net .... 300ll 300ll

moitié passe ici

150 reproduisent net 150 150

moitié, &c.

75 reproduisent net 75 75

37.10 reproduisent net .... 37.10. .... 37.10

18.15 reproduisent net .... 18.15. .... 18.15

9...7...6⁴ reproduisent net .... 9...7...6⁴ .... 9...7...6⁴

4.13...9 reproduisent net .... 4.13...9. .... 4.13...9

2...6.10 reproduisent net .... 2...6.10. .... 2...6.10

1...3...5 reproduisent net .... 1...3...5. .... 1...3...5

0.11...8 reproduisent net .... 0.11...8. .... 0.11...8

0...5.10 reproduisent net .... 0...5.10. .... 0...5.10

0...2.11 reproduisent net .... 0...2.11. .... 0...2.11

0...1...5 reproduisent net .... 0...1...5. .... 0...1...5

&c.

REPRODUIT TOTAL...... 600 *ll* de revenu; de plus, les frais annuels de 600 *ll* et les intérêts des avances primitives du Laboureur, de 300 *ll* que la terre restitue. Ainsi la reproduction est de 1500 *ll* compris le revenu de 600 *ll* qui est la base du calcul, abstraction faite de l'impôt prélevé, et des avances qu'exige sa reproduction annuelle, &c. *Voyez l'Explication à la page suivante.*

Fig. 1 The *Tableau économique* (from *Philosophie rurale*, 1767) from the other. When successive rounds of income are added up, they come to £2,000 for each sector (£1,000 + £500 + £250 + £125 + ...). Each sector thus receives an income of £2,000 and spends £1,000 on buying consumption goods from the other sector. There is, however, an important difference between the two sectors. Manufacturing uses the £1,000 that it does not spend on food to purchase raw materials from agriculture, with the result that it generates no surplus. The entire stock of money (£2,000) thus ends up in the agricultural sector. In contrast, agriculture ends up with a financial surplus of £2,000, which is paid to the proprietors as rent.

The reason why Quesnay believed that agriculture could generate this financial surplus is that, unlike manufacturing, it produces a surplus of goods. The 'advance' of £2,000 in corn is used to produce output worth £5,000. Of this, £1,000 is sold as food to the proprietors, and £2,000 is sold to the manufacturing sector, half as food and half as raw materials. This leaves £2,000 worth of corn to replenish agriculture's capital stock for the following year. The accounts balance.

This numerical example is discussed in detail to make an important point. Although the fundamental insight about the circulation of income came from Boisguilbert and Cantillon, Quesnay tried to develop his argument with a degree of rigour that was absent from their work. Quesnay's numbers may seem arbitrary, but they were not. They reflected such statistics as were available about the French economy of his day. The figure of 100 per cent for the surplus, for example, reflected Quesnay's belief about what could be achieved in capitalist farming if sufficient capital were available to employ the most efficient techniques (using horses). These techniques were used on large farms in southern England and parts of northern France, but many French farmers could not afford them. Such numerical examples also enabled Quesnay, in successive versions of the *Tableau*, to explore the sensitivity of the economic system to various changes. For example, he showed that if a tax of £25 were imposed on both sectors, the result would be a decline in the annual advance in agriculture from £50. Agriculture would lose £25 directly and £25 indirectly through reduced sales to the manufacturing sector. The result would be economic decline, for less output would be produced the following year. Similarly, he could

show that a fall in productivity (perhaps due to government intervention or keeping the price of corn low) or the diversion of spending
from agriculture to manufacturing would reduce output.

The physiocratic system, centred on the *Tableau économique*, was
used to defend a clear and controversial political agenda. The state
was needed to maintain markets and the circular flow of income.
Quesnay performed exercises with the *Tableau* to show how output
would be reduced if his initial assumptions were not satisfied. Taxation,
interference with agriculture, artificial stimulation of manufacturing,
keeping food prices low – all policies pursued by the governments of
Louis XIV and Louis XV – were all harmful and should be abandoned. The laws of nature provided constraints on what the state
could undertake without undermining the prosperity on which it
depended. However, this did not rule out all state activity. The surplus
accruing to the proprietors could be taxed (as was necessary to raise
the funds needed to support the market), but taxation could not rise
too far. The reason was that the proprietors' spending was necessary
to maintain the annual flow of income and spending.

TURGOT

Not all reformers belonged to the physiocratic school. One group that
stood apart from the physiocrats, though it supported them on economic policy, was centred on Vincent de Gournay (1712–59). Gournay
was a businessman who made himself a public servant by purchasing
the office of Intendant of Commerce, a position he held from 1751 to
1759. His work involved visiting different parts of France to investigate trade and manufacturing there. Gournay popularized the phrase
Laissez faire, laissez passer, and he probably arranged for the publication of Cantillon's *Essay*. He wrote little, but exerted an important
influence on others – including Turgot.

Anne Robert Jacques Turgot (1727–81), in a eulogy written in
1759, argued that Gournay saw himself not as a systematizer but as
someone who offered common-sense maxims. Regulations that
allowed one city in France to treat citizens of other cities as foreigners,

preventing them from working within its precincts, or that ruined a weaver because his cloth was inferior to that produced by a guild, did not make sense. Turgot claimed that, though Gournay saw matters as common sense, there was a principle underlying them: that 'in general every man knows his own interest better than another to whom it is of no concern'. Gournay, he argued, reached the conclusion that

> when the interest of individuals is precisely the same as the general interest, every man ought best to be left at liberty to do what he likes. Now in the case of unrestrained commerce, M. de Gournay thought it impossible for the individual interest not to concur with the general interest.[10]

The government should therefore restore liberty to all branches of commerce – removing barriers to trade, simplifying taxes, and giving everyone the right to work. This would 'excite the greatest competition in the market, which will infallibly produce the greatest perfection in manufacturing, and the most advantageous price to buyers'.[11]

Turgot's first contribution to economics was a critique of Law's monetary theory in 1749. In the 1750s, however, he met Gournay and worked with him, translating a book by the English economist Josiah Tucker (1712–99), and accompanying Gournay on tours of inspection in the provinces. In 1761 he was appointed intendant in the Limousin, then a backward region in France, where he engaged in a process of reform. Areas affected included taxation, the system of forced labour during the harvest and the road system. It was during this period that his main contributions to economics were written. His commitments as a government official meant that these were mostly letters and reports. The two exceptions were *Reflections on the Formation and Distribution of Wealth* (1766) and an unfinished essay, 'Value and Money' (1769).

In 1774 Turgot was promoted to Controller-General of Finances and moved to Paris. Here, too, he engaged in reform. His response to the perennial problem of food shortages was to free the grain trade, though he still prohibited the export of corn and made special provision for the supply of grain to Paris. He replaced the inefficient private company that held the monopoly of saltpetre (needed in the manufacture of gunpowder) with a state-owned firm, run by the chemist

Lavoisier. Postal services were also transferred to a government department, and further similar reforms were projected. In 1776 Turgot sought to liberalize the corn trade still further, to abolish the guilds that restricted access to many industries, and to fund road building through a tax on landowners instead of through forced labour. He also spoke up in favour of tolerating Protestants. These measures, however, trampled on numerous vested interests. As a result, Turgot lost the support of other ministers and was attacked in the *parlements*, restored by his predecessor. He tried to force through his reforms using the king's authority, but his opponents managed to turn Louis XVI against him and he was dismissed. Many of his reforms were abandoned.

Though Turgot's reforms may have been pragmatic, they were consistent with the view of economic phenomena outlined in his two most systematic writings on economics. The early sections of the *Réflections* could have been written by a physiocrat. They discuss the origins of exchange and the pre-eminence of agriculture – of the husbandman over the artisan – and distinguish between a productive and an unproductive class. Like Quesnay, Turgot discusses different ways in which agriculture can be organized, arguing that farming by tenant-entrepreneurs is the most efficient, but that it is possible only if there is sufficient capital. However, he takes the discussion in a different direction when he argues that lending money can also contribute to the creation of wealth. This leads into a discussion of the role of money in commerce, and eventually to a very unphysiocratic perspective on the role of industry in creating wealth.

When people save, they accumulate capital that they can then use in a variety of ways: they can lend it at interest, purchase land (which yields rent), or employ it as an advance in industry (which yields profit). Because people have this choice, Turgot argued, the returns on all three of these uses of capital will be linked. They will not be equal, because the risks are different. If you lend money the borrower may fail to repay you, but if you purchase land you are secure. Land will thus yield a lower return than lending at interest. Similarly, investing in industry is more risky and will carry a higher return. Competition will therefore establish an equilibrium between the returns on these different ways in which capital can be employed. If, for example, the value of land is too high (equivalent to the return being too low) compared with other uses of capital, owners will exchange it for other types of capital and its price will be pushed down.

The equilibrium rate of interest is determined by supply and demand: it 'depends directly on the relation between the demand of the borrowers and the offer of the lenders'.[12] Thrift increases the number of lenders and reduces the number of borrowers, while luxury consumption has the opposite effect. Europe's falling rate of interest, Turgot argued, showed that thrift had prevailed over luxury, producing a rise in the amount of capital. This view led him to insist that the rate of interest was a price like any other and should therefore be determined by 'the course of trade', like the price of any commodity. The rate of interest would determine which lands were sufficiently profitable to cultivate and which industrial activities were sufficiently profitable to be undertaken.

Important features of this view can be found in seventeenth-century writing, notably by Locke on the rate of interest and by Mun on capital. However, Turgot integrated the various elements of this theory better than any of his predecessors. Furthermore, he used the theory to answer more clearly than anyone at that time the question of what constitutes a nation's wealth. His answer was that it comprises, to use modern terminology, the present value of the net revenue from land (the value of the land) plus the stock of movable goods. This, in essence, is the answer any modern economist would give. Turgot pointed out explicitly that to include 'capitals on loan' (financial assets) would involve double counting and that, though money was the object of saving, specie (gold and silver, a movable good and therefore part of wealth) was but a very small component of wealth.

In the course of this argument about the nature of wealth, Turgot explored the nature of value, a theme he developed in his later unfinished work. He started from the assumption that the value, or worth, of a good was unique to each individual. It depended on the fitness of the good to serve the purposes for which it was required, and on the difficulty of obtaining it. This concept of value could be described as 'esteem value', for value depended on the esteem in which a good was held. Turgot argued that there is no natural unit in which to measure value, and that the value of one good had to be measured in terms of another good. It is possible, for example, to say how many armfuls of firewood have the same value as a measure of grain. In practice, given that there are many goods, value is measured in terms of an arbitrary unit given by convention – a *numéraire*. If all goods are measured in terms of the same *numéraire*, then the relative value of any pair of goods can readily be calculated.

Turgot's discussion of 'esteem value' was applicable to an isolated person. From there he proceeded to consider exchange between two people who would generally value goods differently. He assumed that two goods would be exchanged at the average of the two parties' esteem values. If this were not the case, one would benefit less than the other from the exchange and would force the other to come closer to his price. This established what Turgot called 'exchange value'. Though conceptually different from the term 'price', which denotes the sum paid for a good, exchange value and price are numerically the same and can, in many contexts, be used interchangeably. Finally, Turgot introduced a second pair of traders, so that he had four people in communication with each other, two selling wood and two selling corn. He outlined how competition would force both sellers of each good to accept the same price.

Turgot was not alone in developing a subjective theory of value – a theory of value in which goods are worth as much as people consider them to be worth. On the contrary, there was a long tradition of such theories, going back through natural-law philosophers such as Samuel Pufendorf and Hugo Grotius (1583–1645) to the scholastics and Aristotle. In the eighteenth century, however, the clearest statements of subjective-value theories came from Italian economists, of whom Ferdinando Galiani (1728–87) is perhaps the outstanding representative. In 1751 Galiani published *Della Moneta*, one of the few works cited by Turgot in his essay on value. In 1759 he was appointed to the Neapolitan embassy in Paris, where he stayed for ten years. This decade was precisely the time when, due to Quesnay, political economy had become fashionable. Galiani, however, was not a physiocrat, and criticized the policy of allowing free export of corn while there were still extensive barriers to internal trade. *Della Moneta* clearly states the doctrine, taken up by Turgot, that value is subjective and measurable only in relation to the value of other goods. Utility and scarcity are the main factors explaining value. Galiani's argument that man is the common measure of value was, Turgot claimed, 'one of the newest and most profound truths which the general theory of value contains'.[13]

ECONOMIC THOUGHT UNDER THE *ANCIEN RÉGIME*

When the once-strict French censorship laws were relaxed sufficiently to allow the publication of writings that could be used against the government, the main issue driving economic analysis was reform. Taxes and regulations were seen by many to be stifling trade. Against this background it is not surprising that the doctrine of laissez-faire was developed by a wide variety of writers, from Boisguilbert at the start of the century to Turgot on the eve of the French Revolution. The effects of government restrictions on agriculture no doubt provide part of the reason (though not the whole reason) why the physiocrats emphasized the productivity of agriculture so strongly. They needed to counter the assumption, underlying Colbertism, that resources had to be shifted into manufacturing.

However, though economic thought was largely stimulated by urgent policy questions, many abstract ideas were developed. Cantillon's main work was on the nature of commerce *in general*. The physiocrats went even further, developing an abstract numerical model of economic activity. Turgot, even while involved in the running of the French state, and trying to reform it, probed into the meaning of abstract concepts such as wealth and value. The result was that the French economists of this period produced ideas that proved able to be taken up and used in very different contexts in the following century. French ideas fed into English political economy through Adam Smith, who was strongly influenced by Quesnay and Turgot, as well as through writers working after the Revolution, such as Jean-Baptiste Say. Though their economic views could hardly be more different, the *Tableau économique* inspired Karl Marx (pp. 169–77) and, even later, Wassily Leontief (pp. 230–31).

6

The Scottish Enlightenment
of the Eighteenth Century

BACKGROUND

The Scottish Enlightenment is the name given to the remarkable flour-
ishing of intellectual activity in what, at the time, was a very backward
part of Europe. It was sufficiently remarkable that even contemporaries were aware of it. David Hume was not alone in observing, in 1757,
that it 'really is admirable how many Men of Genius this Country
produces at present'.[1] The universities in Edinburgh, Glasgow and
Aberdeen were central to this activity, out of which arose some of the
eighteenth century's most notable contributions to economic thought
(and to social thought more generally).

The social thought associated with the Scottish Enlightenment had
several features which, if not unique, were taken further in Scotland
than by thinkers in other countries. It was secular. It did not deny the
tenets of established religion (such denial was still dangerous at this
time, especially for people in university positions and in the early decades of the century), but it focused on the mundane, everyday aspects
of reality. It was also committed to detachment and scientific objectivity rather than to orthodoxy. The thinkers of the Scottish Enlightenment
were consciously the heirs of Bacon, Newton and the scientists of the
seventeenth century, as well as inheriting important elements of
natural-law philosophy. In addition, and more distinctively, the Scottish Enlightenment had a clear social and above all historical focus. Its
writers were aware that different societies had different customs,
and they sought to discover the causes of these. In this they were following Montesquieu's *Spirit of the Laws* (1748), a work Hume was

responsible for translating into English. However, the Scottish writers – in particular Adam Smith – went further than Montesquieu in that they also sought to explain how human societies changed. They sought to provide an account of the history of civil society.

A major theme in these studies was that human nature was the same at all times. History, Hume argued very clearly, could be used to discover what these 'constant and universal principles of human nature' were.[2] The writers of the Scottish Enlightenment, however, also sought to examine the changing environment in which human nature operated. Man's action could change the environment and produce a new situation in which behaviour was different, even though the underlying human nature had not changed. The Scottish writers were led to the view that society had progressed through several historical stages. Primitive society was based on hunting and gathering the fruits of nature, without any antecedent social organization. Pasture followed from the domestication of animals and because property could now be appropriated, the result was inequality and differences in social status. This was followed by the agrarian stage, in which land became regarded as property that could be appropriated. This was the stage in which inheritance became important. The legal system developed accordingly. Finally, there was the exchange economy, in which society became divided into classes who gained their livelihoods in different ways. Division of labour raised productivity and made people more dependent on each other. This was an evolutionary theory of social organization in which economics, politics and law were all bound up together.

The fact of social evolution led both to a belief in progress and to a historical relativism. Adam Ferguson (1723–1816), a historian prominent in the Scottish Enlightenment, could write that 'the present age is perfecting what a former age began; or is now beginning what a future age is to perfect'.[3] Such an outlook had clear political implications. The Jacobite Rising of 1745, which attempted to restore the Stuarts to the throne, was backward-looking; the future lay elsewhere. At the same time, however, the writers of the Scottish Enlightenment became convinced that it was important to judge societies according to the customs of each society's own age. It was inappropriate to judge them according to the customs of modern society.

One factor behind the Scottish Enlightenment was an awareness that Scotland was backward in comparison with the south and east of England. The Scottish supporters of the 1707 Act of Union had hoped that the act would stimulate their economy. They were also confronted with the dramatic contrast between the relatively developed Lowlands and the very backward Highland regions. However, despite union with England, Scotland remained different in key respects. The Church of Scotland was Presbyterian, with a Calvinist emphasis on decisions made by the individual. More importantly, the Scottish legal system was, unlike the English, based on Roman law. Natural law, not common law, was fundamental. Feudal elements had survived (as was still the case in the twentieth century). There was thus great interest in comparisons with England, where Roman law was not recognized.

HUTCHESON

Francis Hutcheson (1694–1746), who held the chair of moral philosophy at Edinburgh from 1729 until his death, is generally regarded as the originator of the Scottish Enlightenment. However, he owed much to his predecessor Gershom Carmichael (1672–1729). It was Carmichael who had introduced the German natural-law philosopher Samuel Pufendorf to Scotland, publishing an edition of one of his most important works together with a set of substantial and influential notes. The link from Aristotle to Adam Smith came through Pufendorf and Carmichael. Carmichael's doctrine that the value of a commodity depended both on the commodity's scarcity and on the difficulty of acquiring it, and that a good could be of value only if it was either useful or imagined to be useful, was very squarely in the Aristotelian tradition. Given Carmichael's views, it is not surprising that Hutcheson had what was essentially a supply-and-demand theory of value.

Hutcheson, like many of his fellow Scots, viewed people as driven by a variety of motives. These included the desire to look after oneself, feeling for others, and the desire to better one's condition. As a moderate Christian, he was extremely critical of Bernard Mandeville, whom he saw as irreligious. Neither was he a supporter of Fénélon's reformed Salentum, for he believed that, without the incentive given by goods that provided pleasure, people would be idle much of the time. He sought a middle way between universal gratification of desires and suppressing them altogether. He did this through distinguishing between 'appetites' such as hunger and thirst, and 'desires or passions' that produced pleasure. The range of 'necessaries' continually increased, and increased demand for such goods would make it possible for trade to increase without a high demand for luxuries enjoyed only by the rich.

HUME

David Hume (1711–76) is now best known for his philosophical writing, but to his contemporaries he was known as a historian, for his *History of England* (1754–62). A historical perspective permeates his approach to economics, contained in a series of nine essays published in 1752 as part of a volume of *Political Discourses*. In view of contemporary scepticism about the value of abstract reasoning in economics, it is interesting to note that Hume opens this group of essays with a defence of applying what he calls 'refined and subtle' reasonings to such 'vulgar' subjects as commerce, money, interest, taxes and public credit. He appeals to his readers not to be prejudiced against what he has to say merely because his ideas are 'out of the common road'.[4] The public good, Hume argues, depends on a multitude of causes, not on chance and the caprices of a few individuals. This means that the type of historical account that one might give to explain, say, foreign policy, is inappropriate to this subject matter, and that more general reasoning that may yield unfamiliar conclusions is required.

Hume's concern in these essays is with the greatness of a state. He started by distinguishing between this and the happiness of the state's subjects. The latter will be increased by luxury consumption and will thus be reduced if the state diverts resources from this into defence and foreign ventures. In this sense, there is a trade-off between the happiness of the people and the power and influence of the state. However, luxury spending is important to the state, for it is necessary to persuade people to work. This is the reason that manufacturing is needed – the manufacture of luxury goods provides husbandmen (farmers) with an incentive to work more than the minimum amount required to subsist. Without such an incentive, they would prefer to be idle for much of the time. This desire for luxury goods benefits the state because, if husbandmen are producing a surplus over what they need for their subsistence, resources are available to which the sovereign can lay claim in order to raise fleets and armies. In a society of self-sufficient farmers, there would be no surplus available to be appropriated. Hume supported this claim with evidence from ancient Greek and Roman history.

The basis for Hume's argument about commerce and wealth is the theory that labour is the basis for wealth and that labour will be supplied only if people have an incentive to do so. He writes, 'Every thing in the world is purchased by labour; and our passions are the only causes of labour.'[5] Manufacturing is valuable because it enables labour to be stored up, available for use in times of need:

> [M]anufactures encrease the power of the state only as they store up so much labour, and that of a kind to which the public may lay claim, without depriving anyone of the necessaries of life. The more labour, therefore, is employed beyond mere necessaries, the more powerful is any state; since the persons engaged in that labour may easily be converted to the public service. In a state without manufactures, there may be the same number of hands; but there is not the same quantity of labour, nor of the same kind. All the labour is there bestowed upon necessaries, which can admit of little or no abatement.[6]

For much the same reason, foreign commerce is valuable. It increases the stock of labour in a nation.

Having established that the strength of a state depends on labour and commerce, Hume proceeds to demolish the argument that money is wealth. Money, he claims, is simply 'the oil which renders the motions of the wheels [of trade] more smooth and easy'[7]. There is no benefit to be had from having a greater quantity of money, for prices will be higher in the same proportion. The only exception to this is that, if gold and silver are plentiful, the sovereign will have more resources that can be drawn upon in times of war. In other respects, a large quantity of money is a disadvantage – higher prices will cause manufacturing industries to shift abroad, where costs will be lower. Labour will be lost to the state. Hume was thus opposed to the use of paper money, for this harmed manufacturing without the offsetting benefit of raising the state's stock of gold and silver.

However, although the quantity of money was of no importance, a rising money supply did make a difference – inflation could be beneficial. 'Accordingly we find, that, in every kingdom, into which money begins to flow in greater abundance than formerly, every thing takes a new face: labour and industry gain life; the merchant becomes more enterprising, the manufacturer more diligent and skilful, and even the farmer follows his plough with greater alacrity and attention.'[8] The explanation was that, although money raises prices, it does not do so immediately. There is thus an interval during which the money supply has increased by more than prices, and during this interval industry will be stimulated. Conversely, a falling money supply will have damaging effects on industry – a conclusion that Hume was able to support with much historical evidence.

Hume concluded that the best policy was to keep the money supply continually increasing. However, he was strongly opposed to trying to do this through restricting trade. Attempting to maintain a balance-of-payments surplus would be self-defeating, for the inflow of money would raise prices, causing manufacturing to go abroad, thus undermining the policy. He likened money to water in the sea: it is possible to raise the water level in one region only if it is cut off from the rest of the sea. If there is communication between different regions, money will, like water, find its own level. The only effect of mercantilist policies, therefore, was to interfere with trade. Furthermore, if one wanted to increase reserves of gold and silver for use in wartime, the right method was to hoard it, not to spend it. If money disappeared from circulation into hoards, it would no longer affect prices. This was in contrast with the view exemplified by Mun, that the purpose of increasing the money supply was to increase the circulation.

Hume's discussion of the balance of trade can be read as if it were a piece of pure economic analysis. However, as his discussion of hoarding money for time of war indicates, he was also concerned with national rivalries – with politics as much as with economics. This becomes even clearer in his essay 'Of the jealousy of trade'. This term echoed a remark made by Hobbes, that, even when not at war, kings were 'in continuall jealousies, and in the state and posture of Gladiators; having their weapons pointing, and their eyes fixed on one another; ... which is a posture of war'.[9] In using it, Hume was disparaging the notion that trade should be a matter of competition between nations, for the logic of trade, involving reciprocal advantage, was fundamentally different from the logic of war. Unlike Hobbes, who ignored commerce, Hume was concerned with the interaction between politics and economics, which was, for him, the defining feature of modern politics.

> Trade was never esteemed an affair of state until the last century; and there is scarcely any ancient writer on politics, who has made mention of it. Even the Italians have kept a profound silence with regard to it, though it has now engaged the chief attention, as well of ministers of state, of speculative reasoners.[10]

Hume's position was that there was no reason for jealousy in trade, because improvements in one country would benefit other countries. A nation can find markets for its exports only if its neighbours are prosperous, and emulation between rival nations will promote industry in all of them. The only exception was a country like the Netherlands, which had no natural advantages.

SIR JAMES STEUART

Many themes from the work of Hutcheson and Hume can be found in the book that has been described as the first systematic treatise on economics in the English language, the full title of which was *An Inquiry into the Principles of Political Oeconomy: Being an Essay on the Science of Domestic Policy in Free Nations, in which are Particularly Considered Population, Agriculture, Trade, Industry, Money, Coin, Interest, Circulation, Banks, Exchange, Public Credit and Taxes*

(1767). The title introduced into English the term 'political economy', a translation of the term *économie politique* used by Antoyne Monchretien (*c.*1575–1621) in the title of a book published in 1615. This was to become the standard name for economics as the subject began to achieve a separate identity during the nineteenth century. The English book was also the first work to use the phrase 'supply and demand' to explain how prices were determined:

> The nature of demand is to encourage industry; and when it is regularly made, the effect of it is, that the supply for the most part is to be found in proportion to it ... And when it is irregular, that is, unexpected, or when the usual supply fails, ... [this] occasions a competition among the buyers and raises the current, that is, the ordinary prices.'[11]

This explanation of prices was followed up with a detailed account of competition. Particular attention was paid to what the author called 'double competition', in which there was competition both between buyers and between sellers. This was important because it set upper and lower limits to price and caused the interests of different individuals to balance each other. This balance, however, vibrated, with the result that buyers and sellers could not observe it exactly. Their decisions had to be based on the price for which they expected to be able to resell the goods. The conclusion was drawn that forestalling (buying goods in order to resell them when there was a shortage) was a crime because it diminished the competition that ought to take place and that would ensure that goods sold for their real value.

The author of the book was Sir James Steuart (1712–80). He was part of the Scottish Enlightenment but stood apart from other writers in that he was a Jacobite, and supported the 1745 rebellion. Sent by Charles Edward Stewart, the Young Pretender, as an ambassador to France, Steuart remained in exile after the defeat of the Jacobites at Culloden, not returning to Scotland until 1763. During this period he travelled widely in Europe.

Steuart's experience during his exile influenced his outlook. He became very sceptical about general rules concerning political matters, on the grounds that everything needed to be considered in relation to the circumstances of the country in question. Different countries had different customs, and these needed to be taken into account. He thus wrote that the merit of his book, in so far as it had any merit, arose from 'divesting myself of English notions, so far as to be able to expose in a fair light, the sentiments and policy of foreign nations, relatively to their own situation'.[12] Continental influences account for Steuart's emphasis on the role of the statesman (used as a shorthand for the king, Parliament, or whoever was ruling a nation). His book was, as he put it, 'addressed to a statesman', even though its object was 'to influence the spirit of those whom he governs'.[13] This went against the prevailing mood, which was in favour of liberty and playing down the importance of state action.

Steuart's historical perspective echoed that of Hutcheson, though he distinguished only three stages in history: hunting and gathering, agriculture, and exchange. Growth was seen in terms of an increase in population, this being limited by the supply of food. In the first stage of history, population was limited by the spontaneous fruits of the earth, but, when 'labour and industry' were applied to the soil, a further quantity of food could be produced, enabling a larger population to be supported. However, if farmers were to be induced to produce more than they needed for their own consumption, there had to be a market for their produce – the third stage. This led Steuart to state two principles:

[1] Agriculture among a free people will augment population, in proportion only as the necessitous are put in a situation to purchase subsistence with their labour . . . [2] That agriculture, when encouraged for the sake of multiplying inhabitants, must keep pace with the progress of industry; or else an outlet must be found for all superfluity.[14]

These principles, he claimed, were confirmed by experience. We can see him here arguing for a balance between the more extreme views of mercantilist support for industry and physiocratic support for agriculture – views that he would obviously have encountered during his stay in Europe.

Like Hume, Steuart saw a close link between labour and wealth.

However, in line with the trend in English economic thought from the late seventeenth century, he placed much greater emphasis on the need to keep people employed. He recognized that employment would fail from time to time, and he believed that the state should seek to mitigate this as much as possible. Maintaining employment required that there should be a balance between supply and demand: 'The greatest care must be taken to support a perfect balance between the hands in work and the demand for their labour.'[15] Demand must be neither too high nor too low, and it was the statesman's duty to see that this was achieved.

Steuart had what has come to be called a 'Malthusian' view of population growth. Procreation was not the same as multiplication of the population, for, if the birth rate were too high, fewer children would survive. It followed that population could grow in response to the demand for labour, but only if agriculture could produce more food. There were, however, limits to what agriculture could provide, the main one being rising agricultural costs. Rising food prices would raise the price of subsistence and hence wage costs. The statesman would then be caught in a dilemma between encouraging 'expensive improvements of the soil' (which require high food prices) and cheap imports which enable wages costs to be kept low. This dilemma could be resolved, Steuart argued, only by 'right application of public money'.[16] This is one example of the ways in which Steuart believed that the state might have to use government spending or alterations to the money supply in order to achieve a balance between supply and demand. Public money could be used to raise demand and reduce unemployment, but care had to be taken not to lean too far the other way.

Given such an attitude, it is not surprising that Steuart did not accept the quantity theory of money. The theory of the relationship between money and prices proposed by Montesquieu and Hume, he conceded, was 'so simple, and so extensive, that it is no wonder to see it adopted by almost everyone who has written after them'. However, he argued that 'in this, as in every other part of the science of political economy, there is hardly such a thing as a general rule to be laid down'.[17] The reasons he gave for this were that demand and competition determined prices, and that these depended on wealth and on the circumstances of the economy, not on how much coin people happened to have:

> Let the specie of a country, therefore, be augmented or diminished, in ever so great a proportion, commodities will still rise and fall accord-ing to the principles of demand and competition; and these will constantly depend upon the inclinations of those who have *property* or any kind of *equivalent* whatsoever to give; but never on the quan-tity of *coin* they are possessed of.[18]

Throughout his *Principles*, Steuart emphasized the role of the statesman. It would, however, be a mistake to see him either as a totali-tarian planner or as someone who was simply looking back to a pre-market era. Not only did he assume people to be self-interested, he regarded this as essential if government policy were to be effective:

> The principle of self-interest will serve as a general key to this inquiry; and it may, in one sense, be considered as the ruling principle of my subject ... This is the main spring, and only motive which a states-man should make use of, to engage a free people to concur in the plans which he lays down for their government ... [W]ere every one to act for the public, and neglect himself, the statesman would be bewildered, and the supposition is ridiculous.[19]

One can see from this passage that Steuart lies firmly in the approach to politics that goes back, through Hobbes and Locke, to Machiavelli. For a few years, Steuart's *Principles* was well received. Hume wel-comed the book, and Steuart's advice was sought by the British government. However, the book rapidly fell into oblivion, at least in Britain. The main reason was clearly the publication of Adam Smith's *Wealth of Nations* only a few years later. Smith's work caught the public imagination far more effectively than Steuart's, and Smith adopted the effective rhetorical strategy of completely ignoring the earlier book. Part of the reason, however, may have been Steuart's ram-bling style, which did not always make his message clear. In Germany, however, where Steuart's ideas about the need to regulate the economy found a more receptive audience, the book continued to be read, and his discussion of supply and demand received considerable attention in the early nineteenth century.

ADAM SMITH

Adam Smith (1723–90), who came from an influential Scottish family, was a student of Hutcheson's and, after a year holding the chair of logic, he held the chair of moral philosophy at Glasgow from 1752 to 1764. During this time, he lectured on rhetoric and belles-lettres, jurisprudence and moral philosophy. His work on economics arose out of this and formed part of a broader inquiry into the science of society. This inquiry was squarely in the tradition of the Scottish Enlightenment, with its focus on history and on the foundations of civil society. He was also influenced by French writers, having spent two years as tutor to a young aristocrat, the Duke of Buccleuch, whom he accompanied on a Grand Tour, meeting and conversing with luminaries including Voltaire. In Paris he turned to Quesnay as a physician, becoming familiar with physiocratic ideas and acquiring key works by French writers for his library.

The book that sustained Smith's reputation for subsequent generations, dominating nineteenth-century economics as did the work of no other economist, was *An Inquiry into the Nature and Causes of the Wealth of Nations*, first published in 1776, the year of the American Declaration of Independence. In Smith's lifetime, however, his reputation was based not on this book, but on *The Theory of Moral Sentiments*, published in six editions between 1759 and 1790. Smith regarded both books as part of his broader inquiry into what we would now describe as social science. The relationship between the two books was described at the beginning of the sixth edition of *The Theory of Moral Sentiments*:

> In the ... first Edition of the present work, I said, that I should in another discourse endeavour to give an account of the general principles of law and government, and of the different revolutions which they had undergone in the different ages and periods of society; not

only in what concerns justice, but in what concerns police, revenue and arms, and whatever else is the object of law. In the *Inquiry concerning the Nature and Causes of the Wealth of Nations,* I have partly executed this promise; at least so far as concerns police, revenue and arms. What remains [is] the theory of jurisprudence.[20]

This last part of his project was never completed.

The main concern of *The Theory of Moral Sentiments* was with the criteria on which moral judgements can be based. Smith thus explored the basis for the sense of propriety, the sense of approbation, and judgements of merit and virtue. A key element in his approach was provided by the concept of sympathy – the ability to see things from someone else's point of view, and to see our own behaviour from the perspective of an impartial spectator. The reason why this is relevant to social science is that, in undertaking this inquiry, Smith was exploring the question of what makes it possible for men to live in society. How is it that selfish desires can be restrained in order to prevent men from injuring one another? The simplest answer is the desire to please others – a desire for the approbation of other people. We view our own behaviour from the point of view of the impartial spectator, and act accordingly. This motive, however, will not be strong enough. When we contemplate our actions before we act, 'eagerness of passion' – the desire to do things – will bias our judgement. After an action has been taken, on the other hand, the desire not to think badly of ourselves will lead to bias. Neither beforehand nor afterwards, therefore, can we take an unbiased view of our actions. Further guidance is needed. This is provided by moral rules – generalizations from our experience of what types of action are approved of and disapproved of. However, moral rules are in themselves insufficient and need to be backed up, in some cases, by positive laws.

If people are held together by mutual affection and give each other the support that they need 'from gratitude, from friendship, and esteem', society can flourish. However, Smith argued that such motives are not necessary:

Society may subsist among different men, as among different merchants, from a sense of its utility, without any mutual love or affection;

and though no man in it should owe any obligation, or be bound in gratitude to any other, it may still be upheld by a mercenary exchange of good offices according to an agreed valuation.[21]

A commercial society can flourish even though people do not have strong affections for each other. On the other hand, this is emphatically not the same as saying that a society can flourish if there are no limits to behaviour:

> Society, however, cannot subsist among those who are at all times ready to hurt and injure one another . . . If there is any society among robbers and murderers, they must at least . . . abstain from robbing and murdering one another. Beneficence, therefore, is less essential to the existence of society than justice. Society may subsist, though not in the most comfortable state, without beneficence; but the prevalence of injustice must utterly destroy it.[22]

This is the context for *The Wealth of Nations*. Smith is exploring how a commercial society can prosper, even though men are pursuing their own interests. He is, however, assuming a framework of justice, without which society would be destroyed. The society he is talking about is fundamentally different from a Hobbesian state of nature in that men are assumed to be guided by morality and restrained by a just legal system. Within this framework Smith explains the benefits that arise from a system of natural liberty.

DIVISION OF LABOUR AND THE MARKET

More clearly than any previous writer, Smith was concerned with the process of economic growth. Of the five 'Books' that make up *The Wealth of Nations*, the first discusses 'the causes of improvement in the productive powers of labour' and how produce is distributed among the different classes of society. This improvement could not happen without capital accumulation, the subject of Book 2. In Book 3, Smith turns to 'the different progress of opulence in different nations', showing how different policies have promoted or retarded growth. This leads naturally into a discussion of government policy and in Book 4 he offers critiques of both the 'mercantile system', a system he believed had done much harm, and the 'agricultural system' of the physiocrats, which had done little harm because it had never been applied. He ends with Book 5, on government revenue and taxation. It is a systematic account of the causes of economic growth, encompassing what would today be considered economic theory, economic history, and policy advice. Its variety and range provide part of the explanation of why subsequent generations have been able to interpret it in very different ways.

The most important cause of economic growth, Smith claimed, is the division of labour. On introducing the idea, he illustrated it with a 'very trifling manufacture' – pin (or nail) making. He pointed out that, without being trained in the industry and without the assistance of the right machinery (and both training and machinery were the result of division of labour), a worker could probably make no more than one pin per day and certainly no more than twenty. In contrast, in the modern industry, where the task of making a pin was divided into eighteen different operations (drawing the wire, straightening it, cutting it, grinding it, putting the head on, whitening the pin, putting the pins into paper, and so on), a team of ten men could make upward of 48,000 pins per day. Division of labour was, Smith claimed, carried furthest in the most advanced countries.

However, although Smith introduced the division of labour by considering its application within a single factory, just as important for his case was the social division of labour, where different people perform different tasks, obtaining what they need through exchange. The division of labour, he argued, was 'the necessary, though very slow and gradual consequence of a certain propensity in human nature . . . to truck, barter, and exchange one thing for another'.[23] This led him to the proposition that the division of labour was limited by the extent of the market. In a village, people had to perform for themselves many of the tasks that, in a city, would be performed by specialists. A country carpenter, Smith observed, was not only a carpenter, but a joiner, a cabinetmaker, a wood carver and a wagon maker, each of which would be a separate trade in a larger market. The development of water transport, Smith observed, was crucial to this process of opening up more extensive markets.

Having established the link between economic growth and the expansion of markets, Smith then turned to the question of how markets operated. This took him into the fields of value and the distribution of income. Three concepts are particularly important to his analysis of these problems. The first is the distinction between the real and the nominal prices of commodities. In an exchange economy it is more convenient to use money than to engage in barter and, as a result, prices are measured in terms of money (the nominal price). However, the real price of a commodity is 'the toil and trouble of acquiring it'. This is a quantity of labour, not a quantity of money – though, given the problems involved in measuring labour, it might best be measured in terms of other commodities. Variations in the value of gold and silver would cause the nominal and real prices of commodities to differ from each other. It is the real price that matters and that his theory of value sought to explain.

The second important concept in Smith's value theory is the breaking down of the prices of commodities into their component parts – wages, profits and rents, the returns to labour, capital and land. This is the basis for the third key concept: the distinction between the market price and the natural price of commodities. The market price of a commodity is the price it fetches in the market, which will depend on supply and demand. If supply is insufficient to meet demand at the going price, the market price will rise; if there is a surplus of goods, the market price will fall. Because prices can be broken down into their component parts, it follows that, if the market price rises, so too must at least one of the components of price. The natural price of a commodity is thus defined as the price at which labour, capital and land are all receiving their natural prices. It is, Smith argued, 'the central price, to which the prices of all commodities are continually gravitating'.[24] The mechanism that causes this to happen is competition. If, for example, the rate of profit in producing hats is higher than the natural rate of profits, and if capitalists are free to move their capital from one industry to another, they will move into hat-making. This will increase the supply of hats and bring the price of hats down to the natural price. Alternatively, if workers in mining are earning more than the natural rate of wages, other workers will become miners, pushing wages downward.

Smith's theory was thus a cost-of-production theory, not a labour theory in which value depended on the quantity of labour alone. The only time when the labour theory applied was in a very simple society in which there was no capital or privately owned land, for in such a society labour was the only cost of acquiring a commodity. This explains his claim that if it took two days to catch a deer but only one day to catch a beaver, then a deer would be worth two beavers. However, in order to measure standards of living over centuries, he needed a yardstick. He considered three possibilities, concluding that because the values of silver and corn varied greatly from year to year, neither of them would serve. This left labour time, which best performed this function because it measured the toil and trouble involved in obtaining commodities.

This process is the reason why self-love can produce an outcome that is in the interests of society – why a commercial society can prosper even though people have no affection for each other. Its crucial element is what Smith called 'liberty', the freedom of individuals to move their capital and labour from one activity to another as they choose. It was a concern to promote liberty that led Smith to denounce restrictions on industry and trade that had usually been introduced in the interests of merchants. Such restrictions would benefit particular individuals but would hinder the operation of competition. He consistently referred not to self-interest but to 'self-love', or looking after oneself, a motive crucial to the survival of any animal. It is important to note that Smith was neither advocating selfish behaviour nor claiming that people were selfish: that would be inconsistent with *The Theory of Moral Sentiments*.

Some modern commentators associate Smith's argument about the working of the price mechanism with his phrase 'the invisible hand'. He did use this term – three times – but not to explain the price mechanism. In *The Theory of Moral Sentiments*, he argued that, although they keep for themselves 'what is most precious and agreeable', the rich consume little more than the poor. Through employing the labourers, 'They [the rich] are led by an invisible hand to make nearly the same distribution of the necessaries of life, which would have been made, had the earth been divided into equal portions among all its inhabitants.'[25] Note that the equality involved is limited, for it covers only 'necessaries', goods that people need, not 'conveniences', goods which motivate people to improve their condition. In *The Wealth of Nations*, he used the phrase to refer to people's preference for investing in domestic industry over investing in much riskier foreign trade; because domestic industry produced goods of greater value, this meant that people were 'led by an invisible hand' to produce the outcome that was best for society.[26] Smith's only other use of the phrase was in a completely different context – the history of astronomy, in which it was the invisible hand of Jupiter. Significantly, Smith did not use the phrase where much modern commentary suggests he should have used it.

ACCUMULATION OF STOCK AND THE NATURAL PROGRESS OF OPULENCE

Book 1 of *The Wealth of Nations*, with its emphasis on division of labour and the link between labour and wealth, falls squarely within the Scottish Enlightenment tradition. In Book 2, on the other hand, Smith emphasizes the role of 'stock', or capital, in a way that makes him much closer to Turgot than to Hutcheson or Hume. A precondition for the division of labour, Smith contended, is the accumulation of what he called 'stock'. This includes both the tools that workmen need and also the provisions that they need while they are working. If growth is to occur, stock has to be increased, and to achieve this it is necessary to employ labour productively. This leads to Smith's distinction between productive and unproductive labour.

The basic idea underlying this distinction is that productive labour 'adds to the value of the subject on which it is bestowed'. It 'fixes' itself 'in a permanent subject or vendible commodity' that is there when the labour is finished, and which can then be sold to obtain more labour.[27] Unproductive labour, however, does not add to the value of anything. Thus the labour of a manufacturer who adds to the value of the materials with which he works, or of the farmer who produces a tangible output at the end of the year, is productive. In contrast, the labour of the menial servant or even of the sovereign or judges or the army is unproductive. Given that all labour has to be maintained by annual produce, the accumulation of capital depends on the proportion of labour employed productively. Consider the extreme cases. If the entire labour force were employed unproductively, there would be no produce at all the following year. At the other extreme, if labour were all employed productively, produce must be higher.

The need for capital accumulation is the reason why Smith sees a link between saving and economic growth. 'Capitals are increased by parsimony, and diminished by prodigality and misconduct.'[28] He argues forcefully that there is no need for luxury spending to maintain demand, for savings are spent just as much as is expenditure on consumption goods:

> What is annually saved is as regularly consumed as what is annually spent, and in nearly the same time too; but it is consumed by a different set of people. That portion of his revenue which a rich man annually spends, is in most cases consumed by idle guests, and menial servants, who leave nothing behind them in return for their consumption. That portion which he annually saves, as for the sake of profit it is immediately employed as capital, is consumed in the same manner, and nearly in the same time too, but by a different set of people, by labourers, manufacturers, and artificers, who re-produce with a profit the value of their annual consumption ... The consumption is the same, but the consumers are different.[29]

In other words, saving (which for Smith means investment, for if savers did not invest their money, they could not earn a profit, which is their objective) is employing productive labour, whereas consumption is employing unproductive labour.

Smith's view was that there was a natural sequence in which growth took place – 'a natural progress of opulence'.[30] The development of agriculture naturally came first, because its products were necessary for human subsistence. It was only when agriculture produced a surplus over its own needs that towns could develop, producing conveniences and luxuries that could be exchanged for this surplus. Towns and the countryside therefore contributed to each other's prosperity. The way in which this happened should depend on the circumstances of each nation, such as whether or not there existed large tracts of uncultivated, fertile land. However, unwise policies could divert nations from this pattern, impeding growth. One problem was that there had been attempts, from the Roman empire onwards, to stimulate the growth of towns and of industry in the countryside beyond what was natural, causing growth to be less than it might have been. Given that capital should be invested at home before being employed in less productive uses abroad, supporting trade and the development of colonial systems also served to divert capital from the industries to which it would most naturally flow.

Smith also had the idea that a country's resources and institutions determined a limit to the quantity of stock that could be employed in it – its 'full complement of riches'. He thought that China had long since been in this situation: stationary, with the level of riches consistent with its laws and institutions. However, even with the same soil and climate, but with improved institutions, it might be capable of supporting higher levels of riches. Another example of a country that had achieved its full complement of riches was the Netherlands, where, because the rate of interest had been pushed so low, making it impossible for any but the very wealthy to live on property income alone, people with more modest fortunes had no choice but to work. The result was that it had become 'unfashionable not to be a man of business or engage in some sort of trade'.[31] Wages were typically highest in countries that had not reached this situation and where there were still opportunities to invest stock profitably.

SMITH AND LAISSEZ-FAIRE

Smith advocated what he described as the system of 'natural liberty', to be contrasted with the other two systems of political economy that he discussed: the mercantile system and the system of agriculture (physiocracy). To understand his attitude here it is important to remember that, in passages that may have been written with the French Revolution in mind, he was critical of 'the man of system' who 'is so often enamoured with the supposed beauty of his own ideal plan of government, that he cannot suffer the smallest deviation from any part of it'.[32] He favoured the use of reason and persuasion to change prejudices and, if they could not be changed, advocated accommodating them rather than the use of violence. His system of natural liberty was, therefore, not something imposed but involved simply the freedom of any individual to bring his capital into competition with that of anyone else, unimpeded by artificial barriers, allowing the processes described in the previous section to operate. In contrast, 'perfect liberty', akin to the modern concept of perfect competition, was a more demanding condition which was hard to achieve. He strongly opposed monopoly, which in his day was normally the result of privileges granted by the government: 'Monopoly ... is a great enemy to good management, which can never be universally established but in consequence of that free and universal competition which forces every body to have recourse to it for the sake of self-defence.'[33] In a system of natural liberty, resources would be directed into activities most beneficial to society, even though individuals were pursuing their own interests. Smith's contribution to the debate on what holds society together, opened up by Hobbes over a century earlier, was therefore to argue that what he called 'expediency' – doing things because they were useful – could contribute to this end. However, Smith was not arguing for complete laissez-faire, for he saw an important role for government.

The main reason why government was needed was that the arguments of *The Wealth of Nations* presupposed a system of justice. Without justice, the system of natural liberty would be unable to function. Men would be insecure, continually being damaged by each other. Spending on the legal system and on the armed forces might be classified as unproductive, but it was nonetheless essential for the system to work. For Smith, to maintain law and order was therefore the first duty of the sovereign. It is worth noting that this involved some significant exceptions to the principle of laissez-faire. In particular, Smith supported the Navigation Acts (which severely restricted competition in shipping), on the grounds that they contributed to the strength of the Royal Navy.

Defence and justice, however, were not the only exceptions Smith saw to the principle of laissez-faire. The third duty of the sovereign was that of

> erecting and maintaining those publick institutions and those publick works, which, though they may be in the highest degree advantageous to a great society, are, however, of such a nature, that the profit could never repay the expence to any individual or small number of individuals, and which it, therefore, cannot be expected that any individual or small number of individuals should erect or maintain.[34]

His main examples concerned transport (bridges, roads and canals) and primary education. However, although he argued the case for intervention, he sought to make use of tolls and fees wherever possible. This was for two reasons. He wanted users (for example of roads) to pay as much as possible, and he wanted employees (such as teachers) to have an incentive to do their work properly. Thus, immediately after saying that the cost of education might 'without injustice' be met out of public funds, he declared that it would be better for it to be paid by those who benefited from schooling. His view was that privately provided education was, in his day, better than public education. He was scathing in his criticism of universities, in which teachers failed to teach and students failed to learn.

One area where Smith saw no role whatsoever for the government was in maintaining the level of employment. Writers from Misselden (in the early seventeenth century) to Steuart (writing only a few years before Smith) had seen the disruption that fluctuations in trade could produce and had sought to design policies that would mitigate the resulting underemployment. The policies that he criticized under the label of 'the Mercantile System' can be seen, at least in part, as attempts to reduce unemployment by increasing the circulation of money. The defence of luxury consumption by numerous writers in the seventeenth and eighteenth centuries was also a response to periods when demand was seen to be inadequate. Smith, on the other hand, with his doctrine that saving constituted spending, denied that there was a problem. If there were perfect liberty, men would move into occupations where there was a demand for their services. Monetary economics thus played a minor role in Smith's system. In separating monetary economics from problems of value, income distribution and growth, Smith was taking a position very different from those of many of his predecessors.

ECONOMIC THOUGHT AT THE END OF THE EIGHTEENTH CENTURY

For many contemporaries, as much as for subsequent generations of economists, the crowning achievement of eighteenth-century economic thought was Smith's *Wealth of Nations*. This book arose out of the long-standing controversies over the significance of luxury spending and the relationship between commerce and national rivalries. These debates concerned what we would now consider economic questions, but moral and political questions were never far from the surface. The role of morality – in particular Christian morality – in holding society together was central. Smith was therefore contributing to debates to which Hobbes, Fénelon and Mandeville had made such dramatic contributions. Even his *Wealth of Nations* should be seen as an exercise in moral philosophy.

Smith combined this with a focus on the interdependence of the various sectors of the economy. This was a pervasive theme in eighteenth-century thought, in both Britain and France, and it can even be found as far back as the sixteenth century (as in the *Discourse on the Common Weal*), but it was Smith's version of it that caught the imagination of his contemporaries. Over time, however, the origins of *The Wealth of Nations* in this debate over the morality of commercial society became forgotten, resulting in Smith's work being seen in a different light. He became seen as the advocate of laissez-faire – a perspective that would have surprised his contemporaries, who would have been aware how much further he was from such a position than, for example, many French authors. For him, perfect liberty was an ideal, for he wrote that 'If a nation could not prosper without the enjoyment of perfect liberty and perfect justice, there is not in the world a nation which could ever have prospered.'[35]

Smith's debts to his predecessors and contemporaries are so great that some commentators have gone so far as to argue that *The Wealth of Nations* contains not a single original idea. Supply and demand as the explanation of value has a history too long to summarize briefly. Elements of the labour theory of value can be traced to Petty and to some scholastic writers. The phrase 'division of labour' was used by Hutcheson, and the concept was widely understood in Xenophon's day. The importance of capital was recognized by Turgot. The notion of a spontaneous order can be found in Mandeville and Cantillon. And so on. It was, however, Smith's interpretation of these themes and his integration of them into a system that found its way into nineteenth-century economics, especially in Britain. His originality lay in the way he synthesized these ideas into something new.

7
The Emergence of Political Economy

FROM MORAL PHILOSOPHY TO
POLITICAL ECONOMY

Smith's *Wealth of Nations* was part of a much broader inquiry into the foundations of society. It was inseparable from moral philosophy – from the project of seeking to find a basis on which people could live together when the Church no longer provided an unquestioned set of answers to questions about how society should be organized. Smith's economics should therefore be seen as a response to Mandeville, and before him Hobbes, as much as to the physiocrats or the many merchants, administrators and philosophers who had written about trade. In the half-century or so after Smith's death, however, political economy, though dominated by the framework set out in *The Wealth of Nations*, became independent of moral philosophy. It acquired a more 'scientific' character that appealed to a class of radicals, many of whom wanted to explain social phenomena without reference to a deity.

To understand this transition, it is important to remember that the discipline was thoroughly involved with politics, and that the political context changed dramatically during this period. Among the political-economic issues facing Smith were the relationship between Britain and the American colonies (especially trade and tax policies), restrictions on both domestic and foreign trade caused by the creation of monopolies, and the appropriateness of intervention in the market for food in order to prevent famine. In the 1780s and 1790s, as the growth rate of the population increased, the problem of poverty and its alleviation increased, with the phrase 'the labouring poor' coming into widespread use to describe a supposedly new category of workers who were unable to achieve a decent standard of living even though they were able-bodied and had work. (The need for public support for the old, the sick and children was never questioned.) The 'Speenhamland System', introduced in the 1790s, involved the payment of allowances linked to the price of bread to men earning low wages. These payments were financed from local taxation, and aroused great controversy. Some people argued that the system depressed wages, exacerbating the position of the poor instead of relieving it.

The French Revolution in 1789 and the ensuing wars (1793–1815) had a profound effect on economic thought. The war created acute economic problems in Britain. A financial crisis in 1797 led to the suspension of the convertibility of sterling into gold, and Britain remained on a paper currency until 1819. During the decade and a half after the suspension, the number of banknotes issued by the Bank of England increased and prices rose. A particular problem was the rise in the price of grain, which raised agricultural rents and caused changes in the way land was used. Farmers and landlords prospered. At the same time, people were becoming aware that the 'manufacturing system' was growing rapidly. Steam power, though still used only on a small scale, was spreading, and mechanization was rapidly transforming the long-established woollen textile industry and making possible the dramatic growth of the newer cotton industry. The mix of social unrest caused by high food prices and the social dislocation caused by industrial change was a potent one, especially when combined with fear of French republicanism.

The Revolution raised the spectre of republicanism, and popular unrest was a constant worry for the ruling classes in Britain, especially after the outbreak of war in 1793. When Smith died he was widely associated with radical ideas. His *Wealth of Nations* was cited approvingly by Thomas Paine (1737–1809) in *The Rights of Man* (1791) and by Mary Wollstonecraft (1759–97) in *A Vindication of the Rights of Woman* (1792) and, judging by obituaries, his death was more keenly felt in revolutionary France than in Britain. In 1791, Condorcet published a substantial summary of *The Wealth of Nations*. However, as English public opinion turned against the revolution, especially after the outbreak of war and the Jacobin Terror, it became dangerous to hold such ideas. Towns that had previously been home to republican clubs saw Paine being burned in effigy. The reason Smith did not share this fate was that he was reinterpreted as a conservative figure – as a supporter not of 'liberty' (a dangerous idea associated with the Jacobins) but as an advocate of 'free trade'. Economic freedom was separated from political liberty, a separation Smith himself did not make.

A key figure in the transition from the moral philosophy of Hume and Smith to political economy was Thomas Robert Malthus (1766–1834). In the 1790s, radicals, of whom William Godwin (1756–1836) and the Marquis de Condorcet (1743–94) were most prominent, argued that private property was the root of social ills and that resources should be distributed more equally so as to provide everyone with a decent standard of living. Given Condorcet's links with the policies that developed in France, under Robespierre, into the Terror (in which Condorcet was killed), this was regarded as a seditious doctrine by much of the British establishment. Malthus, a clergyman in the Church of England, responded to such arguments with his *Essay on the Principle of Population*. This was published as a small, anonymous, tract in 1798, then considerably expanded and published under his name in the second edition of 1803. In it, Malthus offered a series of related arguments against the claims made by socialists such as Godwin, which he considered utopian. Far from being a source of harm, Malthus argued, private property was essential, for otherwise self-love would fail to have the beneficial effects that Smith had pointed out. Giving money to the poor would not improve their condition unless someone else was prepared to consume less, for it would have no effect on the quantity of resources available. Furthermore, any extension of poor relief would increase the dependence of the poor on the state – something Malthus viewed with apprehension. Under the Poor Laws, the poor were 'subjected to a set of grating, inconvenient, and tyrannical laws, totally inconsistent with the genuine spirit of the constitution ... utterly contradictory to all ideas of freedom ... [and adding] to the difficulty of those struggling to support themselves without assistance'.[1]

Though it was only one among many ideas presented in the *Essay*,

Malthus has become most widely associated with the argument that there is a continual tendency for population to outstrip resources. He expressed this by claiming that, if unchecked, population would grow according to a geometric progression (1, 2, 4, 8, 16, . . .), whereas food supply could grow only in an arithmetic progression (1, 2, 3, 4, 5, . . .). Population was held down by two types of check: preventive checks, which served to lower the birth rate, and positive checks, which raised the death rate. These two types of check fell into two categories: misery (war, famine) and vice (war, infanticide, prostitution, contraception). In the second edition of the *Essay* he added a third category, moral restraint, which covered postponement of marriage not accompanied by 'irregular gratification'. This third category enabled him to reconcile his theory with the evidence he had collected, between 1798 and 1803, that his original theory was not supported by the facts. Moral restraint was very important because it opened up the possibility of progress. However, although Malthus softened the hard line taken in the original *Essay*, he never shared Godwin's or Condorcet's optimism, for he did not share their belief in the goodness of human nature. People required moral guidance, and Malthus sought to provide it. The term 'moral' restraint was carefully chosen.

The Wealth of Nations, with its optimism about the prospects for growth, offered little guidance to politicians facing the problems of wartime. Malthus reoriented political economy so as to respond to these problems, and in doing this he helped lay the foundations on which political economy developed. After the war, when Britain faced problems of depression in agriculture and industry, he argued, in his *Principles of Political Economy* (1821), that growth required what he called 'effective demand' in addition to population growth and capital accumulation, opening up a positive role for consumption spending. However, in much of his writing he still operated within the sphere of eighteenth-century moral philosophy. He based his case against utopians such as Godwin on laws of society – the security of property and the institution of marriage. Socialism was at fault because it violated natural laws. In arguing along these lines, Malthus was arguing that Christianity, properly interpreted, was consistent with the Enlightenment – indeed, that it was the highest form of enlightenment.

In contrast, other economists, though they acknowledged an equally great debt to *The Wealth of Nations*, did not share this perspective and sought to turn political economy into a secular science.

Though Malthus disagreed with Godwin's and Condorcet's conclusions, he shared with them a belief in reason, presenting himself as applying Newtonian principles to the art of politics. He criticized them for endangering the enlightened, Newtonian, view of science by fostering hopes of progress that could never be realized. This belief in the power of reason was not shared by Malthus's 'Romantic' critics, Robert Southey (1774–1843), Samuel Taylor Coleridge (1772–1834) and the other 'Lake poets'. During his own lifetime, the term 'Malthusian' came to be used as a term of abuse, referring to the materialistic, spiritually impoverished outlook of what was also called 'modern political economy'. This was a reaction that continued throughout the nineteenth century, notably with Thomas Carlyle (1795–1881), who coined the phrase 'the Dismal Science' and, much later, John Ruskin (1819–1900). The term 'economist' came to denote someone with an identifiable approach to politics and a congenitally hard heart.

SMITH, SAY AND POLITICAL ECONOMY

Two French writers were also important for the emergence of political economy in the tradition of Smith. In 1802, Germain Garnier (1754–1821) translated *The Wealth of Nations* into French, the language universally spoken by the educated classes. This was the version of the book that Karl Marx was to read. Also, in 1805, Garnier's introduction to the book was translated into English. He praised Smith for his discovery of the 'great truth' that it was labour, not land, that lay behind the creation of all wealth.[2] In doing so, Smith connected political economy with the other social sciences, dealing with phenomena that could be improved by careful design (in contrast to the natural sciences, which dealt with factors outside human control). However, he accused Smith of being unsystematic, claiming that the first two of the five 'Books' that made up *The Wealth of Nations* could stand alone, for they contained the whole of Smith's views on how wealth was created and distributed, the last three doing little more than 'confirm and develop' his opinions.[3] Garnier then argued that Smith's argument fell into three parts: the determination of values; the nature of national wealth; and finally the way in which the growth and distribution of national wealth takes place. In short, he was criticizing Smith for not writing a systematic text on the principles of political economy, something that Smith had not been trying to do.

Garnier was important for popularizing the view that *The Wealth of Nations* was muddled, but although Garnier wrote his own textbook, the author who did most to shape the way early-nineteenth-century political economy was conceived was Jean-Baptiste Say (1767–1832). A member of the Tribunat, until removed by Napoleon, and a businessman who had worked in Britain and France, he wrote *Traité d'économie politique* (1803), which went through many editions. Say is well known for his theory of entrepreneurship and for the doctrine that there cannot be a shortage of demand in the economy as a whole, a position supported by Ricardo but opposed by Malthus, who believed that there could be a shortage of demand. However, his book is arguably more important for its having framed political economy as dealing with the production, distribution and consumption of wealth, in that order. Not only was the *Traité* widely used as a textbook, both in France and elsewhere (an English translation was published in 1821, which, like the French original, remained in print for many years), the organization of his material, adopted from the second edition onwards, became the standard structure for principles of political economy for most of the nineteenth century.

UTILITARIANISM AND THE
PHILOSOPHIC RADICALS

Say's *Traité* taught that the value of a good depended on its utility – on its ability to satisfy mankind's wants – but the main proponent of the doctrine of utility was Jeremy Bentham (1748–1832), a man idolized by his followers. His utilitarianism arose out of the natural-law tradition, though Bentham rejected the idea of natural law. Moral codes did not reflect natural laws but arose to serve the needs of society. Civil laws, needed to provide rules by which conduct was to be governed, should be based on moral codes, but both might become outdated and need to be changed. The standard by which moral rules and civil laws should be judged was 'the principle of utility' – the maximization of the sum of the happiness of the individuals that make up a society. This was also the standard that should be used to judge government actions.

Bentham's interpretation of utilitarianism rested on some clear-cut value judgements. (1) Society's interest is the sum of the interests of the members of society. (2) Every man is the best judge of his own interests. (3) Every man's capacity for happiness is as great as any other's. These resulted in a philosophy that was both egalitarian and individualist and served as the foundation for Bentham's elaborate schemes for legal and penal reform. For Bentham, however, the principle of utility did not reduce policymaking to a simple rule. Utility had several dimensions (intensity, duration, certainty and nearness), and it was necessary to balance these against each other. The utilitarian principle nonetheless provided a rough guide that policymakers could follow.

Bentham wrote on economic questions, acknowledging his debt to Smith, but his major influence was indirect, through his followers, the Philosophic Radicals. Among these, the most eminent were James Mill (1773–1836), Mill's intellectual protegé, David Ricardo (1772–1823), and John Stuart Mill (1806–73). James Mill studied divinity in Edinburgh and briefly became a Presbyterian preacher before turning to teaching. In 1802 he moved to London to pursue a career as a journalist and writer. His major work was *A History of British India* (1818), after which he obtained a post in the India Office, rising to the position of Chief Examiner, the senior permanent post in the government of India. In London he became a close associate of Bentham. Ricardo, the son of a stockbroker, came from a Jewish family. He married a Quaker and was subsequently disowned by his father. At Mill's instigation, he became a Member of Parliament. John Stuart Mill was the son of James Mill and received a very rigorous education from his father. At three he started to learn Greek, and at eight Latin, algebra, geometry and differential calculus. Political economy and logic came at twelve. He spent many years working at the India Office, rising to the same position as his father, and in 1865 he became a Member of Parliament.

The Philosophic Radicals were actively engaged in politics, using utilitarianism as the basis for criticizing the institutions of society and advocating policies of reform. By the standards of the day, they were genuine radicals, even though their schemes were far removed from the socialism of Godwin and Condorcet or of some of their contemporaries such as Robert Owen (1771–1858), author of the New Lanark socialist experiment. They remained, like Malthus, Whigs. However, though James Mill and Ricardo were close to Malthus on many issues (Ricardo and Malthus were close friends, constantly debating economic issues), they did not share his commitment to economics remaining a moral science. For them economics was *political* economy, but they sought to make it a rigorous discipline offering conclusions as certain as those offered by Euclidean geometry. This resulted in the subject becoming, in Ricardo's hands, more abstract and less inductive than in the hands of either Smith or Malthus. This was at a time when there was widespread scepticism about 'theory', which was associated with 'enthusiasm', conceived as taking ideas to dangerous extremes.

Political economy also reached a wider public though the work of two women, both of whom were prolific writers on other subjects. Jane Marcet's (1769–1858) *Conversations on Political Economy* (1816) was extremely successful in promoting political economy to a wide audience. It is interesting to note that her book begins with a discussion of Fénélon's *Telemachus*, testimony to that book's long life. Because of her gender, the book was published anonymously, advertised as being by the author of the even more successful *Conversations on Chemistry* (1805). She minimized her own originality and presented her ideas as having been obtained from the 'great masters' of the subject, including Smith, Malthus, Say and Ricardo.[4] Harriet Martineau (1802–76) wrote the extremely successful *Illustrations of Political Economy*, a subject about which she had learned through reading books by Marcet and James Mill. This was a series of stories, each of which had a clear economic moral. A supporter of laissez-faire, she argued for married women's property rights and later applied economic analysis to the problem of American slavery, arguing that it was an illegitimate form of property.

RICARDIAN ECONOMICS

Ricardo's economics was a response to the situation in Britain during the Napoleonic Wars (1804–15), when the price of corn (wheat) and agricultural rents rose dramatically. Ricardo sought to demonstrate two propositions: that, contrary to what Smith had argued, the interests of the landlords were opposed to the interests of the rest of society, and that the *only* cause of a declining rate of profit was a shortage of cultivable land. It is easy to see how such a perspective arose from Britain's wartime experience. Influenced by James Mill, with his desire to make political economy as rigorous as Euclidean geometry, in his *Principles of Political Economy and Taxation* (published in three editions, 1817–21) Ricardo constructed a system and a series of arguments that were too abstract for many of his contemporaries to understand.

Ricardo opened his *Principles* by stating that the principal problem in political economy was to determine the laws that governed the distribution of produce between rent, profits and wages, a subject that Turgot, Smith, Say and others had failed to address satisfactorily. The key element was the theory of differential rent, which he attributed to Malthus, although it had been simultaneously developed by Malthus, Ricardo, Edward West (1782–1828) and Robert Torrens (1780–1864) in 1815. To provide an account of how the shares of these three types of income changed, he combined the theory of rent with a Smithian account of capital accumulation and Malthus's theory of population.

Malthus's theory of rent rested on two assumptions: that different plots of land were of different fertility, with the result that applying the same labour and capital to them would yield different quantities of corn, and that agricultural land had no alternative use. Competition would ensure that the least fertile plots of land under cultivation would earn no rent: the corn produced would sell for just enough revenue to cover production costs, with the result that there would be nothing left for the landlord. If there were a surplus, more land would be brought under cultivation; if costs were not covered, the land would not be cultivated. All other plots of land, however, because they must by definition be more fertile, would yield a surplus. Being the owner of the land, the landlord would be able to demand this surplus as rent. The result was that rent emerged as the surplus earned by land that was more fertile than the least fertile land under cultivation.

The theory of differential rent explained the share of national income that was received by landlords. The Malthusian population theory was then used to explain the share of income received by workers. While wages might rise above or fall below this level if the population were growing or declining, they were linked, in the long run, to the subsistence wage rate. The residual after deducting rent and wages was profit, the share of income accruing to capitalists. From there it was a short step to a theory of economic growth. High profits would encourage capitalists to invest, raising the capital stock. This would raise the demand for labour, keeping wages high and causing population growth. However, as the population grew, so too would the price of corn, the result being that the margin of cultivation would be extended: more land would be cultivated, and plots already under cultivation would be cultivated more intensively. As this happened, rents would rise, eating away at profits (wages could not fall, at least for very long, below subsistence, so could not be reduced). This fall in profits would cause the rate of capital accumulation, and hence the rate of growth, to fall.

It was thus apparently a short step to Ricardo's two key propositions. As capital accumulated, rents rose but profits fell. Given that capital created employment, this was bad for the workers too. In addition, Ricardo had shown that falling productivity in agriculture, caused by the need to bring decreasingly fertile land into cultivation, was the cause of a declining profit rate. However, if it were possible to import food cheaply, it would no longer be necessary to extend the margin of cultivation and there would be no need for the price of food to rise. These imports would have to be paid for through exports of manufactured goods. The result would be that continued economic growth would turn Britain into a manufacturing nation – the workshop of the world, a prospect with social implications about which Malthus had great concerns.

The existence of manufactured goods created problems for Ricardo's claim that diminishing agricultural productivity was the *only* cause of a declining profit rate. If workers consumed only corn, this would be true. Agriculture would be self-contained (corn would be the only output and the only input), and the rate of profit would not depend on conditions in manufacturing. Competition would ensure that the rate of profit earned in manufacturing, and hence in the whole economy, would equal that earned in agriculture. On the other hand, if workers' subsistence were to include, say, clothing as well as food, then the subsistence wage would depend on the cost of producing clothing as well as the cost of producing food. Agriculture would not be self-contained. The result would be that the rate of profit would depend on conditions in manufacturing as well as on those in agriculture. Ricardo's theorem that agricultural productivity was the *only* determinant of the profit rate would be undermined.

Ricardo also developed the labour theory of value into something very different from Smith's theory, arguing that the prices of commodities will be proportional to the labour required to produce them. The problem with this theory, cutting through an immensely technical issue, is that, under competition, prices will be proportional to production costs and production costs will depend on the amount of capital used as well as on the quantity of labour. It is not enough to include the labour used in manufacturing capital goods, because there will be an interest charge on top of this. It follows that the ratio of price to labour cost will vary according to the ratio of capital to labour in an industry. The result is that, except under very special circumstances, unlikely to be found in reality, the labour theory of value will not hold. Ricardo struggled to find a way out of this problem, looking for a standard of value that would not itself change when distribution of income between wages and profits changed. In the end he had to resort to an act of faith – he used a numerical example to argue that, in practice, variations in labour time explained virtually all variations in relative prices (93 per cent in his example).

Smith had also been concerned with a standard of value, but Ricardo's purpose was very different. He was concerned with the analytical problem caused by differences in the capital–labour ratio across commodities. This same problem was later to confront Marx.

It is clear, even from this account, that in Ricardo's economics we are dealing with a level of analytical rigour that is to be found in few, if any, of his predecessors. Ricardo simplified the world he was analysing to the point where he was able to show with strict logic that his conclusions followed. When account is taken of the aspects of his system that are not discussed here (notably his theories of international trade and money) these remarks apply a fortiori. This is not to say that his logic was perfect. It was not. His problems with the labour theory of value have already been mentioned. A further problem was that he failed to see that, even if he was correct in arguing that agricultural improvements would not raise rents overall, individual landlords would have an incentive to make improvements to their land, raising agricultural productivity and thereby softening his conclusions about the falling rate of profit.

Ricardo's theory, though rooted in wartime conditions, had clear political implications in the nineteenth-century post-war world. After the war, corn prices remained high because of the Corn Laws, which prevented imports of corn when prices were below 80 shillings a quarter (in the late eighteenth century, the normal price had been considered to be around 60 shillings). His message that the interests of the landlords were opposed to the interests of the rest of society resonated with many political agitators: workers wanted cheaper corn so that their wages would buy more, and manufacturers wanted cheaper corn in the belief that it would reduce wages. Furthermore, Ricardo's theory argued that, unless the Corn Laws were repealed, profits would fall and growth would come to a halt. However, even if the Corn Laws were repealed, there would still be problems: if Ricardo's theory were correct, growth would involve the progressive expansion of manufacturing relative to agriculture. Britain would become the workshop of the world, exporting manufactured goods and importing corn. This was unacceptable to Malthus, who favoured a balance between agriculture and manufacturing.

Ricardo and his contemporaries wrote against the background of what Toynbee (see p. 199) was later to call the 'industrial revolution' – a period of industrial and social change. An important development was the use of steam power and the mechanization of the cotton textile industry, which had expanded rapidly since the 1780s. A symptom of this was the emergence of the Luddites, who saw mechanization as threatening their livelihoods. One of the few ways in which workers could protest was breaking the machines that they believed were making it possible to replace them with cheaper, less highly skilled labour, destroying their jobs. In the first two editions of his *Principles*, Ricardo stuck to the view, common among political economists, that the introduction of machinery could not reduce unemployment, but in the third edition (1821) he changed his mind. He presented a numerical example in which a capitalist decides to employ half his workforce in building a machine instead of producing output. Circulating capital – the capital used to employ labour – is converted into fixed capital, thereby enabling the capitalist to employ fewer workers while earning the same level of profit. The introduction of machinery could, Ricardo argued, harm the working class. This was a controversial conclusion and many economists refused to accept it. Ricardo's numerical example rested on very special and arguably questionable assumptions. Even Ricardo continued to support mechanization, arguing that the alternative was for capital to flow abroad, reducing employment even further. The debate resurfaced periodically over the next two centuries, though economists have generally taken the view that, even though there may be short-run costs – people whose skilled jobs disappear are clearly worse off – in the long run mechanization will not reduce employment because new jobs will be created.

Ricardian economics made a deep impression. In the words of one commentator, it 'burnt deep scars on to the classical-economic consciousness'.[5] It was also the origin of Marx's economic theory and of many concepts that were used in more orthodox economics in the nineteenth and twentieth centuries. The idea that the rate of profit depended on the marginal cost of growing corn (the cost of growing an additional unit of corn, which would typically be higher than the unit cost of the corn that was already being grown) – arguably the defining theme in Ricardian economics – persisted throughout English economics up to the 1880s. In this sense, Ricardo had a lasting influence.

However, Ricardian economics in its purest form (including the labour theory of value, Ricardo's deductive method and the theory of population) were influential for only a brief period in the early 1820s. The labour theory of value was strongly criticized by Samuel Bailey (1791–1870) in 1825. Bailey argued for a subjective theory of value in which value depended, not on costs, but on 'the esteem in which an object is held'.[6] Nassau Senior (1790–1864), appointed to the first chair of political economy at Oxford, moved away from both the Malthusian population doctrine and the labour theory of value. He introduced the idea that profits were not a surplus but a reward to capitalists for abstaining from consuming their wealth. He also formulated the idea that the value of an additional unit of a good (the concept that, in the 1870s, came to be called marginal utility) declined as more of the good was consumed. John Ramsay McCulloch (1789–1864), professor of political economy at University College London from 1828 to 1837 and the most prolific economic writer in the Whig *Edinburgh Review*, was at one time a staunch Ricardian. However, he substantially modified his views, placing a much greater emphasis on history and inductive research than did Ricardo. He rejected Ricardo's view of class conflict. He considered it fallacious on the grounds that individual landlords would always have an incentive to introduce improvements. This would raise the productivity of land and would offset the tendency of the rate of profit to fall.

In short, even English political economy in this period was not purely Ricardian. It reflected the work of a variety of individuals and encompassed a plurality of views on most questions. If one work dominated, it was not Ricardo's *Principles* but Smith's *Wealth of Nations*, with its more catholic blending of theory and history. Even in 1900 there were still textbooks organized on Smithian lines, as mediated by Say's organization of the subject. Outside England, the influence of Ricardo was even less strong. In France, Smith's main interpreter was Say, widely considered the leading French economist of his generation. Though a supporter of Smithian ideas, he advocated a subjective theory of value, consistent with a long-standing French tradition going back at least to Condillac.

GOVERNMENT POLICY AND THE ROLE OF THE STATE

In early nineteenth century Britain, economics (more correctly political economy) was not yet an academic discipline because the universities of Oxford and Cambridge had yet to move away from a classical curriculum. The main writers on political economy were linked by organizations such as the Political Economy Club (a group, founded in 1821, that met each month to discuss economic questions), the Royal Society, the British Association for the Advancement of Science (founded in 1833) and the Royal Statistical Society (founded in 1834). The journals in which their ideas were published did not specialize in economics but addressed the educated classes in general and were frequently identified by their political leanings, not by their disciplinary coverage. The *Edinburgh Review* was Whig, the *Westminster Review* was Benthamite, and the *Quarterly Review* was Tory. Some economists held academic posts (often for short periods, not as a lifelong career), but most did not. For example, Ricardo was a stockbroker; Torrens had served in the army and was a newspaper proprietor; West and Mountifort Longfield (1802–84) were lawyers; and McCulloch (a professor for a brief period) was a civil servant and for a short time editor of the *Scotsman*. Many had a legal training, and many held government appointments at some stage in their careers. However, though abstract issues were discussed, political economy was never far from questions of economic policy. Many economists and many members of the Political Economy Club were Members of Parliament. Even when they were not involved in policymaking, however, almost all the economists formed part of the circles in which policymakers moved, and they played an active role in discussions of economic policy. In the 1830s, after the Reform Act of 1832 (which extended the franchise to most of the propertied classes), the Philosophic Radicals formed an identifiable group in Parliament.

Though there were enormous differences between economists, it is a fairly safe generalization to say that they were, in general, pragmatic reformers. Like Smith, they opposed what he called 'the mercantile system'. In so far as there was an ideological dimension to this, it stemmed from opposition to the corruption associated with regulations on trade as much as to any commitment to non-intervention. It was generally accepted that government had an important but limited role to play in economic life. Even the Philosophic Radicals, who favoured more radical reforms than most economists, were utilitarian – adhering to a philosophy that placed utility above freedom. They were quite willing to see the government regulate, provided that legislation did not undermine the security of private property, an institution they regarded as crucial in stimulating economic growth. Their attitudes and the changes that took place in the political context are best illustrated by considering some of the major questions that arose in the first three quarters of the century: trade policy, poor relief, and labour-market policies.

Most British writers on political economy were basically free-traders and produced a wide range of arguments to support their stance. Not only did they use arguments about how markets worked, they also pointed to the opportunities that protection provided for corruption and the distortion of domestic industry in favour of powerful groups. There were debates over whether free trade should be imposed unilaterally or on the basis of commercial treaties but, on the whole, they supported unilateral free trade. The most contentious issue in trade policy, however, concerned the Corn Laws. Ricardo's theory was aimed at precisely this issue and provided a strong case for repeal, but this was not the ground on which most economists argued. They were influenced more by Smith. Thus, McCulloch and Senior rejected Ricardo's arguments that the interests of the landlords differed from those of other classes in society. Some economists even supported the levying of tariffs to raise revenue, so long as these were not sufficiently high to distort trade flows.

The Poor Law was an issue for which the Malthusian theory had direct implications. Malthus and Ricardo favoured the abolition of the Poor Law, though both wanted this to be done gradually. Others thought this solution impracticable and favoured radical reform. Senior, for example, argued for the policy embodied in the Poor Law Amendment Act (1834), under which relief for the able-bodied poor was confined to those living in workhouses and which tried, in vain, to enforce the principle of less eligibility (that those out of work should be worse off than anyone in work), basing his argument on a highly selective and misleading use of evidence. Most political economists, however, were more relaxed about the provision of poor relief, being sceptical about the Malthusian argument that it would inevitably stimulate growth in the number of paupers. They wanted to continue 'outdoor' relief and were not insistent on enforcing the principle of less eligibility.

Urbanization was changing dramatically the conditions under which an increasing proportion of people worked, and there was pressure for government regulation. In addition, trade unions began to be formed after the repeal of the Combination Laws (under which the formation of unions was illegal) in 1824. On neither issue did the economists adopt a doctrinaire position. The first act regulating factory conditions had been passed in 1802, and during the following decades a series of acts was passed increasing the degree of regulation. In much of this legislation the main target was children's and women's hours and conditions of work, but legislation here inevitably affected men too. There was a tendency to refrain from regulating adult men's hours, on the grounds that this would interfere with the principle of freedom of contract, but in general the economists were pragmatic and responded to events. They kept up with public opinion rather than leading it. On trade unions, the economists' position was generally to favour high wages and to view unions as counterbalancing employers' higher bargaining power.

There was widespread acceptance of the Smithian case for free enterprise, and many writers on political economy viewed the encroachments of the state on individual liberty with great suspicion. On neither, however, were they doctrinaire. They judged particular cases according to the principle of utility. The result was a pragmatic outlook in which the role of laissez-faire was severely circumscribed.

MONEY

Monetary policy was a major concern of British political economists from the 1790s onwards. In 1793 and 1797 serious financial crises took place against the background of a banking system that had changed significantly since Hume's work on the subject. These formed the background to *An Inquiry into the Nature and Effects of the Paper Credit of Great Britain* (1802) by a banker, Henry Thornton (1760–1815). Thornton viewed banknotes and bills of exchange as assets that people hold, with the result that he placed great emphasis on confidence. If people became uncertain about the value of the assets they were holding (whether bills of exchange or notes issued by banks outside London), they would increase their holdings of the more secure asset. In Thornton's day this meant not only gold but also notes issued by the Bank of England. Thornton thus perceived that there was a hierarchy within the banking system. In times of crisis, when they experienced a run on their reserves, the country banks (outside London and generally small) would turn to their correspondents in London for support. These in turn would turn to the Bank of England for liquidity. The Bank of England thus stood at the apex of a pyramid of credit.

This had enormous implications for the policy that the Bank of England should pursue. The normal practice for a bank facing a loss of reserves is to cut back on its lending. However, Thornton argued that this was exactly the wrong policy for the Bank of England, which should increase its lending to the country banks when it experienced a loss of reserves. The reason was that, if there were a crisis of confidence, an increase in the availability of credit from the Bank of England would serve to restore confidence and provide reserves that the rest of the banking system required. This was different from the case of the country banks – an increase in their note issue would reduce confidence in their ability to redeem their notes. In other words, the Bank of England, Thornton argued, should be acting as a central bank, taking responsibility for the financial system as a whole.

After 1804 the price of gold bullion rose significantly above its par value, established by Newton in 1717 (see p. 90). Put differently, the value of the Bank of England's notes had fallen in relation to gold. Ricardo, in 1810, argued that the rise in the price of bullion reflected the overissue of notes by the Bank of England. He argued that the directors of the bank could not be trusted to manage the issue of notes, and that convertibility should be restored – albeit gradually. This was the strict bullionist position – that notes should be convertible into bullion. This was also Thornton's position, though unlike Ricardo he accepted that the link between note issue and the price of bullion might be weak in the short run. In the short run it was possible for factors that affected the balance of payments – such as bad harvests (which caused an increase in imports of corn), subsidies to foreign governments, or overseas military expenditure – to raise the price of bullion independently of the note issue.

The anti-bullionist position can be found in the writings of the directors of the Bank of England. They denied that the quantity of banknotes in circulation bore any relationship to the price of bullion. Their argument was the so-called 'real-bills doctrine'. This was the theory that, provided a bank lent money against 'real bills' (bills issued to finance genuine commercial transactions, not to finance speculation), the bills would automatically be repaid when the transaction was complete. The amount of currency in circulation would therefore exactly equal the demand for it. It was assumed that no one would borrow money and pay interest if they did not need to.

The answer to this was offered in Thornton's *Paper Credit*. Thornton pointed out that the decision on whether to borrow money from a bank would depend on how the interest rate on the loan compared with the rate of profit that could be obtained through investing the money. If the interest rate were below the profit rate, people would have an incentive to increase their borrowing, the circulation of banknotes would increase, and prices would rise. This process would continue for as long as the interest rate was below the profit rate. Conversely, if the interest rate exceeded the profit rate, the quantity of notes issued and the price level would fall. The real-bills doctrine, with its assumption that no one would borrow money unnecessarily if interest had to be paid on it, was thus flawed.

A parliamentary report into the currency in 1810, largely drafted by Thornton, supported the bullionist case, and as a result the government took the decision to return to convertibility, this being achieved in 1819. However, this did not end discussions of monetary policy. The period after 1815 was one of severe deflation – of depression and falling prices. Although the policy of maintaining convertibility of sterling into gold was not questioned, it became clear that this in itself was not enough. The Bank of England's policy had to be organized so as to ensure that its bullion reserves were always sufficient for convertibility to be maintained. This led into a debate over what would nowadays be termed countercyclical policy: economists debated the merits of alternative ways of coping with fluctuations in the demand for credit.

The banking school argued that monetary policy should be conducted according to the needs of the domestic economy. In a depression there was a shortage of credit, and so the note issue should be expanded. If too many notes were issued, they would be returned to the Bank of England – the so-called 'doctrine of reflux'. It stressed that notes were merely one among many forms of credit. One of the main supporters of the banking school, Thomas Tooke (1774–1858), countered Thornton's argument that low interest rates led to inflation with extensive statistical evidence to show that inflation typically occurred when interest rates were high. In opposition to this view, the currency school, of which Lord Overstone (1796–1883) was the leading member, advocated the so-called 'currency principle', or 'principle of metallic fluctuation'. This was the principle that a paper currency should be made to behave in the same way as a metallic currency would behave. This meant that, if the Bank of England lost gold, it should reduce its note issue pound for pound. The money supply would thus be linked to the balance of payments. This was, like the banking school's proposal to meet the needs of trade, a countercyclical policy, for it was designed to ensure that corrective policies would be implemented before an expansion had gone too far. Without the currency principle, the currency school argued, action would be taken too late. Thus, whereas the banking school focused on policy to alleviate depressions, the currency school sought to design a policy that would make them less likely to occur.

CONCLUSIONS

In the first few decades of the nineteenth century the term 'political economy' was widely used as the name for what was seen as a new science. Though this chapter has focused on Britain, its supporters were found in many countries in Europe. It was widely held that the new science originated with Smith's *Wealth of Nations*, but it had become much restricted in scope. Smith's moral philosophy, in which analysis of economic growth was rooted in analyses of commercial society, was, by a narrower set of principles, focused on the determination of value and the distribution of produce between social classes. Although there were counterarguments from socialists such as Owen and from Romantic critics of political economy, there was a widespread commitment to free trade and non-interference, often drawing on broader Smithian arguments as well as Malthusian arguments about population and Benthamite utilitarianism. Political economy became the subject of widespread debate, creating the body of ideas on which the two great synthesizers of the mid-Victorian era – John Stuart Mill and Karl Marx – could build.

8

Mid-Victorian Political Economy

'CLASSICAL' POLITICAL ECONOMY

In the first chapter of the only major work published during his life-time, Karl Marx wrote, 'by classical Political Economy, I understand that economy which, since the time of W. Petty, has investigated the real relations of production in bourgeois society in contradistinction to vulgar economy, which deals with appearances only'.[1] Its most important representatives, he argued, were Smith and Ricardo. The term stuck, and by the early 1890s (shortly after the English translation of Marx's book, though that may be a coincidence) it appears to have become an accepted term to describe English political economy in the first half of the nineteenth century. However, the meaning of the term had changed. Instead of running from Petty to Ricardo, as Marx had argued, classical political economy was generally taken to have begun with Smith, and to have ended not with Ricardo but with the advent of marginal utility theories of value in the 1870s. What remained constant in most of these accounts, however, was the importance attached to Ricardo, whose work was seen as central to the economics of this period. As we saw in Chapter 7, that was not the case. The term 'classical political economy' can be used to denote no more than the work of a particular period or the ideas of a particular community, but it is potentially misleading because it suggests a homogeneity, based on abstract Ricardian theorizing, that did not exist.

The reason such attention came to be paid to Ricardo was the importance attached to his work by two later writers, John Stuart Mill (widely taken to be the culmination of classical political economy) and Karl Marx. For both of them, Ricardo provided an important starting point and, without them, Ricardo's reputation would have been very different from what it is today.

JOHN STUART MILL

That Ricardian economics exerted an influence on English political economy beyond the early 1820s is due primarily to John Stuart Mill. Educated by his father to be a strict disciple of Bentham, and a member of the Philosophic Radicals, around 1830 he wrote a series of essays on economics in which he built upon the Ricardian approach to economics. However, he had problems in finding a publisher and the book was not published till 1844, after the great success of his *System of Logic* (1843). After his father's death in 1836, and probably influenced by Harriet Taylor (1807–58), whom he married in 1851, Mill moved away from a narrow utilitarian position and became much more sympathetic to socialism – albeit a form of socialism very different from what is now meant by the term, in that he did not advocate state ownership of the means of production.

Taylor's precise role in the ideas with which Mill is associated is unknown, for the evidence is contradictory. Mill praised her in the strongest terms, suggesting she might have been effectively a co-author of several of the major works that bear his name alone (they certainly co-authored some minor works). However, other statements, both by Mill and by people who knew them well, suggest that her role was much less, perhaps confined to raising questions to which Mill compiled answers. The consensus among their friends seems to be that he exaggerated her importance, but that leaves a lot of scope for her having played a very significant role.

Mill's main contribution to economics was his *Principles of Political Economy with Some of their Applications to Social Philosophy*, published in several editions between 1848 and 1873. This served as the point of departure for most British and many American economists until the publication of Alfred Marshall's *Principles of Economics* in 1890.

Mill's achievement in the *Principles* was to retain the Ricardian framework but at the same time to take into account the many points made by Ricardo's critics. Given that Mill did not lay claim to originality and that he said he was doing little more than updating Smith's *Wealth of Nations*, the book has been dismissed as eclectic. This, however, is to understate Mill's originality and creativity. The basic theory of value, income distribution and growth was Ricardian, but Mill modified it in important ways. He placed much greater emphasis on demand in explaining value, and the way in which he conceived demand (as a schedule of prices and quantities) marked a significant change from the Smithian and Ricardian concept. When applied to international trade (in his theory of reciprocal demand), the result was a theory that went far beyond Ricardo in two ways. It allowed for the possibility that costs might change with output, and it explained the volume of goods traded. He followed Senior in accepting that profits might be necessary to induce capitalists to save.

Perhaps the main significance of Mill's *Principles*, however, was that, although it contained many ideas taken from Ricardo, it embodied a radically different social philosophy. Mill wrote of seeking to emancipate political economy from the old school, making it less doctrinaire than it had become in many quarters. In this he was strongly influenced by socialist writers, notably a group known as the Saint-Simonians, named after Claude Henri Saint-Simon (1760–1825), who advocated a form of socialism in which the class structure of society was changed but in which production was controlled by industrialists. Mill reconciled his adherence to Ricardian theory with a social outlook that verged on socialism through introducing, at the start of the *Principles*, a distinction between the laws of production and the laws of distribution. After a survey of the evolution of societies, reminiscent of the Scottish Enlightenment, he argued that the production of wealth depended on factors beyond human control:

> The production of wealth ... is evidently not an arbitrary thing. It
> has its necessary conditions. Of these, some are physical, depending
> on the properties of matter, and on the amount of knowledge of those
> properties possessed at the particular place and time ... Combining

these facts of outward nature with truths relating to human nature it [political economy] attempts to trace the secondary or derivative laws, by which the production of wealth is determined.[2]

These laws of production were based on the physical world, knowledge of that world, and human nature. In contrast, the laws governing the distribution of wealth depended on human institutions:

Unlike the laws of production, those of distribution are partly of human institution: since the manner in which wealth is distributed in any given society, depends on the statutes or usages therein obtaining.

He added, however, the qualification that

though governments have the power of deciding what institutions shall exist, they cannot arbitrarily determine how these institutions shall work.[3]

Political economy could discern the laws governing economic behaviour, enabling governments to create appropriate institutions. Social reform therefore involved redesigning the institutions of capitalism.

The institutions through which Mill sought to improve society were ones that gave individuals control over their own lives. He supported peasant proprietorship, giving small farmers the incentive to improve their own land and raise their incomes. He advocated producers' co-operatives and industrial partnerships (involving profit-sharing) as institutions that would enable workers to share responsibility for the successful conduct of business. These schemes all had the characteristic that they maintained incentives. He described such schemes as socialist – the difference between socialism and communism, as he used the terms, being that socialism preserved incentives whereas communism destroyed them. He still accepted the Malthusian theory of population growth, but he believed that education of the working classes (including education about birth control) would lead them to see the advantages of limiting family size and that living standards would then be able to rise. This outlook also affected his view of the stationary state. Growth might slow down, but if workers turned to self-improvement there would be no cause for concern.

As his book *On Liberty* (1859) makes clear, Mill was a liberal in the classical nineteenth-century sense. He believed in individual freedom. His commitment to the emancipation of women, his opposition to slavery in the Confederacy, and to fair treatment of emancipated slaves was consistent with this. He was even prepared to argue that there should be a general presumption in favour of laissez-faire. However, he was far from an unqualified supporter of laissez-faire, going so far as to describe the exceptions as 'large'. He listed five classes of actions that had to be performed by the state, ranging from cases where individuals were not the best judges of their own interests (including education) to those where individuals would have to take action for the benefit of others (including poor relief) if the state were not involved. He argued that anything that had to be done by joint-stock organizations, where delegated management was required, would often be done as well, if not better, by the state. Even more radically, Mill argued that there might be circumstances in which it became desirable for the state to undertake almost any activity: 'In the particular circumstances of a given age or nation, there is scarcely anything, really important to the general interest, which it may not be desirable, or necessary, that the government should take upon itself, not because private individuals cannot effectually perform it, but because they will not.'[4] Having made the case for laissez-faire, Mill thus qualified it so heavily as to leave open the possibility of a level of state activity that many would regard as socialist.

KARL MARX

The other mid-nineteenth-century economist to build on Ricardo's economics was Karl Marx (1818–83). Nowadays, Marx is generally considered a towering figure, and it would seem odd to discuss the nineteenth century without covering his work. Catalogues list many books by Marx, and the literature interpreting Marx is vast. However, to form a correct view of Marx, it is important to remember that, aside from pamphlets and short works, including the *Communist Manifesto*, only one of these books was published in his lifetime; the others were edited and published posthumously. In his own time, he was one of many socialist theorists and agitators, and it was not obvious that his would be the one that would come to be seen as standing far above the others. His work received significant attention in the closing decades of the nineteeenth century, but it was only after the Soviet Revolution of 1917, with its adoption of Marxist-Leninist ideology, that it achieved the place that it held for most of the twentieth century.

Whereas Mill remained within the framework laid down by Smith and Ricardo, Marx, although he drew on the same sources, sought to provide a radical critique of orthodox 'bourgeois' political economy. His starting point was the study of ancient philosophy at the University of Berlin, then dominated by the ideas of Georg Wilhelm Friedrich Hegel (1770–1831). Central to Hegel's work was the idea of dialectics, according to which ideas progressed through the opposition of a thesis and an antithesis, out of which a synthesis emerged. However, whereas Hegelian dialectics applied to the realm of ideas, Marx offered a dialectical analysis of the material world and the evolution of society (historical materialism). Each stage of history produced tensions within itself, the outcome of which was a move to a new, higher, stage of society. Feudalism gave way to capitalism, which in turn would give way to socialism and eventually to communism, the highest stage of society. This dialectical analysis of the material world is Marx's historical dialectics.

Marx's writings fall into several distinct stages. In the early 1840s Marx worked as a journalist in the Rhineland, where he had to tackle economic issues such as free trade and legislation on the theft of wood. The theoretical framework that underlies his later work was completely absent – he considered the notion of surplus value (an idea central to his later work) an 'economic fantasy'. In 1844, however, Friedrich Engels (1820–95), a cotton manufacturer with interests in Britain and Germany who became Marx's lifelong friend, supporter and collaborator, introduced him to English political economy. His distinction between the 'classical', scientific, political economy of Smith and Ricardo and the vulgar apologetics for capitalism of his followers was a convenient way to avoid engaging seriously with his contemporaries. He referred to the 'shallow syncretism' of Mill, claiming that he tried to reconcile ideas that were fundamentally incompatible with each other.[5]

In an article published the previous year, Engels had argued that the intensity of competition among workers impoverished them. Capitalists could combine to protect their own interests and could augment their industrial incomes with rents and interest, whereas workers could do neither. Marx, in 1844, went on to explain low wages in terms taken straight from Smith. If demand for a product falls, at least one component of price (rent, profits or wages) must fall below its natural rate. He argued that, with division of labour, workers became more specialized and therefore found it harder to move from one occupation to another. The result was that when prices fell it was the workers whose incomes were reduced below the natural rate. Capitalists were able to keep the competitive price of their product above the natural price – to charge more than the value of their produce, and hence to extract a surplus.

In the next three years Marx studied Ricardo further and adopted the labour theory of value. However, whereas Ricardo had used the term 'value' to mean the price of a commodity, Marx defined value as something that lay beneath price: the labour time required to produce a commodity. Value and price were distinct. The significance of this was that it provided him with a rigorous explanation of how exploitation could arise, even in equilibrium. Exploitation was inherent in the basic relationships of capitalist production.

The year 1848 saw publication of The Communist Manifesto and Marx's involvement in the revolutions that took place (especially the one in Paris), followed by his exile to Britain. In London he turned again to economics and started work on a more systematic, scientific treatment of the subject. The main manuscript dating from this period, the Grundrisse, was a series of notebooks never finished for publication (though it was published many years later). By the end of the 1850s all he had published was a short introduction to the subject, A Contribution to the Critique of Political Economy (1859), his first significant economic work. In correspondence with Engels, he outlined a project involving six volumes, dealing with capital, landed property, wage labour, the state, international trade and the world market. His major work, *Capital*, was thus conceived as the first volume of a much larger study. *Capital* itself grew to three volumes, only one of which was published in Marx's lifetime, in 1867; the remaining two volumes were published by Engels in 1885 and 1894. (Marx also wrote the material on the history of economic thought in notebooks later published as *Theories of Surplus Value*, which his editors Engels and Kautsky presented as a fourth volume of *Capital*.) In short, although Marx has a reputation as a prolific writer, he developed a habit of making promises on which he later failed to deliver.

Capital is characterized by the method of inquiry that some scholars have termed 'systematic' dialectics. In this method, ideas are criticized from within (as Marx was analysing capitalism from within a capitalist society) in a series of stages that lead from the abstract to the concrete. However, because the analysis starts with very abstract categories, it could explain only very general phenomena in its early stages. At each stage, it failed to explain more complex empirical phenomena but this failure carried the analysis forward to more complex and concrete categories. This movement from the abstract to the concrete is reflected in the organization of the three volumes of *Capital*. Volume 1 starts with the concept of a commodity and the process of capitalist production. It discusses value and the production of surplus value (explained in the next paragraph) and analyses the antagonism between capital and labour. Volume 2 discusses the circulation of capital and the various forms that capital can take. Volume 3 investigates competition and the antagonism between capitalists. Whereas Marx dealt with capital and surplus value as very abstract concepts in Volume 1, by Volume 3 these categories have become much more complex. The result is that he was able to explain many more empirical features of capitalism, such as the division between interest payments and entrepreneurial profits, and the tendency of the rate of profit to fall.

Marx's argument about exploitation rested on the distinction between labour and labour power. The value of an individual's labour power was, like the value of anything else, its cost of production (measured in labour time). If it took, for example, six hours' labour to produce the goods a worker needed in order to subsist and reproduce, the value of his labour power was six hours. However, it might be possible to force the worker to work for ten hours – his labour. If this happened, the worker would produce goods to the value of ten hours' labour, but his wages would be only six hours' labour, for this was the value of his labour power. The result would be the creation of surplus value equal to four hours' labour. This surplus value, Marx contended, was the source of profit. The reason why capitalists could exploit labour in this way was that they owned the means of production. Because capitalists owned the means of production, workers could not undertake production themselves. They were forced to sell their labour power to the capitalists. Exploitation thus lay at the heart of the capitalist system: it was not an accidental feature that could be removed without affecting its entire structure.

The surplus value created by extracting unpaid labour from workers and fixing it in commodities was realized by the capitalist as a sum of money. Capital, however, was not simply money. To function as capital, it had to be transformed first into means of production and labour power, then into capital in the production process, then into stocks of commodities, and finally, once the commodities were sold, into money again. The simplest form of this circuit was summarized by Marx as M–C–M (money–commodities–more money). He analysed this in two stages. The first was 'simple reproduction', in which an economy reproduced itself on an unchanged scale. The second was 'extended reproduction', where capital was increasing. He agreed with Smith that capital accumulated not because capitalists hoarded money but because they used money to employ labour productively.

In Volume 2, after an extensive discussion of the circulation of capital and the different forms that capital took in the process of circulation, Marx illustrated the process with some numerical examples – his reproduction schemes – inspired by Quesnay's *Tableau*. These were based on a division of the economy into two 'departments' or sectors. Department 1 produced capital goods, and Department 2 produced consumption goods that might be consumed by either capitalists or workers. He also distinguished two of the forms that capital could take: constant capital (machinery, etc.) and variable capital (used to employ labour). The economy started with given stocks of constant and variable capital. Simple reproduction occurred when, after capitalists had used their surplus value to purchase consumption goods, the produce of the two departments was exactly sufficient to reproduce the capital used up in production. Extended reproduction occurred when stocks of capital at the end of the process were larger than at the beginning, with capitalists turning part of their surplus into constant and variable capital. Marx was using what would nowadays be called a 'two-sector' model to analyse the process of capital accumulation.

Volumes 1 and 2 remained at a very abstract level, analysing the movement of capital as a whole. In Volume 3 Marx considered the concrete forms taken by capital – notably costs of production, prices and profits. He analysed the way in which surplus value was converted into various forms of profit and rent. Here he addressed the problems that Ricardo had encountered when working out his labour theory of value. Prices would be higher than values in industries that employed a high proportion of fixed capital, and lower in industries where little fixed capital was used. Prices, therefore, would not be proportional to labour values. For Marx, this arose as the transformation problem – the problem of how values were transformed into prices. As he defined values in terms of labour time, this problem did not undermine his labour theory of value as it did Ricardo's.

Marx's analysis of the dynamics of capitalism went far beyond his reproduction schemes. It is not possible to cover all the details, but several points need to be made. The first is that Marx predicted that capitalist production would become more mechanized and more centralized. Increased mechanization led to what Marx called a rising 'organic composition of capital' – a rising proportion of capital would take the form of constant (fixed) capital, and a lower proportion would take the form of variable capital. Because surplus value was produced by variable capital (by exploiting living labour), this meant that surplus value per unit of capital would fall and with it the rate of profit. Capitalists would attempt to offset this by increasing the exploitation of workers by means such as increasing the length of the working day and forcing workers to work more intensively.

Marx was also led into analysing economic crises and the business cycle. Capitalists, he argued, were forever striving to accumulate capital. From time to time capital would accumulate so rapidly that they would be unable to sell all the output that they were producing. The result would be a crisis in which they failed to realize their profits. Capital would be liquidated as some businesses failed and others simply failed to replace the capital that was wearing out. Eventually the rate of profit would rise to the point where new investments were started and the system would move from depression into a new period of expansion. Marx therefore saw capitalism as undergoing successive periods of depression, medium activity, rapid expansion, and crisis. There would be a cycle, the period of which depended on the turnover rate or life cycle of capital goods. He assumed that this had increased, and that by the time he was writing it was around ten years in the 'essential branches of modern industry'.[6]

It is also important to note that Marx saw capitalism as containing the forces that would lead to its downfall. The main force was the concentration of capitalistic production:

This expropriation is accomplished by the action of the immanent laws of capitalistic production itself, by the centralization of capital. One capitalist always kills many. Hand in hand with this centralization, or this expropriation of many capitalists by few, develop, on an ever-extending scale, the cooperative form of the labour process, the conscious technical application of science, the methodical cultivation of the soil, the transformation of the instruments of labour into instruments of labour only usable in common, the economizing of all means of production by their use as the means of production of combined, socialized labour, the entanglement of all peoples in the net of the world-market, and with this the international character of the capitalistic regime.[7]

This centralization would at the same time increase the misery of the working class and cause it to become more organized:

Along with the constantly diminishing number of the magnates of capital, who usurp and monopolize all advantages of this process of transformation, grows the mass of misery, oppression, slavery, degradation, exploitation; but with this too grows the revolt of the working class, a class always increasing in numbers, and disciplined, united, organized by the very mechanism of capitalist production itself.[8]

Eventually capitalism, which up to that point had been a progressive force, would become an impediment to further development and would be overthrown:

The monopoly of capital becomes a fetter upon the mode of production, which has sprung up and flourished along with, and under it. Centralization of the means of production and socialization of labour at last reach a point where they become incompatible with their capitalist integument. This integument is burst asunder. The knell of capitalist private property sounds. The expropriators are expropriated.[9]

Marx never finished *Capital*, let alone the other books that would have filled out his analysis of the capitalist system. After his death, Volumes 2 and 3 of *Capital* were edited by Engels from his unfinished manuscripts. There were further delays of around twenty years before these volumes were translated into English. His early writings were not published in German until 1932, and the *Grundrisse* not until 1953, with English translations of these appearing only during the 1970s. The result of the delay in publication was that for many years much of his work was virtually unknown. Though written much earlier, and reflecting the situation of the 1860s and 1870s, Marx's economics became widely known only in the 1880s and 1890s. During the twentieth century, interpretations of his work changed as new evidence became available. Given that Marx's writings extended far beyond economics, into philosophy and social science, any interpretation of Marx offered here is inevitably very limited: it is one among many different possibilities.

The first point to make about Marx is that his economics is built upon the economics of Smith and Ricardo. Marx's labour theory of value clearly owes much to his reading of Ricardo. It is therefore possible to view Marx as a Ricardian. To do this, however, is to miss the point that, though he started with Ricardo's analysis, he transformed it and produced a radically different type of economics. For Ricardo and many of his followers, the laws of production were laws of nature. For Marx, on the other hand, the laws of production were based on the laws and institutions of capitalism, a specific historical stage in history. Capital could exist only because people had the right to own the produce of other people's labour. Wage labour – common in British industry, but in Marx's time less widespread than it is today – was another institution central to the process of exploitation. Exploitation, the circulation of money and goods, capital, and the institutions of capitalism were therefore intertwined.

Despite its roots in English political economy, Marxist economics developed largely independently of the mainstream in economic thought. Its other roots in Hegelian philosophy were foreign to the Anglo-Saxon traditions that increasingly dominated the economics profession. The association of Marxian economics with socialist political movements and, after 1917, with Russia and the Soviet Union provided a further barrier. As economics distanced itself from other branches of social thought, the Marxian amalgam of economic and sociological analysis became remote from the concerns of most economists.

Marx's economics was, however, important even for non-Marxian economists. The obvious reason is that attempts were made by non-Marxian economists to rebut Marx, and Marxists responded. The most notable example was perhaps the debate between the Austrian economist Eugen von Böhm-Bawerk (pp. 204, 235) and the Marxist Rudolf Hilferding (1877–1941) following the publication of Volume 3 of *Capital*. Much more importantly, however, Marxian ideas fed into non-Marxian thinking – sometimes directly, sometimes indirectly. Marx's analysis of the business cycle in terms of fixed-capital accumulation fed, via the work of the Russian economist Mikhail Ivanovich Tugan-Baranovsky (1865–1910), into twentieth-century business-cycle theory, which came to focus on relations between saving and investment (see p. 235ff.). His analysis of the waste caused by competition between capitalist producers was a crucial input into the debates over the possibility of rational socialist calculation in the interwar period (pp. 308–12). Marx's vision of the future of capitalism stimulated economists to offer their own alternatives, as in Joseph Alois Schumpeter's *Capitalism, Socialism and Democracy* (1942) (pp. 231–2).

FRANCE AND GERMANY

In France there was a long tradition of applying mathematical analysis to economic problems. Condorcet had paved the way with his analysis of voting theory. He had shown, for example, that if there were three or more candidates in an election, majority voting might result in the election of a candidate who would lose in all two-candidate contests. However, the person who made what to modern economists is the most remarkable contribution was Antoine Augustin Cournot (1801–77). Cournot was briefly professor of mathematics at Lyon but spent most of his career as a university administrator. Assuming that each producer maximized profit, and that sales in the market were constrained by demand, he derived equations to describe the output that would result if there were different numbers of firms in an industry. Starting with a single producer (a monopolist) he showed how output would change as the number of firms rose, first to two, and then towards infinity. For Cournot, competition was the limiting situation as the number of firms approached infinity. In a competitive market, no firm could affect the price it received for its product.

Cournot is also considered to have been the first economist to use a diagram to explain how supply and demand determine price in a competitive market. The demand curve (MN in Cournot's diagram, shown in Fig. 2) shows that the amount that people wish to buy falls as price rises.[10] The supply curve (PQ) shows that the amount that producers wish to sell increases as price rises. The market price (ST) is the price at which supply and demand are equal. Cournot went on to show how the diagram could be used to show how market price would change in response to events such as the imposition of a tax on the commodity.

An emphasis on demand for goods was also characteristic of the work undertaken by engineers at the École des Ponts et Chaussées (School of Bridges and Highways). Their work was prompted by the need to find a basis for deciding the merits of civil-engineering projects. In the 1820s, the conventional view was that such projects

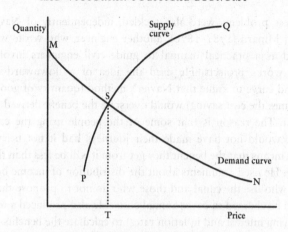

Fig. 2 Supply and demand curves

should be self-liquidating – that they should completely cover their costs. Claude-Louis Marie Henri Navier (1785–1836), well known to engineers for his work on mechanics, challenged this in an article, published in 1830 in *Le Génie civil* (a civil-engineering journal) and in 1832 in the *Annales des ponts et chaussées*. His argument was that a public work, such as a canal or a bridge, could raise public welfare. Taxpayers would get goods more cheaply, and the expansion in trade caused by the project would increase tax revenues in general. He estimated benefits derived from a project by multiplying the quantity of goods carried using the canal or bridge by the reduction in transport cost produced. If these benefits were greater than the ongoing annual cost of the project, the construction cost should be financed out of taxation. Navier thought that tolls should be zero but, if they had to be levied, they should cover only interest payments and regular maintenance. He extended these ideas in later articles and in his lectures at the École des Ponts et Chaussées, taking account of such things as the relation between costs and the length of a railway line. He also considered whether public works should be provided by the state or franchised to private firms, and the type of regulation that should be imposed.

These problems were also tackled, independently of Navier, by Joseph Minard (1781–1870), another engineer, who wrote what he viewed as a practical manual to guide civil engineers involved in public-works projects. He used the idea of a downward-sloping demand curve to argue that Navier's method (quantity of goods carried times the cost saving) would overstate the benefit derived from a project. The reason is that some of the people using the canal or bridge would not have made their journeys had it not been built, which means that the benefit they get from it will be less than the cost saving. He used arguments about the distribution of income between those who use the canal and those who do not to propose that tolls should be charged to cover annual costs. He also produced a formula (involving interest and inflation rates) to calculate the benefits from a project that took time to build, would not last for ever, and had an annual maintenance cost. However, though Minard wrote his manuscript in 1831, the course for which he planned to use it was not approved for many years, with the result that he did not publish his work until 1850. By that time, other articles on the subject had appeared.

Jules Dupuit (1804–66), another engineer concerned with methods by which the benefits of public-works projects could be estimated, also argued, in a series of articles in the 1840s and 1850s, that Navier's method overestimated the benefits. First, what mattered was not the reduction in transport costs but the reduction in the price of products. When production rose following the construction of a new bridge or canal, goods would be transported over longer distances. The result was that production costs would not fall as much as the cost of transport over a given distance. Second, and here he was making a point similar to Minard's, Dupuit argued that the utility of an additional unit of a good could be measured by the price the consumer was willing to pay for it. This price would fall as consumption rose. Dupuit went on to argue that the benefit obtained from building a canal or bridge could be measured by subtracting the cost of the project from the area under the demand curve. The demand curve, used by Cournot simply to analyse behaviour, could be used as a measure of welfare.

The three engineers discussed here form part of a long, well-established tradition at the École des Ponts et Chaussées in the middle decades of the nineteenth century. Starting with the practical problem of evaluating civil-engineering projects, they developed an alternative to the orthodox theory of value associated with Smith and Say. Some of Dupuit's later articles were published in the *Journal des économistes*, but much of the engineers' work was published in journals where economists would not see it. Say did express an interest in Minard's work in 1831, but he died a year later.

Another tradition, owing little to Ricardo, is found in the writers of economics textbooks in Germany, notably Karl Heinrich Rau (1792–1870), Friedrich Hermann (1795–1868), Hans von Mangoldt (1824–68) and Wilhelm Roscher (1817–94). These were Smithian in that they accepted Smith's ideas about the importance of saving and division of labour for economic growth. However, they rejected the labour theory of value. Instead, they took from Steuart the idea that prices are determined by supply and demand. Unlike most British writers on political economy, they attached great importance to demand. Hermann, for example, wrote explicitly about how changes in demand can cause changes in costs. Their textbooks discussed demand before supply and explored the connections between demand and human needs. The result was a subjective theory of value in which the value of a good depended on what other goods people were prepared to forgo in order to obtain it – subsequently known as an opportunity-cost theory.

As in the French engineering tradition, supply and demand were represented graphically. Independently of Cournot, Rau used a supply-and-demand diagram in the fourth edition (1841) of his textbook. (He began the convention, followed in most of the modern literature, of putting quantity on the horizontal axis and price on the vertical axis.) Unlike Cournot, he analysed not only the equilibrium (where demand and supply are equal) but also the stability of this equilibrium. If price were too high, supply would exceed demand, pushing price down; if price were too low, demand would exceed supply, pushing price up. These ideas were taken further by Mangoldt in his textbook (1863). He argued that the shape of the supply curve would depend on the behaviour of costs as output increased and he used his curves to see how prices would change in response to changes in supply or demand.

For most of the nineteenth century, Germany was not a single country but a mosaic of small states. It is thus not surprising that different approaches to economics could coexist alongside each other. One such tradition is represented by Johann Heinrich von Thünen (1783–1850). Thünen was a farmer who became, by 1827, an internationally known authority on agriculture. His main work, *Der isolierte Staat* (*The Isolated State*), was published in three instalments between 1826 and 1863. It is best known for its analysis of location, in which the profitability of agriculture (and hence the level of rent and the type of agriculture that will be undertaken) depends on how far farms are from the city. He took as his starting point a city located in the centre of a large, fertile plain in which there were no rivers or other natural factors affecting transport costs. On such a plain, farming would be organized in a series of concentric circles. Closest to the city would be horticulture and market gardening, the produce of which cannot be transported far. Furthest away would be hunting, for which large tracts of land were needed and where transport costs were not a problem. In between would be various types of forestry, arable farming and pasture.

Perhaps as significant as Thünen's theory of location was his method. He tackled the question of how much capital and labour to use by regarding it as a maximization problem. Farmers use the quantities of capital and labour that will maximize their profits. Thünen formulated this problem using algebra and solved it using differential calculus. By these methods he obtained the result that the wage paid will equal the contribution to output made by the last worker to be employed – the marginal-productivity theory of distribution. These methods also led him to see the problem of forest management as one involving time and the rate of interest. If the essence of capital is seen as being that it allows production to take place over time (a view later developed by Austrian economists), this can be seen as a marginal-productivity theory of the rate of interest.

CONCLUSIONS

Early-nineteenth-century political economy comprised a great variety of theories and ideas. Many of these ideas were held together by their roots in Smith's *Wealth of Nations*. Ricardo had created a far more rigorous system based on much more abstract reasoning, but neither his deductive style of argumentation nor the assumptions on which this reasoning was based won widespread support. Even Mill – responsible for sustaining the Ricardian tradition after interest in it waned in the 1820s – reverted in his *Principles* to the combination of inductive, historical analysis and deductive reasoning that characterized *The Wealth of Nations*.

Political economy was never far from issues of economic policy: academics formed part of the same intellectual community as politicians, journalists and men and women of letters. At one end of the political spectrum were supporters of doctrinaire laissez-faire, and at the other were the Ricardian socialists. Most economists, however, fell between these two extremes. They succeeded in using the framework laid down by Smith to address first the policy problems arising during the revolutionary and Napoleonic wars, and later those arising from industrialization and the immense social changes that accompanied this. In Smith's day, Britain was ruled by a narrow oligarchy, whereas by the 1870s, although corruption had not been eliminated, its scope had been very much reduced by reforms such as the extension of the franchise, secret voting and competitive examinations for the civil service. The extension of the franchise to include the working classes – a process started in the 1867 Reform Act and extended in 1884 – placed socialism much higher on the political agenda than it could ever have been in the days of Smith and Bentham. Mill and Marx, in radically different ways, showed that the Smithian structure, modified by Ricardo, could still be used in this changed environment.

However, although political economy proved adaptable, it was becoming outdated. Even Mill had no analytical tools suitable for tackling problems of monopoly. Towards the end of the nineteenth century, problems of big business became more and more prominent, especially in Germany and the United States. Competition between industrial nations meant that free trade could not be taken for granted in the way that it had been as late as the middle of the century. Above all, real wages had, at least since the 1850s, risen substantially, with the result that the Malthusian population theory, which up to that point had been the basis for much economic argument, was becoming hard to defend. On top of this, Romantic critics of economics, such as John Ruskin, were questioning the value judgements on which the subject was based. Thus, by the 1860s, the confidence in the subject that had enabled Senior to describe the Great Exhibition of 1851 as a triumph of political economy had dissipated, setting the scene for developments in the 1870s.

9

The Split between History and
Theory in Europe, 1870–1914

THE PROFESSIONALIZATION OF
ECONOMICS

In the closing decades of the nineteenth century, economics in both Britain and the United States, like many other disciplines, became professionalized. It came to be dominated by men (there were few women) who specialized in the subject. Most of them were full-time academics. This marked a dramatic contrast with the world of Smith, Malthus, Ricardo and their contemporaries. In addition, research began to be published in specialist journals, such as the *Quarterly Journal of Economics*, established in 1886, the *Economic Journal* (1890) and the *Journal of Political Economy* (1892).

In continental Europe these changes had taken place earlier. In Germany, with a long tradition of *Cameralwissenschaft* (the science of economic administration) centred on the training of public servants, academics had dominated economics for much of the century. The Humboldt University of Berlin, as it later came to be known, founded in 1810, had established a strong research tradition on the basis of providing professors with security and freedom from pressure to teach particular doctrines. This freedom was later extended to other German universities by Bismarck. Specialist academic journals had been established much earlier than in the English-speaking world – the *Zeitschrift für die gesamte Staatswissenschaft* (which has since become the *Journal of Institutional and Theoretical Economics*) in 1844 and the *Jahrbücher für Nationalökonomie und Statistik* (*Yearbook of Economics and Statistics*) in 1863. In France, economic ideas had been developed by university professors such as Say and Cournot, and by engineers in elite colleges such as the École des Ponts et Chaussées.

There were also important changes in the intellectual environment in which economic ideas were developed. Newtonian ideas inspired economists for much of the eighteenth and nineteenth centuries. Smith and Malthus both saw their work as deriving laws applicable to the social realm that were analogous to Newton's laws about the physical realm. Even in the seventeenth century, science had influenced the way in which economic questions were tackled. In the nineteenth century, however, the idea of the 'scientist' became established, the term being coined by William Whewell (1794–1866) in 1833. People stopped referring to science as 'natural philosophy', and the gap between science and philosophy widened. This affected economics in several ways. People with backgrounds in natural science turned to economics. They sought to emulate the achievements of natural science, notably physics, widely regarded as the most successful science. Some sought to strengthen the foundations of economics through basing it on experimental psychology (very different from Bentham's psychology). Others were inspired by biology – by ideas about evolution.

The publication of Charles Darwin's *Origin of Species* in 1859 had a profound effect on the environment in which economic discussions took place. By making possible a purely secular account of human origins, the theory of evolution by natural selection had potentially dramatic implications for religion, which in turn raised questions about the basis for ethics and morality. Just as influential were the evolutionary arguments of a contemporary, Herbert Spencer (1820–1903), a philosopher who knew Mill and Martineau and who developed the idea of social Darwinism and invented the phrase 'survival of the fittest'. His evolutionary theory differed from Darwin's in that it was teleological, leading from lower to higher forms. Inspired by Darwin, Francis Galton (1822–1911) developed the theory of eugenics. Starting from the proposition that mental as well as physical traits could be inherited, advocates of eugenics argued that selective breeding could improve the population. These ideas were widely entertained in both Britain and the United States. Interest in eugenics spanned the political spectrum, its social Darwinist underpinning appealing to conservatives and liberals alike. The term abruptly went out of fashion after the Second World War and the use of eugenic arguments to justify genocide.

Ideas from the new biology were taken up by economists as varied as Marshall in Britain and Veblen in the United States, for whom evolutionary ideas were central to their thinking about how economic activity developed. Many economists also followed the wider fashion for eugenics, a development that is not surprising, given that they can be seen as a development from the Malthusian ideas that had been influential in the early nineteenth century. (Darwin had been influenced by reading Malthus.) For example, the later counterpart of the Malthusian idea that population would grow until wages were pushed down to the subsistence level was that if birth rates among the poor were higher than birth rates among the elite (especially artists, musicians and scientists), the average quality of the population would decline. Such arguments were extended from class to race. For some economists this did little more than add to their doubts about the wisdom of redistributing income to the poor. Others, such as Irving Fisher (pp. 223–7), were more committed to advocacy of eugenic policies.

These developments were associated with changes in the way in which economics was conceived. Though many of the questions tackled by the subject remained the same, economics moved, or at least appeared to move, away from its origins in political philosophy. By 1900 the term 'economics' was beginning to displace 'political economy' as the generally preferred label for the discipline. The use of mathematics was becoming more common (although it remained a minority activity), and the idea that students should be able to specialize in economics, rather than coming to it through mathematics or philosophy, was gaining ground.

JEVONS, WALRAS AND MATHEMATICAL ECONOMICS

Throughout the nineteenth century there had been French and German economists who had used mathematics. In France this tradition went back to Condorcet's social mathematics and included Cournot and the engineers at the École des Ponts et Chaussées (pp. 178–80). In Germany there were the examples of Thünen and Hermann Heinrich Gossen (1810–59). The bulk of the subject, however, remained non-mathematical. In Britain, if we leave aside Ricardo's use of numerical examples, few if any economists in the first half of the century used mathematics. From the 1870s, however, mathematical analysis began to be used much more widely, as economists sought to follow the example set by physics. Along with this came several other changes: there was a greater focus on individual behaviour, and the subject moved away from the Smithian theme of long-term development to focus on narrower problems. Two people were at the forefront of this process: in Britain, William Stanley Jevons (1835–82) and, at Lausanne, the French economist Léon Walras (1834–1910).

Jevons was a meteorologist, a chemist and the author of *The Principles of Science* (1874), a widely read textbook on scientific method. He was also a utilitarian. These elements in his background had a major influence on his approach to economics. Although his training in economics was (typically for the time) based on Mill's *Principles*, he reacted strongly against Mill and the Ricardian tradition in economics in *The Theory of Political Economy* (1871). He disagreed with Ricardo over the theory of value. Ricardo had argued that, although a good must have utility if it is to have value, its value is determined by its production cost, not by its utility. Jevons argued that this was wrong, and that value depended entirely on utility. In particular, value depended on the benefit a consumer received from the last unit consumed (the marginal utility or, as Jevons put it, the 'final degree of utility'). There was a link between value and cost of production, but it was indirect. He summarized it as follows:

> Cost of production determines supply; Supply determines final degree of utility; Final degree of utility determines value.[1]

Jevons started *The Theory of Political Economy* by arguing that economics was inherently mathematical because it dealt with quantities. He was optimistic about the possibilities of measuring economic quantities, pointing out that numerical data abounded – in account books, price lists, bank returns, government data and so on. The problem was not the absence of data but that economists did not know how to use them, and that the data were incomplete. Establishing economics as a science was, for Jevons, closely linked to the exact measurement of economic quantities.

Jevons's starting point was Bentham's theory of utility, in which utility was defined as the ability to increase pleasure or to reduce pain. Though feelings and motives could not be measured directly, Jevons argued that it was possible to measure them indirectly. The goods someone buys or sells will depend on comparisons of the pleasure to be obtained from various goods, which means that comparative pleasures can be measured by observing behaviour in the marketplace. He used an analogy with the measurement of gravity through measuring the movements of a pendulum. Jevons thus devoted much attention to the problem of defining utility and working out how it might be measured, drawing extensively on contemporary psychology. Only then could he use the theory to analyse economic phenomena.

In *The Theory of Political Economy* Jevons used utilitarianism to explain behaviour. This involved assuming that individuals sought to maximize their utility – to increase pleasure and reduce pain as much as possible. He suggested four ways in which this might be accomplished and analysed each in turn: (1) allocating stocks of a good between different uses in the best possible way; (2) exchanging goods with other people; (3) working to produce goods; and (4) through employing capital. He used differential calculus to express the conditions for utility maximization in each of these four settings. In the context of exchange, for example, he derived the condition that utility would be maximized when the ratio of the marginal utility of two goods was equal to the relative price of the two goods. For example, if an apple costs twice as much as a banana, the pleasure obtained from the last apple purchased must be twice as large as the pleasure of an additional banana. If it were less, the individual would give up an apple to get two extra bananas. With labour, the equivalent result is that a worker works the number of hours such that the pain of an additional hour's work is exactly equal to the pleasure obtained from the additional commodities that that hour's labour enables them to purchase.

Walras, too, was concerned to make economics scientific through making it mathematical, and he developed many of the same results as Jevons concerning consumer behaviour and the determination of prices in competitive markets. However, he reached these conclusions by a very different route, and his focus was also very different. Walras was not a utilitarian but instead started from the notion – well established in the French tradition going back through Say to Condillac – that value depended on scarcity. The dominant influence on his work, however, was neither of these authors, but his father, Auguste Walras (1801–66). Responding to Say, he argued that scarcity, not utility, was the source of value. People were entitled to the wealth that derived from their own labour, but land was also a source of wealth; this meant that rents on land would always exist, but he argued that land could not belong to an individual, because it existed before the individual was born and continued after their death. Rents on land, therefore, belonged to the community as a whole – to the state. Thus where the Saint-Simonians sought to prohibit all inheritance, Auguste Walras focused on land rents, arguing that, because land was the property of the community, they should be the source of government revenues.

On the death of his younger brother in 1958, Léon Walras inherited the task of completing his father's work. His first book, *L'Économie politique et la justice* (1860), was a criticism of the doctrines of the socialist-anarchist writer Pierre-Joseph Proudhon (1809–1865) famous for the remark 'Property is theft.' Walras's dependence on his father is illustrated by the fact that he did not read Proudhon's work himself, but relied on his father's notes. Ironically, given their subsequent reputations, the young Marx had also engaged with Proudhon, in *The Poverty of Philosophy* (1847).

Walras wrote of scarcity as *rareté* – the intensity of the last want satisfied. Using this, he derived conclusions similar to those worked out by Jevons. However, whereas Jevons analysed markets in terms of exchange between two individuals (allowing for competition with other potential traders), Walras focused on an organized market in which everyone faced a market price. In this situation, an individual would decide how much of each commodity they wished to buy or sell. This led Walras to construct demand-and-supply curves relating desired purchases or sales to price: as price rose, demand would typically fall and supply would typically rise. The market would be in equilibrium where the two were equal.

Up to this point there were only minor differences in the conclusions reached by Jevons and Walras. The main difference between them was that Walras went on to discuss the problem of multimarket equilibrium – the problem of how prices are established in a large number of markets at the same time. He started by deriving demand-and-supply curves for the case of two-commodity exchange. People have stocks of two commodities and exchange them with each other so that they end up with the combination of the two commodities that they prefer, given the relative price of the two commodities. Walras then extended his analysis to the exchange of many commodities. After that he introduced production, assuming that entrepreneurs moved resources from one activity to another until all opportunities for profits were eliminated. Introducing production meant bringing in markets for factor services (markets for renting the labour and machinery used to produce goods). Finally, he added a market for credit, in order to explain the rate of interest. This was then used to link the rental rates on capital goods to their purchase price.

The end result was a set of simultaneous equations describing an entire economy in which everything, in principle, depended on everything else. For example, a change in fashion might reduce demand for beer and increase demand for tea. This could affect not just the prices of beer and tea but the prices of all other goods, wages, and even the rate of interest. Given the complexity of the set of equations and the very abstract level of his analysis, Walras confined his attention to doing two things. First, he sought to show that his set of equations had a solution: that there was a set of prices and quantities that satisfied all his equations. This is the problem of *existence* of equilibrium. He achieved this by counting the number of equations and showing that it was equal to the number of unknowns (the prices and quantities). Second, he sought to show that the solution to his set of equations was stable in the sense that, if the economy started with any arbitrary set of prices, it would end up with the set of prices that satisfied his equations. This is the problem of *stability* of equilibrium. Walras's method was to postulate that if supply of a commodity exceeded the demand the price of the commodity would fall, and vice versa. This was the *tâtonnement* process, through which an economy 'groped' its way towards the equilibrium.

Walras knew that real economies did not solve sets of simultaneous equations. He claimed that the *tâtonnement* described the trial-and-error process through which real-world economies determined prices but argued that the economist could reach the same solution by solving the simultaneous equations. Both methods gave the same answer. The theory he had derived was 'pure' economics, and it needed to be applied. However, despite this, the foundations of Walras's system were normative. In theorizing about a competitive system, he was not claiming to describe the world, but was constructing a system that conformed with principles of commutative justice, or justice in exchange, which required that the same good must always sell for the same price. And he used his system to derive conclusions about a just system of taxation. His father had made the moral case for taxation of rents on land, and Walras developed this by deriving the Ricardo-like conclusion that, over time, the share of rents in national income would rise. This meant that it would be enough to tax the increase in rents, because the rising share of rents in income meant that such a tax would yield progressively more revenue. This proposal for what was effectively gradual land nationalization would, he contended, provide a way to reconcile individualism and socialism.

Jevons also saw his abstract mathematical theory as comprising only part of economics. His applied economics was statistical and inductive. This was consistent with his view about science being to do with measurement. He became famous for *The Coal Question* (1865), in which he examined the effects of Britain's coal reserves becoming exhausted. When Britain ran out of coal, he concluded, growth would cease. He made this case with detailed statistics, not only on stocks of coal but also on the expansion of British industry. He was, however, wrong, for he failed to appreciate how technological change would transform the situation. In the 1860s he also tackled the question of the effect of the discovery of gold in California on its price. The main characteristic of this work was his novel use of index numbers to quantify the rise in prices that had taken place during the 1850s. However, perhaps Jevons's most innovative work was on the trade cycle. He used statistical series to establish the existence of fluctuations in economic activity every ten years. At the time, sunspots were believed to affect the weather, and so he sought to establish a correlation between sunspot activity and the business cycle on the assumption that there were strong links between the weather and the harvest. To test this idea he collected and analysed large quantities of data on prices.

Walras and Jevons came to their ideas about marginal utility and prices independently (Jevons had presented his ideas almost a decade earlier, but no one had taken any notice of them). They discovered each other's work in the mid-1870s and agreed to cooperate in furthering mathematical economics and opposing Ricardian doctrines. During the following decade, however, the spread of mathematical economics was slow. They were both social reformers, Walras considering himself a socialist, Jevons using his utilitarianism as the basis for a series of piecemeal, pragmatic suggestions for reform, much in the manner of J. S. Mill.

ECONOMICS IN GERMANY
AND AUSTRIA

In the second half of the nineteenth century, German economists attached greater importance to history than did most of their British counterparts. A distinction is often drawn between an 'older' historical school headed by Wilhelm Roscher and a 'younger' historical school headed by Gustav Schmoller (1838–1917), though the notion of a 'historical school' is problematic. What gives the impression of a historical school is their emphasis on detailed empirical studies and their scepticism about abstract theorizing. Other approaches to economics were found in their work, but they drew on Smith and French theorists such as Condillac rather than on Ricardo. The term 'Smithianismus' or 'Smithianism' was, like 'Manchesterism', associated with an extreme variety of liberalism and support for free trade. As in Britain, there were also 'Romantics' (given the hostility of some writers to economics, it is not clear whether they should be classified as economists or not).

The historical movement in German economics was established by Roscher with his *Grundriss zu Vorlesungen über die Staatswissenschaft nach geschichtlicher Methode* (*Outline of Lectures on Political Economy According to the Historical Method*) of 1843. In this book, Roscher argued not that English political economy was wrong, but that it was inappropriate given the political and industrial conditions in the Germany of his day. Economic theories needed to take account of the circumstances in which different countries found themselves. It was, furthermore, important to work out laws and stages of historical development. However, despite such views, the works of the older historical school did not differ markedly from those of Smith or Mill, both of whom mixed extensive empirical and historical material with their theoretical arguments.

Schmoller was more radical in that he sought to broaden the subject to include what would now be termed economic sociology. He was sceptical about the idea of laws of history, arguing that they were frequently no more than dubious generalizations or psychological truths – they bore no relationship to the laws of the natural sciences. It was, he argued, important for economic propositions to be based on detailed empirical observation, for only then could proper account be taken of the circumstances of particular times and places. He was not opposed to theory, but he argued for extreme caution in ascertaining the facts of the case before making any generalizations. The method by which the necessary empirical basis would be established consisted of detailed historical studies.

Politically, Schmoller was conservative, a supporter of the Hohenzollern monarchy. However, he was a social reformer committed to the view that economists should be involved in the process of economic and social change. To this end, he organized committees that would work out desirable social policies within the Verein für Sozialpolitik (Union for Social Policy), founded in 1872. The members of this organization became known as academic socialists. They were liberal but were supporters of the existing regime and equally opposed both to communists and to ultra-liberals. They were committed to piecemeal studies that could result in social reform on topics such as working hours, social insurance and factory legislation.

In Austria, a different type of theoretical economics was offered by Carl Menger (1840–1921), in his *Grundsätze der Volkswirtschaftslehre* (1871, translated into English as *Principles of Economics*). Though an Austrian, based in Vienna, he drew on the German tradition of supply-and-demand analysis established by writers such as Rau, Hermann and Roscher. In contrast to Jevons and Walras, Menger was not seeking to make economics scientific according to the standards of contemporary physics. Rather, his approach was closer to Aristotelian philosophy with its desire to uncover the essence of economic phenomena – to discover their real nature. However, despite this radically different perspective, he also argued that value was determined at the margin by the value of an additional unit of a commodity.

Menger started from the presupposition that the purpose of economic activity was the satisfaction of human needs. Goods were things that contributed to this purpose:

> If a thing is to become a good ... all four of the following propositions must be simultaneously present:
>
> 1. A human need.
> 2. Such properties as render the thing capable of being brought into a causal connection with the satisfaction of this need.
> 3. Human knowledge of this causal connection.
> 4. Command over the thing sufficient to direct it to the satisfaction of the need.[2]

To be a good, not only must a thing be able to satisfy human needs, but also people must know about how they can use it to this end, and they must have sufficient control over it.

What about things that appear to satisfy no human needs? Menger's answer is that goods may satisfy needs either directly (he called these low-order goods) or indirectly (higher-order goods). Goods can thus be arranged in a hierarchy, with goods that satisfy needs directly at the bottom and ones that satisfy them extremely indirectly at the top. Bread would be at the bottom, whereas steelworks would be much higher up.

From here, Menger went on to define value as the importance of a good in satisfying needs: it is the satisfaction derived from command over a good. The value of a particular commodity is thus the needs that would not be met if the good were not available. Menger assumed that this value fell as the quantity of the good increased – the concept of diminishing marginal utility. This was a concept that could easily be extended to higher-order goods – to goods that do not satisfy human needs directly: 'The value of a given quantity of a particular good of higher order . . . is equal to the importance of the satisfactions provided for by the portion of the product that would remain unproduced if we were not in a position to command the given quantity of the good of higher order.'[3] What Menger is saying here is that if a higher-order good (for example, a kilogram of wheat) is not available, a certain quantity of lower-order goods (two loaves of bread) will not be produced. The value of the kilogram of wheat is the human needs satisfied by the two loaves of bread.

As defined by Menger, the concept of value does not involve either exchange or price. Price enters only with exchange, and is determined by values. In an exchange between two isolated individuals, all that can be said about price is that it will be between the limits set by the values which the two individuals place on the goods being exchanged; otherwise, one of them would opt out. Where there is competition, the level of indeterminacy will be less.

Menger's verbal analysis of price determination can be compared with the mathematical analysis of Jevons and Walras. All three assumed that prices depended on marginal utility and rejected the Ricardo–Marx labour theory of value. However, simply to bracket Menger with the other two is to overlook important points to which his, less formal, analysis drew attention. Menger did not assume that markets were in equilibrium, with individuals maximizing utility. On the contrary, individuals would frequently have limited knowledge of the possibilities available to them. Entrepreneurs emerge as people who seek out and take advantage of opportunities for profit, creating goods that previously did not exist and finding new ways to create existing goods. Competition, therefore, was for Menger a dynamic process that had much more in common with Adam Smith's view of competition than with the static concept found in Walras or Jevons. For Menger, competition was not the absence of monopoly but a process through which monopolies were progressively eliminated: 'the need for competition calls forth competition, provided there are no social or other barriers in the way'.[4]

A further characteristic of Menger's economics was his stress on the way in which institutions arose from the nature of goods. The most important of these institutions was private property itself. Property, he argued, 'is not an arbitrary invention, but rather the only practically possible solution to the problem that is . . . imposed upon us by the disparity between requirements for, and available quantities of, all economic goods'.[5] The legal order, therefore, had an economic origin. However, while institutions might have had economic origins, they had often not been designed by anyone. Rather, they emerged as the unintended consequences of individuals' actions. For example, money, Menger claimed (seemingly overlooking the substantial evidence concerning the role of the state in setting monetary standards), was not planned, but arose unplanned from the actions of individuals seeking to satisfy their needs as best they could.

Menger's *Grundsätze* was dedicated to Roscher, widely seen as one of the originators of the historical approach to economics. His subjective-value theory continued the earlier German tradition and met with little resistance. There was no sense of a break with the past. In 1883, however, Menger published a methodological critique of historicism as it was developing under Schmoller. He sought to provide a rigid distinction between theoretical and historical economics. Theoretical economics, he argued, dealt with 'exact' laws based on assumptions of pure self-interest, omniscience and freedom of movement. To test the resulting theory involved a misunderstanding, because it was based on abstractions: in the real world, 'pure self-interest' cannot exist any more than can 'pure oxygen'. Menger also objected to mathematical economics, on the grounds that all mathematics could demonstrate was relationships between quantities: it could not establish the essence of economic phenomena, which was his concern. To analyse interdependence and mutual determination, as did Walras, was to lose sight of causal connections. Menger also put forward two doctrines that, though minor themes in the book, subsequently became very important in Austrian economics. One was methodological individualism (the idea that all analysis must start with the individual, not with aggregate or collective concepts). The other was the idea that there is a spontaneous order underlying social phenomena.

Schmoller reviewed Menger's book very critically, and the outcome was a bitter controversy – the *Methodenstreit*, or 'Struggle over method'. In the ensuing discussion, many issues were confused. It has been argued that the dispute was as much to do with policy (Schmoller supporting protection and Menger opposing it) and jockeying for dominance as with substantive issues. It is arguable that Schmoller and Menger could otherwise have agreed that different methods were needed to answer different questions. The disagreement had, however, the effect of splitting the economics profession in Germany.

HISTORICAL ECONOMICS AND THE MARSHALLIAN SCHOOL IN BRITAIN

In Britain, historical methods were advocated by Richard Jones (1790–1855), who used them to criticize Ricardo's theory of rent. With Malthus he established the Statistical Society of London, later the Royal Statistical Society. However, the writer who bore most responsibility for stimulating debate on the issue of whether economics should be a historical subject was Thomas Edward Cliffe Leslie (1827–82). In 1870 Leslie took up the point, made by the German historical economists, that economic laws were not universal but varied from place to place. He also challenged the prevailing conception of Smith's *Wealth of Nations*, reinterpreting the book as an exercise in historical economics. Smith, Leslie contended, had adopted an inductive approach (though he had not taken this far enough) and he had not assumed that behaviour was selfish. Leslie called for the replacement of abstract political economy with a more inductive, historical approach that took into account the whole variety of human motivations and the evolution of economic, political and social institutions.

Competition and movement of capital were increasing the complexity of the world and also increasing uncertainty, undermining the assumptions of orthodox theory.

These arguments – that economics had become too abstract and that the conclusions of political economy were of limited relevance – were developed by other writers in the following years. The 1880s also saw the appearance of pioneering works on English economic history by J. E. Thorold Rogers (1823–90), William Cunningham (1849–1919) and William James Ashley (1860–1927). One of the most influential (perhaps because he died so young and came to be regarded by many of his generation as a saint) was Arnold Toynbee (1852–83), who popularized the term 'the Industrial Revolution' in lectures given shortly before his death. Toynbee was committed to social reform and succeeded in inspiring a generation of Oxford students to take up economics in order to achieve this end. He refused to accept that ethics could be separated from economics, at least on questions of distribution, and he insisted that to understand current economic and social problems it was necessary to consider their history. He argued the case for economic and social history as autonomous from, though dependent on, other types of history.

Though there were sharp differences between the advocates of theoretical and historical economics, British economics avoided being split in the same way as the German profession. One reason for this was the attitude of Alfred Marshall (1842–1924), the economist who, from his position as professor of political economy at Cambridge, dominated the British economics profession from the 1880s until around 1930. He had a vision for establishing economics as a professional discipline, at the heart of which would be an engine of economic analysis, which could be applied to different problems. Central to his thinking was the idea that economics was not a body of truths, but an apparatus for discovering truths about the world. To further this ambition he was instrumental in establishing the *Economic Journal* and an economics degree in Cambridge, separating economics from its place among the 'moral sciences', where it had been taught alongside logic, ethics and politics. He also devoted years to preparing eight editions of his textbook, *Principles of Economics* (1890–1920).

However, although he had some brilliant pupils, notably Pigou and Keynes, who kept Cambridge at the centre of developments in economics in the interwar period, he was unable to fulfil his vision. Too few students chose to specialize in the subject.

After early work on psychology, including a paper on the structure of cognition, Marshall came to economics through translating Mill's doctrines into mathematics, a task he undertook during the late 1860s. This involved geometric representations of demand and supply. In attempting this, he was strongly influenced by the German writers, notably Rau, Hermann and Thünen. After reading Jevons's *The Theory of Political Economy*, he grafted utility theory on to his theory of supply and demand by using it to explain the demand curve. The result was a system of equations describing a static equilibrium, comparable to those of Jevons or Walras. However, whereas Walras's analysis remained at a very abstract level, Marshall continually sought to be realistic. In particular, he wished to take proper account of time. To do this, he could not analyse general equilibrium, allowing for all the possible instances of interdependence in the economy, but had to deal with one market at a time. He therefore developed the method of partial-equilibrium analysis, in which one part of the economy (typically a single industry) is analysed on its own.

There was, however, a further reason why Marshall adopted this approach. Like many of his contemporaries, he was obsessed with biology, and in particular evolutionary ideas. Biological metaphors were, he argued, more useful than mechanical ones in dealing with economics. This meant that he was sceptical about the mathematics used by Jevons and Walras, so closely linked with mechanics. This passion for evolutionary ideas came out in several ways. He considered continuous, gradual change as typical of economics, adopting the motto *Natura non facit saltum* ('Nature does not make jumps'). He did not take individuals' behaviour as given but assumed that their behaviour would be modified in response to their environment. Thus, if workers spent their income on wholesome goods and activities, the result would be an increase in their strength and intelligence, and their productivity would rise. In contrast, if they indulged in ways of living that were unwholesome, both physically and morally, neither efficiency nor character would improve. Evolution also affected Marshall's view of firms, which he saw as progressing through a life cycle analogous to that of the individual. They began young and vigorous, but after a period of maturity they became old and were displaced by newer, more efficient firms. An industry, therefore, was like a forest – it might remain the same when seen as a whole, even though every tree in it was changing.

The foundation of Marshall's economics was the theory of supply and demand. He took time into account through the device of distinct periods. These are defined not in terms of calendar time but in terms of what is free to change within each period. The calendar time involved in each period might vary from one problem to another. The shortest possible time period is defined as the market period. There is a certain quantity of goods available, as there is no time to produce more. If the commodity is perishable, such as fish (before the advent of refrigeration), it will be sold for whatever it can fetch. Price will be determined entirely by demand. But if the commodity can be stored without great expense (for example, wheat), price will be governed primarily by the price that sellers expect to prevail in the future: sellers will be reluctant to accept a lower price, even if demand is low. The result is that demand will determine sales, not price.

Marshall's next time period, the short run, is sufficiently long to allow variations in the level of production to take place. In the short run, firms can alter the quantity of unskilled labour they employ, but not the amount of skilled labour and machinery, or their production methods. The result is that output can be increased, but only at increasing unit cost. Supply and demand therefore determine price. If demand increases, price will rise, because of rising production costs caused by the limited stock of skilled labour and machinery. In the long run, Marshall's next longest time period, however, firms have time to change the skilled labour and machinery they use and to organize in different ways. Under these circumstances, Marshall believed, expansion of output will result in falling costs. An increase in demand will therefore result in output increasing and price falling. Finally, Marshall postulated a very long period, in which 'there are very gradual or *secular* movements of normal price, caused by the gradual growth of knowledge, or population, or capital, and of the changing conditions of demand and supply from one generation to another'.[6]

Like Toynbee and so many others of his generation, Marshall came to economics because he believed it offered a way to improve society. Social reform was providing a partial replacement for the Christian faith that was being lost. However, Marshall was equally concerned that economics be established as a scientific discipline. This meant that he was extremely reluctant to get involved in public controversy, for he believed that this would undermine the authority of the subject. The role of the economist was not to propound truths about the economy, but to develop an agreed body of economic principles that could be used to tackle economic problems. This was one of the reasons why, in his *Principles of Economics* – a book that was still used by a few students as a textbook in the 1950s – he presented his results verbally in the text. Diagrams were relegated to the footnotes, and algebra was banished to an appendix. In this way, he hoped, the subject could be made accessible to those in business as well as to professional economists. Such an arrangement also accorded with his suspicion of mathematical arguments.

Marshall was trained as a mathematician and developed his economics using mathematics. He was an innovative theorist, developing many of the theoretical concepts that have become standard in modern economics. However, he always remained very sceptical about the use of mathematics in economics. He wanted economics to be realistic, but the use of mathematics made it very easy to derive results that had no foundation in reality. If mathematical results could not be translated into English, he was suspicious of them. His papers, for example, contain a mathematical model of economic growth, but, because he was doubtful about the value of the equations, he did not publish it. His methodological pronouncements emphasize the need for quantitative and statistical methods, but, unlike with Jevons, the empirical evidence he used appears anecdotal rather than statistical, and illustrative rather than essential. This is true not only of the *Principles* but also of *Industry and Trade* (1919), a volume that contained an enormous amount of information on the organization of industry. This attitude towards evidence must have arisen, at least in part, from his strong desire to keep theory and reality close together.

A similar ambiguity underlay Marshall's attitude towards history. As a young lecturer, Marshall was enthusiastic about history. In the first edition of the *Principles* he began with economic history. He mixed factual material and history in most chapters of the book and argued that only one part – on the general relations of supply, demand and value – should be considered 'theory'. However, in later editions the historical element was played down and moved into appendices. When the time came to appoint a successor to the chair at Cambridge, Marshall supported A. C. Pigou (1877–1959), strongly inclined towards theory, in preference to the historian H. S. Foxwell (1849–1936). The historical content of the first edition of the *Principles* had been strongly criticized by Cunningham (his review was entitled 'The perversion of economic history'). Marshall may have decided that it was safer to avoid controversy and to accept a disciplinary division of labour, in which history was left to historians.

EUROPEAN ECONOMIC THEORY, 1900–1914

By the start of the twentieth century, marginalist economics – economics based on marginal utility and individual maximization – had become well established. Walras's successor in the chair at Lausanne, Vilfredo Pareto (1848–1923), had developed and refined his general-equilibrium system. In Sweden, Knut Wicksell (1851–1926) had integrated Walras's general-equilibrium theory with Böhm-Bawerk's capital theory. In their work, marginal-productivity theory displaced the Malthusian explanation of wages and the notion that profits were a residual. In England, Marshall had imposed his view of economics on Cambridge and dominated the discipline, promoting a supply-and-demand analysis that built on the French and German traditions as well as on British writers. In keeping with the goal of becoming a scientific discipline, the term 'economics' was displacing 'political economy'. At the London School of Economics (LSE), established by the historians, social investigators and socialists Beatrice and Sidney Webb (1858–1943 and 1859–1947), and at Oxford, a slightly more historically minded economics was being pursued, but these institutions were dwarfed by Marshall's Cambridge. Furthermore, because LSE, despite the socialist element in its origins, was committed to free inquiry, it also included economic theorists and supporters of laissez-faire. By the 1930s, with the appointment of Lionel Robbins and Friedrich Hayek, the latter become very prominent. Theory and history, despite Marshall's desire to keep them together, had separated. In England (unlike in the United States), historical economics was about to turn into economic history, leaving economics behind. In the German-speaking world, the *Methodenstreit* had split the profession and reduced chances of cooperation.

Not only was mathematics, in particular differential calculus, increasingly used, but economics had almost lost the older concern with long-run dynamics. Static theory, more amenable to treatment with the mathematical tools economists had begun to use, received more attention. However, some economists were still concerned with dynamics. There was much research on the business cycle, notably by Tugan-Baranovsky (see p. 177); Arthur Spiethoff (1873–1957), a student of Schmoller's; and Albert Aftalion (1874–1956), a professor in France, though born in Bulgaria. In 1912 Joseph Alois Schumpeter (1883–1950), an Austrian working in the tradition of Friedrich von Wieser (1851–1926), and Böhm-Bawerk (Menger's two disciples), published *Theorie der Wirtschaftlichen Entwicklung* (*The Theory of Economic Development*), in which he argued that technical progress was the motive force underlying the cycle and economic growth. Innovation moves the economy out of equilibrium, creating new opportunities for entrepreneurs to make profits and causing an expansion as these are taken up. When these opportunities are exhausted, slower growth and depression occur as the economy settles down to a new equilibrium before it is disturbed by a new wave of innovations. Such ideas, however, can be regarded as marginal to the pure theory that was becoming increasingly prominent.

Most of the economists involved in these developments were social reformers. Though they were far from being Marxists, they were not content with the status quo. If their work was ideologically motivated, their goal was to develop policies that would reduce poverty and improve the condition of the working class. They generally favoured piecemeal reform and were opposed to radical schemes such as those of Marx or the American Henry George (1839–97), whose enormously successful and widely read book *Progress and Poverty* (1879) proposed replacing all taxes with a single tax on rent. But they were by no stretch of the imagination doctrinaire defenders of capitalism. Even the Austrians, who were such strong critics of Marx, wrote of the need for capitalism to be reformed.

By the twentieth century, economics was on the way to becoming an academic discipline. Economists might be motivated by social concern, but the discipline had become much more clearly separated from politics than was the case for much of the nineteenth century. This separation of economic analysis from politics was, however, not complete. This was starkly revealed in England in 1903 when fourteen British economists (including Marshall, Francis Ysidro Edgeworth (1845–1926) and Pigou) wrote a letter to *The Times* supporting free trade. This was an attempt to bring the authority of economic science to bear on an urgent political issue. However, its effect was to show that British economists were divided along political lines.

10

The Rise of American Economics,
1870–1939

US ECONOMICS IN THE LATE
NINETEENTH CENTURY

In retrospect, the most significant development towards the end of the nineteenth century was the rapid development of Economics in the United States. There is still dispute about whether American economics in the mid-nineteenth century should be considered derivative of European economics. However, by the 1880s, if not earlier, economics was expanding rapidly in the United States, and American economists were clearly making original contributions to the subject. Furthermore, the context of US economics was significantly different from that in Europe. With the expansion of the frontier, many states were setting up institutions of higher education, and in some of these a culture where research was important was becoming established, though the quality of different institutions was extremely variable. More significantly, a small number of universities were making research central to their mission, creating the research universities that were to become very important in the twentieth century. There was no central control of higher education, and personal and institutional rivalries were strong. Academics were regarded as employees who could be dismissed very easily if what they said was unacceptable to their sponsors, but at the same time they were expected to undertake work that was relevant to the problems facing their society. American economists were therefore subject to pressures different from those facing their European counterparts. Though this was an extreme case, in the 1880s the University of Pennsylvania insisted that its economists were not to support free trade. Popular interest in economic and social questions was high, and academic economists were expected to have 'sound' opinions to offer about them. The result was a tendency towards a professional (though not political) conservatism.

For most of the nineteenth century the tariff had been the dominant issue in US economic policy. Manufacturers generally favoured high taxes on imports of manufactured goods, whereas farmers complained that such tariffs raised the prices they had to pay. By the 1890s, however, it had become clear that there was no possibility of protective tariffs being removed and the issue received less attention than money and the control of business.

Money was a perennial issue in American history. The Civil War, financed by the issue of inconvertible currency (the greenbacks), focused attention on the question. Rapid territorial expansion, a weak banking system, the deep depression of the late 1870s and continued depression during the 1880s ensured that monetary problems remained on the agenda. Opinion was divided between those who regarded paper currency as tantamount to fraud and the cause of much speculative activity and those who welcomed the additional purchasing power it created. The former ranged from those who wanted the issuing of paper currency severely curtailed to those who wanted it abolished altogether, or at least wanted all currency to be backed 100 per cent by gold reserves. The latter included farmers and others who wanted higher prices. On top of this there was the silver question, relating to the terms under which silver should enter the currency alongside gold. Given the interests of states that produced the two metals and the uneven distribution of agriculture and manufacturing across the continent, sectional interests were strong.

Control of business was a more important issue than in Britain because of the concentration that had accompanied the growth of railroads. Not only were railroads large organizations in themselves, but control of them was widely used to further the tycoons' interests in other industries. Pools, trusts and other devices were used to counteract the potentially damaging effects of competition. Farmers and industrialists alike complained, with good reason, about high and discriminatory freight rates. Consumers and rival industrialists objected to trusts because they raised prices to take advantage of monopoly positions. In response, the operators of cartel arrangements responded that these were essential in industries where unlimited competition would force prices below cost, creating instability in the industry. Competition was thus high on the agenda facing economists.

American economics changed very significantly in the 1880s as a result of several developments. The first independent university department was established at Harvard in 1879, responsible for the *Quarterly Journal of Economics* a few years later. The American Economic Association was established in 1885. This was soon designed as a broad, inclusive organization, open to anyone sufficiently interested to pay a membership fee, and served as a focus for serious discussion of economic questions. Although the *American Economic Review* did not start until 1910, the American Economic Association immediately began a series of scholarly publications that amounted to a journal. The University of Chicago started publishing the *Journal of Political Economy* in 1892.

The main European influence during this period came from Germany, not Britain. The historical approach adopted by many German economists, with its notion that economic theories needed to be adapted to fit different historical situations, had strong appeal to those who believed that economic conditions in the United States were different from those in Europe. Though postgraduate training developed in the United States, especially after the establishment of Johns Hopkins University in 1876, many economists had gone to Germany for their postgraduate work. The Verein für Sozialpolitik, with its emphasis on social reform, was the model underlying the American Economic Association. Though it expressed a commitment to non-partisan inquiry, the first constitution of the association expressed opposition to doctrinaire laissez-faire and, as a result, several economists of the 'old school' refused to join. By the 1890s, however, the offending clauses had been removed and most of the 'old school' economists were members.

JOHN BATES CLARK

One of the most eminent figures during this period of American economics was John Bates Clark (1847–1938). Like many American economists of his generation, he was educated in Germany, studying in Heidelberg under Karl Knies (1821–98), often considered a member of the older historical school. It is thus not surprising that in his first book, *The Philosophy of Wealth* (1886), he sought to broaden the premisses on which economics was based. He wanted to take account of elements in human nature that were more ethical and less mechanical than those taken into account in conventional theory. In addition, he sought to apply to economics an organic concept of society. Thus, although he proposed a theory of marginal utility (which he attributed to what he had learned from Knies, not from Jevons, Menger or Walras), he understood 'effective utility' (his name for marginal utility) somewhat differently from others. The market, he argued, measures the value that society, not just the individual, places on a commodity. This shift of attention from the individual to the social reflected his organic conception of society and was something that the European marginal-utility theorists would not have considered.

The American context explains Clark's treatment of competition, for he brought in ethical considerations to distinguish between 'conservative' competition – competition in which competitors try to provide a better or cheaper service than each other – and 'cut-throat' competition – in which ethical constraints on behaviour are abandoned. The idea of competition without moral restraints was, for Clark, absurd. To find it we would have to go back to 'the isolated troglodyte, the companion of the cave bear'.[1] Ethics also entered his analysis of what he saw as the dominant problem facing contemporary American society – highly aggressive 'competition' between firms that eventually forced all but one of them out of business, thereby creating a monopoly. The solution, he suggested, lay in cooperative ventures and profit-sharing, with arbitration being available until these were more widely developed. Such institutions would result in a just outcome and, once imposed, society would accept them.

In *The Distribution of Wealth* (1899), based on articles written over the previous decade, Clark proposed a theory of income distribution in which each factor of production (land, labour and capital) received a reward equal to the marginal value of its contribution to output. The wage rate, for example, would be equal to the money that an employer would lose if they had to employ one fewer worker. Clark applied the theory to capital by likening this to a fund: individual capital goods (machines, buildings, etc.) come and go, but the fund remains intact. The rate of interest, he argued, was the marginal product of this fund of capital – the additional revenue that could be obtained if capital increased by one dollar. There was no essential difference between land and capital goods: they both yielded a return that was determined by the rate of interest. As in his previous book, he drew ethical conclusions – in this case the conclusion that, if there is competition, each agent of production gets what it is entitled to. This was a potentially conservative doctrine, criticized by radicals for justifying the profits earned by capitalists. It countered socialist claims that capitalists took a share of the produce that rightfully belonged to labour.

Clark defended the use of static theories (in which prices and quantities settled down to values that did not change) by using the analogy of an ocean. Oceans are continually in motion, but provided we are not concerned about fine detail a static theory is adequate:

> A static ocean is imaginary, for there was never such a thing: but there has never been a moment in the history of the stormiest seas, when the dominant forces that controlled them were not those which, if left entirely alone, would reduce their waters to a static condition. Gravity, fluidity, pressure, and nothing else, would have the effect of making the sea level and motionless . . . If we take a bird's eye view of the ocean, we are tempted to say that a static philosophy of it is sufficient and that we may treat waves and currents as minor aberrations due to 'disturbing causes'.[2]

This is a clear statement of the view to which Keynes (p. 247) was later to object when he claimed that it was useless for the economist to say that, when the storm had passed, the sea would be calm again.

Clark was concerned not with short-run fluctuations but with what he believed to be the underlying phenomena.

Like his European contemporaries Marshall and Schumpeter, Clark regarded the study of statics as the prelude to studying dynamics. An innovation, he argued, would move the economy out of equilibrium, creating profits for entrepreneurs. In time, wages would respond, reducing profits back to their normal level; but before that could happen another innovation would usually occur, disturbing the equilibrium again.

Clark illustrates very clearly the characteristics of American economics during this period. Ethical considerations permeated his approach, and, although he was a critic of American society, his stance could be described as conservative, not breaking radically with established methods. He was driven by a concern with the problem of big business, and he adopted an approach to competition that was the result of this concern. In his earlier book he, like many of his contemporaries, was alarmed by the problem of monopoly, and he proposed cooperation as the means of tackling it. In his later book he was much less concerned about the problem. 'Latent' or potential competition would prevent firms from raising prices too far, and the growth of capital would lead to new competition. Furthermore, the costs to consumers of higher prices would be offset by the benefits that would accrue from the accumulation of capital. He became distinctly more optimistic about capitalism, and moved away from the Christian socialism of his youth.

MATHEMATICAL ECONOMICS

Other American economists proposed more mathematical versions of marginalism. Simon Newcomb (1835–1909), an astronomer and mathematician, defended the methods employed by Jevons (though he argued that Cournot was superior) and criticized the old school of American economists for deprecating them. He claimed that these economists criticized mathematical theory because they did not understand it: their own theories were substantially the same, even though they did not use mathematics. His own use of mathematics in economics was prompted by the currency question, in particular the problems after the Bland–Allison Silver Act of 1878, which reintroduced and increased the coinage of silver. He argued that fluctuations in prices were harmful because, when prices changed, people did not realize that the value of the dollar had changed. In a time of falling prices, such as the 1880s, workers would resist cuts in wages because they did not realize that prices had fallen even more than their wages were being cut. If prices fell but wages did not, employment and production would be reduced. Newcomb's remedy was the creation of a dollar whose value was linked to an index number of prices – a novel idea in the United States. This dollar would be a paper currency, and the amount of precious metal it represented would be changed from time to time, to compensate for changes in prices. Contracts in such dollars would be index-linked, reducing the problems that arose from ignorance about what was happening to prices. This was a scheme that had already been proposed in Europe, but Newcomb developed it in more detail.

Newcomb was also responsible for a mathematical formulation of the quantity theory of money. His equation was $V \times R = K \times P$. This stated that, in any period, the quantity of currency in circulation, R, multiplied by its velocity of circulation (the number of times that each dollar is, on average, used to make a transaction), V, equals the amount of business undertaken, K, times the price level, P. (In different statements of the quantity theory, K might be replaced with total transactions or total income. Though the interpretation might differ, the essentials of the theory were the same.) Newcomb used this equation to argue that, if the quantity of currency increased and other things stayed the same, the price level would rise. However, his main interest was astronomy and, although he remained an ardent supporter of mathematical methods, he did not develop his economic ideas or continue publishing in economics after around 1886.

The first American with a rigorous training in mathematics to pursue a full-time career in economics was Irving Fisher (1867–1947). He was taught by Willard Gibbs (1839–1903), a chemist and physicist, known for his work on statistical mechanics. Fisher's doctoral dissertation, *Mathematical Investigations in the Theory of Value and*

Prices (1892), provided a rigorous mathematical treatment of the marginal-utility theory of value. However, although he used the concept of utility in his mathematics, he stripped it of any connection with pleasure and pain: it was merely a way to describe individuals' behaviour and was not based on psychology. The only psychological assumption necessary for the theory was that 'each individual acts as he desires'. Utility meant simply 'intensity of desire' and implied nothing about the psychology underlying desires for different goods. Fisher's greater proficiency in the use of mathematics meant that his theory was more general than that of Jevons or Walras and that he was able to tackle some of the technical problems they had ignored.

Fisher's mathematical approach to the theory of value had much in common with the approach that came to dominate the subject after the 1930s. At the time, however, it gained little support. Other versions of marginalism, such as those of J. B. Clark or Frank Albert Fetter (1863–1949), which offered ethical or psychological interpretations of utility, and which eschewed the use of mathematics, were more widely used. It was thought that special genius was needed to be able to handle economics mathematically without being led astray into making unjustified speculations. Thus Arthur T. Hadley (1856–1930) suggested that the use of the mathematical method made it possible to frame a hypothesis and then end up treating it as a rigorously verified proposition. Only exceptional men, such as Jevons, Walras or Fisher, could avoid this trap. It is interesting to note how close this objection was to Marshall's reservations about the use of mathematics in economics.

In contrast to his early work on value theory, which was not widely appreciated, Fisher's work on money, capital and interest attracted widespread attention and respect. He developed his ideas in a series of books written after his move from the mathematics department to the economics department at Yale in 1895. They included *Appreciation and Interest* (1896), *The Nature of Capital and Income* (1906), *The Rate of Interest* (1907, later much extended as *The Theory of Interest* (1930)) and *The Purchasing Power of Money* (1911). In them he tackled a series of fundamental conceptual issues in economic theory relating to capital, prices, the rate of interest and money. *Appreciation and Interest* developed the idea of the real rate of interest. If interest is 10 per cent, for example, and the inflation rate is 8 per cent, the real return on the loan is only 2 per cent. Given that it is the real rate of interest that matters to people, if inflation were to change, one would expect the nominal rate to change by the same amount. He then offered a theory of the real rate of interest as the outcome of decisions to save and invest. These depended on two things. The first was individuals' attitudes towards consumption now and in the future. If people were more impatient, they would need a greater inducement to save (i.e. they would have to be paid a higher rate of interest) than they would if they were more content to postpone their consumption. The second was the productivity of capital – how much additional income could be created by postponing consumption in order to invest the resources. Fisher produced a mathematical theory to show how the real rate of interest was determined by these two forces of time preference and productivity.

In *The Purchasing Power of Money* Fisher took up Newcomb's mathematical version of the quantity theory of money, extending it to cover bank deposits as well as currency and providing a more thorough exposition, linking it with his theories of capital and interest. He also attempted to provide a statistical verification of the theory. His central thesis was that changes in the money supply would, in the long run, produce corresponding changes in the price level, but that there would be what he termed 'transition periods' during which everything would change. His theory of the relation between inflation and the rate of interest played an important role in his analysis of these transition periods and the processes that caused the level of production to change.

Fisher approached economics as a mathematician who was concerned to make economics scientific along the lines of physics and mechanics. One effect of this was his ability to use what, for economists of his generation, were advanced mathematical techniques. Possibly more important, however, was his persistent use of mechanical analogies. This is perhaps clearest in his work on money, where he persistently uses two types of analogy. One is the idea of a balance (in the sense of scales, shown in Fig. 3) in which money appeared on one side and commodities on the other. (Here, Fisher was simplifying by focusing purely on transactions that involved buying and selling commodities, ignoring the use of money to support transactions in financial assets, property and so on.) The lengths of the arms correspond to the velocity of circulation and the price level. The other, shown in Fig. 4, is the levelling of fluids in a system of cisterns. In the diagram below, stocks of gold and silver are represented by the levels of liquids in two barrels. Both barrels have leaks (corresponding to losses of metal to non-monetary uses) and inflows (gold and silver entering the circulation). Liquid is free to flow from each of these into the central cistern, in which a movable membrane keeps them separate from each other. The pressure from each liquid will ensure that the level of the liquid is the same in all three cisterns. This illustrates the operation of a bimetallic system. If a model were constructed, it could be used to illustrate changes such as the effects that a silver discovery would have

Fig. 3 Fisher's balance model of the quantity theory of money[3]

Fig. 4 Fisher's cistern model of bullion flows[4]

on the equilibrium. This use of diagrams, representing physical models, was also a feature of Fisher's doctoral dissertation.

Much of Fisher's work dealt with relatively abstract conceptual issues. However, he was also an ardent reformer and felt impelled to offer solutions to the problems his books discussed and to some problems his books did not cover, even when colleagues complained that these were sometimes quick fixes rather than solutions to the basic difficulties. His work on economic policy formed part of a programme that included causes such as health, eugenics, prohibition (arguing *against* allowing the sale of alcohol) and world peace. On all of these he was an active campaigner and organizer, and on some of them he could be regarded as a fanatic. The Stable Money League, which propagated his views on money, was merely one of many such organizations in which he was involved. He worked hard to get his scheme for a 'compensated dollar' implemented. This would have varied the weight of gold in the dollar in order to stabilize an index number of prices.

THORSTEIN VEBLEN

Another major figure in American economics in the first half of the twentieth century was Thorstein Bunde Veblen (1857-1929). Like Marx, Veblen was a strong critic of bourgeois society and of orthodox economics. However, whereas the background to Marx's work was the England of the 1840s and 1850s, vividly described in the novels of Charles Dickens, Veblen was concerned with American capitalism at the very end of the nineteenth century. He spent the first sixteen years of his life in an isolated, almost self-sufficient Norwegian community in Wisconsin. This community was then destroyed by technological change in the flour industry, which caused farmers to switch to producing a single crop and brought railroads and an extension of the money economy. Even as he developed his career as an academic economist, many of his attitudes remained those of an outsider to the mainstream of American society. This was clearly reflected in his writing. In *The Theory of the Leisure Class* (1899) he satirized the lifestyles and mores of the capitalists of his day, developing the concepts of conspicuous consumption and pecuniary emulation. Consumption had, for the very wealthy, ceased to be undertaken for its own sake but had instead become part of a process whereby people sought to establish their place in society – certain types of consumption were desirable because they were expensive and demonstrated success in acquiring wealth. Such behaviour, he argued, was a relic of a predatory, barbarian past.

This perspective on the wealthy classes in America was part of an attempt to apply Darwinian evolutionary ideas systematically to the analysis of society. Human behaviour developed in response to circumstances, including the prevailing technology. Habits of thought, or 'institutions', as Veblen termed them, could become stuck, remaining even when the circumstances that produced them had disappeared. People become conditioned to accept certain ideas, and these ideas persist, often because of vested interests. A modern example might be attitudes towards the environment and the use of energy. These attitudes, which have their origins in an era when resources appeared plentiful, have become strongly entrenched in the institutions of society and do not change even though they are ill suited to a world in which the environment is threatened. Sometimes, however, technological developments result in the creation of new habits of mind that are strong enough to overthrow existing institutions. But in time these too become entrenched and out of phase with the material environment.

Veblen's analysis of American industrial society as he found it in the 1890s rested on the distinction between two institutions: the machine process and business enterprise. The machine process denoted the entire system of production in which mechanized processes were used. It comprised a set of delicately balanced sub-processes, none of which was self-sufficient. The values it required and which it engendered reflected the instinct of workmanship and included precision and uniformity – mechanical standardization was more important than craftsman-like skill in enabling the machine process to operate efficiently. These values were very different from the pecuniary standards of business enterprise, concerned not with making goods but with making money. Businessmen might gain not by enabling the machine process to run smoothly but by disrupting the system, opening up opportunities for profitable speculation. Depression and the manipulation of markets could make it possible to buy business assets cheaply, enabling their purchasers to make money without undertaking any productive activity. The creation of monopoly power, through acquisition of other businesses or through advertising, would raise profits though contributing nothing to production. Advertising, for example, was competitive, and businesses were forced to undertake it even though it added nothing to the value of the goods produced. Veblen was therefore critical of the emergence of what he called 'parasitic' lines of business that were useless or harmful to the community at large but were profitable for individual businessmen.

It followed that the machine process and business enterprise would engender completely different spiritual attitudes. The machine process, with its enforcement of a standardization of conduct, would engender the habit of explaining things in terms of cause and effect: 'Its metaphysics is materialistic, and its point of view is that of causal sequence.'[5] In contrast, business enterprise is centred on the concepts of ownership and property: 'The spiritual ground of business enterprise . . . is given by the institution of ownership. "Business principles" are corollaries under the main propositions of ownership; they are the principles of property – pecuniary principles.'[6] In the United States, Veblen contended, business enterprise was dominant, for it provided the mechanism whereby different parts of the machine process were linked. The machine process, though it had a logic of its own, had been extended to meet the objectives of business enterprise – making money. The habits of mind associated with business enterprise had affected American culture, conspicuous consumption by the very wealthy being but one manifestation of this.

However, there was a potentially disruptive element in this process. The machine process inculcates habits of mind that conflict with those of business enterprise. Veblen therefore predicted that two types of people would emerge: one employed in running business and the other in running the machine process. These two groups would have different ways of thinking: the former in terms of natural rights, the latter in terms of cause and effect. The working classes would cease to think in terms of natural rights and would thus be unable to understand the justification for business enterprise. They would turn to socialism, threatening the status quo. In *The Engineers and the Price System* (1921) Veblen saw the possibility that the regime of business might be overthrown not by workers but by the engineers on whom the system depended but whose values were so different from those of the businessmen for whom they worked. He wrote:

> And there is the patent fact that such a thing as a general strike of technological specialists in industry need involve no more than a minute fraction of one per cent of the population; yet it would swiftly bring a collapse of the old order and sweep the timeworn fabric of finance and absentee sabotage [disruption of industry by absentee owners] into the discard for good and all.[7]

Like Marx, Veblen held out the prospect that internal contradictions within capitalism would lead to its overthrow. The nature of these contradictions and the manner of this overthrow, however, were different for Marx and for Veblen.

Veblen's critique of orthodox economics followed naturally from this evolutionary perspective. Orthodox economics, which included the whole line running from Ricardo to Marshall, was castigated as pre-Darwinian. It took human nature as given, not as changing in response to material conditions, and it explained society in terms of natural laws. It was hedonistic (individuals were assumed to be motivated solely by the pursuit of pleasure), teleological (changes in society were explained as movement towards an ideal) and taxonomic (involving mere classification without explanation). It had emerged at an earlier stage of industrial development, antedating the emergence of business enterprise, and had become entrenched even though it was no longer appropriate. Orthodox theory might be defended as hypothetical speculation, but it nonetheless influenced the way the world was perceived:

> Of course, this perfect competitive system, with its untainted 'economic man' ... is an expedient of abstract reasoning; and its avowed competency holds ... only in so far as the abstraction holds. But, as happens in such cases, having been once accepted and assimilated as real ... it becomes an effective constituent in the inquirer's habits of thought, and goes on to shape his knowledge of facts.[8]

These criticisms applied equally to 'classical' political economy (Smith, Ricardo and Mill) and to modern writers such as Alfred Marshall, for whom Veblen coined the term 'neoclassical', to emphasize the continuity that he saw between the two groups of economists. What was required, Veblen argued, was the replacement of such economics based on a simplified, hedonistic view of human nature by a Darwinian evolutionary economics that took account of changes in human nature and was based on cause-and-effect reasoning. However, he never managed to specify this method clearly.

JOHN R. COMMONS

John Rogers Commons (1862–1945) was an ardent social reformer. He was a student of R. T. Ely (1854–1943), one of the founders of the American Economic Association, who had taken his Ph.D. at Heidelberg with Karl Knies and whose approach to economics was strongly influenced by German historical economics. Because of his radical views, Commons found it hard to find a long-term academic post until, in 1904, Ely managed to create a position for him at Wisconsin, where he remained until his retirement in 1932. In his early work he sought to reconcile Austrian utility theory with the historical school's emphasis on the role of law and the use of statistics.

By the 1920s Commons had come to base his work on the idea that economic activity depended on the underlying legal and institutional relationships, and that these evolved over time. The economist should not take these as given, but must explain them. This led Commons into detailed historical research, notably his four-volume *History of Labor in the United States* (1918–35), a project he took over from Ely, and *The Legal Foundations of Capitalism* (1924). However, although he attached great importance to empirical research, he developed a distinctive theoretical framework, culminating in *Institutional Economics* (1934).

The main feature of Commons's analysis of the legal and institutional foundations of capitalism was that he took transactions as the basic unit of analysis. Transactions involve the transfer of property rights, but do not necessarily take place through the market. In addition to 'bargaining' transactions (ones that do take place through markets), he distinguished 'managerial' transactions (as when a manager orders a subordinate to do something) and 'rationing' transactions (as when the state levies taxes). The main characteristics of bargaining transactions are that, unlike the other two types of transaction, they are between legal equals and there is a double transfer of ownership. Each side has the legal right not to participate, and each party gives something to the other. This focus on transactions led Commons to analyse not just markets but the whole range of institutions through which transactions are organized. These include 'going concerns', such as the state, corporations, trade unions, families and churches, each of which has its own 'working rules'. These rules evolve over time in such a way that the organization is enabled to function.

Commons's view was that collective action was necessary to maintain order. Without external sanctions, including the threat of force, individuals would not respect the institutions on which society relied. This immediately put him at odds with conservatives, who rejected the idea that individual freedom had to be controlled, and led to the charge of socialism being applied to his work. However, he denied that his ideas were socialist. Rather, he emphasized that collective action was necessary to preserve individual freedom. Collective action can prevent people from interfering with the liberties of others, and provides a framework within which people can act. Freedom within a market system, for example, is possible only if property rights exist and if it is possible to make contracts that will be honoured.

The main source of external sanction was provided by the legal system. Commons attached particular importance to property rights, and in *The Legal Foundations of Capitalism* he explored in detail the way in which these had evolved as a result of decisions made by the courts. For example, he showed how the United States Supreme Court had, in the late nineteenth century, dramatically changed the notion of property. It had moved from an interpretation of the law that assigned property rights only to physical objects to one that assigned them to the expected earning power of physical objects. He argued that the courts regularly took account of economic effects when reaching their decisions.

Commons was a pragmatist who devoted much of his career to the task of reform. He did not try to find ideal solutions, but looked for solutions that worked. In this he was extremely successful, influencing legislation both in Wisconsin and at the federal level. This included civil-service reform, factory legislation, workers' compensation, unemployment insurance, interest-rate control, rural credit schemes, inheritance taxation, property-assessment laws, immigration policy and industrial relations. Through his students, many of whom went into government, in the 1930s he had an indirect influence on Roosevelt's New Deal, the programme of economic measures, including large public-works projects, designed to lift the United States out of the Depression.

INSTITUTIONALISM AND NEOCLASSICAL ECONOMICS

J. B. Clark, Fisher, Veblen and Commons represent four of the many approaches that were to be found in US economics in the early twentieth century. Unlike British economics, dominated by Marshall, no single economist or approach to economics was dominant. The movement most closely associated with this period, which began with a session at the 1918 meeting of the American Economic Association, was the 'institutional' approach to economics. Institutional economics has often been contrasted with 'orthodoxy' or with 'classical' or 'neoclassical' economics. Neoclassical economists emphasized individuals' maximizing behaviour and the role of competitive markets, whereas institutionalists, inspired by Veblen, denounced this approach and argued for a more holistic view in which economy and society could not be separated.

However, although institutional economists might see themselves ranged against a neoclassical orthodoxy, such a characterization is misleading, for they were very much part of the mainstream of American economics and in no sense marginal to it. Moreover, there was great diversity within both camps, and some individuals defy classification in this way. Even John Maurice Clark (1884–1963), one of the founders of institutionalism as a self-conscious movement, is best seen as standing on the boundaries between institutionalism and neoclassicism. He supported institutionalism, and yet he saw his work as being continuous with that of his father, John Bates Clark, who, despite his reputation as a neoclassical economist, was no more a straightforwardly neoclassical economist than was Marshall. Allyn Young (1876–1929), who exerted an immense influence in a short career, during which he worked at Chicago, Harvard and LSE, is another such figure whom it is hard to classify as either neoclassical or institutionalist.

Neoclassical economics clearly included mathematical economists such as Fisher. There was, however, a great difference between his approach and the more traditional, non-mathematical and more ethical approach of J. B. Clark. Fisher and Clark had different attitudes towards both the use of mathematics and the meaning of the concept of utility. There were other economists who were closer to Marshall and his English predecessors. These included Jacob Viner (1892–1970), Frank Taussig (1859–1940) and Frank Knight (1885–1972). If such economists are to be described by a single term, 'traditionalist' is probably better than 'neoclassical'.

What united institutionalists was a commitment to making economics scientific through basing it on strong empirical foundations and abandoning theories that rested simply on axioms about human behaviour for which there was little evidence. Though he was not the originator of this approach, the clearest representative of it is Wesley Clair Mitchell (1874–1948). In his presidential address to the American Economic Association in 1924, he spoke of the need to quantify economic theory. Now that economists were in a position to estimate directly relationships such as that between the demand for a quantity and its price, 'it seems unlikely that the quantitative workers will retain a keen interest in imaginary individuals coming to imaginary markets with ready made scales of bid and offer prices. Their theories will probably be theories about the relationships among the variables that measure objective processes.'[9]

In similar vein, Mitchell interpreted Veblen's distinction between business and industry in terms of the relationship between two groups of time series, one group measuring physical quantities of goods, the other sums of money. Quantitative workers would enjoy tackling the relationships between these two groups of data. Such a programme was consistent with Mitchell's role in the National Bureau of Economic Research, founded in 1920. This was an outgrowth of the sense of frustration at the inadequacies of the statistics available during the First World War, and was responsible for a wide range of statistical and empirical investigations into income, wealth and the business cycle.

INTERWAR STUDIES OF COMPETITION

Important features of US economics during the interwar period can be illustrated by the work of three economists: Frank Knight, J. M. Clark and Edward Chamberlin. All three tackled the problem that the theory of competition appeared inadequate to explain the behaviour that was observed in most capitalist economies, but they tackled it in very different ways.

Knight was a social scientist with wide-ranging interests, spanning ethics and political philosophy, but was a traditionalist in economic theory. In his Ph.D. dissertation, published as *Risk, Uncertainty and Profit* (1921), he described his task as being one of 'refinement, not reconstruction',[10] and he argued that the essentials of his arguments differed little from ones to be found in J. S. Mill or Marshall. Critics of the theory of competition had, he argued, never understood it properly. He was also a fervent liberal. In 1927 he moved to the economics department at the University of Chicago. There, with Viner, he was instrumental in consolidating the Chicago school, established by James Laurence Laughlin (1850–1933), later dominated by Milton Friedman and George Stigler, on the basis of a commitment to the virtues of free markets and competition. Knight is therefore a major figure in the history of modern economics, even though his own approach was pluralistic and encompassed ideas that hardly fit into conventional views about how to do economics.

Knight's most well-known analytical contribution was his separation of risk and uncertainty, an idea he attributed to nineteenth-century German writers, in particular Thünen and Mangoldt. Risk is measurable and can be expressed in terms of probabilities. Thus games of chance involve risk – it is impossible to predict which card will be drawn from a well-shuffled pack, but the probability of a particular card is precisely 1 in 52. Uncertainty, on the other hand, cannot be measured. For example, it is impossible to calculate in the same way the probability that a particular new product will be successful, because it depends on too many unknown and unpredictable factors. Having drawn this distinction, Knight went on to argue that there was a connection between uncertainty and profits. Given that the main difference between theory and reality that required explanation was the existence of profits in excess of the normal return on capital, Knight could claim that his theory explained the difference between competition as described in theory and competition as experienced in the United States.

However, although he defended traditional theory, Knight was at the same time acutely aware of its limitations. Like Marshall, he contended that humans are complex creatures, driven by a range of motives and values. Economic analysis is concerned only with actions directed towards the satisfaction of wants, and hence with only a small part of human activity or even of economic behaviour. This limitation, he argued, is far more sweeping in its scope and import than is easily imagined. It raises the fundamental question of how far human behaviour is inherently subject to scientific treatment. In his views on this point the writer is very much an irrationalist. In his view the whole interpretation of life as activity directed towards securing anything considered as really wanted, is highly artificial and unreal.[11] Human behaviour is not predictable, and thus economic laws can be no more than approximations. If science were measurement, Knight claimed, then economic science would not be possible.

Knight also denied that it was possible to separate positive and normative economics – to separate questions about what is from questions about what ought to be. His reasons for this lay in his pragmatist theory of knowledge. 'Reality is not what is logical, but what it suits our *purposes* to treat as real.'[12] Knowledge is simply a way of making sense of the world in order to achieve our objectives. Given that motives are varied, it follows that strict objectivity is impossible. This in turn means that scientific method is of limited usefulness in economics, for it is necessary to take account of human feelings and attitudes even though these cannot be measured or analysed scientifically.

The orthodox theory of perfect competition, defended by Knight, describes a world in which supply equals demand and resources are efficiently allocated, with labour and capital moving freely into those activities where they are most valuable. J. M. Clark, in his first major work, *Studies in the Economics of Overhead Costs* (1923), sought to explain why the actual economic system did not work like that. Why was it that there was instability in many markets and that capital and labour often lay idle? He found the answer in 'overhead costs'. These were costs that the producer incurred whatever the level of output. If overhead costs were sufficiently high, they would cause unit costs to fall as production increased and there would be no such thing as 'normal' costs at which price would settle. Clark argued that the enormous growth in investment in fixed capital had dramatically increased the importance of overhead costs, and that for many businesses full-capacity operation would require a price so low that it would fail to cover them. Theoretical arguments reinforced this conclusion by suggesting that competition would cause price to cover only variable costs such as the costs of labour and materials.

Clark argued that businesses responded to this situation in two ways. They might try to operate price discrimination, charging different prices to different customers. For example, they might establish brands, charge different wholesale and retail prices, or charge different prices in different places. Alternatively, they might engage in cut-throat competition: pushing prices so low as to drive competitors out of the market in order to establish a monopoly and charge higher prices. If this happened, the higher prices might in turn attract new competition.

In *Studies in the Economics of Overhead Costs*, Clark offered a view of competition that was radically different from the world of perfect competition, in which all firms have to accept the going market price, each being too small to have any influence on the market. Clark's world was one in which unrestrained private enterprise offered too many advantages to large-scale production. It was necessary to find ways in which business could be controlled without undermining competition. In *The Social Control of Business* (1926) he explored how this might be done and steps that had been taken to achieve this in the United States since the 1870s. These included anti-trust laws, regulation of public utilities, labour legislation, minimum-wage laws, food standards, urban planning and many other measures. Significantly, he did not see such control as something imposed on business – as an alternative to laissez-faire. Pure laissez-faire, Clark contended, was impossible. Furthermore, social controls were a part of business activity, involving informal agreements and customs, legislation and rules developed by the legal system in the course of settling disputes. This was very close to the perspective of Commons.

Edward Chamberlin (1899–1967), in a dissertation submitted in 1927 and published as *The Theory of Monopolistic Competition* (1933), addressed the same problem of the discrepancy between competition in theory and in practice. His solution, however, was to focus on market structure. He defined monopoly as the ability of a firm to control price through altering supply, and he defined 'pure' competition as competition in which monopoly elements were absent. Pure competition was not necessarily perfect, for knowledge of the future might be limited, or freedom of movement from one activity to another might be limited. He argued that the reason why real-world competition diverged from pure competition was that firms in practice experienced some degree of monopoly power. Markets were both competitive (firms were competing with each other) and monopolistic (firms had control over the price of the goods they sold).

> [I]t is monopolistic competition that most people think of in connection with the simple word 'competition'. In fact, it may almost be said that under pure competition the buyers and sellers do not really compete in the sense in which the word is currently used. One never hears of 'competition' in connection with the great markets [such as those for agricultural commodities], and the phrases 'price cutting', 'underselling', 'unfair competition', 'meeting competition', 'securing a

market', etc., are unknown. No wonder the principles of such a market seem so unreal when applied to the 'business' world where these terms have meaning.[13]

In order to explain the world of business it was therefore necessary to construct a theory intermediate between those of monopoly (where competition was absent) and the pure competition to be found in organized markets such as those for commodities or financial assets. Clark, Knight and others, Chamberlin claimed, had been led into confusion by being insufficiently clear in their assumptions about market structure. He reached the conclusion that the reason why economic theory appeared remote from reality was not that its method was wrong but that its assumptions were too far from the facts.

Chamberlin analysed market structure in terms of two dimensions: the number of firms in an industry and the degree to which each one produced a differentiated product. Small numbers led to the problem of oligopoly, in which each firm has to take account of how its competitors will react to any changes in its pricing or sales policy. Product differentiation means that each firm has a degree of monopoly power in that it can raise its price without losing all its customers. In such a world, advertising and selling costs are important in a way that they are not under pure competition.

In seeking to find a theory intermediate between pure competition and monopoly, Chamberlin wanted to develop a theory of value that was more general than Marshall's. His thesis was that elements of monopoly and competition interact in the determination of most prices, and that a hybrid of these two theories was needed to analyse firms' pricing behaviour. His book thus dealt with the whole of value theory. He brought Marshall's theory up to date by taking into account phenomena that had become increasingly important, such as advertising and product differentiation.

One reason why economists were interested in market structures in the 1930s was that there was a widespread belief that the cause of the Great Depression was a breakdown in competition, with the result that the economic system had become less dynamic – less responsive to new developments. Among the many economists who investigated this problem, Gardiner Means (1896–1988) was particularly influential. His book *The Modern Corporation and Private Property* (1932), written together with lawyer Adolf Berle, analysed the consequences of corporations being owned by shareholders but controlled by managers who often did not own significant numbers of shares. This meant that decisions taken might not be in the interests of shareholders, raising both legal questions relating to corporate governance and economic questions about business performance. Means later investigated 'administered pricing' – where prices are set not in competitive markets but by bureaucracies. Prices set in this way were likely to be changed less often than prices set in competitive markets, supporting the idea that the price mechanism might not be working as efficiently as it could. In contrast with the approach of Clark and Chamberlin, Means's writing was dominated not by theory but by empirical and statistical work.

THE MIGRATION OF EUROPEAN ACADEMICS

The period from 1914 to 1945 was a time of political turmoil in Europe. The First World War led to the Bolshevik Revolution in Russia, and the post-war settlement led to the redrawing of many national boundaries. Many people were uprooted and forced to find new homes. During the 1920s and 1930s this problem was increased dramatically by the rise of the Nazi Party in Germany. Many people were forced to leave Germany and, as Hitler conquered neighbouring countries, to leave the continent of Europe. The result was that, during this period, many economists migrated to the United States. In the 1920s they came mostly from Russia, and in the 1930s and 1940s mostly from German-speaking countries. Not only were they numerically significant, they also included some very prominent individuals who made a significant impact on the profession. They were particularly important in developing mathematical and quantitative economics.

Harvard attracted two of the most prominent such emigrés: Leontief and Schumpeter. Wassily Leontief (1906–99) was Russian. In 1925 he moved to Berlin to complete a Ph.D., and then in 1930 he moved to the

United States, taking up an appointment at Harvard in 1931. While in St Petersburg he had written a paper arguing that Walras's general-equilibrium system could be simplified in such a way as to analyse real-world economies. He spent the rest of his career developing this idea into what is known as input–output analysis. The essential idea is that the economy is divided into a number of industries or sectors, and a table is constructed showing how much each industry buys from each of the other sectors. For example, if there are three industries, the table contains three rows and three columns. If one of these industries is mining and another is the steel industry, one of the cells in the table will contain the steel industry's purchases of coal and iron ore and another will contain the mining industry's purchases of steel. If it is assumed that the proportions in which each industry buys other industries' outputs do not change, it is possible to use the input–output table to calculate the effects on all industries of various changes in the economy. For example, if exports of steel were reduced, this would have repercussions on all other sectors of the economy: less coal and iron ore would be bought, and these industries would in turn have to reduce their purchases from other industries, and so on. The changes can be calculated using an input–output table. The limitation of this technique is that it does not take account of price changes, which limits the range of problems to which it can provide useful answers.

Whereas Leontief devoted his career to input–output analysis, the activities of the Austrian-trained Joseph Alois Schumpeter were much more wide-ranging. Schumpeter's *Theory of Economic Development* (1912) placed the entrepreneur at the centre of the process of capitalist development. Entrepreneurs are responsible for the innovations (new products, new sources of supply, new production methods, new forms of organization) that open up opportunities for profit, disturbing the system. Successful entrepreneurs will earn high profits and will attract imitators. Over time, imitation will eliminate the profits earned by the original innovator and the system will settle down to a new equilibrium until it, in its turn, is disturbed by another innovation. Schumpeter's vision of capitalism was thus one of a system in continuous motion, the impetus for change coming from the entrepreneur.

Schumpeter had a brief political career, at one time being Finance

Minister in Austria, but emigrated to the United States in 1932. During the 1930s he worked on the problem of business cycles, building on his earlier work by explaining the cycle in terms of swarms of innovations that create profits that are subsequently eroded by imitators. The result was *Business Cycles* (1939), in two volumes. However, it received an extremely critical review from Simon Kuznets (pp. 269–70), and in the face of Keynesian economics (pp. 257–60) it failed to attract support. In contrast, *Capitalism, Socialism and Democracy* (1942), which he viewed as a potboiler, was very successful. In this book, Schumpeter argued that Marx was wrong in his diagnosis of why capitalism would break down. The success of capitalism would create rising living standards for all classes. The proletariat would have no reason to rise up and overthrow the system. Nevertheless, capitalism would eventually destroy itself, for it would destroy the values on which its success was based. Entrepreneurs would give way to bureaucracies, self-interested individualism would undermine workers' loyalties, and capitalist values would give way to a desire for security, equality and regulation. By weakening the resistance to change, the Second World War had contributed to this process, as the First World War had done in Europe.

Schumpeter was also the author of one of the classic books on the history of economics – his *History of Economic Analysis* (1954), edited by his wife, Elizabeth Boody Schumpeter (1898–1953), and published posthumously. (Views from this book are discussed in the Epilogue.)

ECONOMICS IN THE MID-TWENTIETH CENTURY UNITED STATES

It is no exaggeration to say that the position of US economics had been transformed since the middle of the nineteenth century. Up to 1914 it was still true that the dominant economic ideas came from Europe and that, although it contained some distinguished and original economists, the United States followed Europe. By the 1940s, however, this was no longer true. Indeed, not only were American economists making important theoretical and empirical contributions to the subject, their numbers had been strengthened by the arrival of migrants from Europe and American universities offered graduate training in economics that was not matched anywhere else in the world. For example, Harvard's economists were strengthened by the arrival from Europe of Schumpeter, Haberler and Leontief. Mitchell's National Bureau of Economic Research was arguably the world's pre-eminent centre for research in economic statistics, and by the end of the 1930s the Cowles Commission (p. 274) was becoming established as the world's most important centre for research in mathematical economics. On the eve of the Second World War, American economics exhibited a breadth of approaches to the subject that was found in no other country. With the effects of the Second World War on the discipline, the strength of American economics was increased still further.

11
Money and the Business Cycle,
1898–1945

WICKSELL'S CUMULATIVE PROCESS

The central figure in early-twentieth-century work on money and the business cycle was the Swedish economist Knut Wicksell. In *Interest and Prices* (1898) and his *Lectures on Political Economy* (1906) he developed a theory of the relationship between money, credit and prices – his so-called 'cumulative process'. Wicksell's theory was based on the theory of capital developed by the Austrian economist (and student of Menger) Eugen von Böhm-Bawerk, in which the rate of interest is essentially the price of time. There are two sides to this coin. If someone is receiving an income, she has a choice to make. She can spend it on consuming goods and services immediately, or she can save it in order to be able to consume goods at a future date. The way people save is to buy financial assets, thereby lending income to someone else, and in return for this they receive interest. The higher the rate of interest, the more future consumption can be 'bought' by deciding to save rather than to consume now. If the rate of interest rises, people have a greater incentive to postpone their consumption by saving part of their income.

The other side of the coin is investment. Businesses have to choose between investing in production processes that yield revenues very quickly and investing in other processes that are more productive but take longer to yield revenue. For example, the owner of a vineyard can choose whether to sell grapes immediately after the harvest or to ferment them and produce wine. Having produced the wine, there is then a choice of how long to store it. If the wine is allowed to mature, it will become more valuable. Wicksell followed Böhm-Bawerk in assuming that 'long' processes of production (ones which take a long time to yield a revenue) will be more productive than 'short' processes. However, because resources are committed for longer, such processes will require more capital. This means that, if the rate of interest rises, long processes of production will become more expensive relative to shorter ones.

The rate of interest, therefore, influences consumers' decisions about whether to consume goods now (using short processes) or in the future (using long processes), and also influences producers' decisions about whether to invest in processes that will produce goods now or in the future. A rise in the rate of interest will cause a rise in saving, as consumers decide it is worth postponing more consumption, and a fall in investment, as producers move towards shorter production processes. Wicksell argued that there will be some rate of interest at which these two types of decision are balanced. This is his 'natural' rate of interest. At the natural rate of interest, the amount that consumers wish to lend is exactly equal to the amount that producers wish to borrow in order to finance their investment: there is intertemporal equilibrium.

This part of Wicksell's theory drew on Böhm-Bawerk. The next stage was to introduce a banking system that created credit. The rate at which banks lent money was the 'market' or 'money' rate of interest. The cumulative process arose when the market rate of interest, for some reason, fell below the natural rate. Businesses would increase their investment, borrowing from the banking system the funds that they could not obtain from savers. The increase in investment would cause an increase in demand for resources, with the result that prices would be bid up. At the same time, the increased supply of credit would enable purchasers to pay these higher prices. Wicksell went on to show that, in what he called a pure credit economy, where goods were bought and sold using only bank money, not gold and silver, this process could continue indefinitely. As long as the market rate of interest was lower than the natural rate, prices would continue to rise. (Conversely, if it were higher than the natural rate, prices would fall indefinitely.) This was his cumulative process. If the country concerned were on a gold standard, the process would be brought to an end when the banks began to run out of gold reserves. This would force them to raise interest rates and cut back their lending, bringing the process to a halt.

Wicksell held a 'real' theory of the business cycle, in the sense that he believed that the cycle arose because of changes in the natural rate of interest. For example, inventions that raised productivity would cause the natural rate to rise, as would wars that destroyed resources. But the interest rate would not respond immediately to such changes, the result being that cumulative rises and falls in prices would be initiated. Furthermore, the quantity of currency (gold) played a purely passive role in the process. The active element in the system was the banking system. There was no fixed link between the volume of credit and the supply of currency. Despite this, however, Wicksell did not consider himself as a critic of the quantity theory but as elaborating on it, showing *how* changes in the quantity of money changed prices.

Though the basic theory was simple, there were several serious problems with it. Two of these were particularly important for subsequent developments. The first concerned the use of the Austrian theory of capital to determine the natural rate of interest. Though the notion of a period of production is an appealing one, capturing the insight that capital is associated with taking time to produce goods, it is riddled with technical problems. There may be no clear link between the period of production and the rate of interest. A fall in the rate of interest may cause the period of production to rise or fall, with damaging consequences for the notion of intertemporal equilibrium. The second major problem can be explained by noting that the natural rate of interest is the rate of interest at which (1) savings equal investment, (2) there is no new credit being created, and (3) prices are constant. However, these three conditions will not necessarily be satisfied at the same rate of interest. For example, in a growing economy, stable prices will require an increasing quantity of credit to finance the growing volume of transactions. This means that some credit creation, accompanied by an inequality of saving and investment, may be compatible with price stability. In addition, if productivity is rising, equality of the money and real rates of interest will lead to falling prices.

Wicksell was aware of these problems, and carefully made assumptions that avoided them. His successors, however, responded to them in very different ways and, as a result, developed very different theories. To understand these, it is necessary to understand some of the economic events of the interwar period.

THE CHANGED ECONOMIC ENVIRONMENT

The interwar period was one of unprecedented economic instability. By the end of the First World War the dominant country in the world economy was clearly the United States. Like much of the world, it experienced a brief boom in 1920, followed by a very sharp depression, when prices fell and unemployment rose, in 1921. For the rest of the 1920s, however, the country experienced unparalleled industrial growth and prosperity. Unemployment remained low, electricity spread throughout the country, with profound effects for industry and domestic life, the number of cars registered rose from 8 million to 23 million, and there was an enormous amount of new building. At the end of the decade, Herbert Hoover, as a presidential candidate, claimed that the country was close to triumphing over poverty. The stock market boomed, and investors thought that prosperity would continue indefinitely. Few other countries fared as well as the United States (Japan and Italy were unusual in growing faster), but most countries prospered during the 1920s. Countries that stagnated included many in eastern Europe (including the newly formed Soviet Union), Germany and Britain.

Britain, like the United States, shared in the immediate post-war boom and the depression that followed. Prices rose by 24 per cent in 1920, and then fell by 26 per cent in 1921. Unemployment rose to 15 per cent of the workforce in 1921, and remained around 10 per cent for the rest of the decade. Prices fell, and industry stagnated. In 1925, by which time US industrial production had risen to 48 per cent above its 1913 level, British industrial production was still 14 per cent below its level in 1913. The British economy had not recovered from the effects of the war.

However, the most spectacular examples of instability in the 1920s were in central Europe. In Germany, prices nearly doubled in 1919, and then more than trebled in 1920. After a brief respite in 1921, they then rose by over 1,600 per cent in 1922. In 1923 the currency completely collapsed. Prices rose by 486 million per cent – true hyperinflation. The value of the mark fell so far that the exchange rate, which had been US$1 = 4.2 marks in 1913, fell to US$1 = 4.2 billion marks. At the same time, unemployment rose to almost 10 per cent of the workforce. At the end of the year a new currency was issued, and prices rose gently for the rest of the decade. However, unemployment remained high, averaging over 10 per cent.

The Great Crash came in October 1929. In the United States, the downturn which had begun earlier that summer developed into an enormous slump in which industrial production, agricultural prices and world trade collapsed. Unemployment rose dramatically. In the next few years US industrial production fell to a little over half of its 1929 level, and unemployment rose to over 25 per cent of the labour force. It was not until 1937 that unemployment fell below 15 per cent, and then a further slump pushed it back up to 19 per cent. Similar levels of unemployment were recorded in many other countries. In 1933, unemployment was 26 per cent in Germany, 27 per cent in the Netherlands, 24 per cent in Sweden, 33 per cent in Norway, and 21 per cent in Britain. It was a problem affecting the entire capitalist world, and it persisted through most of the 1930s. In some countries, such as the Netherlands, unemployment remained at similar levels right up to 1939. In others, such as Britain and Sweden, unemployment recovered slowly to just over 10 per cent by the end of the decade. Only in Germany, under the Nazi regime brought to power by the crisis in 1933, was unemployment brought down to low levels (2 per cent by 1938).

Inevitably, these events attracted the attention of the world's economists. Though the underlying causes of the period's economic instability remained controversial, it became clear to most economists that the dominant theories of the pre-war period were inadequate to explain what was going on. Most important, it became clear that it was necessary to be able to offer a coherent theory of the level of economic activity. Changes in the level of industrial production and unemployment, on both of which statistics were beginning to be calculated during the 1920s, had become too important to be regarded as a secondary phenomenon. It was also clear that, in some way, changes in the level of economic activity were linked to money and finance. The German case, where hyperinflation completely destroyed the value of the currency and rendered normal economic activity virtually impossible, may have been an extreme example, but it was a very important and salutary one. It was also hard not to look for a connection between the financial activities that caused boom and bust in the US stock market and the unprecedented depth of the following depression.

In addition, behind all this was a world economy that was very different from before the war. In particular, intergovernmental debts, almost unknown before 1914, were a major problem. European governments had borrowed heavily from each other and, in particular, from the United States. They sought to recover these costs from Germany through extracting reparations. There was, and is, scope for disagreement over the role played by reparations in the German hyperinflation, or how far the causes of the Crash and the Depression should be sought in Germany and eastern Europe. There was, however, no doubt that the new situation in international finance was an integral part of the world trading system that, after 1929, proved to be so fragile.

The different experiences of the European countries and the United States meant that, though the economists involved formed a single community in the sense that Europeans drew on American literature, and vice versa, their perspectives were different. In the United States it was natural throughout the 1920s to be optimistic about the prospects for the long-term stability of the economy. When the Great Depression came, it was natural to see it, at least at first, as an unusually bad cyclical downturn. In contrast, by the end of the 1920s British economists had come to see unemployment as a structural problem, not a cyclical one. There was a further difference in that, whereas Britain had not experienced financial panic and bank failures since the 1860s, these were still regular events in the United States. The Federal Reserve System, established in 1913, had yet to establish a reputation as lender of last resort comparable with that of the Bank of England. The result was that Americans were much more interested in finding policy rules that would alleviate the cycle. The situation was different again on the Continent. In Germany, for example, memories of the hyperinflation of 1922–3 remained long after the event.

AUSTRIAN AND SWEDISH THEORIES OF THE BUSINESS CYCLE

The main proponents of the Austrian theory of the business cycle were Ludwig von Mises (1881–1973) and Friedrich von Hayek (1899–1992). Both were from Vienna, though Hayek moved to the London School of Economics in 1931. Mises's main ideas were set out in *The Theory of Money and Credit*, first published in 1912, but it was in the 1920s and early 1930s that they came into their own. They were apparently vindicated by the German hyperinflation and the sudden collapse of the American economy after the greatest boom in its history.

Mises and Hayek started from Wicksell's theory but developed it into a monetary theory of the cycle. They placed great stress on the Austrian theory of capital underlying Wicksell's natural rate of interest, and argued that, by artificially lowering interest rates, monetary policy was liable to interfere in the normal working of credit markets and distort the structure of production. In a credit economy, not constrained by the gold standard, bankers would be under pressure to keep interest rates low. If they yielded to this pressure and the market interest rate fell below the natural rate, this would both cause inflation and interfere with the intertemporal allocation of resources. Low interest rates would cause entrepreneurs to invest in production processes that were too long – too capital intensive – compared with what was appropriate given the level of saving. Because investment in capital goods was too high, capital-goods prices would rise relative to the prices of consumer goods. This would cause a problem because, although producers were shifting resources into processes that would yield returns only in the future, consumers were given no incentive to postpone their consumption; low interest rates would encourage them to spend more and save less than if interest rates were higher. The result would be excessive demand for consumer goods.

As long as credit continued to expand, such a situation could continue, possibly for a long time, but eventually the credit expansion would have to end. When this happened, interest rates would rise and the result would be a fall in output and a rise in unemployment. The reason for the rise in unemployment was that the long, capital-intensive production processes that had been started when interest rates were low would suddenly become unprofitable and be closed down. The resources put into them (embodied in stocks of unfinished goods, equipment and so on) would typically be unsuitable for the newly profitable shorter processes and would lie idle.

Mises and Hayek used this theory to condemn the use of expansionary monetary policy as a means of raising the level of economic activity. Credit expansion could be used to sustain a boom, but the result would be that, when the collapse eventually came, it would be worse. This diagnosis fitted the American experience of the 1920s. An exceptionally long boom, sustained by massive credit expansion, had been followed by an equally massive depression. According to Mises and Hayek, the depression was the inevitable consequence of the preceding boom. They advocated non-intervention and a policy of 'neutral' money whereby the rate of interest would be set so as to keep the level of money income constant. Even in a depression as severe as that of 1929–32, it would be foolish to lower interest rates and expand the money supply, for it was important that the structure of production be allowed to adjust.

In contrast, the Stockholm school – Erik Lindahl (1891–1960), Erik Lundberg (1907–89), Gunnar Myrdal (1898–1987) and Bertil Ohlin (1899–1979) – developed Wicksell's theory in a completely different way. They argued that technical problems with Austrian theory of capital meant that it was impossible to argue that the natural rate of interest was determined by the productivity of capital. Such a concept was impossible to define. Instead, they took up the idea, previously developed by Irving Fisher, that capital should be understood as the value of an expected stream of income. The demand for loans would depend on expectations about the future. This perspective led them to take issue with the idea of neutral money, claiming that equilibrium between saving and investment was compatible with *any* rate of inflation. The reason was that, so long as it was correctly anticipated, the rate of inflation could be taken into account in all contracts for the future and therefore need not have any effect. It was unexpected changes in prices that would disrupt the relationship between saving and investment.

Members of the Stockholm school were therefore led to abandon two of the ways in which Wicksell defined the natural rate of interest and, instead, they focused on the relationship between saving and investment. They analysed this through investigating dynamic processes, tracing the interaction of incomes, spending, prices and so on from one period to the next. Among other problems, they analysed how it was that a discrepancy between savers' and investors' plans (termed an *ex ante* imbalance between saving and investment) could be turned, by the end of the relevant period (*ex post*), into an equality. For the most part the processes they analysed started from a situation of full employment, with the result that they analysed cumulative processes similar to Wicksell's. However, they took very seriously the idea that prices and wages might be very slow to change, with resulting consequences for output. They also investigated processes that started with a situation of unemployment, and were able to show how lowering interest rates might lead to a prolonged increase in production.

One reason why the Swedish economists did not reach a more definite view of the cycle was that their theory was very open-ended. They explored a series of related models, showing that a wide range of outcomes was possible. This fitted in with their very pragmatic attitude towards policy. They were open to the idea of using not only monetary policy but also government spending to reduce unemployment. This was in marked contrast to the hostility of the Austrians towards government intervention.

BRITAIN: FROM MARSHALL TO KEYNES

Leaving aside Hayek and his followers at LSE, such as Robbins, British thinking on money and the business cycle had its roots in the work of Alfred Marshall. His first work on the problem was in *The*

Economics of Industry (1879), written jointly with Mary Paley Marshall (1850–1944), a student whom he taught and later married, and strongly influenced by J. S. Mill. In a period of rising demand, confidence is high, the level of borrowing increases, and prices rise. At some point, however, lenders reassess the situation and start to cut back on their loans, with the result that interest rates rise. This precipitates a fall in confidence and prices begin to fall. Businesses are forced to sell their stocks of goods, causing further falls in prices. The reason why this leads to fluctuations in output is that prices fluctuate more than costs, in particular wages and fixed costs. In the boom, prices rise faster than costs, increasing profits and causing firms to increase their production. After the crisis, prices fall more rapidly than costs, cutting profits and causing businesses to reduce output.

The main factor underlying this account of fluctuations in economic activity is confidence. Referring to the depression stage of the cycle, Marshall and Marshall wrote:

> The chief cause of the evil is want of confidence. The greater part of it could be removed almost in an instant if confidence could return, touch all industries with her magic wand, and make them continue their production and their demand for the wares of others ... [The revival of industry] begins as soon as traders think that prices will not continue to fall: and with a revival of industry prices rise.[1]

Crises occur because overconfidence by both borrowers and lenders causes expansions to go on too long.

Over the following forty years, Marshall integrated into his account of the cycle a clear statement of the quantity theory of money and the distinction between real and nominal interest rates. However, the essentials of the theory remained unchanged. In particular he continued to argue that fluctuations in demand caused prices to fluctuate. Output changed only when prices and costs moved in such a way as to raise or lower profits. This was the framework underlying the work of his followers. The most important of these were Arthur Cecil Pigou, Marshall's successor as professor at Cambridge, Dennis Robertson (1890–1963), Ralph Hawtrey (1879–1975) and John Maynard Keynes (1883–1946). The theories they developed were all firmly rooted in the Marshallian tradition, emphasizing the role of expectations and errors made by businessmen in explaining the cycle. However, this tradition encompassed a great variety of views.

Hawtrey, whose most influential book was *Currency and Credit* (1919, revised in 1927 and 1950), held a purely monetary theory of the cycle. His theory had several distinctive features, but the most important was his emphasis on what he termed 'effective demand' – the total level of spending, including both consumers' spending and investment. He argued that changes in the money supply would affect the level of effective demand and that, because prices and wages were slow to respond to this, output would change. The existence of time lags in the various processes involved meant that expansions and contractions of credit would go too far, with the result that there would be cycles, not steady growth.

In contrast, Robertson, in his *Theory of Industrial Fluctuations* (1915), explained the cycle in terms of shocks caused by inventions that raised productivity. Following Aftalion, Robertson used the gestation lag (the time that elapses between undertaking an investment and obtaining the output) and other features of investment to explain why such shocks would produce a cycle. A decade later, in *Banking Policy and the Price Level* (1926), his emphasis shifted. Though he did not abandon the idea that inventions caused fluctuations in economic activity, he switched to arguing that, because of monetary factors, cyclical fluctuations were much larger than they needed to be. Suitable banking policy could mitigate this, but, unlike the Austrians, he did not believe that this could completely stabilize the economy.

Pigou's work is revealing because it illustrates the way in which a major British economist reacted to the persistence of high unemployment during the 1920s. He published a theory of the business cycle, first in *Wealth and Welfare* (1912) and later in *Industrial Fluctuations* (1927). Like several of his contemporaries, he emphasized the importance of entrepreneurs' expectations of profit, and, like Hawtrey, he stressed the role of demand. If demand were sufficiently low, there might be no positive wage rate at which entrepreneurs would wish to employ the whole labour force. However, in discussing the cycle, Pigou was thinking primarily of cycles experienced before 1914. He did not think of himself as explaining the unemployment experience of the 1920s and 1930s, for which a different approach was required. To explain this, he focused much more on wages and the labour market, publishing *The Theory of Employment* in 1933. This was very Marshallian in discussing the problem in terms of supply and demand for labour.

Pigou was also important for his encouragement of Frank Ramsey, a philosopher and mathematician with a keen interest in economics who became an important figure in Cambridge from his arrival as an undergraduate until his death, aged twenty-six, in 1930. His reputation in economics is based on two articles, both published in the *Economic Journal*, edited by Keynes, who took a close interest in both projects, on optimal taxation and on lifetime savings. In both articles he was using his mathematical skills to tackle problems relating to utility maximization using methods that became widely used only in the 1960s and 1970s. The problem of optimal taxation, suggested to him by Pigou, was to determine rates of taxation on different commodities that would minimize the overall loss of utility resulting from raising a given amount of revenue. He derived a rule that related the optimal tax rate on a commodity to the responsiveness of demand for that commodity to changes in its price. The other article concerned the choice between using income to support current consumption and investing resources in order to increase consumption in the future. Ramsey derived a formula for the optimal rate of consumption given assumptions about how society valued current and future consumption. After the 1970s, when economists paid much more attention to problems of intertemporal optimization, Ramsey's equation became a component of many economic models.

However, the significance of Ramsey here is that he exerted a significant influence on Keynes, who was also a mathematician with passions for philosophy and economics. Ramsey persuaded Keynes to abandon the theory of probability on which his early reputation in Cambridge rested, resulting in the move to the treatment of uncertainty on which his arguments in the *General Theory* were later based.

In the early 1920s, Keynes was an orthodox Marshallian. He had achieved celebrity status in 1919 when he resigned from the Treasury team at the Versailles peace conference to write his bestselling book *The Economic Consequences of the Peace*. This provided a devastating critique of the peace treaty and of the way in which the negotiations were conducted, even though he shared responsibility for the outcome. He argued that it was immoral for the allies to demand high reparations payments from Germany, and that Germany would not be able to pay. Then, in 1923, he turned his attention to monetary policy and the cycle in his *Tract on Monetary Reform*, focusing on the decision to return to the gold standard at the pre-war exchange rate. He thought this a mistake, in part because the rate was too high, making British industry uncompetitive, causing unemployment.

However, although this work was very creative, his analytical framework was Marshall's version of the quantity theory. In common with his Cambridge colleagues, he emphasized the role of expectations. Because the demand for cash balances (the key element in Marshall's quantity theory) depended on expectations about the future, it was liable to change at any time. In the absence of suitable changes in the money supply, the result would be fluctuations in the price level. Strict proportionality of the price level to the money supply was true only in the long run. Referring to the notion that doubling the money supply would double the price level, Keynes argued:

> Now 'in the long run' this is probably true. But this *long run* is a misleading guide to current affairs. *In the long run* we are all dead. Economists set themselves too easy, too useless a task if in tempestuous seasons they can only tell us that when the storm is long past the ocean is flat again.[2]

There were also disturbances caused by changes in foreign prices, which were linked to British prices via the exchange rate.

This posed a dilemma for the monetary authorities. If they stabilized the domestic price level (increasing the supply of money when demand for it rose, and contracting it when demand fell), the result might be changes in the exchange rate. Alternatively, if they chose to stabilize the exchange rate (as Britain was then doing by trying to return to the gold standard) the result would be instability of domestic prices. Keynes argued two things. The first was that the evils of falling prices were worse than the evils of either rising prices or changing exchange rates. In the context of the early 1920s, when prices were being pushed downward as the government sought to raise the exchange rate to its pre-war value, this led Keynes to oppose returning to the gold standard. The second was that the authorities had to make a decision about the exchange rate: it was necessary for them to recognize that the economy had to be managed and that they could not claim that the price level was determined by forces beyond their control:

> In truth, the gold standard is already a barbarous relic. All of us . . . are now primarily interested in preserving the stability of business, prices and employment, and are not likely, when the choice is forced on us, deliberately to sacrifice these to the outworn dogma . . . of £3. 17s. 10½d. per ounce [the pre-war exchange rate in terms of gold, set by Newton]. Advocates of the ancient standard do not observe how remote it now is from the spirit and the requirements of the age. A regulated non-metallic standard has slipped in un-noticed. *It exists.* Whilst the economists dozed, the academic dream of a hundred years, doffing its cap and gown, clad in paper rags, has crept into the world by means of the bad fairies – always so much more potent than the good – the wicked ministers of finance.[3]

He developed this idea, that policymakers had to take conscious decisions about managing the economy, in 'The end of laissez faire' (1926), a pamphlet that was political as much as economic. His main argument there was that the state had to do things that would otherwise not get done at all, and that one of those was the regulation of the relation between saving and investment.

During the 1920s Keynes worked closely with Robertson and other Cambridge economists on problems of money and the cycle, and in 1930 he published *A Treatise on Money*, intended to be his definitive treatment of the problem. The core of his analysis was Wicksellian. He effectively defined saving as the amount that people planned to save out of the income they expected to receive, which meant that saving would equal investment only if 'windfall profits' (profits over and above the normal level of profits necessary to keep firms in business) were zero. He then used the relationship between saving and investment to analyse the impact of monetary policy on the level of activity. For example, a low interest rate would cause a rise in investment and a fall in saving. This would raise prices and windfall profits, causing firms to increase production. Conversely, if the interest rate rose, investment would be less than saving, windfall profits would become negative, the price level would fall, and output would contract. As with his previous work, he emphasized the role of expectations in this process. The link between money and interest rates would depend on the level of 'bearishness' – or the degree to which people were worried about the future. If bearishness were high, for example, people would want to hold more money as a hedge against future uncertainty, with the result that an increase in the money supply would be needed to prevent interest rates from rising.

Keynes was to abandon the Wicksellian theoretical framework of the *Treatise on Money* almost as soon as it was published, but the book is significant because it provides the context for his only public debate with Hayek. Hayek reviewed the *Treatise* very critically, and in his reply Keynes criticized Hayek's recent book, *Prices and Production*, equally harshly. Their theories both drew on Wicksell, but because they developed his ideas in different ways, they reached diametrically opposed conclusions about the role of monetary policy. Hayek attached great importance to the damaging effects of artificially low interest rates on the structure of production, an argument that Keynes did not understand and with which he had little patience. They completely failed to understand each other. The debate ended when Keynes, in response to criticisms of the *Treatise* by some of his younger Cambridge colleagues, became dissatisfied with his own book and decided not to continue defending it.

THE AMERICAN TRADITION

For reasons mentioned earlier, there arose a distinctive American tradition in monetary economics. The 1920s were a time of immense prosperity, and the Federal Reserve System was only beginning to work out how it should conduct its operations. The result was that, unlike in Europe, American economists paid great attention to the question of designing rules to govern the conduct of monetary policy. However, although there was widespread support for using monetary and fiscal expansion to combat the depression after 1929, there was no consensus on any underlying theory. There were many different views on how to respond to the depression. In the words of a recent commentator:

> It is difficult to think of any explanation for the event itself [the Great Depression], or any policy position regarding how to cope with it, that did not have its adherents. Moreover, virtually every theme appearing in the European debates ... found an echo somewhere in American discussions.[4]

The variety of ideas discussed means that it is possible to do no more than outline a few of them.

The most prominent exponent of the quantity theory throughout this period was Irving Fisher. He expressed great scepticism about the existence of anything that deserved to be termed a business cycle. Prices fluctuated, which meant that sometimes they would be high and sometimes low (he used the phrase 'the dance of the dollar'). That was not enough to make a cycle, which implied a regular pattern of cause and effect. What was needed was to stabilize prices, which was why he was active in organizing the Stable Money League in 1921 (which subsequently developed into the National Monetary Association and the Stable Money Association). He was also influential, during the 1920s, in promoting legislation to require the Federal Reserve System to use all its powers to promote a stable price level. Consistent with this, in the early 1930s he argued for a series of schemes to raise the price level, thereby helping to restore stability. He continued to argue that the idea of a cycle was a myth, but he produced several theories that might explain how a recession could be so severe. The most prominent was his debt-deflation theory. According to this, falling prices raised the real value of debts, forcing debtors to cut back on their spending, which forced prices still lower, worsening the situation.

At the other extreme were those who argued that there was no link between monetary policy and the price level, justifying this with a version of the real-bills doctrine. They argued that prices normally changed for non-monetary reasons, and that, if the money supply was not allowed to expand to accommodate this, the velocity of circulation would rise instead. Provided the banking system lent money only for proper commercial transactions, the result would not be inflationary. When the Great Crash came, such economists argued that credit had been overextended (a view not unlike that of the Austrians) and that no useful purpose would be served by monetary expansion. Thus Benjamin Anderson (1886–1949) wrote, 'it is definitely undesirable that we should employ this costly [cheap money] method of buying temporary prosperity again. The world's business is not a moribund invalid that needs galvanizing by an artificial stimulant.'[5]

Austrian views were represented in America, but few economists took them up. Gottfried Haberler (1900–1997), who arrived from Europe in 1931, used Hayekian arguments about capital to explain why the Depression was more than a monetary phenomenon and would last a long time. Schumpeter, who went to Harvard in 1932, argued that the Depression was so severe because it marked the coincidence of a number of cycles, all of different length. There was the Kondratiev long cycle (around forty years long), the Juglar cycle (around ten years long) and the Mitchell-Persons short cycle (around forty months long). These were cycles for which previous economists claimed to have found statistical evidence, and all of them turned down in 1930–31. This perspective was shared by Alvin Hansen (1887–1975), an economist from the Midwest who moved to Harvard in 1937. Hansen added the hypothesis that this coincidence of the three cycles came on top of a long-term decline in prices caused by a world shortage of gold and an accumulation of gold stocks in France and the United States. Both Schumpeter and Hansen were sceptical about the possibility of using monetary expansion to get out of the Depression. The Depression might be painful, but it paved the way for improved production methods and higher standards of living.

Another strongly anti-quantity-theory position was that of the underconsumptionists, most prominent of whom were William Truffant Foster (1879–1950) and Waddil Catchings (1879–1967). Foster and Catchings argued that monetary expansion would stimulate activity only if it stimulated consumers' spending. Any other form of monetary expansion, even if linked to rises in government spending, would have no effect. J. A. Hobson (1858–1940), a British economist who had first put forward underconsumptionist theories in 1889, and who had coined the term 'unemployment' in 1896, was widely read in the United States.

Other economists adopted a more moderate position. One of the most influential of these was Allyn Young (who had many students while at Harvard), who was in turn strongly influenced by Hawtrey's *Currency and Credit*. Young argued that monetary policy was needed to stabilize business, but that this required the establishing of sound traditions, not the imposition of a simple rule such as Fisher and others were proposing. He also supported the use of government spending to alleviate the cycle. He was able to show, through a detailed statistical analysis, that bank reserve ratios fluctuated greatly with seasonal movements of funds between New York and the rest of the country. Following Hawtrey, he emphasized the instability of credit – something that a strict quantity theorist would not accept. Young died in 1929, but one of his students, Laughlin Currie (1902–93), applied Hawtrey's theory to the Depression, finding evidence that monetary factors were important. He used statistics on the behaviour of a range of measures of the money supply to argue that the Federal Reserve System could have prevented much of the collapse had it chosen to do so. The claim that it was powerless was not borne out by the evidence.

During this period the economist most firmly associated with empirical research on the business cycle was Wesley Clair Mitchell, director of the National Bureau of Economic Research. He popularized the notion of the cycle, and sought to document, statistically, exactly what happened during cycles. He was sceptical about theories that sought to explain the cycle in terms of a single cause, preferring to analyse individual cycles in detail. However, he was convinced that its causes lay in what Veblen had called the 'pecuniary' aspects of economic life. The cycle could not be divorced from its monetary aspects, though these were not all that mattered. When the Depression came in 1929, Mitchell argued that the only puzzle was why it was so severe and so prolonged. His explanation was that several shocks happened to occur on top of each other: depression in agriculture, the after-effects of excessive stock-market speculation, political unrest, increased tariff barriers and so on. The effects of these shocks were exacerbated by changes that reduced the powers of the economic system to stabilize itself. People were buying more semi-durable goods (such as cars and electrical appliances), with the result that if incomes fell they could more easily reduce their spending. There was less self-sufficiency in agriculture, and large firms were increasingly reluctant to cut prices when demand fell. Mitchell's response to this was that laissez-faire was proving inadequate and that greater national planning was required. However, beyond supporting public-works policies and the dissemination of information and forecasts, he did not work out plans in any detail.

In the early 1930s a number of economists, with very different theoretical views, endorsed the idea of requiring the banking system to hold 100 per cent reserves. Supporters of such a rule included Currie, Paul Douglas (1892–1976), Fisher, and Henry Simons (1899–1946), all for different reasons. Currie supported the rule on the grounds that, if the government issued the entire money supply, this would provide the government with the best possible control over it. It would be easy to expand or contract the money supply as much as was required. In contrast, Simons supported it because he regarded 'managed currency without definite, stable, legislative rules [as] one of the most dangerous forms of "planning"'. In the 'Chicago plan' in 1933, Simons argued for 100 per cent reserves combined with a constant growth rate of the money supply and a balanced-budget rule for government spending. This, he believed, would stabilize prices and restrain government spending. However, by 1936 he had come round to the view that this rule would merely lead to variability in the amount of 'near monies' (assets that do not count as money but which can be used instead of money). As a result, he moved towards setting price stability as the goal of policy.

The history of the support for 100 per cent money illustrates the way in which, even though there was enormous diversity within American monetary economics at this time, there were also great overlaps between the views held by different groups. Simons moved from a money-growth rule towards Fisher's price-stability rule. At the same time, Fisher took up the Chicago position of 100 per cent money. Though the case for 100 per cent money was based on a monetary interpretation of the Great Depression, later associated with Simons and his fellow Chicago economist Milton Friedman (p. 261), this interpretation originated with Currie. He worked within the theoretical framework laid down by Hawtrey and developed by Young, his teacher at Harvard. Other overlaps include the views on monetary policy shared with Austrian economists and the advocates of the real-bills doctrine.

KEYNES'S GENERAL THEORY

In his early work, in the 1920s and before, Keynes was a quantity theorist in the Marshallian tradition. In *A Treatise on Money* he moved away from this to a perspective closer to Wicksell's, focusing on the links between money, saving, investment and the level of spending. However, in that book, his approach remained traditional in that he still considered the price level to be central to the whole process. Changes in spending led to changes in prices and profits, thereby inducing businesses to change their production plans. This raised a technical problem at the heart of his analysis. He had developed a theory to explain changes in prices and profits on the assumption that output did not change, and had then used that theory to explain why output would change. This was unsatisfactory, and soon after the book was published he began to rethink the theory with the help of younger colleagues at Cambridge – the so-called 'Circus', which included, inter alia, Richard Kahn (1905–89), Joan Robinson (1903–83) and Austin Robinson (1897–1993). The results of this process of rethinking were eventually published in 1936 as *The General Theory of Employment, Interest and Money*, the book on which Keynes's subsequent reputation rests.

Perhaps the crucial transition made in the *General Theory* was towards thinking in terms of an economy where the first thing to change in response to a change in demand was not prices but sales. If demand fell, firms would find that their sales had fallen, and that their inventories of unsold goods were higher than they had anticipated. They would then adjust their production plans, even if prices had not changed. One stimulus to this way of thinking came as a result of discussions on employment policy in the 1920s and early 1930s. It was commonly agreed that public-works expenditure could raise employment, but there was no basis for working out by how much employment would rise. This problem was tackled by Kahn, who in an article published in 1931 put forward the idea of the multiplier. (This idea was also found in Hawtrey's work in the 1920s, though not named as such.) The question Kahn asked was the following. If an additional worker is employed on a public-works scheme, and that worker buys goods that need to be produced by other workers, how many additional workers will end up being employed? He found that the mathematics of the problem yielded a clear answer, and that it depended on how much of the newly generated income was spent on consumption goods. In a subsequent article a Danish economist, Jens Warming (1873–1939), framed this in terms of national income, pointing out that if a quarter of income were saved, a rise in investment of 100 million would lead to a rise in income of 400 million. Saving would rise by 100 million – exactly enough to finance the initial increase in investment. The size of the multiplier (the ratio of the rise in income to the initial investment) was determined by the fraction of income saved.

The multiplier provided Keynes with a link between investment and the level of demand in the economy. He based this link on the notion of what he called the 'fundamental psychological law' that, when someone's income rises, their consumption rises, though by less than the full amount. He labelled the ratio of the rise in consumption to the rise in income the 'propensity to consume'. He then needed a theory of investment. He adopted an approach similar to Fisher's, arguing that the level of investment depended on the relationship between the expected return on investment (which he termed the 'marginal efficiency of investment') and the rate of interest. For a given marginal efficiency of investment, a rise in the interest rate would cause a fall in investment, and vice versa. However, although he talked of a negative relationship between investment and the interest rate, Keynes did not consider it to be a stable relationship. He placed great emphasis on the role of expectations and the importance of uncertainty in influencing investment.

He analysed the relationship between uncertainty and investment through arguing that the marginal efficiency of capital depended on what he called 'the state of long-term expectation'. This covered all the factors that were relevant to deciding the profitability of an investment, including the strength of consumer demand, likely change in consumers' tastes, changes in costs, and changes in the types of capital good available. All these had to be evaluated over the entire lifetime of the investment, and were matters about which investors knew little.

> The outstanding fact is the extreme precariousness of the basis of knowledge on which our estimates of prospective yield have to be made. Our knowledge of the factors which will govern the yield of an investment some years hence is usually very slight and often negligible. If we speak frankly, we have to admit that our basis of knowledge for estimating the yield ten years hence of a railway, a copper mine, a textile factory, the goodwill of a patent medicine, an Atlantic liner, a building in the City of London amounts to little and sometimes to nothing.[6]

Faced with this uncertainty, investment would depend not on rational calculation of future returns, but on the state of confidence. In practice, Keynes argued, expectations are governed by conventions – in particular the convention that 'the existing state of affairs will continue indefinitely, except in so far as we have specific reasons to expect a change'.[7] Because expectations are based on conventions, they have the potential to change dramatically in response to apparently minor changes in the news. The situation is made worse in a world, such as Keynes saw around him, where investment policy is dominated by professional speculators. Such people are not trying to make the best long-term decisions but are concerned with working out how the stock market will move, which means they are forever trying to guess how other people will react to news. The result is great instability.

The other determinant of investment is the rate of interest. To explain this, Keynes introduced the idea that money is required not only to finance transactions in goods and services but also as a store of value. People may hold money because they are uncertain about the future and wish to be able to postpone their spending decisions, or because they expect holding money to yield a better return than investing in other financial assets. (If the price of bonds or shares falls, the return may be negative – less than the return from holding money.) This is the theory of liquidity preference, which led Keynes to argue that the demand for money would depend on the rate of interest. He even claimed that, under some circumstances, the demand for money might be so sensitive to the rate of interest that it would be impossible for the monetary authorities to lower the rate of interest by increasing the money supply – the liquidity trap.

When put together, these three components – the propensity to consume, the marginal efficiency of investment, and liquidity preference – form a theory of output and employment that can be used to work out how policy changes will affect output and employment. For example, given liquidity preference, a rise in the money supply will cause a fall in the rate of interest. Given the state of long-term expectations, this will cause a rise in investment and hence a rise in output and employment. It is a theory in which output is determined by the level of effective demand, independently of the quantity of goods and services that businesses wish to supply.

Keynes's strategy in developing his theory was to take the wage paid to workers as given. Then, towards the end of the book he considered what would happen if wages were to change, and advanced a variety of arguments about why changes in wage rates would have no effect on employment. Cutting wages would not raise employment unless doing so raised the level of effective demand. He went through all the ways this might happen, concluding that cutting wages was as likely to reduce unemployment as to increase it.

THE KEYNESIAN REVOLUTION

Keynes presented his book as an assault on an orthodoxy – the 'classical' theory that, he claimed, had dominated the subject for a hundred years, since the time of Ricardo. According to this orthodoxy, the level of employment was determined by supply and demand for labour and, if there were unemployment, it must be because wages were too high. The 'classical' cure was therefore to cut wages. If wages were flexible, the only unemployment would be frictional (associated with turnover in the labour market – if someone loses their job, they will be temporarily unemployed until they have found a new one) or structural (caused, for example, by the decline of certain industries). The classical theory, he claimed, was also characterized by Say's Law, according to which there could be no general shortage of aggregate demand. Keynes went on to argue that the classical theory was a special case, and that his own theory was more general. 'Moreover,' he wrote, 'the characteristics of the special case assumed by the classical theory happen not to be those of the economic society in which we actually live, with the result that its teaching is misleading and disastrous if we attempt to apply it to the facts of experience.'[8]

This dramatic claim, together with Keynes's celebrity status, help explain why the *General Theory* made such an enormous impact on its publication. It appealed in particular to young economists who relished the prospect of overthrowing the orthodoxy supported by their elders. Paul Samuelson (see below) compared Keynesian economics to a disease that infected everyone under the age of forty, but to which almost everyone over forty was immune. In so far as the reaction of the older generation was generally critical, Samuelson's point appears justified. Older economists found fault with Keynes's logic and took issue with his claim to be revolutionizing the subject. There was, however, much more to the Keynesian revolution than this.

For economists who read the *General Theory* for the first time in the late 1930s or the early 1940s, it was a difficult book. For some of the older generation, the reason lay in the mathematics – by the standards of the time, it was a mathematical book. There were, however, deeper reasons. The first was that Keynes spoke of a classical orthodoxy, but, as will not be surprising in view of the wide range of theories surveyed in this chapter, it was not clear just what that classical orthodoxy was. The second difficulty was that the *General Theory* contained many lines of argument, and it was not clear which ones mattered and which could be left to one side. This was a problem not only for non-economist reviewers, many of whom said that they awaited the judgement of Keynes's professional peers, but also for economists who read the book. Even economists had to work hard to make sense of what Keynes was saying.

Some economists tried to make sense of Keynes's central argument by translating it into a system of equations. The first was David Champernowne (1912–2000), who, in an article published in 1936, within months of the *General Theory*, reduced Keynes's system to three equations. Over the next few months, other economists worked with similar sets of equations, trying to use these to explain what Keynes was saying. The most influential of these was John Hicks (1904–89). Hicks's equations were very similar to those developed by Champernowne and others, but he managed to reduce Keynesian economics to a single, simple diagram showing relationships between output and interest rate. One curve (labelled LM in Fig. 5) showed combinations of output and the rate of interest that gave equilibrium in the money market; the other (labelled IS) showed combinations that made savings equal to investment. Equilibrium output is where the two curves intersect. Hicks then argued that, if the LM curve were fairly flat, Keynes was right – increases in government spending would shift the IS curve to the right, and output would rise. On the other hand, if the LM curve were vertical, shifts in the IS curve caused by changes in government spending would simply change the rate of interest, leaving output unaffected. Hicks provided a solution to the puzzle about what the differences between Keynes and the classics really were. His diagram also provided a valuable teaching tool, for students could learn how to manipulate the IS and LM curves to show the effects of a wide range of policy changes. The maze of pre-Keynesian business-cycle theory was apparently simplified into a single diagram.

The myth of the Keynesian revolution, which Keynes himself propagated, is that Keynes overthrew something called 'classical economics' and that his theory involved a complete break with the past: that he was the first to show why unemployment could arise and how changes in government spending and taxation could reduce it. This, however, is a serious distortion of what happened. His theory was novel but, as we have seen, the literature of the 1920s and 1930s contained a wide range of approaches to macroeconomic questions by economists working in many countries, notably the United States, Britain and Sweden. That literature paid attention to problems of expectations – the relation

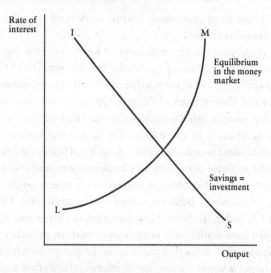

Fig. 5 Curves showing relationships between output and interest rate

between saving, investment and effective demand – and much of it supported the idea that both monetary policy and control of government spending might be needed to alleviate unemployment. The *General Theory* arose out of that literature and did not mark a complete break with what went before it. This resolves the puzzle of how, if the *General Theory* was as revolutionary as the myth suggests, Keynesian policies were being employed in several countries long before the book was published. Roosevelt's New Deal, for example, began in 1932.

THE TRANSITION FROM INTERWAR
BUSINESS CYCLE THEORY
TO POST-SECOND WORLD WAR
MACROECONOMICS

The main reason why post-war macroeconomics was so different from pre-war monetary economics and business-cycle theory is that, from the late 1930s, macroeconomics began to be based, as never before, on working out the properties of clearly defined mathematical models. These include the mathematical models of Keynesian economics associated with Hicks and Champernowne, as well as the dynamic business-cycle models of Ragnar Frisch and Jan Tinbergen (pp. 276–8). This strategy of mathematical modelling affected not just macroeconomics, but also other branches of economics. The reason why Keynesian economics came to dominate macroeconomics so completely is that it provided a framework that could be translated into a mathematical model that proved extremely versatile. In this sense, therefore, the outcome of the Keynesian revolution was the IS–LM model.[9]

However, two important qualifications need to be made. The first is that, though it is arguable that the IS–LM model captures the central theoretical core of the *General Theory*, much is left out. This is an inevitable consequence of formalizing a theory. In the case of the *General Theory*, what was left out included Keynes's discussions of dynamics and of expectations. As a result, there are many economists who argue that Keynes's most important insights were lost, and that the IS–LM model represents a 'bastard' Keynesianism, to use Joan Robinson's phrase. If we make the comparison between post-war economics and the entire business-cycle literature of the 1920s and 1930s, the amount that was forgotten appears even greater. One reason for this may be that, by the 1960s, many economists had (mistakenly) come to believe that Keynesian macroeconomic policies had made the business cycle a thing of the past.

The second, and perhaps more important, qualification is that, despite the triumph of Keynesianism (at least in its IS–LM version), the earlier traditions did not die out completely, even though they became marginalized. Hayek, for example, dropped out of mainstream economics, moving into what is usually considered political philosophy. In the 1970s, however, there was a resurgence of interest in his ideas. More significantly, the institutionalist tradition represented by Mitchell left an influential legacy. The monetary economics of Milton Friedman (1912–2006), one of the major figures in economics after the Second World War, lies squarely in the tradition established by Mitchell at the National Bureau, emphasizing the importance of detailed statistical work of a type very different from much modern econometrics. Friedman and Schwarz's influential *Monetary History of the United States, 1867–1960* (1963) (pp. 373–4) is very much in Mitchell's style, and their explanation of the Great Depression is similar to that offered by Currie in the early 1930s. It can also be argued that the 'Chicago' view of monetary policy, with which Friedman has been so strongly associated, goes back via Simons to Currie, and through him to Hawtrey. Behind all this, however, the influence of Fisher, with his analysis of the rate of interest as the price linking the present and the future, is pervasive.

However, perhaps the best illustration of how post-war macroeconomics was not the creation of Keynes alone is the way Keynesian ideas were taken up by Hansen. By the 1930s, Hansen was established as a business-cycle theorist, working in the institutionalist tradition. He attached great importance to a concept called the acceleration principle. This is based on the idea that, in order to increase output, more capital is needed. From this it can be deduced that the level of investment in new capital will be proportional to the increase in output. He also attached great importance to long-term, structural change in the American economy. In the late nineteenth century, population growth and the westward expansion of the United States and the need for railroad construction had created a demand for new investment. In the early twentieth century, investment was needed because of the spread of electricity and the invention of automobiles.

Hansen believed that by the 1930s these factors stimulating investment had disappeared – the frontier was closed, there were no innovations comparable with electricity and automobiles, and population growth had fallen. The resulting tendency towards long-term (secular) stagnation helped explain why the Great Depression was so severe. When he read Keynes's *General Theory*, Hansen realized that Keynes's theory of the multiplier, which could be used to explain consumption, could be grafted on to his own theory, which explained investment. Putting the multiplier together with the acceleration principle, he constructed a theory of the business cycle. The result was a theory that looked Keynesian in that the multiplier and aggregate demand determined output and employment, but in which the explanation of investment owed much more to the American institutionalist tradition. The result was a distinctively American version of Keynesian economics in which, although many of the equations could be traced back to Keynes, the interpretation placed on them was different. This was the version of Keynesian economics that became established in the most influential post-war textbooks, notably Samuelson's *Economics* (p. 380).

12
Quantitative Economics

THE MATHEMATIZATION OF ECONOMICS

Between the 1930s and the 1970s economics became mathematized in the sense that it became the normal practice for economists to develop their arguments and to present their results, at least to each other, using mathematics. This usually involved geometry (particularly important in teaching) and algebra (particularly differential calculus and matrix algebra). In the 1930s only a small minority of articles published in the leading academic journals used mathematics, whereas by the 1970s it was unusual to find influential articles that did not. Though the speed of the change varied from one field to another, it affected the whole of the discipline – theoretical as well as applied work.

Mathematics is used in two ways in economics. One is as a tool of theoretical research. Algebra, geometry and even numerical examples enable economists to deduce conclusions that they might otherwise not see, and to do so with greater rigour than if they had used only verbal reasoning. This use of mathematics has a long history. Quesnay and Ricardo made such extensive use of numerical examples in developing their theories that they were criticized in much the same way that the use of mathematics in present-day economics is criticized – critics argued that mathematics rendered their arguments incomprehensible to outsiders. Marx also made extensive use of numerical examples. The use of algebra goes back at least to the beginning of the nineteenth century, though in retrospect the most significant development was the use of differential calculus by Thünen (1826) and Cournot (1838). With the work of Jevons, Walras and their turn-of-the-century followers – notably Fisher – the use of mathematics, in particular calculus and simultaneous equations, was clearly established as an important method of theoretical inquiry.

The second use of mathematics – with which this chapter is concerned – is as a tool in empirical research. This involves generalizing from observations (induction) and testing economic theories using statistical data about the real world. Given that calculating averages or ratios is a mathematical technique, this has a very long history. A precondition for the use of such methods is the availability of statistics. This has meant that the scope for such work increased dramatically with the extensive collection of such data early in the nineteenth century by economists and statisticians such as McCulloch, Tooke and William Newmarch (1820–82), Tooke's collaborator on his *History of Prices* (1838–57). More formal statistical techniques, including correlation and regression analysis, were developed in the late nineteenth century by Francis Galton (1822–1911), Karl Pearson (1857–1936) and Edgeworth. Jevons had speculated that it might one day be possible to calculate demand curves using statistical data, and early in the twentieth century several economists tried to do this, in both Europe and the United States. In the period before the First World War, economists began to address the problem of how to choose between the different curves that might be fitted to the data.

Despite these long histories of the use of mathematics in deductive and inductive arguments, the mathematization of economics since the 1930s represents a major departure in the subject. The reason is that it has led to a profound change in the way in which the subject has been conceived. Economics came to be structured not around a set of real-world problems, but around a set of theoretical techniques and empirical techniques. Theoretical techniques involve not just mathematical tools such as constrained optimization or matrix algebra but also received assumptions about how one represents the behaviour of individuals or organizations so that it can be analysed using standard methods. Similarly, empirical techniques involve assumptions about how one relates theoretical concepts to empirical data as well as methods for generating and analysing statistical data.

This new approach can be summed up by saying that economists now talk about 'models'. These may be theoretical models, describing abstract worlds constructed to focus on specific problems or mechanisms, or they may be empirical models, providing a numerical depiction of a specific real-world situation. For example, a model of the market for ice cream might enable one to predict how much higher sales will be on hot, sunny days than on days when it is cold and wet, or what the effect of imposing a sales tax will be. A model of the US economy might predict what would happen to unemployment and inflation if the Federal Reserve raises its interest rate by a percentage point. Where a theoretical model will generate only qualitative predictions – that variables will go up or down, or change in relation to other variables – empirical models will generate predictions that are numerical: that, for example, a one percentage point rise in interest rates will lead to a three percentage point rise in the unemployment rate.

This move towards modelling has had profound effects on the structure of the discipline. The subject has come to be considered to comprise a 'core' of theory (both economic theory and econometric techniques) surrounded by fields in which that theory is applied. Theory has been separated from applications, and, at the same time, theoretical and empirical research have become separated. The same individuals frequently engage in both (mathematical skills are highly transferable), but these are nonetheless separate enterprises. Because this move towards modelling generates technical problems that need to be solved, some research has been driven by an agenda internal to the discipline, even where this has not helped solve any real-world problems. This has led some critics to argue that economics has become divorced from reality, a charge fiercely denied by others.

THE REVOLUTION IN NATIONAL-INCOME ACCOUNTING

One of the most important developments in the 1930s and 1940s was the large-scale, systematic collection of economic statistics and the creation of national accounts. Without accurate national accounts, we do not know how much output is being produced or how that output is being used. In the 1920s, comprehensive national-income accounts did not exist for any country. The pioneering attempts by people such as Petty and King had involved inspired guesses as much as detailed evidence, and were not based on any systematic conceptual framework. Even in the nineteenth and early twentieth centuries, when estimates of national income were made in several countries, including the United States and Britain, gaps in the data were so wide that detailed accounts were impossible. In the United States, the most comprehensive attempt was *The Wealth and Income of the People of the United States* (1915) by Willford I. King (1880–1962), a student of Irving Fisher's. King showed that national income had trebled in sixty years, and that the share of wages and salaries in total income had risen from 36 to 47 per cent. He concluded that, contrary to what socialists were claiming, the existing economic system was working well. In Britain, A. L. Bowley (1869–1957) was producing estimates based on tax data, population censuses, the 1907 census of production, and information on wages and employment. However, this work, like that being undertaken elsewhere, remained very limited in its scope.

In the interwar period, national-income statistics were constructed right across Europe. Interest in them was stimulated by the immense problems of post-war reconstruction, the enormous shifts in the relative economic power of different nations, the Depression of the 1930s, and the need to mobilize resources in anticipation of another war. During the 1930s Germany was producing annual estimates of national income with a delay of only a year. The Soviet Union constructed input–output tables (showing how much each sector of the economy purchased from every other sector) through most of the 1920s and the early 1930s. Italy and Germany had worked out a conceptual basis for national accounting that was as advanced as any in the world. By 1939, ten countries were producing official estimates of national income. However, because of the war, the countries that had most influence in the long term were Britain and the United States. Unlike these two, Germany never used national income for wartime planning, and stopped producing statistics. In complete contrast, by the 1950s, national-income statistics were being constructed by national governments and coordinated through the United Nations and estimates existed for nearly a hundred countries.

In the United States there were three strands to early work on national-income accounting. The first was that associated with the National Bureau of Economic Research (NBER), established by Mitchell in 1920. Its first project was a study of year-to-year variations in national income and the distribution of income. Published in 1921, its report provided annual estimates of national income for the period 1909–19. These were extended during the 1920s, and were supplemented in 1926 by estimates made by the Federal Trade Commission. The FTC, however, failed to continue this work. With the onset of the Depression, the federal government became involved. In June 1932 a Senate resolution proposed by Robert La Follette, senator for Wisconsin, committed the Bureau of Foreign and Domestic Commerce (BFDC) to prepare estimates of national income for 1929, 1930 and 1931.

Little was achieved in the first six months after the resolution, and in January 1933 the BFDC's work was handed to Simon Kuznets (1901–85), who had been working on national income at the NBER since 1929. At the NBER he had prepared plans for estimating national income, later summed up in a widely read article on the subject in the *Encyclopedia of the Social Sciences* (1933). Within a year, Kuznets and his team produced estimates for 1929–32. (Recognizing the importance of up-to-date statistics, they had included 1932 as well as the years required by La Follette's resolution.) Kuznets moved back to the NBER, where he worked on savings and capital accumulation, and subsequently on problems of long-term growth. The BFDC study of national income became permanent under the direction of Robert Nathan (1908–2001). The original estimates were revised and extended, and new series were produced (for example, monthly figures were produced in 1938).

At this time, the very definition of national income was controversial. Kuznets and his team published two estimates: 'national income produced', which referred to the net product of the whole economy, and 'national income received', which covered payments made to those who produced the net product. In order to base estimates on reliable data, they had excluded many of the then controversial items. These estimates of national income covered only the market economy (goods that were bought and sold), and goods were valued at market prices. The basic distinction underlying Kuznets's framework was between consumers' outlay and capital formation.

At the same time, Clark Warburton (1896–1979), at the Brookings Institution, produced estimates of gross national product (GNP). This was defined as the sum of final products that emerge from the production and marketing processes and are passed on to consumers and businesses (i.e. excluding products that are remanufactured to make other products). This was much larger than Kuznets's figure for national income, because it also included capital goods purchased to replace ones that had been worn out, government services to consumers, and government purchases of capital goods. Warburton argued that GNP minus depreciation was the correct way to measure the resources available to be spent. He produced, for the first time, evidence that spending on capital goods was more erratic than spending on consumers' goods. Economists had long been aware of this, but had previously had only indirect evidence.

The third strand in American work on national income was the work associated with Lauchlin Currie. In 1934–5 he began calculating the 'pump-priming deficit'. This was based on the idea that, for the private sector to generate enough demand for goods to cure unemployment, the government had to 'prime the pump' by increasing its own spending. Currie and his colleagues focused on the contribution of each sector to national buying power – the difference between each sector's spending and its income. A positive contribution by the government (i.e. a deficit) was needed to offset net saving by other sectors.

In Britain, the calculation of national-income statistics was the work of a small number of scholars with no government assistance throughout the interwar period. Of particular importance was Colin Clark (1905–89). In 1932 Clark used the concept of gross national product and estimated the main components of aggregate demand (consumption, investment and government spending). This work increased in importance after the publication of Keynes's *General Theory* (1936), and soon after its publication Clark estimated the value of the multiplier (he thought it was about two, a figure Keynes thought plausible). His main work was *National Income and Outlay* (1937). One of his followers has written of this book that it 'restored the vision of the political arithmeticians [Petty and Davenant] ... [It] brought together estimates of income, output, consumers' expenditure, government revenue and expenditure, capital formation, saving, foreign trade and the balance of payments. Although he did not set his figures in an accounting framework it is clear that they came fairly close to consistency.'[1]

Clark's work was not supported by the government. (When he had been appointed to the secretariat of the Economic Advisory Council in 1930, the Treasury had even refused to buy him an adding machine.) Questions of income distribution were too sensitive for the government to want to publish figures. Industrialists did not want figures for profits revealed. The government did calculate national-income figures for 1929, but denied their existence because the estimates of wages were lower than those already available. Official involvement in national-income accounting did not begin until the Second World War. Keynes used Clark's figures in *How to Pay for the War* (1940).

In the summer of 1940 Richard Stone (1913–91) joined James Meade (1907–94) in the Central Economic Information Service of the War Cabinet. During the rest of the year, encouraged and supported by Keynes, they constructed a set of national accounts for 1938 and 1940 that was published in a White Paper accompanying the Budget of 1941. The lack of resources available to them is illustrated by a story about their cooperation. They started with Meade (the senior partner) reading numbers which Stone punched into their mechanical calculator, but soon discovered that it was more efficient for their roles to be reversed. Though the Chancellor of the Exchequer said that the publication of their figures would not set a precedent, estimates were from then on published annually.

During the Second World War, estimates of national income were transformed into systems of national accounts in which different accounts were connected. Its position in the war effort, together with the work of Kuznets and Nathan at the War Production Board, ensured that the United States was the dominant country in this process.

However, the system that was eventually adopted owed much to British work. In 1940 Hicks introduced the equation that has become basic to national-income accounting: $GNP = C + I + G$ (income equals consumption plus investment plus government expenditure on goods and services). He was also responsible for the distinction between market prices and factor cost (market prices less indirect taxes). Perhaps more important, Meade and Stone provided a firmer conceptual basis for the national accounts by presenting them as a double-entry production account for the entire economy. In one column were factor payments (national income), and in the other column expenditures (national expenditure). As with all double-entry accounts, when calculated correctly the two columns balanced.

From 1941 the United States moved away from national accounts as constructed by Kuznets and Nathan to ones constructed on Keynesian lines, using the Meade–Stone framework. This was the work of Martin Gilbert (1909–79), a former student of Kuznets's, who was chief of the National Income Division of the US Commerce Department from 1941 to 1951. One reason for this move was the rapid spread of Keynesian economics, which provided a theoretical rationale for the new system of accounts. There was no formal economic theory underlying Kuznets's categories, which derived from purely empirical considerations. The change also appeared desirable for other reasons. In wartime, when the concern was with the short-term availability of resources, it was not necessary to maintain capital, which meant that GNP was the relevant measure of output. In addition, because of the scale of government spending during the war, it was important to have a measure of income that included government expenditure. Finally, the Meade–Stone system provided a framework within which a broader range of accounts could be developed. After the war, in 1947, a League of Nations report, in which Stone played an important role, provided the framework within which several governments began to compile their accounts so that it would be possible to make cross-country comparisons. Subsequently, Stone was also involved in the work of the Organization for European Economic Cooperation and the United Nations, which in 1953 produced a standard system of national accounts.

THE ECONOMETRIC SOCIETY AND THE ORIGINS OF MODERN ECONOMETRICS

For economics to become a quantitative discipline it was not enough for data to become available; it was necessary for economists to develop techniques for analysing data. Here, a central role was played by the Econometric Society, formed in 1930, in Chicago, at the instigation of Charles Roos (1901–58), Irving Fisher and Ragnar Frisch (1895–1973). Its constitution described its aims in the following terms:

> The Econometric Society is an international society for the advancement of economic theory in its relation to statistics and mathematics ... Its main object shall be to promote studies that aim at a unification of the theoretical-quantitative and the empirical-quantitative approach to economic problems and that are penetrated by constructive and rigorous thinking similar to that which has come to dominate in the natural sciences.[2]

In commenting on this statement, Frisch emphasized that the important aspect of econometrics, as the term was used in the society, was the unification of economic theory, statistics and mathematics. Mathematics, in itself, was not sufficient.

In its early years the Econometric Society was very small. Twenty years before, Fisher had tried to generate interest in establishing such a society, but had failed. So when Roos and Frisch approached him about the possibility of forming a society he was sceptical about whether there was sufficient interest in the subject. However, he told them that he would support the idea if they could produce a list of a hundred potential members. To Fisher's surprise, they found seventy names. With some further ones added by Fisher, this provided the basis for the society.

Soon after the society was formed, it was put in touch with Alfred Cowles (1891–1984). Cowles was a businessman who had set up a forecasting agency but who had become sceptical about whether forecasters were doing any more than guessing what might happen. He therefore developed an interest in quantitative research. When he wrote a paper under the title 'Can stock market forecasters forecast?' (1933), he gave it the three-word abstract 'It is doubtful.' His evidence came from a comparison of the returns obtained from following the advice offered by sixteen financial-service providers and the performance of twenty insurance companies with the returns that would have been obtained by following random forecasts. Over the period 1928–32 there was no evidence that professional forecasts were any better than random ones. With Cowles's support, the Econometric Society was able to establish a journal, *Econometrica*, in 1933. In addition, Cowles supported the establishment, in 1932, of the Cowles Commission, a centre for mathematical and statistical research into economics. From 1939 to 1955 it was based at the University of Chicago, distinct from the economics department, after which it moved to Yale. This institute proved important in the development of econometrics.

Econometrics grew out of two distinctive traditions – one American, represented in the Econometric Society by Fisher and Roos, and the other European, represented by Frisch (a Norwegian). One strand in the American tradition was statistical analysis of money and the business cycle. Fisher and others had sought to test the quantity theory of money, seeking to find independent measures of all the four terms in the equation of exchange (money, velocity of circulation, transactions, and the price level). Mitchell, instead of finding evidence to support a particular theory of the cycle, had redefined the problem as trying to describe what went on in business cycles. This inherently quantitative programme, set out in his *Business Cycles and their Causes* (1913), was taken up by the National Bureau of Economic Research, under Mitchell's direction. It resulted in a method of calculating 'reference cycles' with which fluctuations in any series could be compared. An alternative approach was the 'business barometer' developed at Harvard by Warren Persons (1878–1937) as a method of forecasting the cycle. There was also Henry Ludwell Moore (1869–1958) at Columbia University, who sought, like Jevons, to establish a link between the business cycle and the weather. A few years later, in 1923, he switched from the weather to the movement of the planet Venus as his explanation. Moore's work is notable for the use of a wider range of statistical techniques than were employed by other economists at this time.

The other strand in the American tradition was demand analysis. Moore and Henry Schultz (1893–1938) estimated demand curves for agricultural and other goods. This work did not go very far in bringing mathematical economic theory together with statistical analysis. Fisher's dissertation had involved a mathematical analysis of consumer and demand theory, but this remained separate from his statistical work, which was on interest rates and money. Mitchell was sceptical about the value of pursuing simplified business-cycle theories that emphasized one particular cause of the cycle. For him, statistical work provided a way to integrate different theories and suggest new lines of inquiry which meant that he failed to develop a close link between theory and data. Mitchell was also sceptical about standard consumer theory. He hoped that empirical studies of consumers' behaviour would render obsolete theoretical models, in which consumers were treated as coming to the market with ready-made scales of bid and offer prices. In other words, statistical work would replace abstract theory rather than complement it. Similarly, Moore criticized standard demand curves for being static and for their *ceteris paribus* assumptions (assumptions about the variables, such as tastes and incomes, that were held constant). The result was that as long as the attitude of statisticians was one of scepticism concerning mathematical theory, this theory was unlikely to be closely integrated with statistical work. This unlikelihood was reinforced by the scepticism expressed by many economists (including Keynes and Morgenstern) about the accuracy and relevance of much statistical data.

The European tradition, which overlapped with the American at many points, including research on business cycles and demand, had different emphases. Work by a variety of authors in the late 1920s led to an awareness of some of the problems involved in applying statistical techniques, such as correlation, to time-series data. George Udny Yule (1871–1951), a student of Karl Pearson's, explored the problem of 'nonsense correlations' – seemingly strong relationships between time series that should bear no relation to each other, such as rainfall in India and skirt lengths in Paris. He argued that such correlations often did not reflect a cause common to both variables but were purely accidental. He also used experimental methods to explore the relationship between random shocks and periodic fluctuations in time series. The Russian Eugen Slutsky (1880–1948) went even further in showing that adding up random numbers (generated by the state lottery) could produce cycles that looked remarkably like the business cycle: there appeared to be regular, periodic fluctuations. Frisch also tackled the problem of time series, in a manner closer to Mitchell and Persons than to Yule or Slutsky, by trying to break down cycles into their component parts.

FRISCH, TINBERGEN AND THE COWLES COMMISSION

Slutsky and Frisch had pioneered statistical modelling of the business cycle, but the first statistical model of an entire economy was constructed by the Dutch economist Jan Tinbergen (1903–94), who came to economics after taking a doctorate in physics and spent much of his career at the Central Planning Bureau in the Netherlands. In order to understand what Tinbergen was doing with this model, it is helpful to consider the theory of the business cycle that Frisch published in 1933. He took up the idea (taken from Wicksell) that the problem of the business cycle had to be divided into two parts – the 'impulse' and 'propagation' problems. The impulse problem concerned the source of shocks to the system, which might be changes in technology, wars, or anything outside the system. The propagation problem concerned the mechanism by which the effects of such shocks were propagated through the economy. Frisch produced a model which, if left to itself with no external shocks, would produce damped oscillations – cycles that became progressively smaller, eventually dying out – but which produced regular cycles because it was subject to periodic shocks. Following Wicksell, he described this as a 'rocking-horse model'. If left to itself, the movement of a rocking horse will gradually die away, but if disturbed from time to time the horse will continue to rock. Such a model, Frisch argued, would produce the regularly occurring but uneven cycles that characterize the business cycle.

The distinction between propagation and impulse problems translated easily into the mathematical techniques that Frisch was using. The propagation mechanism depended on the values of the parameters in the equations and on the structure of the economy. In 1933 Frisch simply made plausible guesses about what these might be, though he expressed confidence that it would soon be possible to obtain such numbers using statistical techniques. The shocks were represented by the initial conditions that had to be assumed when solving the model. Using his guessed coefficients and suitable initial conditions, Frisch employed simulations to show that his model produced cycles that looked realistic.

In 1936 Tinbergen produced a model of the Dutch economy. This went significantly beyond Frisch's model in two respects. The structure of the Dutch economy was described in sixteen equations plus sufficient accounting identities to determine all of its thirty-one variables. The variables it explained included prices, physical quantities, incomes and levels of spending. It was therefore much more detailed than Frisch's model, which contained only three variables (production of consumption goods, new capital goods started, and production of capital goods carried over from previous periods). Most important, whereas Frisch had simply made plausible guesses about the numbers appearing in his equations, Tinbergen had estimated most of his using statistical techniques. He was able to show that, left to itself, his model produced damped oscillations, and that it could explain the cycle.

Three years later Tinbergen published two volumes entitled *Statistical Testing of Business-cycle Theories*, the second of which presented the first econometric model of the United States (which contained three times as many equations as his earlier model of the Netherlands). This work was sponsored by the League of Nations, which had commissioned him to test the business-cycle theories surveyed in Haberler's *Prosperity and Depression* (1936). However, although Tinbergen managed to build a model that could be used to analyse the business cycle in the United States, the task of providing a statistical test of competing business-cycle theories proved much too ambitious. The available statistical data was limited. Most theories of the cycle were expressed verbally and were not completely precise. More important, as Mitchell had noted, most theories discussed only one aspect of the problem, which meant that they had to be combined in order to obtain an adequate model. It was impossible to test them individually. What Tinbergen did manage to do, however, was to clarify the requirements that had to be met if a theory was to form the basis for an econometric model. The model had to be complete (containing enough relationships to explain all the variables), determinate (each relationship must be fully specified) and dynamic (with fully specified time lags).

With the outbreak of the Second World War in 1939, European work on econometric modelling of the cycle largely ceased and the main work in econometrics was that undertaken in the United States by members of the Cowles Commission. However, many of the economists working there were European emigrés. A particularly important period began when Jacob Marschak (1898–1977) became the commission's director of research in 1943. (Marschak illustrates the extent to which many economists' careers were changed by world events. A Ukrainian Jew, born in Kiev, he experienced the turmoil of 1917–18. He studied economics in Germany and started an academic career there, but in 1933 the prospect of Nazi rule made him move to Oxford. In 1938 he visited the United States for a year, and when war broke out he stayed.)

Under Marschak, research at the Cowles Commission moved away from seeking concrete results towards developing new methods that took account of the main characteristics of economic theory and economic data, of which there were four. (1) Economic theory is about systems of simultaneous equations. The price of a commodity, for example, depends on supply, demand and the process by which price changes when supply and demand are unequal. (2) Many of these equations include 'random' terms, for behaviour is affected by shocks and by factors that economic theories cannot deal with. (3) Much economic data is in the form of time series, where one period's value depends on values in previous periods. (4) Much published data refers to aggregates, not to single individuals, the obvious examples being national income (or any other item in the national accounts) and the level of employment. None of these four characteristics was new – they were all well known. What was new was the systematic way in which economists associated with the Cowles Commission sought to develop techniques that took account of all four of them.

Though many members and associates of the Cowles Commission were involved in the development of these new methods, the key contribution was that of Trygve Haavelmo (1911–99). Haavelmo argued that the use of statistical methods to analyse data was meaningless unless they were based on a probability model. Earlier econometricians had rejected probability models, because they believed that these were relevant only to situations such as lotteries (where precise probabilities can be calculated) or to controlled experimental situations (such as the application of fertilizer to different plots of land). Haavelmo disputed this, claiming that 'no tool developed in the theory of statistics has any meaning – except, perhaps, for descriptive purposes – without being referred to some stochastic scheme [some model of the underlying probabilities]'.[3] Equally significant, he argued that uncertainty enters economic models not just because of measurement error but because uncertainty is inherent in most economic relationships:

> The necessity of introducing 'error terms' in economic relations is not
> merely a result of statistical errors of measurement. It is as much a
> result of the very nature of economic behaviour, its dependence upon
> an enormous number of factors, as compared with those which we
> can account for, explicitly, in our theories.[4]

During the 1940s, therefore, Haavelmo and others developed methods for attaching numbers to the coefficients in systems of simultaneous equations. The assumption of an underlying probability model meant that they could evaluate these methods, asking, for example, whether the estimates obtained were unbiased and consistent.

In the late 1940s this programme began to yield results that were potentially relevant for policymakers. The most important application was by Lawrence Klein (1920–2013), who used models of the US economy to forecast national income. Klein's models were representative of the approach laid down by Marschak in 1943. They were systems of simultaneous equations, intended to represent the structure of the US economy, and they were devised using the latest statistical techniques being developed by the Cowles Commission. Klein's approach led to the large-scale macroeconometric models, often made up of hundreds of equations, that were widely used for forecasting in the 1960s and 1970s.

This programme of integrating mathematics, economics and statistics promoted by the founders of the Econometric Society was only partly successful. Mathematics and statistics became an integral part of economics, but the hoped-for integration of economic theory and empirical work never happened. Doubts about the value of trying to model the structure of an economy using the methods developed at Cowles remained. It was not clear whether structural models, for all their mathematical sophistication, were superior to simpler ones based on more 'naive' methods. The aggregation problem (how to derive the behaviour of an aggregate, such as market demand for a product, from the behaviour of the individuals of which the aggregate is composed) proved very difficult. The outcome was that towards the end of the 1940s the Cowles Commission shifted towards research in economic theory. (Research into econometrics continued apace, mostly outside Cowles, but without the same optimism as had characterized earlier work.) The commission's motto, 'Science is measurement' (adopted from Lord Kelvin), was changed in 1952 to 'Theory and measurement'. As one historian has expressed it, 'By the 1950s the founding ideal of econometrics, the union of mathematical and statistical economics into a truly synthetic economics, had collapsed.'[5]

13
From Marshall to Mathematical Economics

JOAN ROBINSON

On Marshall's death in 1924, Frank Taussig, a professor at Harvard since 1886 and one of the profession's most eminent economists, wrote that 'economic science [had] lost its most distinguished representative', and that no one would question his primacy in the English-speaking world and probably worldwide.[1] However, over the next decade, economists increasingly questioned Marshall's theories about how firms and markets worked. His imprecise verbal analysis of evolutionary change did not appeal to a younger generation of economists who sought a more rigorous approach. In Cambridge, a particularly important challenge came from an article by a young Italian economist, Piero Sraffa (1898–1983), published in 1926 in the *Economic Journal*, that challenged the coherence of Marshall's assumptions. He argued that Marshall's analysis of one market at a time using the tools of supply and demand was consistent with neither increasing nor decreasing returns to scale (situations in which the average cost of producing commodities fell or rose as output increased). This prompted a debate in the pages of the *Economic Journal* that lasted for several years. In this debate economists explored the problem of how to analyse the behaviour of firms when they had some control over the prices they were able to charge for their products.

This debate involving many British economists culminated in *The Economics of Imperfect Competition* (1933) by Joan Robinson. Robinson had studied at Girton College, Cambridge, and completed her examinations in 1925, though, because of her gender, she could not formally graduate. (The rules changed to allow women to graduate only in 1948.) Faced with such discrimination, she decided that the only way she could advance her career as an economist was through writing a major work on economic theory. What her book achieved was a systematic treatment of the theory of what she called 'imperfect competition'. Competition was imperfect in that, in the short run, each firm had a degree of monopoly power, and was able to choose the price that maximized its profit. However, markets were competitive in that, in the long run, new firms could enter the industry until any monopoly profits had been competed away. Imperfect competition was thus a halfway house between monopoly and competition.

Robinson's book was significant for its method as much as for its content. Where Marshall had used mathematics to support evolutionary arguments that went beyond anything in the mathematics, Robinson provided a logically coherent theory of equilibrium. For example, instead of markets comprising a variety of firms, varying in their size, management and objectives, she assumed that firms were identical, each maximizing profits subject to the conditions they faced. The book used no algebra, relying instead on analytical diagrams, but the verbal reasoning was rigorous.

Robinson's book was published in the same year as Chamberlin's (pp. 228–9) and they were read by many economists as offering essentially the same theory. However, their methods were very different. Robinson turned Marshall's theory into a rigorous theory of economic equilibrium, albeit using very limited mathematics, where Chamberlin sought to construct a more realistic theory. She described her task as developing a box of tools that could be used to analyse economic problems, not as tackling those problems herself. She was not the only economist to develop economics in this way. In continental Europe, Heinrich von Stackelberg (1905–46), Frederik Zeuthen (1888–1959) and others developed theories of oligopoly. However, although their work was known internationally, political developments and language barriers, as well as the accessibility of Robinson's purely geometric analysis resulted in her theory coming to dominate teaching of the subject after the Second World War. Her own work, however, moved in a different direction. She became heavily involved in the Keynesian revolution, and she also developed an interest in Marx. In her book *An Essay in Marxian Economics* (1942) she applied to Marx the logical clarity that she had previously applied to Marshall. After that she became progressively more critical of economics and an enthusiast for a series of communist regimes, increasingly distancing herself from the mainstream of the profession.

LIONEL ROBBINS AND THE DEFINITION OF ECONOMICS

The justification for approaching economics through equilibrium analysis based on precisely stated assumptions about behaviour was provided, in 1932, by Lionel Robbins (1898–1984) in *The Nature and Significance of Economic Theory*. In this book, Robbins argued that economics was not distinguished by its subject matter – it was not about the buying and selling of goods, or about unemployment and the business cycle. Instead, economics dealt with a specific aspect of behaviour. It was about the allocation of scarce resources between alternative uses. In other words, it was about choice. The theory of choice, therefore, provided the core that needed to be applied to various problems.

Robbins also encouraged the view that the major propositions of economics could be derived without knowing much more than the fact that resources are scarce. This suggested that theory could be pursued largely independently of empirical work. Theory came to be seen as fundamental because, without theory, there was no explanation. Robbins emphasized that observation could uncover correlations (it could show how one variable changes in relation to another) but it could not demonstrate causation. This focus on deductive theory resonated with the trend towards viewing theory as involving the construction and use of mathematical models: the analysis of precisely specified relationships, usually expressed in algebra or geometry. This opened up a large research agenda in specifying and analysing theories of the consumer, firms and markets with greater logical rigour than previously. As assumptions were specified more precisely, it became clearer that they were theoretical constructs, not descriptions of the real world, and detailed reference to empirical work was frequently thought not to be necessary. With the emergence of econometrics – more formal methods of analysing statistical data – it became easier for theorists to ignore empirical work, on the grounds that testing theories was a task for econometricians. When economists wrote articles that had both theoretical and empirical content, it became standard practice for these articles to be divided into separate sections, one on theory and another on empirical work.

GENERAL-EQUILIBRIUM THEORY: THE 1930S

In the 1940s and 1950s general-equilibrium theory (also termed competitive-equilibrium theory) became seen as the central theoretical framework around which economics was based. Analysing such models remained a minority activity, requiring greater mathematical expertise than most economists possessed, but one with great prestige. Its roots went back to Walras and Pareto, though during the 1920s, when Marshall's influence was dominant, it had been neglected. Interest in general-equilibrium theory remained low until the 1930s, when several different groups of economists began to investigate the subject.

One of these groups was based on the seminar organized in Vienna in the 1920s and early 1930s by the mathematician Karl Menger (1902–85) – not to be confused with his father, Carl Menger. Another was the so-called Vienna Circle, the manifesto of which, *The Scientific View of The World*, was published in 1929, and helped shape the philosophy of science and broader conceptions of science after the Second World War. Vienna was attracting mathematicians and philosophers from all over Europe. One of these was Abraham Wald (1902–50), a Romanian with an interest in geometry. He was put in touch with Karl Schlesinger (1889–1938), whose *Theorie der Geld und Kreditwirtschaft* (*Theory of the Economics of Money and Credit*, 1914) had developed Walras's theory of money. They discussed the simplified version of Walras's set of equations for general equilibrium found in *The Theory of Social Economy* (1918), written by the

Swedish economist Gustav Cassel (1866–1945). Cassel had simplified the set of equations by removing any reference to utility. Schlesinger noted that, if a good was not scarce, its price would be zero, which led him to reformulate the equations as a mixed system of equations and inequalities. For those goods with positive prices, supply was equal to demand, but where goods had a zero price, supply was greater than demand. In a series of papers discussed at Menger's seminar, Wald proved that, if the demand functions had certain properties, this system of equations would have a solution. Using advanced mathematical techniques (in particular a fixed-point theorem, a mathematical technique developed in the 1910s), and using Schlesinger's reformulation of the equations, Wald had been able to achieve what Walras had tried, but failed, to do by counting equations and unknowns. He proved that the equations for general equilibrium were sufficient to determine all the prices and quantities of goods in the system. In 1937 Wald (like Menger) was forced to leave Austria, and he moved to the Cowles Commission, where he worked on mathematical statistics.

Another mathematician to take an interest in general equilibrium was John von Neumann (1903–57), a Hungarian polymath whose achievements included his work on quantum physics, the atomic bomb and computer architecture. During the early 1930s, moving back and forth between Europe and the United States, where he had obtained a position at Princeton, he became increasingly involved with economic problems, engaging with the work of Wicksell, Cassel and others and wrote a paper proving the existence of equilibrium in a set of equations that described a growing economy. He discussed this work at Menger's seminar, after which it was published in *Ergebnisse eines mathematischen Kolloquiums* (*Results of a Mathematical Colloquium*, 1938) in an issue edited with Wald. Von Neumann focused on the choice of production methods, and he developed a novel way of treating capital goods. This was in contrast to Wald's focus on the problem of allocating given resources. However, they had used similar mathematical techniques to solve the problem of existence of equilibrium.

Initially, however, it was not mathematicians such as Wald and von Neumann who revived economists' interest in general-equilibrium theory. At the London School of Economics, Robbins, who had a greater knowledge of Continental economics than most British economists of his day, introduced his young colleague John Hicks to Walras and Pareto. In the early 1930s Hicks, with Roy Allen (1906–83), reformulated the theory of demand so as to dispense with the concept of utility, believed to be a metaphysical concept that was not measurable. Individuals' preferences were described instead in terms of 'indifference curves'. These were like contours on a map: each point on the indifference-curve diagram represented a different combination of goods, and each indifference curve joined together all the points that were equally preferred (that yielded the same level of welfare). In the same way that moving from one contour on a map to another means a change in altitude, moving from one indifference curve to another denotes a change in the consumer's level of welfare – the consumer is moving to combinations of goods that are either better or worse than the original one. The significance of indifference curves was that, in order to describe choices, it was not necessary to measure utility (how well-off people were – the equivalent of altitude). So long as one knew the shape of the contour lines and could rank them from lowest to highest, it was possible to find the highest point among those that were available to the consumer. Hicks and Allen argued that this was sufficient to describe behaviour.

This was followed by Hicks's *Value and Capital* (1939). This book contained an English-language exposition of general-equilibrium theory. It restated the theory in modern terms (albeit using mathematics that was much simpler than that used by Wald, von Neumann or even Samuelson, discussed below), basing general equilibrium on the Hicks–Allen theory of consumer behaviour. It also integrated it with a theory of capital and provided a framework in which dynamic problems could be discussed. Though Hicks did not refer to the IS–LM model in *Value and Capital*, most readers, at least by the end of the 1940s, understood him to have shown how macroeconomics could be viewed as dealing with miniature general-equilibrium systems. In short, the book showed that general equilibrium could provide a unifying framework for economics as a whole.

There was, however, the problem that general-equilibrium theory was a theory of perfect competition. Hicks dealt with this by arguing that there was no choice: imperfect competition raised so many difficulties that to abandon perfect competition would be to destroy most of economic theory – a response that was virtually an admission of defeat. He followed Marshall in relegating the algebra involved in his work to appendices, confining the mathematics in the text to a few diagrams, so that the book was accessible to economists who would be unable to make sense of a more mathematical treatment. *Value and Capital* was very widely read, and was instrumental in reviving interest in general-equilibrium theory in many countries.

PAUL SAMUELSON AND OPERATIONALISM

At the same time as Hicks was working on *Value and Capital*, Paul Samuelson (1915–2009) was working on what was to become *The Foundations of Economic Analysis* (1947). After studying economics at Chicago, Samuelson did postgraduate work at Harvard, where he became a protégé of the Austrian economist Joseph Schumpeter and learned mathematical economics from E. B. Wilson (1879–1964). As well as being a mathematical economist and statistician, Wilson had an interest in physics, having been the last protégé of Willard Gibbs, a physicist who laid the foundations of chemical thermodynamics and contributed to electromagnetism and statistical mechanics. (Irving Fisher had previously been taught by Gibbs.) Samuelson was also influenced by another physicist, Percy Bridgman (1882–1961), who proposed the idea of 'operationalism', according to which any meaningful concept could be reduced to a set of operations – concepts were defined by operations. Although Bridgman was responding to what he saw as ambiguities in electrodynamics, Samuelson applied operationalism to economics. In the *Foundations*, he interpreted this idea as meaning that economists should search for 'operationally meaningful theorems', by which he meant 'hypotheses about empirical data which could conceivably be refuted, if only under ideal conditions'.[2] Much of the book was therefore concerned to derive testable conclusions about relationships between observable variables.

Samuelson's starting point was two assumptions. The first was that, when considering the behaviour of individuals, there was an equivalence between equilibrium and the maximization of some magnitude. Thus the firm's equilibrium (chosen position) could be formulated as profit maximization, and the consumer's equilibrium could be formulated as maximization of utility. The second assumption was that systems were stable: that, if they were disturbed, they would return to their equilibrium positions. From these, Samuelson claimed, it was possible to derive many meaningful theorems. The book therefore opened with chapters on mathematical techniques – one on equilibrium and methods for analysing disturbances to equilibrium, and another on the theory of optimization – and these techniques were then applied to the firm, the consumer and a range of standard problems.

Unlike *Value and Capital*, *Foundations* placed great emphasis on mathematics. Like his teacher, Wilson, Samuelson believed that the methods of theoretical physics could be applied to economics, because both fields involved optimization, and he sought to show what could be achieved by tackling economic problems in this way. Where Marshall had been suspicious of mathematical reasoning, Samuelson was enthusiastic. Referring to Marshall's dictum that mathematical results needed to be translated into English, he wrote, 'The laborious literary working over of essentially simple mathematical concepts such as is characteristic of modern economic theory is not only unrewarding from the standpoint of advancing the science, but involves as well mental gymnastics of a particularly depraved type.'[3] Of course, not everything could be expressed using mathematics, but Samuelson believed that if something could be simplified using mathematics, it should be expressed in this way.

There were important similarities between *Foundations* and *Value and Capital*. Hicks and Samuelson both emphasized that all interesting results in the theory of the consumer could be derived without assuming that utility could be measured. Hicks used indifference curves and Samuelson used what he called 'revealed preference': the notion that if someone chooses x when they could have chosen y, then they must consider x to be at least as good as y. They both discussed dynamics and the stability of general equilibrium. Samuelson's assessment of the relationship between the two books was that '*Value and Capital* (1939) was an expository tour de force of great originality, which built up a readership for the problems Foundations grappled with and for the expansion of mathematical economics that soon came.'[4]

One of the most significant features of the growth in interest in mathematical economics and general-equilibrium theory in the 1930s and 1940s is that those involved came to it from very different backgrounds. Hicks approached it as an economist, bringing ideas influenced by Robbins and Continental economists into the British context, then dominated by Marshall. Samuelson was also an economist, but his ideas were shaped by Wilson, whose background included mathematical physics as developed by Gibbs, and whose techniques he sought to apply to economics. In emphasizing dynamics and predictions concerning observable variables Samuelson was arguing against the view of Robbins, that economic laws must be true because they were derived from propositions that were known to be true. Notwithstanding this difference, Robbins, Hicks and Samuelson all provided strong arguments in favour of economic theory. In contrast to both Hicks and Samuelson, Wald and von Neumann were mathematicians – outsiders to economics – whose approach to general equilibrium arose directly from their involvement in mathematics.

GENERAL-EQUILIBRIUM THEORY:
THE 1950S AND 1960S

In the first three decades of the twentieth century, enormous changes in mathematical thinking had taken place. Acceptance of non-Euclidean geometry (discovered early in the nineteenth century but not fully axiomatized until 1899) raised questions concerning the foundations of mathematics. It became impossible to defend the idea that geometry simply formalized intuitive notions about space. Non-Euclidean geometries violated everyday experience but were quite acceptable from a mathematical point of view. Euclidean geometry became only one of many possible geometries, and after the theory of relativity it was not even possible to argue that it was the only geometry consistent with the physical world. Another blow to earlier conceptions of how mathematics related to the real world came with quantum mechanics. It was possible to integrate quantum mechanics and alternative theories, but only in the sense that it was possible to provide a more abstract mathematical theory from which both could be derived. Mathematics was, in this process, becoming increasingly remote from everyday experience.

David Hilbert (1862–1943) responded to this situation by seeking to reduce mathematics to an axiomatic foundation. In his programme, in which he hoped to resolve several paradoxes in set theory, mathematics involved working out the implications of axiomatic systems. Such systems included definitions of basic symbols and the rules governing the operations that could be performed on them. An important consequence of this approach is that axiomatic systems are independent of the interpretations that may be placed on them. This means that when general-equilibrium theory is viewed as an axiomatic system it loses touch with the world. The symbols used in the theory can be interpreted to represent things like prices, outputs and so on, but they do not have to be interpreted in this way. The validity of any theorems derived does not depend on how symbols are interpreted. Thus when Wald and von Neumann (whose earlier work included axiomatizing quantum mechanics) provided an axiomatic interpretation of general-equilibrium theory, the way in which the theory was understood changed radically.

In the 1930s, although some economists were involved in Menger's seminar, and Wald had worked with Schlesinger, Wald and von Neumann were essentially outsiders to economics. This changed in the 1940s when they both moved to the United States. At Columbia, Wald worked alongside the mathematical economist Harold Hotelling (1895–1973), who had applied mathematical methods to problems of oligopoly (a small number of sellers) and exhaustible resources. One Columbia student, Kenneth Arrow (1921–2017), though discouraged by Wald from pursuing what he was told was a very difficult subject, took an interest in the problem of the existence of general equilibrium. Shortly afterwards, as a researcher at the Cowles Commission, he discovered that a young French mathematician, Gerard Debreu (1921–2004), had derived some results similar to his own. Debreu was more interested in the mathematics than in the economics, having been trained in what he later described as 'the formalist school of mathematics' in Paris during the Second World War, but they collaborated on an improved existence proof eventually published in *Econometrica* in 1954. Their article was published alongside another article that contained an equivalent proof, developed independently of theirs, showing existence of equilibrium in a model of international trade. Its author, Lionel McKenzie (1919–2010), though American, had been a student of Hicks in Oxford. Substantially the same theorem had been discovered by three economists coming from very different backgrounds.

The Arrow–Debreu–McKenzie model (more commonly known as the Arrow–Debreu model) has since come to be regarded as the canonical model of general equilibrium. It represented a level of abstraction and mathematical sophistication that went even further than what was found in Hicks or Samuelson. Its definitive statement came in Debreu's *Theory of Value* (1959). In the preface, Debreu wrote:

> The theory of value is treated here with the standards of rigor of the contemporary formalist school of mathematics ... Allegiance to rigor dictates the axiomatic form of the analysis where the theory, in the strict sense, is logically entirely disconnected from its interpretations.[5]

This statement echoes his training in Paris with the so-called Bourbaki group, a group of French mathematicians concerned with working out mathematics with complete rigour who published their work under the pseudonym 'Nicolas Bourbaki'. *Theory of Value* could be seen as the Bourbaki programme applied to economics.

Debreu's *Theory of Value* provided an axiomatic formulation of general-equilibrium theory in which the existence of equilibrium was proved under more general assumptions than had been used by Wald and von Neumann. The price of this generality and rigour was that the theory ceased to describe any conceivable real-world economy.

For example, the problem of time was handled by assuming that futures markets existed for all commodities, and that all agents bought and sold on these markets. Similarly, uncertainty was brought into the model by assuming that there was a complete set of insurance markets in which prices could be attached to goods under every possible eventuality. Clearly, these assumptions could not conceivably be true of any real-world economy.

In the early 1960s, confidence in general-equilibrium theory, and with it economics as a whole, was at its height, with Debreu's *Theory of Value* being widely seen as providing a rigorous, axiomatic framework at the centre of the discipline. The theory was abstract, not describing any real-world economy, and the mathematics involved was understood only by a minority of economists, but it was believed to provide foundations on which applied models could be built. It held out the prospect of a general economic theory in that interpretations of the Arrow–Debreu model could be applied to many, if not all, branches of economics. There were major problems with the model, notably the failure to prove stability (to prove that if there was a disturbance, the system would return to equilibrium), but there was great confidence that these would be solved and that the theory would be generalized to apply to new situations. The model provided an agenda for research.

However, this optimism was short-lived. There turned out to be very few results that could be obtained from such a general framework. Most important, it was proved, first with a counter example and later with a general proof, that it was impossible to prove stability in the way that had been hoped. The method was fundamentally flawed. In addition, there were problems that could not be tackled within the Arrow–Debreu framework. These included money (attempts were made to develop a general-equilibrium theory of money, but they failed), information and imperfect competition. In order to tackle such problems, economists were forced to use less general models, often dealing only with a specific part of the economy or with a particular problem. The search for ever more general models of general competitive equilibrium that culminated in *Theory of Value* was over.

GAME THEORY

An alternative unifying framework on which economics can be based is game theory. Though some of the ideas involved can be traced much further back, modern game theory goes back to work by von Neumann in the late 1920s, in which he developed a theory to explain the outcomes of parlour games such as chess, draughts or card games. The simplest such game involves two players, each of whom has a choice of two strategies. There are therefore four possible outcomes. The problem is that, because the optimal strategy for each player depends on what the other player does, if they cannot cooperate they have to assume the worst. If they can cooperate, and there are more than two players, they can form coalitions, so that members of the coalition can achieve better outcomes than if they did not. Von Neumann was able to prove that there will always be an equilibrium in such a game, defined as an outcome in which no player wishes to change their strategy in the light of what the other players do. To ensure this, however, he had to assume that players have the option to choose strategies randomly (for example by tossing a coin to decide which strategy to play). There was thus a parallel between social interaction and the need for probabilistic theories in physics. Such work was an attempt to show that mathematics could be used to explain the social world as well as the natural.

From 1940 to 1943 von Neumann cooperated with Oskar Morgenstern (1902–77) on what became *The Theory of Games and Economic Behavior* (1944). Morgenstern was an economist who succeeded Hayek as director of the Institute for Business Cycle Research in Vienna from 1931, until he moved to Princeton in 1938. In the course of his work on forecasting and uncertainty, he introduced the Holmes–Moriarty problem, in which Sherlock Holmes and Professor Moriarty try to outguess each other. If Holmes believes that Moriarty will follow him to Dover, he gets off the train at Ashford in order to evade him. However, Moriarty can work out that Holmes will do this, so he will get off there too, in which case Holmes will go to Dover. Moriarty in turn knows this ... It is a problem with no solution.

Though expressed in different language from the problems that von Neumann was analysing, it is a two-person game with two strategies.

In Vienna, Morgenstern became involved with Karl Menger and came to accept that economic problems needed to be handled formally if precise answers were to be obtained. Unlike many Austrian economists, he believed that mathematics could play an important role in economics (he had received tuition in the subject from Wald), and he had an eye for seeing points where mathematics would be able to contribute. However, unlike von Neumann, he was critical of general-equilibrium theory and did not believe that it could provide a suitable framework for the discipline. Game theory provided an alternative. In the course of his cooperation with von Neumann, during which he continually put pressure on him to get their book out, he asked provocative questions and offered ideas on equilibrium and interdependence between individuals that von Neumann was able to develop. In developing their theory, von Neumann and Morgenstern were responding to the same intellectual environment – formalist mathematics – that lay behind the developments in general-equilibrium theory during the same period. Indeed, some of the key mathematical theorems involved were the same.

The Theory of Games and Economic Behavior was a path-breaking work. It analysed games in which players were able to cooperate with each other, forming coalitions with other players, and ones in which they were not able to do this. It suggested a way in which utility might be measured. Most significant of all, it offered a general concept of equilibrium that did not depend on markets, competition or any specific assumptions about the strategies available to agents. This concept of equilibrium was based on the concept of dominance. One outcome (call it x) dominates another (call it y) 'when there exists a group of participants each one of whom prefers his individual situation in x to that in y, and who are convinced that they are able as a group – i.e. as an alliance – to enforce their preferences'.[6] Equilibrium, or the solution to a game, comprises the set of outcomes that are not dominated by any other outcome. In other words, it is an outcome such that no group of players believes it can obtain an alternative outcome that all members of the group prefer. Given that the notion of dominance could be interpreted in many different ways, this offered an extremely general concept of equilibrium.

The Theory of Games and Economic Behavior was received enthusiastically, but by only a small group of mathematically trained economists. One of the main reasons was that, even as late as 1950, many economists were antagonistic towards the use of mathematics in economics. Another was the dismissive attitude of von Neumann and Morgenstern to existing work in economics. (Morgenstern had published a savage review of *Value and Capital*, and von Neumann claimed a completetely new type of mathematics was needed for economic problems.) The result was that for many years game theory was taken up by mathematicians, particularly at Princeton, and by military strategists, and later by psychologists and biologists, but was largely ignored by economists. The main source of mathematically trained economists was the Cowles Commission, several of whom wrote substantial reviews of *The Theory of Games and Economic Behavior*, but even they did not take up game theory.

One of the Princeton mathematicians to take up game theory was John Nash (1928–2015). In a series of papers and a Ph.D. dissertation in 1950–51, Nash made several significant contributions. Starting from von Neumann and Morgenstern's theory, he too distinguished between cooperative games (in which players can communicate with each other, form coalitions and coordinate their activities) and non-cooperative games (in which such coordination of actions is not possible). He proved the existence of equilibrium for non-cooperative games with an arbitrary number of players (von Neumann had proved this only for the two-player case), and in doing this he formulated the concept that has since come to be known as a Nash equilibrium: the situation where each player is content with their strategy, given the strategies that have been chosen by the other players. He also formulated a solution concept (now called the Nash bargain) for cooperative games.

During the 1950s there were many applications of game theory to economic problems ranging from business cycles and bank credit expansion to trade policy and labour economics. However, these remained isolated applications that did not stimulate further research. The main exception was due to Martin Shubik (1926–2018), an economist at Princeton, in touch with the mathematicians working on game theory. His work during the 1950s culminated in *Strategy and Market Structure* (1959), in which he applied game theory to problems of industrial organization. It was not until industrial economists became disillusioned with their existing models (notably what was termed the structure–conduct–performance paradigm, which assumed a hierarchical relationship between these three aspects of markets) that game theory became widespread in the subject. During the 1970s, industrial economics came to rely more and more on game theory, which displaced the earlier, empirically driven approach which contained relatively little formal theory. By the 1980s game theory had become the organizing principle for underlying theories of industrial organization. From there it spread to other fields, such as international trade, where economists wanted to model the effects of imperfect competition and strategic interaction between economic agents.

THE MATHEMATIZATION OF ECONOMICS (AGAIN)

In the 1960s and 1970s, economics was transformed. The mathematization of the subject, which had gained momentum in the 1930s, became almost universal. Though there were exceptions, training in advanced mathematics came to be considered essential for serious academic work – not least because without it it was impossible to keep up with the latest research. It became the norm for articles in academic journals to use mathematics. The foundations for this change, which was so profound that it can legitimately be described as a revolution, were laid in the preceding three decades and encompassed econometrics and linear models (p. 322) as well as general-equilibrium theory and game theory. Ideas and techniques from these four areas spread into all branches of economics.

The use of mathematical models enabled economists to resolve many issues that were confusing for those who used only literary methods and simple mathematics. Topics on which economists had previously been able to say little (notably strategic interaction) were opened up. However, the cost was that economic theories became narrower, in the sense that issues that would not fit into the available mathematical frameworks were ignored, or at least marginalized. Even economists such as Joan Robinson who avoided algebra, confining themselves to verbal and sometimes geometric analysis, generally analysed equilibrium systems. For reasons articulated by Robbins, it was increasingly accepted that theory, which generally meant a mathematical model, was essential even in empirical work, for without it there could be no explanation. However, the requirement that phenomena be modelled formally meant that theories became simpler as well as logically more rigorous.

The variety of economists involved is evidence against any very simple explanation of this process. The motives and aims of Hicks, Samuelson, von Neumann and Morgenstern, not to mention Frisch and Tinbergen, were all very different. However, some generalizations are possible. Economics saw an enormous influx of people who were well trained in mathematics and physics. They brought with them techniques and methods that they applied to economics. More than this, their experience in mathematics and physics affected their conception of economics. This extended much more widely than the obvious example of von Neumann. The mathematization of economics was also associated with the forced migration of economists in the interwar period. In the 1920s the main movement was from Russia and eastern Europe, and in the 1930s from German-speaking countries, with some economists being involved in both these upheavals. By the 1950s there had been an enormous movement of economists from central and eastern Europe to the United States. The mathematicians involved in Menger's seminar in Vienna (including Menger himself) were merely the tip of an iceberg. In 1945 around 40 per cent of contributors to the *American Economic Review*, most of whom lived in the United States, had been born in central and eastern Europe, and a significant number of these were highly trained in mathematics.

The aim of the Econometric Society, which fostered much of the early work involving mathematics and economics, was to integrate mathematics, statistics and economics. In a sense, its goals were realized, perhaps more conclusively than its founders had hoped. It became increasingly difficult to study economics without knowledge of advanced mathematics and statistics. However, as explained earlier, less progress was made in integrating economic theory with empirical work. From the late 1940s econometrics and mathematical theory developed as largely separate activities within economics. There have been times when they have come together, and there has been considerable cross-fertilization; however, the goal that econometric techniques would make it possible for economic theory to be founded securely on empirical data, instead of on abstract assumptions, has not been achieved. In part this reflects the influence of formalist mathematics. In part it reflects the overconfidence of the early econometricians and their failure to appreciate the difficulty of the task they had set themselves. The main justification for the key assumptions used in economic theory remains, as for Marshall and his contemporaries, that they are intuitively reasonable.

Economists have responded to this situation in different ways. The one most complimentary to economic theory is to argue that theory is 'ahead' of measurement. This implies that the challenge facing economists is to develop new ways of measuring the economy so as to bring theories into a closer relationship with evidence about real economic activity. An alternative way to view the same phenomenon is to argue that economic theory has lost contact with empirical data – that the theoretical superstructure rests on flimsy foundations. From this perspective the onus is on theorists to develop theories that are more closely related to evidence as much as on empirical workers to develop new evidence.

Doubts about the mathematization of economics have gone in cycles. In the long post-war boom, confidence in economics grew and reached its peak in the 1960s. General-equilibrium theory was the unifying framework, affecting many fields, and, as the cost of computing power fell, econometric studies were becoming much more common. As inflation increased and unemployment rose towards the end of the decade, however, doubts were increasingly expressed. With the emergence of stagflation (unemployment and inflation rising simultaneously) in the mid-1970s, and the failure of large-scale econometric models to forecast accurately, confidence in economics was shaken even further.

In the 1980s confidence returned as game theory provided a new unifying framework for economic theory and the advent of powerful personal computers revolutionized econometrics. However, this increased confidence in the subject has been accompanied by persistent dissent. Outsiders and some extremely influential insiders have argued that the assumptions needed to fit economics into the mathematical mould adopted since the 1930s have blinded economists to important issues that do not fit. These include problems as diverse as the transition of the Soviet Union from a planned to a free-market economy or the environmental catastrophe that will result from population growth and policies of laissez-faire.

CONCLUSIONS

During the 1930s economists developed many of the techniques that were to come to dominate economic theory when it became a more technical discipline after the Second World War. General-equilibrium theory was highly regarded but the techniques that were used by most economists were those laid down by Samuelson in his *Foundations of Economic Analysis*. Students who could not cope with his mathematics could turn instead to the geometric analysis of Joan Robinson's *Economics of Imperfect Competition* augmented by the indifference curve analysis of Hicks and Allen. Between them they provided the theoretical tools with which it was believed most economic problems could be investigated. Underlying all of these approaches was the notion, clearly articulated by Robbins, that economics contained a core of economic theory that could be applied to different fields.

Although many of the techniques used had been developed in the 1930s, the approach remained Marshallian in that it could be seen as an elaboration of the theory of supply and demand, to which Marshall had contributed so much. Analysis of firms' behaviour explained supply while consumer theory explained demand. Because it did not cover the mathematical techniques that economists were now expected to know, and because his evolutionary theorizing was now unfashionable, his *Principles* was thought out of date as a textbook, except in

Chicago, where Milton Friedman still endorsed it. The result was that what people thought of as 'Marshallian' economics – the analysis of individual markets using primarily geometric tools – was arguably much closer to Robinson and Hicks than to Marshall himself.

By the 1960s Robbins's definition of economics, as the study of how scarce resources were allocated, was widely though not universally accepted, and it had become normal to divide economic theory into microeconomics and macroeconomics. Microeconomics concerned the behaviour of individual economic agents (households and firms) and of markets for individual commodities; macroeconomics analysed the behaviour of whole economies and typically dealt with aggregates such as national income and unemployment, or index numbers such as the price level. Like many of the theories used after the Second World War, this terminology originated in the 1930s, when Frisch had coined the term 'macro-dynamics', but it was only in the 1960s that it became institutionalized in the titles of courses and textbooks.

14
Welfare Economics and Socialism, 1870–1945

SOCIALISM AND MARGINALISM

The closing decades of the nineteenth century saw the rise of socialism as a large-scale movement. Socialism could mean many things: at one end of the spectrum was revolutionary socialism, such as that associated with Marx; at the other was 'municipal socialism' involving activities such as provision of gas and water, public parks and libraries, education and the implementation of measures to improve public health. In between these extremes was a wide range of positions. Socialist parties were formed across Europe, and in many countries their support grew rapidly. Extension of the franchise to include the working class led to an expansion of socialist representation in European parliaments. There was great pressure for social reform, both from socialist parties themselves and from conservatives (such as Bismarck, the German chancellor, and Disraeli, the British prime minister) who sought to lessen the pressure for more radical change. Government activity was extended into many new fields, new organizations emerged, and the role of the state increased. Labour unions were expanding to include unskilled as well as craft workers, and were beginning to exact improved working conditions. Though there were clear exceptions, the rise of trade unions and the rise of socialism were strongly linked.

For economists, the rise of socialism presented two types of challenge. The first was to develop principles for working out the appropriate role of the state. When, where and how should the state intervene in economic life? The second was to evaluate socialist and communist schemes for reorganizing society. Could an economy organized on socialist principles operate successfully? Though these questions clearly overlapped, they provide a useful way to think about some of the main lines of economic thought during this period.

The challenges posed by socialism came at the time when economists were increasingly taking up marginalist theories. These theories provided a framework within which problems such as the regulation of industry, the provision of welfare benefits, the establishment of government enterprises and tax policy could be tackled that was very different from that available to previous generations of economists. Smith and J. S. Mill had discussed the problem of state intervention, but their analysis had centred on long-run growth. They offered general principles by which state activities could be judged, and their observations on specific cases contained many perceptive insights, but their ability to tackle specific questions about how resources should be allocated was severely limited. Marginalism, with its mathematical apparatus of utility and profit maximization, appeared to be able to fill this gap.

Some of the early marginalists – notably the Austrians – acquired a reputation for being hostile to socialism. Some undoubtedly were. For the rest, however, although they may generally have been biased in favour of laissez-faire and individualism, this was in practice outweighed by more pragmatic considerations. Most marginalists were on the side of reform, even if their approach was sometimes paternalistic or if they were hostile to radical change. For example, although Jevons started his career a supporter of laissez-faire, by his last book, published in 1882, he had arrived at a position where he saw 'hardly any limits to the interference of the legislator'.[1] What had happened was that, during the 1870s, he found more and more contexts where state intervention was justified, to be financed mostly by continual increases in local taxation: public health, working conditions, education, transport, and many others. Marshall, the dominant economist of the following generation, saw a smaller role for state intervention than did Jevons. However, he still assigned a significant role to the state, going along with the wider movement towards support for progressive taxation (where the rich are subject to higher tax rates than the poor). Though his socialism was somewhat limited, Walras described himself as a socialist. If there was a causal link between socialism and marginalism, therefore, it did not involve marginalism being adopted as a way of defending laissez-faire against socialist criticism. To the contrary, marginalist arguments provided new ways of arguing in favour of social reform.

CAMBRIDGE WELFARE ECONOMICS AND ITS EARLY CRITICS

In the English-speaking world, the dominant approach to problems of social welfare and reform was, for several decades, the Cambridge tradition, which originated not with Marshall but with his one-time mentor, Henry Sidgwick (1838–1900). Sidgwick's main reputation is as a utilitarian ethical philosopher, but his books also covered two of the other legs of the Cambridge moral science degree: political economy and politics.

The fundamental part of Sidgwick's argument about welfare was a distinction between two senses in which the term 'wealth' was used. The first was as the sum of goods produced, valued at market prices. The second was as the sum of individuals' utilities – what we would now term welfare. He offered reasons why these might be different. The clearest example is free goods: goods for which no price is paid. Such goods raise individuals' utilities – people value them – but they do not enter into the first concept of wealth at all, for their price is zero. More generally, the market value of a good to a consumer will measure the value of the last unit consumed. If the value of an additional unit falls as consumption rises, this will be less than the average value of the good to that consumer. If the ratio of price to average utility were the same for all goods, this would not matter at all. However, the ratio of price to average utility will depend on how fast marginal utility falls, and there is no reason to suppose that this will be the same for all goods. Some goods have an average utility that is high relative to their price and will be undervalued in calculations of wealth at market prices. Free goods, which have positive value but a zero price, are enough to make this point.

In developing these arguments, Sidgwick made use of Jevons's utilitarianism, according to which individuals' utilities could be measured and compared. This meant that if the marginal utility of a particular good were higher for one person than for another, total utility could be raised by redistributing goods to those who valued them most. This would leave wealth at market prices unchanged. For example, the value of an additional loaf of bread to a poor person may be higher than its value to a rich person; it may therefore be possible to increase welfare by taking a loaf from the rich person and giving it to the poor person. In other words, a community's welfare depends on how goods are distributed, not simply on the value of goods being consumed.

Having provided reasons why these two concepts of wealth (goods valued using market prices and average utilities) might differ, Sidgwick argued that, for practical reasons, wealth had to be measured using market prices, except in specific cases where 'the standards of the market fail us'.[2] This provided the justification for an approach to welfare economics similar to that of early-nineteenth-century economists such as Smith and Mill, which involved tackling problems of welfare by analysing first the production and then the distribution of wealth. Sidgwick also followed Mill in his analysis of the role of government. The general principle was laissez-faire, but this was subject to numerous exceptions that he explored in detail. These included cases where individuals could not obtain adequate reward for the services they provided to society (lighthouses, afforestation and scientific discovery) and also those where the gains to individuals exceeded those to society (duplicating an existing railway line). There were also cases, such as the control of disease, where cooperation was required. However, even though Sidgwick defended the traditional perspective, his separation of two concepts of wealth made it possible, arguably for the first time, to conceive of welfare economics as something distinct from economics in general.

Marshall followed in the same tradition but made Sidgwick's analysis more precise. He defined wealth very clearly as a sum of money values – national income, or national dividend, as he called it – that was distinct from utility or welfare. He also developed a way to measure utility in terms of money. This was the theory of consumers' surplus. An individual consumer's surplus is the difference between what the consumer is willing to pay for a commodity and what they actually pay. Marshall showed that such surpluses could be added together and used to measure changes in social welfare only under certain circumstances: in particular, the value of an additional unit of income had to be the same for all individuals. In general, this would not be true. His response was to confine his use of consumers' surplus to situations where it could plausibly be argued that it was approximately true. He wrote:

> On the whole, however, it happens that by far the greatest number of events with which economics deals, affect in about equal proportions all the different classes of society; so that if the money measures of the happiness caused by two events are equal, there is not in general any very great difference between the amounts of happiness in the two cases.[3]

Marshall confined his use of consumers' surplus to goods that accounted for only a small proportion of consumers' spending. This meant that a change in price would have a negligible effect on real income and would have only a minor effect on the value to the consumer of an additional unit of income.

This practical, utilitarian approach to welfare economics reached its culmination in the work of Pigou (who gave the subject its name), in his two books *Wealth and Welfare* (1912) and *The Economics of Welfare* (1920). Pigou's welfare economics was utilitarian, in that he regarded the elements of welfare as 'states of consciousness' that could be compared with each other.[4] Like Sidgwick and Marshall, he focused on national income and the way in which it was distributed. National income was linked to what he called 'economic welfare' – 'that part of welfare that can be brought, directly or indirectly, into relation with the measuring rod of money'.[5] This was not the whole of welfare, but he argued that economic welfare was likely to be highly correlated with overall welfare.

Pigou's main innovation was to replace Marshall's concept of consumers' surplus with an analysis of marginal private and social products. If the marginal private product of an activity (the benefits obtained by the person undertaking the activity) was different from its marginal social product (the benefits to society), welfare was unlikely to be maximized because individuals' decisions would be based on their private costs and benefits. There were, Pigou argued, many situations where private and social products would be different from each other. One was where one person owned an asset (for example, land or a building) that was managed by a tenant. If the benefits accrued to the landlord, the tenant might have no incentive to improve or even to maintain the asset. The marginal social product of improving land, therefore, would be higher than the marginal private product to the tenant. Another situation was where one person's activities directly affected someone else's welfare. The obvious examples of this are pollution and traffic congestion. Monopoly would also cause private and social products to differ: instead of simply looking at the value of the additional output, the monopolist will also take account of the effect of increased sales on the price of goods that are already being produced. Economic policy therefore involved eliminating differences between marginal private and social products. Using this approach, Pigou analysed numerous possible interventions by government, including regulation of monopoly, nationalization of industry, compulsory arbitration in industrial disputes, regulation of wages, and redistributing income towards the poor.

Utilitarian arguments could have led to egalitarian conclusions because of the implication that, if everyone had the same utility function, total utility would be maximized by an equal distribution of income. However, Sidgwick, Marshall and Pigou both drew back from such a radical idea. The main reason was that measures to eliminate inequality would reduce incentives, meaning that there would be fewer goods to distribute. They were also acutely aware of the limitations of the capacity of government to increase welfare. For example, according to Pigou, 'It is not sufficient to contrast the imperfect adjustments of unfettered private enterprise with the best adjustments that economists in their studies can imagine. For we cannot expect that any State authority will attain, or even whole-heartedly seek, that ideal.'[6] Two decades later he concluded:

In order to decide whether or not State action is practically desirable . . . [w]e have further to inquire how far, in the particular country
in which we are interested and the particular time that concerns us,
the government is qualified to select the right form and degree of
State action and to carry it through effectively.[7]

Their reasons included self-interested politicians, electoral pressures and incompetent and ill-informed civil servants. It was necessary
to balance the evident defects of laissez-faire against the disadvan-
tages that came with government intervention.

Pigou's *Wealth and Welfare* generated a response from the radical
journalist and underconsumptionist Hobson. Pigou recognized that
'economic welfare', the welfare arising from 'earning and spending
the national dividend', was only a part of total welfare, but he argued
that if all we are concerned with is how policy will change welfare,
then the difference does not matter: if economic welfare increases, we
can presume that total welfare will also have increased.[8] Inspired by
Romantic critics of industrial society and of political economy,
Hobson refused to accept this and, in *Wealth and Life* (1914), he
argued for what he called 'a human standard of value' that took
account of the social, psychological and environmental costs of economic activity: of 'illth' (a term coined by Ruskin) as well as wealth.
In the manner of the Romantics, he denounced the dehumanizing
effects of repetitive factory work and degradation of the environment.
Where Pigou had ignored such costs as unquantifiable and unscien-
tific, Hobson was prepared to make the necessary assessments of the
illth and wealth associated with various activities, claiming that they
rested on generally accepted value judgements.

Hobson was not the only English economist to dissent from the
Cambridge orthodoxy. The most prominent of these dissenters was
Richard Tawney (1880–1962), a Christian Socialist and economic
historian who, like Hobson, was very influential within the emerging
Labour Party. He appealed to knowledge of morality that was 'the
common property of Christian nations'.[9] In *The Acquisitive Society*
(1921) he was critical of societies that prioritized the protection of
property rights over social obligations. He asserted that societies had

common goals and that welfare should be judged according to the contribution made to the public purpose.

THE SOCIALIST CALCULATION DEBATES

In the early years of the twentieth century there began an international debate over socialist planning. Responding to the Marxist Karl Kautsky, Dutch economist Nicolaas Pierson (1839–1909) mounted a critique of central planning. The problem was that orthodox Marxists dismissed speculation about how a future socialist society would be organized as utopian, and so they failed to make an economic case for the revolution they were advocating. Economic arguments were relevant only for a capitalist society. In an article first published in 1902, Pierson pointed out that socialists needed to pay attention to economic theory because the problem of value would remain, even under socialism. Valuation was necessary in order to allocate resources to different activities.

Similar arguments were made by Walras's successor in Lausanne, Pareto, who observed that, even if the state owned the entire stock of capital and prohibited all buying and selling, prices and rates of interest would have to remain, at least as accounting entities:

> The use of prices is the simplest and easiest means for solving the equations of equilibrium; if one insisted on not using them, he would probably end up by using them under another name, and there would then be only a change of language, and not of things.[10]

Without prices and interest rates, 'the ministry of production would proceed blindly and would not know how to plan production'.[11] Individuals' desires and the obstacles to satisfying them would be the same under a collectivist organization of society as under capitalism, with the result that both societies would have to solve similar problems. The main difference between socialism and capitalism was the principles by which the distribution of income was determined. Under capitalism, incomes were linked to ownership of means of production (and hence by the way in which society has evolved), whereas under socialism they were determined according to ethical and social considerations.

Pareto's *Manual of Political Economy* was also important for another reason. He defined a social optimum as a situation in which any change would be 'agreeable to some individuals and disagreeable to others' – in other words, a position where it was impossible to make anyone better off without making someone else worse off.[12] The significance of this is that it enabled Pareto to define a social optimum without having to compare the utilities of different individuals.

The argument made by Pierson and Pareto about the similarity of the problems faced by capitalist and socialist societies was taken a stage further by another Italian economist, Enrico Barone (1859–1924). In 'The ministry of production in the collectivist state' (1908), drawing on the work of Walras and Pareto, he used a mathematical general equilibrium model to show that the same conditions had to be fulfilled in a collectivist economy seeking to maximize the welfare of its members as in a perfectly competitive equilibrium. The ministry of production in a socialist state could start with the prices and wages inherited from the previous regime. It could then raise or lower them, in a process of trial and error, until two conditions were fulfilled: prices were equal to costs of production and costs of production were minimized. These arguments led him to claim that such a ministry would face an immense task, though not an impossible one. His main conclusion was that it was impossible for a collectivist state to be ordered in a way that was substantially different from the way it would be ordered under 'anarchist' production, for the same equilibrium conditions would have to be satisfied.

However, debate over whether rational economic calculation was possible under socialism stemmed from a completely different source. In 1909, Otto Neurath (1882–1945) proposed the idea that the way societies were organized during wartime could be subsumed into a theory of 'war economy'. On the outbreak of the First World War, he was placed in charge of a section of the Austrian War Ministry where he could develop his ideas. After the war, in *Through War Economy to Natural Economy* (1919) he argued that the centralized methods of control used in wartime could be applied to peacetime planning. Replacing a market economy with an administrative economy would make it possible to achieve society's aims more quickly than in a decentralized economy in which there was no plan. 'To socialise an economy,' he wrote, 'means to conduct *planful administration in favour of society through society*.'[13] However, although he held to socialist ideals, his concern was to develop a rational way of organizing society – his 'natural economy' – with little concern for the political structure that would support it.

A key feature of Neurath's 'natural economy' was planning in kind: working directly with quantities of goods without reducing them to money values. By the time his book was published, such an approach had become topical, having been tried in two contexts. German wartime planning, including the Hindenberg programme to double output of munitions in 1916–17, involved a type of planning in kind, applying to government planning methods developed in large-scale German industry. And in Soviet Russia, 'war communism' was a brief attempt to dispense completely with markets and prices. Neither experiment was successful, raising the question of whether such policies were fundamentally flawed.

Two economists responded directly to Neurath's claims for planning in kind: Max Weber (1864–1920) and Ludwig von Mises (1881–1973). Independently of each other, they both argued that prices and money were essential, but they did so from different perspectives. Because it was published earlier, the work that came to be seen as starting the debate was by Mises: 'Economic calculation in the socialist commonwealth' (1920). Here, he argued, in uncompromising terms, that socialism was impossible – it could never work because rational calculation required the existence of freely established money prices for both consumers' and producers' goods. Without such prices it would be impossible for anyone to work out how resources should best be used.

This was, Mises emphasized, not a purely technical problem, as some socialists seemed to assume. The main difficulty arose not with consumer goods (one might not need prices to say, for example, that 1,000 litres of wine was more valuable than 500 litres of oil) but with producers' goods. A railway, for example, is valuable because it reduces costs for other industries, enabling them to produce more of the goods that consumers require. Without money prices, it would be impossible to calculate whether or not it should be built. In a static economy, where nothing changed, rational calculation might be possible. A socialist state could continue the pattern of production that prevailed under a previous competitive system. However, the world is not static. Tastes and technology are forever changing, with the result that new ways of producing goods have continually to be worked out. In a socialist state, there would be no one with the responsibility and initiative to change the way in which activities were organized in response to these changes. Managers of capitalist enterprises, Mises argued, have an interest in the businesses they administer that is quite different from anything that could be found in public concerns. 'Commercial-mindedness' will not exist when people are moved from business into public organizations. Even if human nature could be changed so that people all exerted themselves as much as if they were subject to the pressure of free competition, there would still be a problem. In the absence of prices, people would not know what it meant to economize – to balance the costs and benefits of alternative activities.

Mises approached the problem as a supporter of competitive markets. In contrast, though he was sceptical about socialism, Weber was much less enamoured of markets because he wanted to keep certain areas of life free from the rule of officials who could be found in large businesses as much as in government. Where Mises recognized a single rationality – economic calculation – Weber distinguished between formal and substantive rationality. Formal rationality, which covered economic calculation, involved technical calculation and hence required commensurability and, effectively, money. However, substantive rationality involved showing not only that the effective technical means were being used but also that decisions meet the requirements of 'ethics, politics, utilitarianism, hedonism, social rank, egalitarianism or whatever else'.[14] Formal rationality might be unambiguous, but substantive rationality was 'thoroughly ambiguous'.[15]

The most prominent response to Mises did not come from Neurath but from a group of economists who have come to be known as 'market socialists', including Fred M. Taylor (1855–1932), H. D. Dickinson (1899–1969) and Oskar Lange (1904–65). They accepted Mises's claim that rationality required economic calculation, and hence prices, but they argued that prices could be used in a socialist economy. They proposed systems that would be socialist in the sense that the state owned the means of production and would determine how capital goods were distributed between industries, but in which there were markets for consumer goods and labour. Households would thus be free to sell labour and to buy consumption goods in response to market wages and prices, but the allocation of capital goods would be determined by managers who would be given instructions on the criteria they were to use in making decisions. For example, in Lange's scheme, production would be organized by plant managers, who would be given the task of producing at minimum average cost and setting prices equal to marginal cost (the cost of an additional unit of output). Behind these plant managers would be industry managers, who would make investment decisions, including when to open new plants and close old ones. A central planning board would monitor the whole process, setting the prices on which the decisions of industry managers would be based. Implicitly the market socialists were accepting Barone's claim that capitalist and socialist systems needed to solve the same economic problem and therefore would produce the same outcome. No one disputed that there might be practical problems with socialism, but it was argued that socialism was theoretically possible.

HAYEK AND PLANNING

The most forceful response to this came from Hayek in a series of articles, the first of which appeared in 1935. Hayek argued that the market socialists had not shown that rational calculation was possible under socialism. They had just shown that if one had complete knowledge of all the relevant data (including knowledge of consumers' tastes and of all the technical possibilities for producing goods) it would be possible to solve a set of equations to determine what goods should be produced. To formulate the question in this way did not solve the problem of how efficiency could be achieved under socialism – it showed that it had not been understood. In a real-world economy, full information on technical conditions of production does not exist. What does exist is engineers with techniques of thought that enable them to discover new solutions when confronted with new problems. In other words, the knowledge required by socialist planners does not exist – it needs to be created. This means that the initiative in adopting new methods, developing new products and so on has to come not from planners, but from managers who are aware of new developments and are able to respond to them. The problem with socialism is not merely a computational problem: it is one of generating the information required for the system to operate. The market socialists, by taking technical conditions as given, simply assumed the problem away.

Hayek also raised further problems with the market-socialist arguments. In equilibrium, prices can be calculated by solving a set of simultaneous equations. But the economy is never in equilibrium. It is not clear how the planners should operate out of equilibrium. It might not even be appropriate to start with existing prices, for there was no reason to believe that the transition to socialism would not produce large changes in equilibrium prices. Such problems would be compounded by the problem of new goods: planners would have no idea about which new goods should be produced and in what quantities. Comparisons with state enterprises in a capitalist economy would provide no guidance, for it would no longer be possible to make comparisons with the private sector.

Hayek's most influential publication on socialism was *The Road to Serfdom* (1944), written for a lay audience. In contrast with his previous work, this was an explicitly political book arguing that Britain was in danger of repeating the events that had recently led to totalitarianism in Germany. Nazism was not a reaction against the trend towards socialism, but 'a necessary outcome of those tendencies'.[16] It was an interpretation of history, in particular German history, as much as economic analysis. The book became the bible for many conservatives and libertarians, especially in the United States. For Hayek this marked the beginning of a move away from technical economics into political philosophy. It provoked a sharp critical reaction, its attack on collective action being seen as a dangerous attack on democracy.

The focus of *The Road to Serfdom* was political, claiming that attempts to direct the economy would lead to totalitarianism, but Hayek's arguments still related to ones discussed in earlier debates. He argued that central direction of economic activity presupposes a common goal, but terms such as 'common good' or 'general welfare' have no definite meaning and the more government activity increases, the less is the possibility of universal agreement on what is desirable. He dismissed the idea of a 'middle way' between capitalism and socialism as the planner would 'be forced to extend his controls till they become all-comprehensive'.[17]

This was the key point challenged by Hayek's critics in a debate to which many British economists contributed in the 1940s. For example, Evan Durbin (1906–48), a colleague of Hayek at LSE and a junior minister in the 1945 Labour government, claimed that Hayek had overlooked what contemporary economists meant by planning: planning did not mean the imposition of a rigid and 'arbitrarily determined' programme, but changing the way decisions were made, so that they took account of a wider range of consequences than were taken into account by private decision-makers.[18] Decisions could take into account the distribution of income and wider consequences of economic activities. Plans were drawn up 'only to implement … preferences freely indicated by the consumer in the markets for consumption good and capital goods'.[19] If there were inconsistencies, or if tastes changed, then the plans would be modified. Meade went even further towards advocating a 'middle way' in *Planning and the Price Mechanism* (1948), describing his proposals as 'the Liberal-Socialist Solution'. This involved 'making full use of the money and pricing systems' but controlling them to ensure full employment, a 'tolerably equitable' distribution of income and property, and to prevent anyone from remaining 'uncontrolled in a sufficiently powerful position to rig the market for his own selfish ends'.[20]

PLANNING AND WELFARE ECONOMICS

The reasons for planning in wartime were obvious and accepted even by opponents of peacetime planning: in war there was a common objective and resources needed to be directed to achieving it. In contrast, peacetime planning was concerned with increasing social welfare, raising issues of how that was to be defined and what was implied by maximizing the welfare of a large number of individuals. Pigou's welfare economics could provide one answer, as could the arguments of Hobson and Tawney. However, in *The Nature and Significance of Economic Science* (p. 283), Robbins argued that there was no scientific basis on which the interpersonal comparisons of welfare that were essential for utilitarianism could be made. Though people made such judgements all the time, they should not form part of the science of economics. His main target was those economists inspired by the Romantics, including Hobson and Tawney, whose methods (it is important to stress that it was only methods and not conclusions) he saw as dangerously close to those underlying Nazi and fascist beliefs. However, his argument also undermined the foundations of Cambridge welfare economics. There was therefore a need to rebuild the subject. The outcome was what came to be called the 'new welfare economies', developed by Lange and a group of Robbins's younger colleagues at LSE, notably Hicks, Abba Lerner (1903–82) and Nicholas Kaldor (1908–86).

The starting point for the new welfare economics was Pareto's notion of a social optimum as a situation where it was impossible to improve the welfare of one person without reducing that of at least one other person. In the 1930s, economists worked out the set of conditions that needed to be met if this condition were to be satisfied. This condition was, however, not very useful because in practice virtually any policy change will make at least one person worse off. So, Hicks and Kaldor, again taking up an idea found in Pareto, tried to strengthen this criterion by introducing the idea of a 'compensation test'. A change would be beneficial if the gainers could compensate the losers and still remain better off. If this criterion were met, the result would be a *potential* Pareto improvement. It would not be an actual Pareto improvement, of course, unless compensation was actually paid; however, the concept of a compensation test was thought to provide a way in which the question of whether resources were being used efficiently could be separated from questions of income distribution. Unfortunately, the idea turned out to be flawed. In 1940 Tibor Scitovsky (1910–2012) showed that it was easy to find examples where the compensation test would be satisfied in both directions: it gave contradictory results. The search for a 'value free' welfare economics had failed.

In the course of these discussions, economists had approached the problem of social welfare in many different ways, often deriving different versions of the conditions for a social optimum. One of the main problems was that, though economists wrote of 'optimality' and 'ideal output', it was never made clear exactly what it was that was optimized in a social optimum. A way of thinking about this was provided by Abram Bergson (1914–2003), who proposed the idea of a social-welfare function, which was used by Samuelson in the discussion of welfare in *Foundations of Economic Analysis*. A Bergson–Samuelson social-welfare function is a relationship between social welfare and all the variables on which social welfare may depend. In itself, this is entirely devoid of content: it simply states that social welfare depends on whatever variables it depends on. However, it provides a framework within which different approaches to the problem can be analysed, for it is possible to use the social-welfare function to analyse the implications of different value judgements or ethical criteria. For example, individualism implies that the only variables entering the social-welfare function are variables affecting individuals' levels of well-being. The Pareto criterion implies that if an individual's welfare increases (without anyone else's changing), social welfare must increase, which provides another restriction on the form a social-welfare function can take. Using such arguments, it is possible to clarify the meaning of the conditions for a social optimum and to resolve the paradoxes surrounding compensation tests.

The close relationship between studies of socialism and welfare economics during this period is illustrated in Lerner's *The Economics of Control* (1944), which was based on a Ph.D. thesis written at LSE, where Hayek was one of his teachers. This was subtitled 'Principles of

Welfare Economics'. The rationale he gave for the book's coverage was that he had come to realize that democracy was far more important for socialism than state ownership of the means of production. Hence he focused on ways to design policies that would 'best serve the social interest, without prejudging the issue between collective ownership and administration or some form of private enterprise'.[21] The book provided a systematic review of welfare economics. It was based, as far as possible, on Paretian principles, but in order to analyse the distribution of income he assumed that different people obtained similar satisfactions from doing similar activities. This assumption could not be proved, but Lerner believed that people behaved as if it were true. Lerner's book also demonstrates how questions of welfare and planning had, by then, become influenced by Keynesian thinking, for he tackled planning for full employment as well as planning as it was traditionally understood.

When Bergson surveyed socialist economics for the American Economic Association in 1948, he acknowledged Mises as the economist who had started the debate, though noting that it was now agreed that his arguments were 'without much force', a view that was widely held in the 1950s and 1960s.[22] He turned first to the ends of economic activity and his own concept of a social-welfare function before explaining the conditions for a social optimum. The theory was abstract, but it provided a conceptual framework that might guide the planning board of a socialist economy. Calculating the optimum might be impossible, but it was possible to derive a procedure that would approximate this solution in practice. He argued that it was obvious that a socialist solution *could* work, so the debate had to centre on whether socialism or capitalism was more efficient; it was wrong to compare an ideal competitive system with the reality of the Soviet Union, or to compare an ideal socialist state with monopolistic capitalism.

CONCLUSIONS

The challenge of socialism formed the background to discussions of welfare from the late nineteenth century until the Second World War, but the way socialism was understood and the political context changed dramatically during that period. The carnage of the First World War had a profound psychological effect and turned revolutionary Marxian socialism from an idea advocated by a tiny minority into a real threat to existing societies. This was the background to the socialist calculation debate that emerged in the 1920s, on whether it was possible to have rational economic calculation in a socialist society. This debate was inextricable from welfare economics because it raised the question of what it meant to increase social welfare in a society in which people had different views. A further stimulus came from the palpable failure of capitalist economies in the Great Depression.

The focus in this chapter has been on Germany and Britain, but controversies over socialism were not confined to these countries. For example, in Sweden very different positions were taken by the older and younger generations of economists. Cassel and Eli Heckscher (1879–1952) were market liberals. In his textbook Cassel used a comparison of existing society with socialism to reveal which institutions were essential and which could be dispensed with. This led him to elaborate on Barone's point that, even if a socialist state tried to dispense with prices and wages, these would inevitably re-emerge, for they reflected fundamental economic realities. However, he went further than Barone in arguing that, in the absence of private property and a fully developed system of exchange, a socialist state would be unable to direct production in the best way. The necessary prices would not be available. In contrast, the younger generation, including Ohlin and Myrdal, were supporters of planning.

In the United States the situation was different again. In 1932, one economist wrote:

'Economic planning' recently has become the epigrammatic program of practically every economic interest group in our Nation. From the radicalism of the extreme left to the conservatism of the extreme right, from the Communists to the United States Chamber of Commerce, economic planning has come to be the accepted way out of our economic policy.[23]

However, few wanted to overturn the capitalist system, so planning was about improving it. The impetus towards planning came from the experience of wartime planning, and the motivation from the 1920–21 recession and, above all, from the Great Depression. However, 'American planning' meant different things to different economists. 'Social' planning was about collective action to guide the economy; and macro-economic planning involved managing the level of demand so as to ensure full employment. These both involved government.[24] In contrast, other types of planning involved business: establishing more rational business practices within firms, and reorganizing industry through cartels and trade associations. The focus was generally not on the static resource allocation issues that dominated welfare theory, but on the need to create a dynamic economy. This view of competition as a dynamic process had something in common with the perspective that Hayek developed in the 1930s, in which the market provided a means whereby decentralized decision-making by individual firms could be coordinated. Prices conveyed information that would not otherwise be available to decision-makers. Competition was not only a means of moving the economy towards equilibrium, but also a procedure for discovering new ways of doing things.

Debates over socialism continued into the 1940s, but by then the context had changed dramatically. The political character of Stalin's Soviet Union had become very clear, and in the West planning had clearly been important to the war effort. The world became polarized and debates became less over socialism versus capitalism than about the role to be played by planning in peacetime, and what economic analysis could contribute to that. The range of questions linked to planning was enlarged by the emergence of Keynesian economics and the expanded possibilities for macroeconomic planning. In the United States, as the scale of the expansion of the role of the state became clear, some industrialists turned strongly against the New Deal, eventually creating a receptive audience for Hayek's political arguments.

15

The Second World War and After

MILITARY PROBLEMS

In the 1930s the British Air Ministry started to employ civilian scientists to tackle military problems. Though some of the problems related to physics and engineering, it was increasingly realized that certain questions had an economic aspect, and from 1939 the scientists turned to economists for advice. For example, the question of whether it was worth producing more anti-aircraft shells involved balancing the numbers of enemy bombers shot down (and the damage these might have inflicted) against the resources required to produce the shells. This was an economic question. The US armed forces followed, employing economists through the Office of Strategic Services (the forerunner of the CIA). These economists became engaged in a wide range of tasks, ranging from estimating enemy capacity and the design of equipment to problems of military strategy and tactics. The last of these included problems such as the selection of bombing targets and the angle at which to fire torpedoes. These were not economic problems, but they involved statistical and optimization problems that economists trained in mathematics and statistics proved well equipped to handle. This was, of course, in addition to the role of the economist in planning civilian production, price control and other tasks more traditionally associated with economics.

Many of these tasks involved optimization and planning how to allocate resources, which required the development of new mathematical techniques in order to obtain precise numerical answers. As many of the problems involved random errors, statisticians were particularly important. The result was intense activity on problems that are best classified as statistical decision theory, operations research and mathematical programming. After the war, the US military continued to employ economists and to fund economic research.

These activities by economists had a significant effect on post-war economics. They raised economists' prestige. Many of them were directly related to the war effort and, though less obvious than the achievements of natural scientists, who had produced new technologies such as nuclear weapons, they were widely recognized to have been important. In addition, the economists involved in these activities worked in close proximity with physicists and engineers. The boundaries between statisticians and economists became blurred. Much of these professionals' work was closer to engineering than to what had been traditionally thought of as economics.

Some of the research undertaken to solve problems of specific interest to the military proved to have wider applications. The most important example was linear programming. This is most easily explained using some examples. If goods have to be transported from a series of factories to a set of retail stores, how should transport be arranged in order to minimize total transport costs? If a person needs certain nutrients to survive, and different foods contain these in different proportions, what diet supplies the required nutrients at minimum cost? To solve these problems and others like them, it was assumed that all the relationships involved (such as between cost and distance travelled, or health and nutrient intake) were linear – that they were straight lines.

In the United States, linear programming was developed independently by two people, George Dantzig (1914–2005), working for the US air force, and Tjalling Koopmans (1910–85), a statistician with an interest in transportation problems who also made significant contributions to econometrics at the Cowles Commission. During the war, Koopmans was involved with planning Allied freight shipping, and Dantzig was trying to improve the efficiency with which logistical planning and the deployment of military forces could be undertaken. After the war, linear programming and the related set of techniques that went under the heading of 'activity analysis' proved to be of wide application.

The development of such techniques depended on developments before the war. Dantzig's starting point was the input–output model developed by Wassily Leontief. By assuming that each industry obtained inputs from other industries in fixed proportions, this had reduced technology to a linear structure. Koopmans's interest in transport dated from before the war. Unknown to either of them, Leonid Kantorovich (1912–86), at Leningrad, where input–output techniques had a comparatively long history, had arrived at linear programming as a way to plan production processes. Other techniques developed during the war arose even more directly out of pre-war civilian problems. Statistical methods of quality control, for example, had been used in industry before the war, but were taken up and developed by the military.

In 1946, the United States air force, recognizing that during the war it had been important to have access to research by civilian scientists, established Project RAND, later to become the RAND Corporation, as a think tank based in Santa Monica, California. In addition to employing engineers on projects related to the development of military technology, it employed social scientists, including economists. It employed not only full-time staff but also academic consultants who would visit Santa Monica during vacations or sabbaticals or undertake research for RAND from their university offices. In this way RAND, like its counterpart, the Office of Naval Research, was behind much research into economics in the 1950s. RAND consultants included many of the leading American economists and the organization sponsored a significant amount of economic research especially in the fields of game theory and linear programming. Linear programming was important for solving logistical problems and game theory for analysing problems relating to the nuclear stand-off between the United States and the Soviet Union that dominated the Cold War.

During the 1960s, RAND continued to undertake military research, most notoriously into the appropriate strategy for combating what was termed 'insurgency' in South Vietnam. Thomas Schelling (1921–2016), an economist who had developed the concept of nuclear deterrence, used game theory to theorize about the effects of escalating the bombing of North Vietnam. However, at the same time, responding to the increase in government interest in issues relating to social welfare, such as poverty and urban problems, RAND diversified into much broader social research. 'Systems analyis', involving the application of formal mathematical techniques for evaluating the costs and benefits of policy proposals, which was a distinctive product of RAND, spread throughout the United States government during the 1970s.

THE EXPANDING ROLE OF ECONOMISTS

After the Second World War the number of economists, like the number of social scientists more generally, and their public profile, increased dramatically. There were rises both in the number of economics graduates and in the number obtaining postgraduate degrees. In part this reflected a rise in the number of people entering higher education, and in part a general expansion in the social sciences. Demand for the rising supply of graduates, at both first-degree and Ph.D. levels, came not just from academia but increasingly from business, government and international organizations. Economists were employed as technical experts on a scale unknown before the war. With this came changes in the way the subject has been conceived.

One reason why the Second World War was, in many countries, a watershed in the growth of the profession was that this was when economists first became firmly established in government. In the United States, Lauchlin Currie became economic adviser to the president in 1940 – the first economist to be employed full time at such a high level. The role of economists at the heart of the US government was institutionalized with the establishment, in 1946, of the Council of Economic Advisers. The exact scope and the effectiveness of this varied according to the economic climate and the attitudes of the council's chairman, but its existence indicated that economists had acquired a new role. The list of economists serving on the council or associated with it includes many of those whose academic work shaped the post-war discipline: for example, James Tobin (1918–2002) and Joseph Stiglitz (1943–).

Similar developments occurred in Britain with the establishment, in 1941, of the Economic Section in the War Cabinet Secretariat. After the war, however, the Economic Section and its successor, the Government Economic Service, remained small (around twenty members) until 1964, but by 1970 the numbers employed had risen tenfold. In both countries there was also a large increase in the number of statisticians as governments became increasingly involved in the production of national accounts and economic statistics.

It was not just economics that was changed by the Second World War. A similar story could be told about all the other major social sciences – psychology, sociology, political science, anthropology and human geography. They all became involved in the war effort and after the war the number of social scientists increased. Although the pattern of change varied, all the social sciences had to confront the availability of new techniques that had the capacity to change how disciplines were traditionally conceived. The immediate post-war years were also a period that saw many problem-centered interdisciplinary social science projects, encouraged by the foundations, including Ford, Rockefeller and Carnegie, that were supporting such ventures financially. In this period, there was a tendency for economists to stand aloof from other social sciences, often seeing their discipline as 'more rigorous', or 'more scientific' than 'soft' disciplines such as political science or sociology, but there were nonetheless important examples of cross-disciplinary collaboration.

Examples of economists who interacted with other social scientists in very significant ways are Myrdal, Kenneth Boulding (1910–93) and Herbert Simon (1916–2001). Myrdal was commissioned by the Carnegie Corporation to write a report on the situation of African-Americans. He was an eminent economist but this took him squarely into the field of sociology, psychology and political science, his final report being published in 1944. Boulding became involved in research on conflict and defence, involving sociology and psychology as well as economics. After a thoroughly interdisciplinary education in the social sciences and mathematics, Simon completed a doctoral thesis on administrative behaviour. His subsequent work on artificial intelligence, information processing and decision-making defies compartmentalization, involving economics, political science, computer science and psychology. This list of examples could easily be extended.

Economists were also employed in international organizations. There was a precedent for this in that the League of Nations and the International Labour Organization (ILO) had both employed economists. The League of Nations had sponsored economic research by Haberler and Tinbergen on the business cycle. After 1945, however, the number of such organizations increased dramatically, and with it the employment of economists. In addition to the ILO (established before the war) there were the United Nations, which had regional commissions, the International Monetary Fund (IMF), the World Bank (originally the International Bank for Reconstruction and Development, IBRD) and the General Agreement on Tariffs and Trade (GATT). These were later followed by the Organization for Economic Cooperation and Development (OECD), originally the Organization for European Economic Cooperation (OEEC), and the United Nations Conference on Trade and Development (UNCTAD).

These organizations were largely concerned with practical policy questions, and economists were not always influential. However, despite the fact that the organizations' primary goals were technical, economists based in them undertook important economic research, including theoretical research, and could make an impact on economic thinking. One example was Jacques Polak (1914–2010), who at the IMF in the 1950s was engaged in influential work on exchange rates and the role of money in determining a country's balance of payments (p. 386). Another was Raul Prebisch (1901–1986), who at the UN's Economic Commission for Latin America developed a theory about the relationships between industrial and developing countries.

In its early years the World Bank was concerned more to establish its credibility as a sound banking institution than with applying economic analysis, with the result that, as in most other international organizations, economists were marginalized. This situation did not change until the 1960s, under Robert McNamara (1916–2009), when between 1965 and 1969 the number of economists employed rose from 20 to 120. McNamara also encouraged the idea that, because the World Bank's loans would always be small relative to any country's total investment, the dissemination of ideas was important. As a result the importance attached to economic research increased, and by the early 1990s the World Bank employed around 800 economists, many doing research comparable with that done in universities. Nowhere else was there such a large concentration of economists. Given that these were all working on issues related in some way to development, they had a noticeable influence.

KEYNESIAN ECONOMICS AND MACROECONOMIC PLANNING

These changes in the economics profession were closely linked to the spread of Keynesian ideas. The relationship is, however, not a simple one. Keynes's *General Theory* provided an enormous stimulus to the idea that governments could, and should, take responsibility for controlling the level of economic activity. It was also of great importance to the development of national-income statistics. Interest-rate policy and changes in government spending and taxation could be used to keep unemployment low. In the 1940s the United States and Britain both introduced clear commitments to full employment. However, it is important not to exaggerate the influence of Keynesian ideas on these developments. Roosevelt's New Deal, which began four years before Keynes's book was published, owed much to Rexford Tugwell (1891–1979), an advocate of economic planning. The concept of 'American planning' was widely discussed in policymaking circles during the 1930s as something different from the socialist planning found in the Soviet Union or Nazi Germany. Equally important, in both the United States and Britain, the Second World War showed that economic planning could be used to achieve national goals. Economists played an important role in the war effort, and arguably made a significant contribution to the Allied victory. In addition, a significant number of economists (or people who subsequently entered economics) spent the war working as statisticians. Although they worked on technical problems, such as quality control in munitions production, making the best use of limited shipping resources, or even the design of gunsights, many of the techniques they developed and the attitudes they acquired influenced the discipline when the war was over.

A further factor was that, although Keynesian economics swept through the universities, governments were more resistant. Britain introduced a Budget organized along Keynesian lines in 1940, and the concept of the inflationary gap – described by Keynes in *How to Pay for the War* (1940) – was used to calculate how much could be spent without causing inflation, and hence how much needed to be taken out of the economy by taxation or compulsory saving in order to avoid inflation. However, it is arguable that Keynesian ideas were not fully accepted in the Treasury until 1947. In much of continental Europe (notably France and Germany) Keynesian ideas never dominated the policy agenda.

In the United States, the Employment Act became law, but its provisions were less ambitious than some of its supporters had hoped, for there was considerable opposition to the expansion of the role of the state that had taken place during the New Deal and there was still concern about high federal deficits. It was only after the election of President John Kennedy that Keynesian thinking dominated policy-making. Kennedy sometimes resisted the advice of Walter Heller (1915–87) and the other Keynesian economists he had appointed to the Council of Economic Advisers but his implementation of a tax cut to reduce the gap between actual output and full employment output marked the high-water mark of Keynesian economics. Its goal was to reduce unemployment, which had increased in each of the three recessions under President Eisenhower.

Macroeconomic planning of the type that governments tried to use during the post-war decades was made possible by the revolution that took place in national accounting and the provision of statistics during the interwar period and the Second World War. The use that could be made of national-income analysis was clearly demonstrated by wartime experiences in Britain and the United States. In Britain, the estimates of national income produced by Meade and Stone were used to calculate the inflationary gap. In the United States, Kuznets and Nathan used national income to show that Roosevelt's 'Victory Program', in which he promised vast increases in military production in 1942–3, was achievable. (It was achieved.) After the attack on Pearl Harbor, when the military dramatically increased its demand for hardware, Kuznets and Nathan (at the War Planning Board) continued to apply these methods. This time, however, goals had to be revised down, not up. Gilbert, in charge of national-income accounts, focused on providing rapidly available information on the state of the war economy.

The work of Kuznets and Nathan was a major success. They set targets that turned out to be feasible at a time when military procurement rose from 4 per cent to 48 per cent of US national income in four years. Not only was this a contribution to the war effort, it also provided a clear indication of what could be achieved using national accounting as a tool for economic planning. It amounted to turning military procurement into a science: if too little were demanded, war would be prolonged unnecessarily; if too much were demanded, costs would rise without any more being produced.

Planning also became a major issue in relation to less affluent parts of the world, called at various times 'underdeveloped,' 'less-developed',' or 'third world' countries, 'emergent nations' or simply 'the South'. Development economics, as the study of such places came to be called, emerged in its modern form after the Second World War. The United States, clearly the dominant Western power, was hostile to the continuation of European colonial empires, and from the 1940s many colonies began to achieve independence, receiving a political voice through the United Nations. As a result, the 'colonial economics' of the interwar period, with its stress on the development of resources by colonial powers, was clearly out of date.

Attention had also been focused on the economics of underdeveloped countries during the war. Paul Rosenstein-Rodan (1902–85) had tackled the theory of underdevelopment, focusing on south-eastern Europe. The statistical work of Colin Clark and Simon Kuznets revealed, for the first time, the extent of income differences between rich and poor countries. Finally, governments in North America and western Europe were taking an active interest in measures that might be taken to promote growth (and capitalism) in the rest of the world, partly in response to competition with the Soviet Union, where Stalin's series of five-year plans had succeeded in developing Soviet industry. Various agencies associated with the United Nations had a commitment to economic development from the start, and later the World Bank's remit extended from 'reconstruction' to include 'development'. The Organization for European Economic Cooperation became the broader Organization for Economic Cooperation and Development.

There were strong links between Keynesian economics and early theorizing on problems of development. Keynesian economics was based on the presumption that economies could get stuck in situations of mass unemployment or underemployment (where workers have jobs but are not fully employed) from which they could not escape unaided. Underdeveloped countries were similarly thought to have become stuck in situations from which they needed assistance to escape.

There were several theories about why this was the case. One of the most common focused on the difference between economy-wide growth and growth in a single sector of the economy. If a single industry (or a single business) were to expand, it would soon come up against barriers such as a lack of demand for its products and shortages of skilled labour. In contrast, if it were possible to engineer an expansion of the whole economy, each industry would create demand for other industries' products and would contribute to the growth of a pool of skilled labour on which all industries could draw. Such thinking underlay the theories of Rosenstein-Rodan, economic adviser to the World Bank in its early years, and Ragnar Nurkse (1907–59), an economist at the League of Nations who, after the war, became an advocate of the need for balanced growth.

Not all explanations of underdevelopment were of this type. At the UN Economic Commission for Latin America, Prebisch explained the contrast between rich and poor countries as being the outcome of unequal interaction between a 'core' of industrial countries, exporting mainly industrial goods, and a 'periphery' of poor countries, whose main exports were primary commodities. Because workers in industrial countries had great bargaining power, productivity gains led to rising real wages. In contrast, workers in underdeveloped countries did not have such bargaining power and so were unable to translate productivity gains into wage rises. Instead, wages stayed the same and prices fell. This difference led to primary commodities becoming ever cheaper in relation to industrial goods. The terms on which trade took place thus became more and more favourable to industrial countries, and it became more difficult for countries in the periphery to escape from poverty. Prebisch drew the conclusion that development required state intervention to support industries (protected by tariff barriers) that would compete with goods currently being imported – a strategy of 'import substitution'.

Other economists produced theories of 'dualistic' development. Arthur Lewis (1915–91), for example, distinguished between a modern sector in which firms maximized profits and used mechanized production methods and a 'traditional' sector in which family relationships ensured that everyone was employed on the land, even if their presence did not raise output. Economies that were split between sectors in this way were characterized by surplus labour in the traditional sector. Economic development involved the growth of the modern sector. Labour moved out of a sector in which its productivity was zero into one where it was productive.

Few of these theories went unchallenged. 'Big-push' balanced-growth theories, for example, were vigorously challenged by Albert Hirschman (1915–2012), who argued that development required disequilibrium – unbalanced growth. Expansion of a single industry would create opportunities for other industries and would promote the development of new activities. Prebisch's theories were also challenged. There was a vigorous debate over whether statistical evidence supported the claim of a falling trend in commodity prices. Dualistic theories were vulnerable to the charge that it was in practice very difficult to identify sectors that were as different as the theories required.

The common feature of these theories is that they were 'structural' theories. They attributed the problem of underdevelopment either to the structure of the economies themselves or to the structure of the world economy. These structural features meant that the market mechanism would, on its own, be insufficient to ensure development. Planning and state intervention of some kind were a necessity. This fitted in with the Keynesian perspective in two ways. The first was that different types of theory were seen as being needed for different problems. Just as macroeconomics was needed as a subject distinct from microeconomics in order to tackle problems of unemployment, so development economics was needed to deal with problems specific to underdeveloped countries. The second was that it was believed that markets could not be left alone – that government intervention was necessary if market economies were to operate in a beneficial way.

THE 1960S AND AFTER

After Kennedy's assassination, his successor, Lyndon Johnson, was committed to his 'Great Society' programme, which involved action to reduce poverty and solve problems faced in urban areas. The Equal Pay Act (1963) made it illegal to discriminate on the basis of sex, and the Civil Rights Act (1964) and subsequent legislation sought to reduce discrimination against African-Americans. These developments were against the background of an escalation of conflict in Vietnam, which polarized the country and led Johnson not to run for a second full term.

Towards the end of the 1960s, and even more in the 1970s, the economic environment in the Western world changed dramatically. Johnson was committed to the War on Poverty, which required sub-stantial increases in federal spending. In addition, the escalation of the Vietnam War required increasing resources. Together these fuelled a worldwide boom and rise in commodity prices, which culminated, after the Yom Kippur War between Israel and its Arab neighbours, in an oil crisis in which fuel became more expensive and was rationed (p. 385). In politics, there was a turn to the right, culminating in the election, in 1979–80, of Margaret Thatcher as British Prime Minster, and Ronald Reagan as President of the United States.

There were also intellectual challenges to established ways of thinking about society, most of which could be summarized as chal-lenges to 'positivism' in its various forms. Compared with other social sciences, economics was relatively impervious to these ideas, which paid much more attention to individual identities and saw knowledge as embedded in specific historical contexts. Thomas Kuhn's notion that science develops through a succession of 'paradigms' was perhaps the most influential of these challenges, being taken up by economists seeking to challenge the status quo. His key idea was that shifts from one paradigm to another involved losses as well as gains, meaning that the story of science could not be told simply as one of progress. Feminist and antiracist ideas challenged discriminatory practices within economics (for example, the American Economic Association establishing a Committee on the Status of Women in the Economics Profession in 1971) and were taken up in the research agenda of a minority of economists, but most of economics remained unaffected. This was in marked contrast with the profound effect that such ideas had in other social sciences, notably in sociology.

However, other developments did lead to profound changes in economics. Mathematical economics had been becoming increasingly central to economics since the 1930s, but even in the 1950s and 1960s much economics was still done in a traditional way, focused on verbal analysis of theoretical concepts and analysis of tables and graphs of data. It was not until the 1960s that graduate students were generally expected to have taken a course in mathematics and to be familiar with basic econometric methods and the necessary mathematical statistics. Economists increasingly saw economic theory as involving the construction and analysis of mathematical models in which agents were maximizing utility or profit.

The 1960s was also the time when mathematical economics became more widespread in the USSR, though the context was completely different from in the United States and Europe. The USSR was a planned economy with enormous strength in mathematics. Kantorovich, a mathematician, had developed linear programming as early as 1938 in the context of industrial processes (the production of plywood). He aimed at a purely national audience for his methods because he did not want to assist the USSR's enemies and rivals. As production engineering, this was ideologically acceptable to the authorities, but his ideas about applying optimization techniques to national economic planning was ideologically suspect, for it was seen to challenge key Marxist ideas such as the labour theory of value, and as drawing on concepts such as prices and profits that were deemed relevant only in a capitalist society. As one Soviet economist put it,

'You are talking here about optimum. But do you know who is talking about optimum? The Fascist Pareto is talking about optimum,' a chilling remark in Stalin's USSR.[1] Even to engage in mathematical economics could be seen as anti-Marxist. Kantorovich therefore made his career as a mathematician, working on problems related to military activities.

After Stalin's death in 1953, the situation changed under Nikita Khrushchev. This was a brief period of optimism during which it was widely believed that planning could raise Soviet living standards above those in the West: when there was still confidence in Soviet technological capabilities. The planning agency remained unreceptive, but Kantorovich was able to establish an audience for his ideas among economists and, between the early 1960s and the 1980s, mathematical economics became more widely established. Soviet mathematical economics was more practically and technically oriented than its Western counterpart. 'Economic cybernetics', came to be seen from very early in the 1960s as an ideologically neutral tool for controlling the Soviet economy and comprised techniques of operations research, control theory and mathematical programming. From the late 1960s, other economists, often outside the most important research institutes and university economic departments, conducted research much closer to Western mathematical economics, such as general equilibrium and optimal growth theory.[2]

Kantorovich and Koopmans were awarded the Nobel Prize for linear programming in 1975, the year that the award of the Nobel Peace Prize to the dissident physicist Andrei Sakharov made all the prizes politically controversial. In their Nobel lectures, Koopmans spoke of the universality of the problem of resource allocation, whereas Kantorovich sought to differentiate their work by emphasizing that the problems facing socialist and capitalist economies were fundamentally different. Thus, although this period arguably marked the high point of mathematical economics in both the United States and the Soviet Union, with similar problems being pursued in both countries, convergence in thinking was significantly limited by the different institutional and political situations in the two countries.

The Cold War stimulated research by American and European

economists on the Soviet Union, with many universities setting up Centres for Russian or Soviet Studies (part of a wider growth in Area Studies). One reason for concern was that, if Soviet statistics were correct, the Soviet Union was growing faster than the United States, creating the danger that it would overtake it within a few years. When the Soviet Union launched Sputnik, the first satellite to orbit the Earth, there was panic that American science was falling behind. American economists, both in the CIA and in universities, produced separate estimates of Soviet economic growth, often coming up with growth rates that were much lower than the official ones. This was important not only because of the direct military implications of relative incomes (the productivity and efficiency of American industry had been crucial to victory in the Second World War) but also because of competition between the two systems in the Third World: would currently 'non-aligned' countries, such as India, adopt socialism or become free-market economies? It was a time when 'comparative economic systems' – the study of different forms of economic organization, including Soviet and Chinese forms of socialism, Yugoslav socialism, 'Rhenish' capitalism and American capitalism – became a field in which some economists specialized.

The changes in economics that accompanied these political and economic events are discussed in chapters 16 and 17, but one way in which they played out can be seen in development economics. In the 1970s, the ways of thinking about development that were fashionable in the 1950s – what could be called 'Grand Theories' of development – fell out of favour. Attempts to plan development, whether they involved import substitution, export promotion, balanced or unbalanced growth, or the creation of disequilibria, had not been particularly successful. It also became increasingly clear that 'developing' countries were far from homogeneous: sub-Saharan Africa had problems that bore little if any relationship to those faced by South-East Asia or Latin America. It had become apparent that economic growth did not automatically reduce poverty. The result might simply be the emergence of an affluent modern sector amid poverty that was as great as before, or even greater. There was also an ideological shift against planning and in favour of solutions that placed greater emphasis on markets.

The success stories of economic development were seen as arising from free-market economies such as those of Singapore, Taiwan and Korea (even though these had strong and authoritarian governments that intervened actively in industry). The assumption, central to many structural theories of development, that people in developing countries behaved in some way differently from people in developed countries became harder to sustain. The result was an increasing tendency to apply to problems of developing countries the same analytical techniques as were being used to analyse problems of developed countries. Everyone, whether rich or poor, was assumed to behave according to the precepts of rational behaviour.

There was therefore a significant change in the way in which development was tackled in the 1970s. Grand theories, often based on Keynesian macroeconomics, increasingly gave way to microeconomic theories in which prices played a much greater role. In 1969 Ian Little (1918–2012) and James Mirrlees (1936–2018) produced a manual on project evaluation for the OECD. In this widely used manual, it was argued that projects should be evaluated not on the basis of market prices, which might be seriously distorted, but on so-called 'shadow prices' that reflected the constraints facing developing countries. In a similar vein, the concept of effective protection, first developed in the 1960s, came into more widespread use: this was an attempt to reduce the many ways in which countries might protect domestic industry (tariffs, quotas or various regulations) to a common measure. Economists also focused more on the concept of poverty, seeking better ways to measure it. 'Basic needs' indices, taking account of factors such as nutrition levels, mortality and literacy rates, became more prominent. Economic growth, though still important, was no longer the sole criterion by which development was measured. As development economists came to accept that people in 'third world' countries behaved in much the same way as people in developed countries, the theoretical tools used were increasingly those of contemporary microeconomics. For example, in the 1970s development economists took up models of risk and incomplete information. In the 1980s, again following macroeconomics, these were extended to include imperfect competition and the latest developments in growth and trade theory. Parallel changes took place both in academia and in international organizations, though there was no uniformity, even among the latter. For example, in the 1970s the OECD and UNIDO (the UN Industrial Development Organization) took up Little–Mirrlees methods of project appraisal and cost–benefit analysis, but the World Bank did not.

One of the main developments during the 1980s was the increasing prominence of the World Bank in setting the agenda for development. In 1980 it abandoned its earlier policy of lending only to finance specific projects and introduced 'structural-adjustment lending'. This was lending designed to help countries get over medium-term balance-of-payments problems without impeding growth. Loans were made on condition that the borrowing countries implemented a programme of reform, including measures such as allowing exchange rates and interest rates to be determined by world markets, reducing the size of the public sector, deregulating markets, and removing controls on investment. This was based on the so-called 'Washington consensus' – the idea that development required free markets and a trade-oriented development strategy. The debt crisis of the early 1980s worsened the situation for many developing countries, and the World Bank's insistence that lending be accompanied by measures to liberalize trade and capital flows and open up domestic markets became a major issue. Critics of the World Bank argued that structural-adjustment policies served to place the burden of adjustment on the poor in developing countries, for the result would frequently be unemployment and cuts in public services. Supporters focused on the need for such reforms if developing countries' problems were to be solved.

The context of development economics changed even more dramatically with the fall of the Soviet Empire in 1989–91. Economists – including both academics and those in international organizations – turned on a large scale to problems of 'transition' and 'emerging markets'. The establishment of market economies in Eastern Europe and the former Soviet Union had clear parallels with the situation of 'traditional' developing countries facing structural adjustment. It was believed that, in the long run, the establishment of a market economy would raise living standards, but the short-term effects were high unemployment and extreme poverty alongside extreme affluence causing life expectancy to plummet.

EXPANDING THE BOUNDARIES OF ECONOMICS

During the 1960s and 1970s, the boundaries of economics were extended in that economists increasingly analysed problems traditionally considered to lie in the realm of other social sciences, notably sociology and political science. One of the stimuli for this was Johnson's War on Poverty, which not only made research into urban problems, crime, delinquency and poverty topical but also opened up opportunities to obtain funding for research into social problems.

During the 1950s, it was widely assumed that poverty could not exist in an affluent society such as the United States: the word was generally avoided, especially during the 1950s, when Joseph McCarthy's anti-communist witch hunt was at its height. There was also widespread political opposition to research on poverty, even from unions who, a decade earlier, had been more concerned with the problem. Term such as 'low-income families' were used instead of 'poverty'.[3] There was, however, an informal network of economists, mostly in government agencies, who were aware that America's rising wealth was not shared by everyone, and who sought to document the problem, creating statistics on numbers of low-income families and their incomes. These economists included many women, for this was a time when many universities would not appoint women to faculty positions. Examples include Dorothy Brady (1903–77), who worked on family budgets at the Bureau of Labor Statistics, Ida Merriam (1904–97) and Mollie Orshansky (1915–2006), at the Bureau of Research and Statistics of the Social Security Administration, where they developed measurements of poverty. Because they were in government agencies, disciplinary boundaries were less significant than they would have been in university departments.

Research on poverty became easier after Kennedy's election and, in 1962, Robert Lampman (1920–97), a specialist on the problem, was appointed to the Council of Economic Advisers. Following Johnson's declaration of a War on Poverty, he wrote a substantial chapter on the problem of poverty in the 1964 *Economic Report of the President* that documented its extent and the characteristics of those in poverty. It offered a long list of strategies by which poverty could be reduced. However, the work that drew public attention to the problem of poverty was not by Lampman but by a socialist political activist, Michael Harrington (1928–89), in his book *The Other America* (1962). Drawing on the research of the network of government economists analysing the problem, Harrington painted a vivid picture of what poverty meant for those experiencing it in the hope that, once people were aware of the problem, there would be strong political pressure to tackle the problem.

A very different approach to social problems was taken by Gary Becker (1930–2014). He applied standard price theory to the problems of discrimination, crime and divorce. These were modelled as optimization problems in which people weigh up the gains to be obtained from different activities. For example, crime happens when people decide that the rewards from crime exceed the potential losses they would incur in the event of being caught and convicted. Given that, even if they are guilty, they are not certain to be caught and convicted, this can be formulated as a standard problem of choice under uncertainty. It is possible to use such models to decide, for example, how effective increased sentences are likely to be in deterring crime, and Becker's work influenced sentencing guidelines in the United States. Similar models can be used to analyse racial discrimination and decisions within the family, such as the circumstances under which husbands or wives are more likely to go out to work, and even whether changes in economic factors will raise or lower the chances of couples deciding to marry or to divorce. These developments have been controversial, some economists taking them very seriously while others have been dismissive.

At roughly the same time, similar methods were also applied to political decisions, resulting in the field of 'public choice', spanning economics and political science. It originated with the work of James Buchanan (1919–2013), Gordon Tullock (1922–2014), Anthony Downs (1930–2021) and Mancur Olson (1932–98) around 1960, applying standard economic techniques to decisions made by people involved in bureaucracies, government and political processes. Voters, politicians and bureaucrats were all assumed to be agents who maximized their own utility rather than doing what was in the best interests of society. The result was government failure. Even revolutionary activities, such as the ongoing 'insurgency' in Vietnam, were analysed in terms of individual optimization, in contrast to traditional explanations that treated them as collective events, typically motivated by ideology. Initially many economists were resistant to such work, seeing their subject as concerned with prices and markets, but from the 1970s, public choice became an increasingly accepted part of economics.

There were several reasons for the distinctive path taken by public-choice theory. The fact that the two most influential public-choice theorists, Buchanan and Tullock, were to the right of the political spectrum may have helped them obtain funding more easily than might otherwise have been the case. Probably more important, however, was the fact that they preferred verbal arguments to mathematical models, which set them apart from the bulk of the profession and may, at least in part, explain why they initially found it difficult to get their work published in the major journals.

These activities – poverty research, economic analysis of social problems and public choice – raise difficult questions about where the boundaries of economics should be drawn. Should rational-choice sociology, which has affinities with Becker's work, be regarded as economics? Should public-choice theory be regarded as economics or political science? In themselves, these questions are not interesting because the boundaries of academic disciplines are artificial constructions. However, the fluidity of the boundaries of modern economics echoes similar changes that have taken place over the history of the subject. It could hardly be otherwise when the identities of 'neighbouring' disciplines (such as psychology, sociology, geography and political science) were also not clear.

The process of differentiation continued throughout the twentieth century as new disciplines and new fields in economics emerged. The development of management science raised a fresh set of boundary questions. For example, personnel management – now clearly located in management – was at one time considered part of economics. Another example is economic history, settled uneasily on the boundaries of economics and history, with its place influenced by institutional factors as well as by intellectual developments. In the field of development, economics, politics and sociology continually confronted each other. (Hirschman described his career as involving 'crossing boundaries' and 'trespassing'.)[4] Demography, associated with economics since Petty and Graunt, has almost dropped out of the discipline, even though it thrives elsewhere. New developments such as public-choice theory and rational-choice sociology continually challenge conventional assumptions about where boundaries should be drawn.

Economists have never had a monopoly of theorizing based on arguments about rational choice but, especially when combined with the use of advanced mathematics, they have often claimed that these methods define economics. The notion that these developments at the boundaries between social-science disciplines involve the application of economic methods to problems lying within the domain of other social sciences has led some critics to describe it as 'economics imperialism'. This view has been reinforced by the belief of many economists that their discipline is more rigorous than 'softer' disciplines such as sociology. The term is, however, inappropriate, for rational-choice theory is not the exclusive property of economics and, as will be seen in Chapter 16, much important work transgressing conventional disciplinary boundaries has originated outside economics including from within those disciplines that economics has been accused of colonizing.

HETERODOX ECONOMICS

Growing acceptance of the notion that people should be modelled as optimizing individuals (rational-choice theory) and that such behaviour should be analysed using mathematical models, as was the case in fields ranging from economic development to public choice, was associated with a certain narrowing of economics. When economics became professionalized towards the end of the nineteenth century, there was still great variety within the discipline. It encompassed historical economics (especially in Germany), a wide variety of interpretations of marginalism (from the mathematical approach of Walras and Fisher to the less mathematical and very different approaches of J. B. Clark and the

Austrians), Veblen's evolutionary economics, and Commons's law-based institutional economics. There is obviously a sense in which these were all 'economics', but it is hard to claim that this plethora of approaches rested on a single foundation. The differences between, for example, Fisher, Commons and Veblen were simply too great.

After the Second World War, with the increased use of mathematical modelling, this situation began to change. Most noticeably, historical economics was either assimilated (it became applications of standard economics) or pushed aside into other fields, and institutionalism withered away as a significant force in the discipline. However, there was still no uniform approach to the subject. It was accepted that general-equilibrium theory – the dominant paradigm in microeconomics – could not explain everything. As a result, Keynesian macroeconomics and development economics were regarded as distinct, each being appropriate to its particular subject matter. Even industrial economics, centred on what was known as the structure-conduct–performance paradigm (the notion that market structure determined the way firms behaved, and that this in turn determined how well markets worked), developed as a partly autonomous, empirically driven discipline.

From the 1970s, however, there was a narrowing of the subject as field after field came to be based on rigorous rational-choice foundations. The mathematical level of the discipline moved up a step. For many economists, especially those trained after 1950, who took for granted the need for mathematics in economics, these changes constituted progress. Even when economists disagreed with the assumptions being made, or believed that important phenomena were being neglected, most of them could accept the principle that mathematically more rigorous analysis was a legitimate strategy. There were, however, minorities whose dissent from the dominant methods was more radical.

Some dissenting groups have a long history. Marxist economics, sustained by its political dimension, goes back to the nineteenth century. American institutionalism never completely died out. John Kenneth Galbraith (1908–2006), whose *The Affluent Society* (1958) offered a withering critique of consumerism and the role of large corporations in American society, fits into the institutionalist tradition. However, though he became president of the American Economic Association, and though his books were bestsellers, his ideas were never part of the mainstream. (For example, in 1950, on the eve of what became known as the German economic miracle, he told the American Economic Association that removing price controls, a move favoured by many economists, would wreck the German economy.) In the 1970s, however, the coalescing of economics around a central core stimulated the rise of new 'heterodox' groupings that brought together economists who felt that their ideas were being systematically excluded from the profession's main journals. In 1973 Alfred Eichner (1937–88) and Jan Kregel (1944–) argued the case for a 'post-Keynesian' alternative to orthodox economics. This was to integrate Eichner's theory of oligopoly pricing with Keynesian economics as interpreted in particular by Joan Robinson. Robinson had never accepted the IS–LM interpretation of the *General Theory*, and in her later career she repudiated neoclassical economics, including her own work on imperfect competition, as paying insufficient attention to problems of time and uncertainty. Using Kuhn's notion of a paradigm, Eichner and Kregel argued that post-Keynesian economics offered a new paradigm for the subject: a radically new conceptual framework within which to think about economic problems.

Shortly before this, in 1968, the Union of Radical Political Economy (URPE) had been established, drawing together a network of 'radical' economists. The immediate context was disillusion with the American establishment and opposition to the Vietnam War, but there was a deeper concern that issues such as class and power were systematically ignored by most economists. In their emphasis on exploitation, discrimination and the inequalities produced by American society, and their criticism of the role of the military in the American economy, radical economics had much in common with Marxist economics. However, it did not commit itself to the Marxist theoretical framework, and sought new ways to analyse these issues, for example by emphasizing that power relations should be at the centre of the analysis of markets, and criticizing neoclassical economists for not having a theory of power.

At around the same time, 'Austrian' economics began to coalesce into an organized, heterodox school of economics. A conference in 1974 brought together a wide-ranging group of economists, united in finding inspiration in the work of Carl Menger and his followers, in particular Mises and Hayek, who had been marginalized by post-war developments. Politically, the Austrians were conservative (in contrast with the radicals and post-Keynesians, who identified clearly with the Left), and they had considerable success in raising private funds. They emphasized methodological individualism (the doctrine that economic theories should be based on theories about individual behaviour), and they viewed individuals as economizing (making choices in response to the prices and opportunities they faced). However, like Menger, they refused to model this using mathematics, preferring to rely on verbal logic. They took up Hayek's view, which had largely dropped out of orthodox economics with the demise of interwar American institutionalism, of competition as a dynamic process – a discovery procedure – viewing the market as a means for disseminating information in a changing, uncertain world.

Another example was feminist economics, concerned with analysing the economic structures that affect the position of women. Although the journal *Feminist Economics* was not established until 1995, with some scholars dating the establishment of the field to just a few years before that, there is a much longer history of concern with issues related to gender. In the nineteenth century there was discussion of the 'woman problem' and there was much work on relevant issues under headings such as 'household' or 'home' economics.

A significant reason why heterodox groups began to organize was the perceived trend towards greater homogeneity of the mainstream. This posed a problem because, in so far as rigour came to be equated with mathematical modelling based on rational choice, much hetero-dox economics, which challenged such methods, appeared to lack rigour. The result was that heterodox economists found it increasingly difficult to publish in the most prestigious journals. In an academic world where recruitment and promotion decisions were increasingly based on publication in these journals, economists with unorthodox views felt threatened, and organization was important for their survival. One reason that they were able to organize was a result of the profession having become sufficiently large that it could accommodate dissenting groups. Dissenters were not spread uniformly across universities, but relied on particular institutions for support. Chicago (with Friedman, George Stigler (1911–91), Becker and Lucas) was the centre of orthodox free-market economics, and Yale, Harvard and MIT (Massachusetts Institute of Technology) were the centres of orthodox Keynesianism. Public-choice theory (close to being heterodox, though not quite deserving of the label) was centred in Virginia, and Austrian economics in the New York and Auburn universities. Centres of radical and Marxist economics included the New School, in New York, and the University of Massachusetts at Amherst. The variety of the American university system was vital.

CONCLUSIONS

After the Second World War, economics became a much more technical subject, and mathematical techniques were systematically applied to all its branches. This was not a neutral development but was accompanied by a transformation of the subject's content as theories were refined in such a way that they could be treated using the available mathematical tools. The meaning attached even to such basic terms as 'competition', 'markets' and 'unemployment' changed. These developments were something that could happen only in an academic environment, for many theories were developed that had only tenuous links, if any, with real-world problems. Comparisons with 'basic' or 'blue-sky' research (not aimed at any specific use) in science and medicine were used to justify such inquiries.

At the same time as economics became more technical, it also became more international. (Cause and effect are hard to tie down, but there were many causes of internationalization other than the spread of mathematical techniques.) While there are still many economists who can be identified with a single country, there are many who cannot. It became common for an economist to be born in one country, to study in another country (or in two other countries), and to spend their career moving between institutions in a variety of other countries. Communication networks have also become international. The result is that the nationality of economic ideas has become harder than ever to pin down – there is a real sense in which it has become a meaningless concept. Economic ideas have become essentially international. Even where schools have retained national labels (such as 'Austrian' economics) they have become international.

The country at the centre of this process was the United States. Universities, even in countries with long-established academic institutions such as Germany and Britain, have increasingly modelled their graduate teaching on the US model. American textbooks have been widely used in all countries. American criteria for academic advancement, emphasizing the publication of articles in learned journals, have become widespread. In addition, because of the sheer size of the US academic system, American economics has increasingly dominated the pages even of European academic journals. Economists based in the United States clearly dominate the list of Nobel Prize winners and have been responsible for the most influential new ideas in the subject. The process therefore seems to be one of Americanization rather than internationalization. However, against this has to be set the fact that the ideas on which the current consensus is based have significant European roots: mathematical economics in German mathematics of the 1920s; econometrics in Tinbergen's work in the Netherlands; and macroeconomics, through Keynes, in Cambridge, England. In addition, one of the reasons for the apparent American dominance has been the migration of economists from Europe and elsewhere in the first half of the twentieth century. Many of the key players in the transformation of the subject came from German-speaking countries or eastern Europe. If economics has been Americanized, there is a sense in which this is because the American academic system has been so large, so wealthy and so open to international influences.

This, however, is only one side of the story of economics becoming more technical. The other is the increased involvement of economists in government, international organizations and business. Economists have come to be seen as technical experts whose advice is essential to decision-making.

16
Markets and the State since 1945

THE ROLE OF THE STATE

By the end of the Second World War, the size of government and its role in managing the economy were far greater than had been the case before the Great Depression. In the United States, this was the result of the New Deal and wartime mobilization. Britain had mobilized fully for war, and from 1945–51 had a Labour government committed both to a socialist programme involving nationalization of key industries and the creation of a welfare state along the lines that William Beveridge (1879–1963) had proposed in a widely read report published in 1942. The latter was so popular that even Conservative governments hesitated to reverse it. In the United States opposition to the increased role of the state was much stronger, and a government agency that had produced a report advocating a 'bill of economic rights' was disbanded in 1943. Even during Dwight Eisenhower's Republican administration, there was still extensive government intervention, such as building the interstate highway system, as well as the military spending associated with the Cold War and the nuclear arms race. In continental Europe, several countries, notably the Netherlands and France, created planning systems that went beyond anything found in Britain or the United States.

Hayek, who had denounced the move towards collectivism in *The Road to Serfdom* played an important role in organizing opposition to these trends. Taking the view that an intellectual case had to be developed, in 1947 he convened a meeting, which turned out to be dominated by economists, to develop a philosophy of freedom. This

347

was the basis for the Mont Pelerin Society, which provided a network linking economists hostile to socialism and advocating a more limited role for government. He was also instrumental in founding the Institute of Economic Affairs, in London in 1956, the function of which was to turn such ideas into clear policy advice. This eventually developed into a worldwide network of free-market think tanks committed to spreading 'free-market' ideas. These came into their own with the election of governments more sympathetic to their cause after the economic turmoil of the 1970s. The break-up of the Soviet empire in 1989–91 provided a further boost to anti-collectivist thinking in that it was widely held, whether correctly or not, that socialism could not work.

WELFARE ECONOMICS AND SOCIAL CHOICE THEORY

The purpose of welfare economics was to provide guidance as to what this ever-growing state should and should not be doing. Samuelson's *Foundations of Economic Analysis* (p. 287) systematized the field. Addressing Robbins's notion that value judgements were not part of economic science, he argued that it was nonetheless legitimate for economists, in their role as economists, to analyse the implications of alternative values. He did this through using Bergson's concept of a social-welfare function, said to describe 'some ethical belief – that of a benevolent despot, or a complete egotist, or "all men of good will," a misanthrope, the state, race or group mind, God etc'.[1] In general, people will make different judgements about what is good and what is bad, but Samuelson argued that some value judgements were likely to be widely accepted, so he started with those. For example, the judgement that each individual is the best judge of their own welfare (individualism), and that if a change makes one person better off and no one worse off (the Pareto criterion), then social welfare is higher. He worked out the implications of such judgements for the conditions that would maximize social welfare.

Samuelson deliberately said nothing about how the social-welfare function should be determined. In contrast, this was the problem that concerned Kenneth Arrow. In *Social Choice and Individual Values* (1951) he proposed a social-welfare function that was very different from Bergson's. He thought of a social-welfare function (or social-choice function) as being similar to a voting mechanism. Every voter has a preference for a particular political party and a voting mechanism is a rule that translates such individual preferences into a social choice (a government is elected). Possible mechanisms include simple majority voting as well as much more complicated procedures. Arrow viewed the problem of social choice in exactly the same way – as the problem of getting from individuals' views about how society should be organized to a social decision.

The way in which Arrow managed to say anything about such an abstract problem was by specifying a list of conditions that any voting procedure, or social-choice function, should satisfy. These included conditions such as 'If everyone prefers A to B, then A should be chosen' (the Pareto principle); 'No individual should be a dictator'; and so on. He then proved that, although every condition looked extremely reasonable, there was no social-welfare function – no voting procedure or decision rule – that would satisfy all of them. This was his so-called 'impossibility' theorem. A very similar result was also obtained by a British economist, Duncan Black (1908–91), who was concerned with how committees reach decisions.

At around the same time, Arrow and Debreu formulated what have become known as the two 'fundamental theorems of welfare economics'. These results formalized what had been discovered in the 1930s with the new welfare economics. The first theorem is that every competitive equilibrium is efficient in the sense defined by Pareto. In other words, that in a competitive equilibrium it is impossible to make anyone better off without making someone else worse off. The second theorem approaches the problem the other way round. It is that any Pareto-efficient allocation of resources can be made into a competitive equilibrium, provided that income is distributed in an appropriate manner. In 1950, Little coined the term 'Pareto optimum' to denote the optima defined by these conditions.

The Arrow–Debreu theorems mark the culmination of a particular approach to welfare economics, as their inventors' existence proof did for the theory of general competitive equilibrium. Given the value judgements that economists are generally prepared to make – broadly liberal values such as that individuals are the best judges of their own welfare – they establish all that can be said about the merits of perfect competition as a way in which to allocate resources. However, their scope is limited in several ways. The first is that there will typically be many Pareto optima (often an infinite number), each with a different distribution of income, and no guidance is provided on how to choose between them. Indeed, a Pareto optimum is not necessarily better than points that do not meet the optimality conditions. Another problem is that theorems about Pareto optimality provide no guidance about what happens when some of the criteria for optimality are not satisfied. For example, if there are monopolies in several industries, will it be socially beneficial to remove a tax that distorts incentives in another industry? In 1956 Richard Lipsey (1928–) and Kelvin Lancaster (1924–99), worked out their theory of the 'second best', which showed that this would generally not be the case. If there were distortions, such as monopolies or taxes, in some markets, then removing a distortion in another market was as likely to make the overall situation worse as to improve it.

The result of these developments was that by the end of the 1950s the outlook for welfare economics looked very bleak. The new welfare economics had failed to provide any welfare criterion stronger than Pareto optimality. Arrow's impossibility theorem had shown that there was no acceptable way to get from individual preferences to a social preference. Lipsey and Lancaster had undermined the idea that piecemeal reforms could be shown to be beneficial. Arrow and Debreu had established the precise relationship between perfect competition and Pareto efficiency, but nothing could, in general, be said about whether actual policy changes would raise or lower social welfare. This was why, at the end of a survey of the theory of welfare economics, Jan Graaf (1928–2015) wrote that 'the possibility of building a useful and interesting theory of welfare economics ... is exceedingly small'.[2] He deduced that economists could best contribute to human welfare not through normative welfare theory but through making

clear the consequences of possible actions: through positive economics. A slightly less pessimistic view was taken by Little, who was later
involved in working out criteria for project appraisal. He considered
'rigour and refinement [to be] probably worse than useless', all that
was required was 'rough theory, or good common sense'.[3] For example, if the market value of a tricycle is twice that of a bicycle and it
does not cost more than twice as much to manufacture, it is probably
worth producing tricycles.

Tony Atkinson (1944–2017), the founding editor of the *Journal of
Public Economics*, noted that although economists frequently made
statements about what would or would not improve social welfare,
after the 1950s they stopped analysing the criteria underlying such
judgements. What had happened was that welfare economics had
become a specialized field, closely related to the field of social-choice
theory – the study of the normative principles underlying choices
made by groups of people – involving philosophers and political scientists as well as economists. Because the literature in the field became
technically demanding, using mathematical techniques with which
many economists were unfamiliar, it became partly disengaged from
economics more generally, meaning that people could be trained in
economics without engaging in serious discussion of such issues.

The starting point for much social-choice theory and modern welfare economics was Arrow's impossibility theorem. Not only did this
show how new types of mathematical logic could be used, but the
theorem also provided a challenge, to work out conditions under
which democratic decision rules were possible. Although Arrow's
assumptions seemed to be reasonable, further investigation might
show them to be problematic. For example, during the 1950s, several
economists showed that, making apparently weak value judgements,
it was possible to argue for a utilitarian social-welfare function, in
which cardinal measures of individual welfare were added up to get
social welfare. A further stimulus came from *A Theory of Justice*
(1971), by the philosopher John Rawls. He used the device of a 'veil
of ignorance' – the idea that people decide on how society will be
organized without knowing what their position in that society will
be – to argue for an egalitarian concept of social justice. He concluded

that a just distribution of resources is the one that maximizes the consumption of basic goods by the worst-off person in society. This added the issue of justice to that of social welfare.

A particularly influential contributor to this literature was Amartya Sen (1933–), an Indian economist whose career spanned India, Britain and the United States, and whose interest in welfare economics arose out of a concern with problems of poverty and famine in the country of his birth. He challenged the nihilism that was widespread in welfare economics by the 1960s, claiming that apparent differences in values were often dependent on factual assumptions and that it was therefore possible to have a rational discussion about ethics, contrary to what Robbins had argued. He also challenged what he called 'welfarism' – the notion that social welfare depended only on individuals' judgements of their own welfare (their utilities). People might have views about the way collective choices were made. For example, if someone had a commitment to democracy, and they knew that everyone else in society favoured x over y, even though they personally preferred y they might agree that x should be chosen. Individual rights add a further complication to the problem. One interpretation of liberalism is that every individual has a private domain within which they have the right to make decisions. It can be proved that this is inconsistent with the Pareto criterion, for people may have 'nosy' preferences: many people care about what other people are doing.

In the 1980s, Sen, along with the philosopher Martha Nussbaum (1947–) began to develop the notion that it was appropriate to analyse the standard of living in terms of what he called 'capabilities'. Rather than focus on goods that people consume, economists should focus on what people are able to do. This perspective, acknowledging the social dimension of well-being, affected his approach to poverty, for he argued that poverty was not simply about the quantity of goods people consumed. Poverty, Sen argued, could be seen as

> the failure of basic capabilities to reach certain minimally acceptable levels. The functionings relevant to this analysis can vary from such elementary physical ones as being well-nourished, being adequately clothed and sheltered, avoiding preventable morbidity, etc., to more

complex social achievements such as taking part in the life of the community, being able to appear in public without shame, and so on. These are rather 'general' functionings, but . . . the specific form that their fulfilments may take would tend to vary from society to society.[4]

This broadening of the way welfare was considered, and its relation to urgent problems of poor people in India, is consistent with his analysis of the Bengal famine, where he argued that the problem was not a shortage of food but that people were short of entitlements to food; the food was there, but those who needed it were unable to get hold of it. Understanding famine required looking at an entire society, not simply the supply of food.

Sen's welfare theory was very abstract and mathematical, but it arose out of practical concerns: famine (in his work for the International Labour Organization), gender inequality (a particularly acute problem in India), and the meaning of human development (for the United Nations Development Programme). However, he claimed that his more abstract work on social-choice theory had 'helped him investigate the demands of justice, along with 'general – and non-mathematical – political and moral philosophy.'[5]

A particularly important development was the human development index (HDI) created by Sen together with Mahbub ul Haq (1934–), a former finance minister in Pakistan, who was commissioned by the United Nations Development Programme to direct the team responsible for the first UN *Human Development Report* (1990). The report opened by stating that it was concerned with the way in which development enlarged people's choices, a process which involved not only increased income but also a longer and healthier life and being better educated. Though recognizing that human development also involved political freedom, self-respect and guaranteed human rights, and that averages concealed significant inequalities within countries, the report proposed that it be measured by an index (the HDI) that included life expectancy, measures of education and per capita income, constructed so as to take account of levels achieved in developed countries. The *Human Development Report* became an annual publication; the basic HDI remained the same, but was supplemented by other indexes believed relevant for human well-being. By 2021–2, these included HDI adjusted for inequality, an index of gender inequality and a poverty index which also took into account sanitary conditions and access to services such as electricity and water. That year's *Human Development Report* placed great emphasis on the mental distress and uncertainty driven by factors ranging from global environmental problems to political polarization.

MARKET FAILURE AND GOVERNMENT FAILURE

The displacement of the 'old' welfare economics of Sidgwick, Marshall and Pigou by a 'new' welfare economics that did not rest on interpersonal utility comparisons did not mean that the old problems were neglected. To the contrary, some of the issues with which the Cambridge economists had grappled became even more urgent when the size of the state and its role in society increased. A key issue was the justification for providing certain goods at public expense. In 1954 Samuelson, as an exercise in showing the usefulness of mathematics, worked out the theory of pure public goods. Public goods are goods (like the services of a lighthouse, a healthy environment, or a public fireworks display) that, if they are provided at all, are provided for everyone. People cannot be excluded from benefiting from them, and one person can benefit from them without reducing the benefits available to anyone else. (The qualification 'pure' is used to acknowledge that these conditions describe an ideal – problems of congestion, for example, mean that after some point many goods cease to exhibit these characteristics.) The significance of public goods is that, as Samuelson showed, the amount supplied will typically be less than the amount that is socially desirable. Everyone benefits, but no one has an incentive to pay because they will benefit from the public good even if they do not pay for it.

Another circumstance where a decentralized market system is likely to fail to produce an optimal allocation of resources is where one person's activity either harms or benefits someone else. Examples include factories that emit carcinogenic chemicals into the air or the water supply (harmful), or beekeepers whose bees pollinate orchards (beneficial). Such cases had been analysed in detail by Pigou and others. In 1958, Francis Bator (1925–2018) proposed the term 'externality' to denote such effects and explored the various reasons why they might occur. One reason was the public goods problem analysed by Samuelson: the provision of a good by one person or a group of people would inevitably affect others. Another was that, although the producer could in principle charge or compensate those affected by the externality, the administrative costs of doing so would be prohibitive.

Public goods and externalities are both reasons why even competitive markets fail to allocate resources in a Pareto-efficient way. A similar case is that of common-property resources, such as common land on which anyone is allowed to graze their animals, or fisheries that are open to anyone. In a famous article in 1968, the ecologist Garrett Hardin described this as 'the tragedy of the commons'. Resources that were open to all would be over-used.

These concepts of public goods, externalities and common-property resources have been widely used to justify government intervention. It has been argued that government has a responsibility to provide public goods that the market will not supply in sufficient quantities, to use its power to tax in order to compensate for externalities, and to regulate the use of common-property resources. For example, a tax could be imposed on goods associated with negative externalities such as pollution, correcting the defect in the market mechanism, or quotas could be used to prevent overfishing. Such taxes are often described as Pigovian, even though Pigou was much more cautious in proposing intervention than this terminology would suggest. In the 1960s such attitudes fitted in well with the belief that the government also had to intervene at the macroeconomic level to ensure full employment. With the rise of concerns about the environment in the 1970s, the relevance of such theories became even greater.

In 1960, a significant theoretical challenge to the Pigovian approach to externality problems came from Ronald Coase (1910–2013). He made the point that most discussions of externalities, like Pigou's, failed to take account of the legal framework within which economic activities were undertaken. The failure of markets to allocate resources efficiently should, Coase argued, be attributed not to a failure of competition but to the absence of clearly defined property rights and the transaction costs associated with negotiating and enforcing contracts. If property rights were clearly defined and contracts could be negotiated costlessly, negotiation could replace direct government intervention. For example, if the rights over the use of a river were clearly established, a factory owner wishing to pollute the river and anglers with an interest in clean water could negotiate over the amount of pollution that would be allowed. If the factory owner held rights over the river, the anglers could pay them to limit pollution; if the anglers held the rights, the factory owner could buy the right to pollute. The result of this perspective was that Coase saw a much greater scope for the market and a more limited role for the state than did Pigou.

Coase had drawn attention to the importance of such analysis for the law, analysing how the courts in Britain and the United States had tackled the problem. As Commons had done thirty years earlier, he claimed that the way in which judges had interpreted phrases such as 'reasonable' and 'common or ordinary use' frequently reflected economic considerations. A year later, Guido Calabresi (1932–), a legal scholar, made the implications for law even clearer in an article on the law of torts (accidents), written independently of Coase's article. Citing numerous legal cases, Calabresi argued that the goal should be to minimize the costs resulting from accidents rather than to pursue some vague notion of 'justice' and, therefore, that liability for accident damage should fall on the party who could most easily (cheaply) have taken steps to avoid the accident. For example, in the case of road traffic accidents, should the driver automatically be liable for damages caused by injury to a cyclist, or should liability depend on the circumstances of the accident? Calabresi explained that if markets were functioning well, the outcome would be decisions that took into account all costs associated with accidents: an efficient outcome should be reached, whoever is liable. However, he noted that in reality markets do not work this smoothly, in part because of information problems and costs of negotiation. His conclusion was that the law governing liability had important implications for the allocation of resources. Placing liability on the least-cost avoider was thus seen as a useful correction for this market failure.

These results, derived by Coase and Calabresi, in what became two extremely widely cited papers, were important in the growth of the field of law and economics. A key institution was the University of Chicago Law School, to which the economist Aaron Director (1901–2004) was appointed in 1946. Supported by Hayek, he headed a free-market study building on Hayek's *Road to Serfdom* and then, in the 1950s, a study of anti-trust policy. Until his retirement in 1965, he taught an influential course in anti-trust law, arguing that many activities traditionally thought to be anti-competitive might actually be efficient. Together with George Stigler (1911–91) he promulgated the argument that, contrary to the widely held belief at the time, monopolies were transient and that there was no need for active anti-trust policy. The market would allocate resources most efficiently without government interference. Coase was the second economist appointed to the Chicago Law School in 1964.

It was Stigler who first wrote of 'the Coase theorem', a term that has since become ubiquitous. This theorem suggests that, in the absence of transaction costs, there would be no externalities because any inefficiencies would be negotiated away by the parties involved. This was a very powerful theorem because it had the potential to make the case for market solutions to most economic problems. However, in formulating the theorem in this way, Stigler was parting company with Coase, who never liked the terminology 'Coase theorem'. Coase's goal was to draw attention to property rights and the role of transaction costs, and the importance of institutions and the role played by institutions in promoting efficiency (or in not doing so). The 'Coase theorem', on the other hand, suggests that institutions do not matter at all when it comes to efficiency.

One of the most prominent contributors to the emerging field of law and economics was Richard Posner (1939–). Making the assumption that people behave rationally in relation to issues that involve the law, he argued that legal rules could function as prices, deterring certain behaviours in the same way that high prices deter consumption. The law would take account not only of justice (the traditional view) but also economic efficiency. For example, if breaches of contract resulted in resources being used more efficiently, then this should be allowed. Later in his career, his approach softened and he adopted a more pragmatic approach, taking the view that, when faced with a dispute, rather than being obsessed with precedent a judge should start by asking 'what is a sensible resolution of this dispute?'[6] Only then should they check whether there was any legal obstacle. Strongly influenced by Stigler, his focus was on how economic analysis could be important for the law, rather than Coase's emphasis on what understanding the law could contribute to economics.

Conventional views of the role of government were also challenged, also around 1960, with the development of theories of how voters, governments and bureaucracies behaved (pp. 339–40). In these theories, governments were not treated as disinterested organizations that acted in the public interest but were assumed to be made up of individuals who are seeking to achieve their own ends. Politicians offer policies that will maximize support in elections. Managers run their organizations in ways that increase their own status and income. Taxes and government spending came to be seen as the outcome of political processes in which competing interests were expressed. The result was that the concept of government failure came to be placed alongside that of market failure.

An important problem linked to government failure is 'rent seeking', a concept introduced by Anne Krueger (1934–). A business has two ways it can increase its profits: it can invest in productive activity, purchasing new machinery, developing new products or more efficient techniques; alternatively it can invest in lobbying politicians, or bribing them, for example, to increase tariffs on imported goods or taxes on rival products which will enable it to charge higher prices. The latter is an example of rent-seeking, by which the firm increases its own income even though its activities do not benefit, and may harm, society. This activity of rent-seeking may even be competitive, as rival businesses compete for the favours of politicians. It is clearly a problem for society if it is more profitable for firms to invest in rent-seeking than in productive investment. Krueger used the examples of Turkey and India to argue that in some countries, rent-seeking was potentially large enough to be a significant problem.

Taken together, theories of market failure and government failure raise questions about whether efficient resource allocation will ever be possible – that self-interested behaviour is an impediment to efficiency in both government and the market. Against this pessimistic view, Elinor Ostrom (1933–2012), a political scientist and the first woman to receive the Nobel Prize in Economic Science, argued that in practice societies do often find ways of solving such problems. The problem she tackled was common-property resources, such as common land on which anyone is allowed to graze their animals. This was the problem that ecologist Garrett Hardin had described, in 1968, as 'the tragedy of the commons'. Resources that are open to all will be over-used because if one person chooses, for example, to limit the number of cows they graze on common land, the benefits will be shared with everyone else who uses the land. Or if an angler leaves fish in the sea, most of the benefit will accrue to others. Individuals have an incentive to over-use such resources.

Ostrom approached this problem through looking at how such problems were solved in practice. This involved moving away from theoretical generalizations towards detailed analysis of institutions, the rules governing common-property resources and mechanisms for enforcing those rules. It was, she argued, an oversimplification to see 'the market' and 'government' as the only types of organization. Local communities such as parishes can establish rules and monitor compliance in ways that national governments cannot. Similarly, the ownership of property (property rights) could typically be broken down into different rights (the right to enter a property; the right to harvest resources; the right to manage resources; the right to exclude people; and the right to sell or lease assets), each of which could be governed in a different way. For example, Ostrom found that a Swiss village avoided problems of overgrazing by imposing the rule that farmers could graze only the number of cattle that they were able to look after over the winter. She found that people can see that it is in their own interest to commit themselves to collective action and to devise methods to ensure that people cooperate. Also, people are sometimes altruistic.

TRANSACTION COSTS AND INFORMATION

Coase's argument about negotiated solutions to externality problems drew attention to the idea of transaction costs – the costs of transferring ownership from one person to another. They arise for many reasons:

> The parties to a contract have to find each other, they have to communicate and to exchange information. The goods must be described, inspected, weighed and measured. Contracts must be drawn up, lawyers may be consulted, title is transferred and records have to be kept. In some cases, compliance needs to be enforced through legal action and breach of contract may lead to litigation.[7]

The term 'transaction cost' was first used by Marschak in 1950, but the idea has a long history. Economists frequently referred to 'frictions' and used the metaphor of money being the oil that reduces such frictions. In the 1920s Commons argued that transactions (which he defined very broadly, to include much more than the exchange of goods and services) should form the focus of economists' attention. In 1937 Coase argued that transaction costs could explain the existence and size of firms. He pointed out that activities could be organized in two ways: through the market or through management within a firm. Both methods involve costs, but the costs are different. He then argued that the boundary of the firm – the dividing line between activities organized managerially and those that are organized through the market – should be the one that minimizes transaction costs. In other words, transaction costs explain why firms should exist (why some transactions are undertaken outside the market) and why the economy is not organized as one giant firm (a centrally planned economy). Around 1970 economists began to appreciate the significance of Coase's idea. Oliver Williamson (1932–2020) and others began to find ways to make the idea of transaction costs operational in analysing firms and industrial structure. They used it to answer questions such as why certain industries are vertically integrated (the same firm controls the supply of materials, production and distribution) whereas others are not.

The significance of this idea was that it offered an alternative to the conventional theory of the firm. The traditional view saw the firm as a technical unit for transforming inputs into outputs. Its size was determined by technology – steel firms are large because production costs are lower for larger firms than for smaller ones, whereas greengrocers can be small because small shops can be as efficient as large ones. Coase, instead, saw the firm as an organization or, as Williamson put it, as a governance structure. This is, of course, obvious. However, it was not until Coase introduced the idea of transaction costs that economists had any way in which to analyse this. Many economists had studied the organization of industry (a classic example is Marshall's *Industry and Trade*, 1919), but such work was largely descriptive. Economists had not found a theoretical framework that could explain why industries were organized as they were. 'Industrial organization' existed as a field within economics, and courses were taught, but they focused on problems such as monopoly, regulation and anti-trust laws: the way industry was organized as a datum.

A related idea with the potential to transform thinking about markets was the notion that information was limited and that not everyone might have the same information. If this is the case, markets may not operate as the traditional theory of supply and demand, based on perfect competition and the assumption that everyone is fully informed, suggests.

Knight had pointed out, in 1921, that the standard theory of perfect competition assumes perfect information. In 1961, Stigler challenged this assumption on the grounds that information was costly to acquire and, because not all sellers asked the same price, consumers typically have to search for the best price for products they want to buy. This raises the question of what is the optimal searching strategy: how many stores should someone visit before deciding where to make a purchase? Searching raised issues of advertising and reputation that had typically been neglected, or treated very informally in economic theory.

One field in which information plays a particularly important role is medical care, a problem analysed by Arrow in 1963. Arrow was not the first to analyse the problem of health-care provision, Selma Mushkin (1913–79) having tried to define the field of health economics some years before, but he analysed two issues that are fundamental to the market for health care: adverse selection and moral hazard. Adverse selection is the problem that, if a company offers medical insurance for a fixed price, because it cannot tell who is healthy and who is not, people with poor health are more likely to purchase insurance than people who are in good health. Moral hazard is the problem that, if people have insurance, they are less likely to take care of themselves than if they are uninsured. These problems, both relating to asymmetric information (people know more than the insurance company about their health and their behaviour), make it difficult for efficient markets to exist.

Information and information processing were also central to Simon's work. He introduced the notion of 'satisficing'. Faced with the cost of processing information, it would be rational for people to decide that it was not worth trying to find the best possible solution to a problem because, after a certain point, the gains from making a better decision would not be enough to make the cost of doing so worthwhile. Instead, it was sensible to aim for a satisfactory solution. For example, a firm might decide, at the outset, what would constitute a satisfactory rate of profit and then search for a way to organize production that achieved that. In other words, decision-making was costly. Though known among economists for the concept of satisficing, this theory was, for Simon, part of a much broader and deeper investigation into decision-making that encompassed artificial intelligence and computing.

Even more fundamental problems were introduced by asymmetric information – situations where one party to a transaction knows more than the other. In 'The market for lemons', George Akerlof (1940–) looked at the market for used cars (automobiles). If the seller knows whether the car being sold is a lemon (American slang for a bad car) but the buyer does not have this information, it is possible that there will be no price at which a sale can be agreed. For the market to work it is necessary for there to be devices such as warranties and inspections. This is a general problem, a particularly important example being employment contracts, where an employer will often not know whether a worker is hard-working until after they have been hired. In such situations, as Michael Spence (1943–) showed, education may serve as a signal: because it is more difficult (more costly) for an unproductive worker to acquire, an educational qualification may serve to signal that someone is a productive worker. This signalling function of educational qualifications can work even if education has no effect on someone's productivity.

The most general statement of this was by Sanford Grossman (1953–), and Stiglitz, who showed that, once information was introduced, markets could not be completely efficient. If someone tried to use information they possessed (say by trading on the stock exchange), the very act of trading would reveal information to others, reducing its value. Differences in the information available to different agents were shown to produce results that were far removed from the perfectly competitive ideal. For example, if banks were unable properly to monitor the performance of businesses to whom they had made loans, it might be rational for them to maintain a low rate of interest and ration borrowers, behaviour inconsistent with the standard theory of supply and demand.

MECHANISM DESIGN AND THE ROLE OF MARKETS

Information is central to the problem of how economic activity should be organized. In the 1930s, Hayek had argued that the schemes designed by market socialists such as Oskar Lange would not work because they had tried to design a socialist system that would allocate resources as efficiently as would a competitive capitalist economy, but Hayek had argued that no central planning authority could have the information necessary to do this. Leonid Hurwicz

(1917–2008), a Polish emigré, provided a formal analysis of the problem, showing first that a system in which supply and demand responded to prices (as in competitive markets) required much less information than one in which a central authority allocated quantities in response to information on how people valued different goods and services. The crucial step came in a paper published in 1972 when he took account of the fact that people may cheat and that information may not be truthful – that, in order to achieve an outcome that is better for them, an agent may pretend that their preferences are different from what they really are. For example, if someone knows that an arbitrator will split the difference between what the seller asks and what the buyer offers to pay, a seller will have an incentive to ask more, and a buyer an incentive to offer less, with the result that the outcome will be based on incorrect information. This means that systems have to be designed so that people have an incentive to behave in the desired way that takes into account the costs both of collecting information and of ensuring that people have the right incentives.

This work came at the same time that other economists were advocating increased use of market mechanisms. The most prominent of these was Friedman, who argued for the virtues of the market in the columns he wrote for *Newsweek* between 1966 and 1984, and in his mass-market books *Capitalism and Freedom* (1962) and *Free to Choose* (1980), the latter co-authored by Rose Friedman (1910–2009). He claimed that more activities should be left to the market, and that the state should do less. The move towards such policies is associated with the coming to power of conservative politicians such as Thatcher and Reagan, but such moves had broader support. In the 1960s Robert McNamara, Secretary of Defence under Kennedy and Johnson and previously president of Ford Motor Company, had brought RAND's systems analysis into his department. In the 1970s such methods involving quantified cost–benefit analysis spread within the United States government under Presidents Ford and Carter as well as Reagan. Many of the economists advocating deregulation were trained not in Chicago but in Harvard, by Edward Mason (1899–1992). At the political level, critiques of government were mounted not just by conservatives but, just as forcefully, by consumer advocates such as Jane Jacobs and Ralph Nader.

One of the lessons learned in the 1980s and 1990s was that, contrary to the claims of those who simply wanted government regulations abolished, attention had to be paid to the design of markets: to how markets worked. Nowhere was this more obvious than during the collapse of the Soviet Union, where the planning structure was removed before alternative institutions had been put in place. In Russia, the result of the transition was economic chaos, poverty and a dramatic reduction in life expectancy. The economists who advocated 'shock therapy' and a quick transition to a market economy did not come out of the episode well, even if the reality was that the Russian government lost control of the situation. Thus even if the collapse of the Soviet Union appeared, to some, to vindicate the claim made by Mises and Hayek that socialism could not work, it raised doubts about whether simply removing state control was sufficient.

It is tempting to argue that economic theory proved of little help in designing a rational transition from socialism to capitalism. One might claim that the most important lesson the reformers needed was to be found in Adam Smith, who emphasized the importance to any capitalist system of a secure framework of law, morality and property rights, which simply did not exist in the former Soviet Union. Most contributions to the socialist-calculation debate, along with most welfare economics, missed the importance of effective institutions entirely. In contrast, the creation of the single market in the European Union, completed in 1992, shortly after the fall of the Soviet empire, was more successful. It was a much simpler exercise, involving the harmonization of regulations rather than the creation of a market economy from scratch. In addition, a lot of attention was paid to creating appropriate institutions, with numerous regulations aimed at ensuring fair competition, maintenance of standards and other social goals.

Where economists have had more success is with narrower, more well-defined problems where, in a literature that traces its roots back to the work of Hurwicz, they have been able to pay close attention to how markets are designed. This literature, which includes work by Nobel Prize winners Paul Milgrom (1948–), Eric Maskin (1950–),

Roger Myserson (1951–) and Alvin Roth (1951–), focuses on creating incentives so that people behave in ways that achieve the outcomes that market designers are trying to achieve. It draws extensively on both game theory and experimental economics. Game theory is central because it focuses on what it is rational for people to do when faced with given situations and hence on how they are likely to behave; and experimental economics is important because it proved necessary to work out many of the details on which outcomes depended. The relative credit awarded to game theory and experimental methods has varied between applications even where both were clearly involved has been disputed.

One apparent success of a newly designed market relates to the problem of acid rain in the United States, caused by sulphur dioxide emissions, primarily from power stations. Attempts at regulation during the 1970s had not been successful and some had even backfired. For example, imposing limits on the amount of sulphur that could be emitted by new power stations caused companies to extend the life of old ones; imposing limits on emissions led companies that were below the legal limit to burn cheaper coal with a higher sulphur content. The solution, imposed in 1990, was to institute a market in sulphur dioxide emissions – permits to pollute. The result was that emissions fell and companies had an incentive to implement more efficient methods that reduced emissions.

Another example was the use of auctions to allocate rights to use parts of the radio spectrum for mobile telecommunications. Previously this had typically been done largely by 'beauty contests' in which companies submitted proposals and the authorities decided how to allocate rights on the basis of how these would achieve whatever objectives they had in mind. In the 1990s governments turned instead to auctions, economists being involved in designing them, drawing on economic theory and even the results of experiments. The rationale for auctions was that, in addition to raising revenue, they would result in a more efficient allocation of resources, for rights to the radio spectrum would be sold to the firms that valued them most highly. However, the complexity of the problem meant that very close attention needed to be paid to how the auction was designed. There are many possible types of auction (for example, ascending or descending; open or sealed bids; are different lots auctioned simultaneously or sequentially; and are there opportunities to revise bids?) and, in choosing between them, account had to be taken of the complexity of the resources being auctioned. Spectrum rights could be bundled in different ways and the values of different bundles to a company would depend on what other rights they either owned or were able to purchase. It became clear that the choice of auction was critical to achieving the desired objectives and, in order to decide what would work best, the economists involved used a combination of game theory and experiments. Some auctions were considered failures, but others were believed to be highly successful in that they raised large amounts of revenue, though it was harder to establish that the efficiency goals were achieved.

There was also much privatization and deregulation from the 1980s onwards. A prominent example was air travel, where the aim of deregulation was to reduce prices through increasing competition. Though this was politically contentious, involving strikes and opposition from companies that lost out, and though there is room for debate over the extent to which services improved for passengers, increasing competition in air travel was comparatively straightforward. Ticket prices fell, lower-cost carriers were able to enter the market and many new services were provided. In contrast, there were other industries where the infrastructure imposed severe constraints, making it necessary to design new types of market to ensure competition. Examples here include the UK privatization of rail travel, and of the gas and electricity supply industries. Privatization took the form of dividing up the rail system, with different companies owning the track and the rolling stock, with elaborate contractual arrangements governing the relations between these companies and the companies involved in running the services. Because companies had monopolies of services in different areas, regulations and price controls were needed. In the gas and electricity industries, where all suppliers fed energy into a common grid, there was a clear need for regulations on how firms could compete. Economists were involved in designing new forms of regulation and sometimes in the regulatory process itself.

CONCLUSIONS

After the Second World War, socialism was still an issue in some countries and there was considerable debate over the appropriate extent of government intervention, but there was widespread acceptance of a mixed economy: a market economy in which government intervened in order to secure socially acceptable outcomes. Scepticism about government intervention increased from the 1970s, with economists producing theoretical arguments about government failure to explain why government policies had often been less successful than had been hoped. There was extensive deregulation and privatization, greatly expanding the role of the market. However, this did not mean that technical economic analysis became irrelevant. To the contrary, economic theory played an important role in designing the new markets – in designing institutions that would achieve the outcomes that expanding the role of the market were designed to achieve. In order to achieve this, many of the new developments in economic theory – including game theory, theories of asymmetric information and transactions costs – proved essential, for they showed that, even in competitive markets, the intuitions resulting from simple supply-and-demand models might be misleading.

17

Macroeconomics and Policy, 1939–2008

THE 'NEW ECONOMICS'

The so-called 'new economics' brought together what, in the interwar period, had been two fields: monetary economics and business-cycle theory. Economists came to call this field 'macroeconomics', a term that in the late 1940s was sometimes placed in quotation marks, indicating that it was still novel, but which by the early 1960s was being used in the titles of textbooks. It deals with the behaviour of aggregates: as Boulding put it, macroeconomics 'deals with large aggregates of economic quantities, with price levels, output levels, wage levels, and the broad relationships of classes, industries, and nations'.[1] It was widely believed that this new field should be traced back to Keynes's *General Theory*: that macroeconomics *was* effectively Keynesian economics. For example, in a survey of contemporary economics organized by the American Economic Association at the end of the 1940s to help with training returning servicemen, Keynes was far and away the most frequently cited author.

However, although Keynes's work was undoubtedly very important, it is an exaggeration to see macroeconomics as originating solely in his work, for the field also drew on the work of many other economists. The interwar period had, not surprisingly, seen a proliferation of theories on problems relating to the level of economic activity and unemployment, and many of these found their way into post-war economics. Some did so because Keynes drew on previous work; others came in as economists tried to make sense of Keynes's ideas, reinterpreting them in the process. Although the IS–LM model (p. 259) was often taken to be synonymous with Keynesian economics, this is misleading. The IS–LM model and other models that emerged in the 1940s were both less and more than a summary of Keynes's ideas. They were less in that they omitted ideas that Keynes thought central to his theory, and they were more in that they drew on resources not found in Keynes's work. The example of Hansen and Samuelson, who brought Keynesian and institutionalist ideas together, illustrates this.

In addition, to see the new economics as synonymous with Keynesian economics is to ignore the drive towards quantitative economics that was a major factor in the emergence of post-war macroeconomics. Post-war macroeconomics was centred on measures of national income and its components (notably consumption and investment), which had not existed for most of the interwar period. Because Keynesian ideas had been developed and applied during the war, when many American economists were working in government agencies, there was a focus on practical application and on data, with the result that the development of theory had come to be tied up with the revolution in national accounting, a process in which British and American economists collaborated. There was also a greater emphasis on dynamics than was found in Keynes's *General Theory* as well as interest in the construction of quantitative models. This is best illustrated by the work of Tinbergen and Klein (pp. 267–8).

During the 1940s, one of the main exponents of the 'modern theory of income analysis' (a politically less provocative label than 'Keynesian economics') was Samuelson,[2] whose elementary textbook, *Economics: An Introductory Analysis* (1948), became a bestseller and changed the way economics was taught. It went through nineteen editions. He simplified Keynes's theory of the multiplier into a simple diagram, a version of which is shown in Figure 6. Saving increases with income, whereas investment does not. There will therefore be a level of income at which saving and investment are equal. If investment rises (if the horizontal line shifts upwards), but the saving function remains unchanged, the level of income at which saving and investment are equal will rise. The amount by which income rises depends on the slope of the saving function.

Fig. 6 Samuelson's saving and investment diagram

The rate of interest does not come into this diagram. One reason for playing down the importance of interest rates is that these ideas were developed during the 1940s, and since 1942 American interest rates had been pegged at very low levels to allow the federal government to borrow cheaply during the war and to protect the value of war bonds after the war (when the rate of interest goes up, the price of bonds goes down).

Other economists, including Franco Modigliani (1918–2003) and Don Patinkin (1922–97), both students of Marschak, continued the process of making sense of Keynes's theory by translating it into mathematical models that made microeconomic sense, working out just what had to be assumed in order to get Keynesian results. In 1953, Hansen, the leading exponent of Keynesian ideas in the 1940s and 1950s, produced *A Guide to Keynes*, a book that explained the theory using Hicks's diagram, giving the curves the labels used in Figure 5. The diagram came to be known as the IS–LM model and became central to macroeconomics for many years.

In the 1940s and 1950s, a major limitation on the construction and use of empirical models such as those of Tinbergen and Klein was the limited power of computers, but during the 1960s, as electronic (mainframe) computers became more widely available, these models grew in both size and sophistication. For example, in 1964 Klein produced a model of the United States based on quarterly data, comprising thirty-seven equations and estimated using more advanced statistical techniques than had been employed in his earlier work. The larger size of the model was the result of a much more detailed modelling of variables such as consumption (broken down into durable goods, non-durables and services) and investment (where Klein took account of inventories and new orders). Klein became a central figure in macro-econometric modelling. Not only was he responsible for the Wharton model, produced by the Wharton School of Business at the University of Pennsylvania, but he had connections with many other modelling groups.

Developing such large and complex models generally involved large teams of economists, for which funding was needed. An important model was the Brookings model (produced by the Brookings Institution, a think tank established in the 1920s). The first version, published in 1965, contained around 200 variables, later increased to over 400, and provided a much more detailed analysis of the economy than smaller models could provide. For example, it had separate equations for automobile sales and for spending on food and drink. Housing was distinguished from non-residential construction, and several industries were analysed. Equally important, it was the result of a collaborative research effort involving economists from different universities and other institutions. This was followed by a series of other models on a similar scale during the 1960s and 1970s. For example, the FMP (Fed–MIT–Penn) model was produced through collaboration between MIT, the University of Pennsylvania and the Federal Reserve in Washington. Not surprisingly, the Federal Reserve's involvement meant that the banking and monetary sector of the economy was modelled in more detail than was the case in many other models.

Unlike the earlier models, several of the new ones were produced by commercial organizations while others were taken over by commercial organizations when their original sponsors ceased to support them. As this happened, the emphasis shifted away from exploring new techniques and developing new concepts towards keeping the models up to date so that they could provide business with the forecasts that were being demanded. The hope was that, by using an increasingly detailed model, estimated by ever more sophisticated statistical techniques, more accurate forecasts would be produced. Though there were national differences, similar developments occurred in other countries. In the

Netherlands and France, for example, modelling was part of a more extensive apparatus of national economic planning.

Though there were exceptions, these models were generally Keynesian in their broad structure: aggregate demand for goods and services was modelled in great detail, being broken down into various categories following the national accounts. These accounts adopted the Keynesian categories of consumption, investment, government spending on goods and services, exports and imports. Each of these was then subdivided into a more detailed classification. This core, in which national income was determined by the level of aggregate demand, was supplemented by other equations to determine variables such as productive capacity, prices, wages and interest rates. Many of them could be seen as vastly more elaborate versions of either the IS–LM model or Samuelson's saving–investment diagram.

MONETARY ECONOMICS

During the 1950s and 1960s, monetary economics developed in two main ways. One approach was the revival of the quantity theory of money by Friedman that began with a widely read article in 1956. This theory argued that the main factor explaining inflation was increases in the quantity of money (the stock of currency in circulation plus the stock of bank deposits). Friedman sought to prove his case through extensive empirical work on the relationship between money, prices and interest rates, much of it written jointly with his long-time collaborator Anna J. Schwartz (1915–2012), a researcher at the National Bureau who became a leading authority on monetary data. They argued that the money supply did not respond passively to other developments in the economy but was an important source of disturbance; and that changes in the money supply exerted a powerful effect on the economy. In the short run a rise in the money supply would raise output, but eventually output would return to its original level and the only effect would be on the price level.

One place where Friedman and Schwartz made this argument was *A Monetary History of the United States, 1867–1960* (1963).

They provided evidence that the money supply in the United States had often changed for reasons that had nothing to do with the demand for money: that the money supply depended, primarily, not on how much money people needed to engage in their day-to-day activities, but on the actions of the authorities. A particularly important case study was their analysis of the Great Depression. The conventional view was that the Federal Reserve had been powerless to stop the slide into depression, but they claimed that this was wrong: what might have been a regular cyclical depression turned into the Great Depression because the Federal Reserve allowed the money supply to collapse. The extreme depth of the Great Depression was caused not by impotent monetary policy but by incompetent monetary policy.

Another important claim made by Friedman and Schwartz was that, although the money supply has a powerful effect on economic activity, it was not possible to use this relationship as the basis for controlling the business cycle, because the effects of monetary changes were felt only after a long and unpredictable lag. If a central bank were to raise the money supply, the effects might be felt a year, or even three years, later, by which time it might be the wrong policy. This, Friedman argued, was fatal for Keynesian demand-management policy. He concluded that the aim of policy should be to prevent money from being a source of disturbance, and the way to do this was to ensure that the stock of money grew at a constant, known rate. For example, if the money supply grows at 5 per cent per annum, and the real economy grows at 3 per cent, then inflation will be 2 per cent.

Friedman's view of money as controlled by the Federal Reserve fitted with a fairly mechanical view of the creation of money. The bulk of the money supply, bank deposits, was created by commercial banks, but their ability to lend was constrained by the availability of reserves issued by the central bank: the monetary base, or high-powered money. The reason for the latter name was that if reserves increased by $1 million, and commercial banks had to keep 10 per cent of deposits in the form of reserves, they would be able to expand their lending by $9 million: a $1 million increase in reserves would result in a $10 million increase in the money supply. Such 'money multipliers' (not to be confused with the Keynesian multiplier) were central to Friedman and Schwartz's *Monetary History*.

Friedman proposed to deal with the problem of financial instability by two policy changes. The first was a monetary rule: that policy should be aimed at achieving a constant growth rate of the money supply. Though often seen as an anti-inflation measure, preventing excessive monetary growth, such a rule would also have prevented the collapse of the money supply that occurred during the Great Depression. The other was 100 per cent reserve banking, in which commercial banks were required to hold cash or risk-free government debt to back all of their liabilities, removing their ability to destabilize economic activity.

In contrast, Tobin, a prominent Keynesian economist, developed a different view of money. He explained the money supply as the result of supply of and demand for different assets: the volume of bank deposits depended on how much people wanted to keep in the bank. During the 1960s, together with colleagues at the Cowles Commission, now at Yale, he constructed models of the financial sector that were much more elaborate than Friedman's, recognizing that there were many types of bank deposit and that securities with different times to maturity carried different rates of interest. For example, in those days a demand deposit (checking or current account) with a commercial bank was very different from a savings deposit at a savings and loan association or even from a time deposit (deposit account) at the same bank. If there is a spectrum of bank deposits, each of which is slightly different from the next, it does not make sense to pick out certain accounts and say 'these are money but the others are not'.

Tobin's approach has several advantages. It makes it possible to analyse the effects of a wider range of policy measures that cannot be analysed in a simple quantity-theory framework: increases in the supply of bank reserves, payment of interest on checking accounts, central bank purchases or sales of short- and long-term bonds (including what was later called quantitative easing), and restrictions on bank lending. It also moves attention away from aggregates, such as the various definitions of money (M1, M2, M3, etc., each of which involves a different set of bank deposits) towards interest rates, on the grounds that these are what influence people's behaviour. For Tobin, a particularly important variable was one that he called q – the ratio of the rate of return on productive capital (machinery, buildings, etc.) to the cost of capital (the cost of raising funds through either borrowing or issuing equity). Tobin's q measures the incentive to invest in productive assets and hence is important in explaining the level of investment, central to the Keynesian explanation of unemployment.

Another critique of Friedman came from Ben Bernanke (1953–). He accepted the view of Friedman and Schwartz that monetary policy errors were responsible for the depth of the Great Depression, though he argued that the mechanism involved was different. Where Friedman and Schwartz blamed the collapse of the money supply, Bernanke's argument, in a paper published in 1983, was that bank failures caused production to fall because they disrupted the supply of credit to businesses. Even if other banks were able to provide credit, it would take time for those businesses to build relationships with them. This involved a different view of banks, not simply as creators of money but as conduits through which funds were channelled from savers to potential investors. The policy of 100 per cent reserve banking advocated by Friedman would make it impossible for them to perform this function.

One of the difficulties with this role for banks is that savers typically want to be able to access their funds at short notice. Emergencies happen, causing people to need money very quickly. In contrast, businesses that want to invest in productive assets (factories, machinery and so on) need to borrow for longer periods; if they had to liquidate their investments in order to repay their loans at short notice, they would often make a loss, or at least not make as much profit as if they kept funds invested as originally planned. This imbalance between the liquidity of assets (loans to investors) and liabilities (deposits which may have to be repaid), which is inherent in acting as an intermediary between savers and investors, necessarily makes banking a risky activity. Douglas Diamond (1953–) and Philip Dybvig (1955–), in a paper also published in 1983, provided a formal model of this problem. In their model, banking was socially beneficial because it provided an efficient mechanism for channelling funds, but there could be bank runs, unless institutions were in place to prevent this. For example, government-provided insurance of bank deposits, ensuring that if a bank failed, depositors would not lose their money, could eliminate the motive for bank runs.

INFLATION AND THE PHILLIPS CURVE

During the 1950s the conventional view of inflation was that it was caused by excessive demand in the economy, as was clearly the case during the Second World War and, a few years later, the Korean War. It was well understood that there was a relationship between the level of economic activity, which could be measured by either real national output (national income adjusted for price changes) or by the level of employment and the rate of inflation. However, towards the end of the 1950s, United States inflation rates began to creep upwards even though there was, apparently, plenty of spare capacity. To explain this, economists turned to what they called 'cost push' – the notion that, independently of the level of demand, powerful unions might push wages and costs upwards, generating inflation. It was common knowledge that if the cost of living was rising, unions would be likely to demand higher wages and that, anticipating higher prices for their products, firms would be more likely to agree to wage increases.

The relationship between inflation and unemployment eventually came to be known as the Phillips curve, named after an LSE economist, A. W. Phillips (1914–75). He was an engineer who had turned to economics and used his engineering skills to create the 'Phillips machine', a physical model of an economy in which coloured water was pumped through a system of transparent pipes and tanks. Flows of water represented flows of income in the Keynesian system. Samuelson had used such a diagram in his textbook, but the Phillips machine was 'hydraulic Keynesianism' in the most literal sense of the term: the metaphor of a circular flow of income was translated into real flows of water. If the machine went wrong, the laboratory or classroom could literally be flooded.

As an engineer, Phillips was interested in the mathematics of how to

Fig. 7 The Phillips curve

control dynamic systems. In an article on the subject he drew a curve depicting the generally accepted negative relationship between inflation and unemployment: that when unemployment rose, inflation fell, and vice versa. And then in 1958, he wrote an article that estimated such a curve from British data on wages and unemployment. Because unemployment could not fall below zero, however high inflation might be, and because wages fell by little, even when unemployment rose to 20 per cent during the Great Depression, the result was a curve rather than a straight line, as shown in Fig. 7.

The shape of the curve was soon given a theoretical interpretation by Lipsey. His explanation of the curve was based on the idea that if supply of any good (including labour) exceeds demand, the price will fall, and if demand is greater than supply, the price will rise. This explains the negative relationship between unemployment and inflation but not why it should be so strongly curved. To explain this, he introduced the notion of 'frictional unemployment': unemployment that arises because workers are different from each other and have to be matched with the right job before they can be employed. If there are lots of unemployed workers but few vacancies, employers will easily be able to find suitable recruits. Similarly, if there are many vacancies and a small number of unemployed workers, those workers will easily be able to find jobs. It is in between these situations that frictional unemployment will be highest.

In the same year as Lipsey's article, Samuelson and Solow found a similar relationship for the United States, though they were doubtful that it held in the long run, as appeared to be the case in Britain. Reviewing theories of inflation, they were looking for ways to establish whether inflation was caused by 'cost push' or 'demand pull'. Explanations of inflation and the Phillips curve could provide a framework within which to do this. If the curve were stable, movements along it might be attributed to changes in demand, and changes in inflation caused by shifts in the curve could be attributed to trade-union power and 'cost push'.

Though describing their estimates as 'guesses', they calculated that 5 or 6 per cent unemployment would be necessary to generate stable prices, and that in order to keep unemployment under 3 per cent, it would be necessary to have 4 or 5 per cent inflation.[3] However, if policymakers tried to run a 'low-pressure' economy in order to have stable prices, expectations might change so as to shift the curve. Unfortunately, there was no conclusive evidence on how the curve would shift. Persistent high unemployment might reduce expectations, pushing it down, or it might create an increasing amount of structural unemployment, pushing the curve up. It would therefore be 'overhasty' to draw clear conclusions from their estimates of the Phillips curve.[4] During the 1960s, as inflation increased, and as electronic computers became more accessible to economists, there was a surge in empirical work on what determined inflation, trying to measure factors such as union power. However, no consensus emerged.

Lipsey had provided a theoretical explanation of the shape of the Phillips curve, and Samuelson and Solow had argued that 'imperfect competition is the essence of the [cost-push] problem', but neither of them provided an explanation based on utility-maximizing individuals.[5] This step was taken by Edmund Phelps (1933–) in the late 1960s. In one paper he assumed, like everyone else, that inflation depended on the rate of capacity utilization (the unemployment rate), but he also took explicit account of expected inflation. The rationale is that if people expect a given rate of inflation, this will be the starting point in decisions over wages and prices. The result was that he drew a different Phillips curve for each expected rate of inflation: if expected inflation rose by one percentage point, then the curve shifted upwards by one percentage point. It can be shown that there will be only a single unemployment rate at which people's expectations of inflation turn out to be correct. In another paper, he built on Lipsey's theory, developing a theory of labour-market turnover based on the assumption that information was limited, and that firms had to form expectations of the wages that would be offered by other firms. He provided a formal theoretical explanation of why the labour market would not be in equilibrium with zero unemployment.

The approach taken by Phelps of assuming that inflation depended on what people expected inflation to be as well as on unemployment, with its implication that there would be just one unemployment rate consistent with a constant inflation rate, became more prominent when it was used by Friedman in his 1967 presidential address to the American Economic Association. Making an analogy with Wicksell's 'natural rate of interest' (pp. 235–7), Friedman called the unemployment rate at which inflation was constant (the rate of unemployment at which inflation is correctly anticipated, with the result that people will not change their expectations) the 'natural rate of unemployment'.[6] He argued explicitly that if the authorities aimed for any rate of unemployment less than the natural rate, the result would be accelerating inflation.

This approach to the problem of inflation came to be widely adopted. Some economists took up Friedman's terminology of the 'natural' rate of unemployment, though others, perhaps because they objected to the normative implications of the word 'natural', or because they were concerned to explain the level of unemployment, used more descriptive terms such as the NAIRU (Non-accelerating Inflation Rate of Unemployment). When unemployment rose in Europe in the early 1980s and remained high for the rest of the decade, the problem was widely framed in terms of why the NAIRU had risen.

RATIONAL EXPECTATIONS AND DYNAMICS

Macroeconomists had always wanted their theories to be based on theories about the behaviour of individuals, but most economists had in practice adopted an eclectic approach to theory construction. During the late 1960s and 1970s, attitudes changed, in that there was greater scepticism towards theories that were not grounded in this way. An increasing number of economists took the view that macroeconomic theories could be taken seriously only if they had what eventually came to be called 'microfoundations'. They pursued this goal in different ways. One was to develop 'disequilibrium' microfoundations, in which supply and demand might differ, the justification for this being that changing prices inevitably took time, meaning that there would be times when markets were not in equilibrium. However, this raises the problem of why prices do not adjust to bring about equilibrium of supply and demand. Here the 'equilibrium' approach taken by Phelps, of assuming rational, maximizing individuals who would typically have limited information, proved attractive.

One of the first economists to take up this idea was Robert Lucas (1937–2023). In a series of papers starting in the 1970s, he argued that macroeconomic models ought to be based on the assumption that individuals were completely rational and that they took advantage of all opportunities open to them. He interpreted this to imply that all markets must be modelled as being in equilibrium, with supply equal to demand. If supply were greater than demand, for example, some suppliers would be unable to sell all the goods they wanted to sell. They would thus have an incentive to undercut their competitors, causing prices to fall, so bringing the market into equilibrium. To assume that markets were not in equilibrium, therefore, was to assume that people were not being fully rational. Similarly, he argued that if people were fully rational, their expectations would take account of all the information that was available to them. Here Lucas added the novel twist that modellers should assume that agents in their model know the true structure of the model. There are several ways in which this assumption can be justified, the most convincing of which is the argument that, if they do not do this, agents will make mistakes and change their behaviour. The only possible equilibrium, therefore, is one where people know the true model of the economy.

In the 1970s, in the wake of the first oil crisis, macroeconometric forecasting models began to forecast very badly and, in 1976, Lucas used the notion of rational expectations to provide an explanation. The essential argument in what has come to be called the 'Lucas critique' is that the behaviour of the private sector depends on people's expectations of what the government is going to do. For example, consumption patterns will depend on the tax and social-security policies that consumers expect to face. This means that a consumption function estimated under one tax regime will no longer work when tax policy changes. Thus, even if forecasting models offered accurate accounts of the way the economy operated when they were built in the 1960s, they were bound to break down when policy changed during the 1970s. Lucas concluded that a different type of model was required.

One reason why the new classical macroeconomics had such a big impact was that it appeared to many economists to be a natural development from what had been happening in microeconomics since the 1930s. It was mathematically rigorous and it assumed competitive markets in which supply and demand were equal and modelled as the outcome of optimizing behaviour – firms maximized profits and individuals maximized utility. In such a world, everything ultimately rests on technology and individual tastes. Whereas it was previously assumed that some phenomena emerged only at the macroeconomic level, with the result that macroeconomics and microeconomcs were fundamentally different, in many new-classical models the behaviour of aggregates was the same as the behaviour of individuals, multiplied many times over. This reduced the distinction between microeconomics, dealing with the behaviour of individual firms and households, and macroeconomics, dealing with the economy as a whole.

The twin assumptions of 'continuous market clearing' and 'rational expectations' have dramatic implications. They undermine the idea, basic to Keynesian economics, that people are unemployed because they cannot find work. Instead it is assumed that, if people would accept a lower wage rate, they would find work – that they have 'chosen' to be unemployed in that they have decided that the wage they would obtain from working is not enough to compensate them for the leisure they would lose. Fluctuations in output and employment arise because unanticipated shocks cause people to make mistakes in their estimates of inflation. It follows from this that systematic changes to government policy (such as following a rule that says to expand the economy when unemployment is high and contract it when unemployment becomes low) will have no effect. The effects of such a rule will be predictable and hence will not affect output. The private sector will discount the policy changes in advance.

The business cycle presents a major challenge to such a theory. Though precise changes in output cannot be predicted, the economy generally follows a rough cyclical pattern of boom and slump, with the cycle lasting several years. In the 1970s Lucas tried to explain this as the result of monetary shocks. These would raise or lower demand, causing people to make mistakes that would cause output to fluctuate around its long-term trend. Much effort was put into measuring these shocks and explaining how they might produce fluctuations similar to those observed in the real world. Eventually, however, Lucas's explanation was abandoned in favour of one which explained the cycle in terms of 'real' shocks: primarily shocks to technology (new inventions and so on). The result was the 'real business cycle' theory first proposed by Fynn Kydland (1943–) and Edward Prescott (1940–). This was based on the same assumptions as Lucas's theory (notably continuous market clearing and rational expectations) but differed in its assumptions about the source of shocks to the system.

Though many economists remained sceptical about the extreme policy conclusions reached by what came to be called the 'new classical macroeconomics', the main thrust of the new classical argument, that economic models should assume fully rational behaviour, came to be widely accepted. Keynesians, who in the 1970s had been exploring models where markets were generally out of equilibrium and traders faced rationing, changed their research strategy. They started to search for explanations of unemployment that did not violate the assumption of rationality. They built models using assumptions such as asymmetric information (where workers know more about themselves than potential employers know) or imperfect competition (where firms or unions have power to influence the prices at which they buy or sell). These models were based on the main new-classical assumptions but produced Keynesian conclusions. Prominent examples of such 'New Keynesian' macroeconomists include Phelps and Stiglitz (discussed earlier) and Janet Yellen (1946–), an exponent of 'efficiency wage theory' – the theory that workers who are paid more may be more efficient than ones who are paid less.

During the 1990s, the distinction between real-business-cycle and new Keynesian theories diminished. In order to explain real-world data, real-business-cycle theorists needed to introduce frictions and lags, which made their models behave more like new Keynesian models; and new Keynesian economists adopted many of the techniques employed by real-business-cycle theorists. Some economists described this as the emergence of a new synthesis, which went under the name of DSGE (Dynamic Stochastic General Equilibrium) modelling, summed up in Michael Woodford's *Interest and Prices* (2003). The models were dynamic in that people were assumed to maximize utility over their entire lifetime; they were stochastic in that there were random shocks; and they were general-equilibrium models, albeit based on imperfect competition, an assumption found to be necessary in order to explain why monetary policy could affect behaviour in a world where expectations were rational.

MACROECONOMIC POLICY

The 1960s saw the high tide of Keynesian economics. In the United States, as was explained in Chapter 15, under President Kennedy, Keynesian policies were used to move the economy towards full employment by the end of the decade. This coincided with the escalation of the war in Vietnam and an enormous rise in military expenditure. In the rest of the world, too, the late 1960s and early 1970s were a period of rapid expansion, and inflation began to rise rapidly. The collapse of the Bretton Woods system, dating from 1944, which had fixed exchange rates for the previous quarter-century, meant that countries could expand without worrying about the effect it would have on their balance of payments. An important feature of this boom was a rise in commodity prices. In 1973 the Organization of Petroleum Exporting Countries (OPEC) contributed to this rise by successfully reaching an agreement to cut supplies of crude oil in order to raise its price. The Yom Kippur War, between Israel and the Arab states, disrupted oil supplies. The outcome was that oil prices rose by 66 per cent in October 1973 before doubling again in January 1974, and there was an acute shortage of oil. Furthermore, because oil revenues rose more rapidly than oil exporters could spend them, there was a sudden shortage of demand in oil-importing countries, which found themselves with unprecedented balance-of-payments deficits. The world was plunged into recession.

The novel feature of this depression was that inflation and unemployment rose simultaneously, a phenomenon for which Samuelson coined the term 'stagflation'. The Phillips curve had 'broken down' and Keynesian theory no longer provided clear guidance for policymakers. Cutting back demand to curb inflation and reduce expected inflation would increase unemployment, but unemployment was already too high, posing the problem of how to find the appropriate balance. This is difficult because it involves estimating the trade-off between unemployment and inflation and value judgements about the costs of unemployment and inflation. In contrast, Friedman's prescription that the authorities should set and stick to a target for the growth rate of the money supply, ignoring any transitional unemployment cost, was clear.

During the 1950s and 1960s, only a minority of economists had found Friedman's arguments about inflation and the money supply persuasive, but against the background of 1968–73, when many governments had allowed the money supply to increase, Friedman's analysis of inflation became much more convincing. Rapid monetary expansion around 1971 had been followed, about two years later, by an equally rapid rise in inflation. (Inflation in 1973 was clearly linked to the oil price rises of that year, though monetarists could argue that, were it not for monetary expansion, prices would not have risen so much.) During the 1970s, therefore, government after government broke with Keynesianism and implemented targets for the growth of the money supply.

In some countries, such as Britain, this process was assisted by pressure from the IMF, which had for some years been working on the links between money and the balance of payments. At the IMF, Jacques Polak started from the circular flow of income central to Keynesian economics but chose to focus on its monetary implications. In his theory, the money supply and national income could be increased either by rising exports (which would cause an inflow of money) or by an expansion of domestic credit. The latter could be a problem because, unlike an increase in exports, it led to a loss of foreign currency reserves and potentially a fall in the exchange rate. In the 1970s, the main exponent of this approach was Harry Johnson (1923–77), a Canadian specialist in international economics who simultaneously held chairs at the University of Chicago and the London School of Economics. Like the quantity theory of money, the monetary approach to the balance of payments focused on the money supply but, because of its focus on international payments, recognized that export promotion and devaluation of the currency could provide alternatives to reducing domestic credit expansion. Such arguments explain why, in Britain, where monetary targets were first introduced in 1976 after the government received IMF support following a crisis, the target adopted was for Domestic Credit Expansion (DCE) rather than the money supply as a whole.

Friedman's earlier arguments in favour of targeting the growth rate of the money supply were greatly strengthened by his arguments about the natural rate of unemployment. If governments could not control unemployment and faced the danger of accelerating inflation, there was a strong case for using monetary policy to control the one variable they could control, namely the rate of inflation. This doctrine came to be known as 'monetarism', a term previously used in Latin America but introduced into American discussions by Karl Brunner (1916–89). Though the quantity theory of money was a doctrine about the relationship between money and inflation, many of its supporters, such as Friedman, combined it with more general support for free markets and non-intervention. 'Monetarism' therefore came to be associated, especially in the minds of non-economists, with measures such as privatization, deregulation, income-tax cuts and reductions in social-welfare provision. The meaning of the term became even looser where, as under Margaret Thatcher's government in Britain in the 1980s, attempts were made to implement so-called 'monetarist' policies using methods (namely cuts in government spending) that were far removed from those advocated by Friedman.

During the 1980s, inflation was brought under control, mainly because of tight monetary policy. However, this was less of a vindication of monetarism than it might seem because it was found necessary to pay attention to much more than the money supply. The problem was financial innovation – the development of new financial products and changes in the way people used financial assets. Deregulation of the financial sector and the ending of foreign-exchange controls made financial innovation much easier. If, for example, the authorities set a target for a particular definition of the money supply, banks had an incentive to invent types of bank deposit that were not part of that definition that people could use instead. The result was that the target would become irrelevant. Charles Goodhart (1936–) formulated the law that if government tries to rely on a statistical regularity, such as a relationship between the growth rate of M3 and inflation, that regularity will collapse. In Britain this happened repeatedly, as the government shifted from one target to another.

Public-choice arguments were increasingly used to argue that politicians could not be trusted with monetary policy. Economists increasingly argued in favour of independent central banks which would be immune to electoral pressures. However, this was hardly a victory for monetarism because, instead of mandating them to control the growth rate of the money supply, they were given other goals such as achieving a target rate of inflation. The mechanism for doing this was the central bank discount rate (the rate at which banks can borrow from the central bank). Changing this rate would have knock-on effects on other interest rates and hence affect private spending. If inflation was above target, the discount rate should be raised to induce people to spend less, and if inflation was too low, it should be reduced to stimulate activity. This came to be known as the 'Taylor rule', after John Taylor (1946–), who proposed that interest rates should depend on two gaps: between the actual and target rates of inflation and real GDP. As the title of Woodford's book *Interest and Prices*, the same as used by Wicksell over a century earlier, suggested, such a policy could be seen as a return to the theory of Wicksell (p. 235).

CONCLUSIONS

The Second World War ushered in the so-called 'age of Keynes'. Although post-war macroeconomics drew on many sources, notably the econometric approach of Frisch and Tinbergen, the field came to be associated with the name of Keynes and the framework he had provided in his *General Theory*. Ideas from earlier generations remained, but they were mediated by Keynesian economics as interpreted by economists such as Hicks, Hansen and Samuelson. Even economists such as Friedman who disagreed with Keynesian policies found his theoretical framework useful. Policymakers were more resistant to Keynesian thinking, but Keynesian views on managing the economy fitted well with the move, especially strong in Europe, towards a welfare state. Not only did high employment contribute directly to social welfare, but it also made the welfare state more affordable, keeping taxes high and the need for social security benefits low. Keynesianism was thus pervasive. There were of course economists who challenged this. They had limited success until the economic turbulence of the 1970s called Keynesian ideas into question and monetarist policies proved more attractive. The age of Keynes ended abruptly in 1973.

However, the ideas that dominated macroeconomics from the 1970s until the beginning of the twenty-first century were not Friedman's. They were based on the more mathematical theorizing initiated by Lucas, emphasizing the importance of theories that were consistent with microeconomic theory. Although much empirical work was adduced to support the new theories, it seems likely that the main impetus was theoretical: a belief that mathematically rigorous theories must somehow be more reliable than ones based on less precise models of human behaviour. Neither was Friedman successful at the level of policy, except in so far as there was a move away from giving politicians discretion to manage the economy. Policy in the twenty-first century arguably owed as much to Wicksell and Tobin than to Friedman.

For over a decade, these policies appeared to be successful. In the same way that, during the age of Keynes, many economists believed that the business cycle had been tamed, the period from the mid-1980s to the end of the century came to be known as the Great Moderation. At least, it looked that way in the United States and Europe, for the period looked very different in other parts of the world. Output collapsed in the former Soviet empire during the 1990s; in Japan the 1990s came to be known as the 'lost decade' on account of persistent stagnation; and economies in East Asia experienced a major financial crisis at the end of the 1990s. Leaving aside whether they should have done, none of these exceptions was sufficient to dent the widely held view that macroeconomics had made great progress since its failure in the 1970s.

18
Economics in the Twenty-first Century

THEORY AND APPLICATION

Writing in the 1940s, Schumpeter distinguished between different types of applied field. The first type comprised fields such as money and banking that were widely considered part of general economics but were taught separately so that they could be treated in more detail. A second type included fields such as actuarial science and insurance that were separate from economics for purely historical reasons (he might have added that there is a clear vocational element to training in both fields). The third included fields based on public policy, such as agriculture, labour, transport and public finance. Some fields, such as socialism and comparative economic systems and area studies fell into both the last two categories. Reflecting on this, he commented:

> There is evidently no permanence or logical order to this jumble of applied fields. Nor are there definite frontier lines to any of them. They appear or vanish, they increase or decrease in relative import-ance, and they overlap with one another as changing interests and methods dictate. And ... this is as it should be.[1]

It would be possible to make very similar remarks about the situation at the beginning of the twenty-first century.

However, an important change between 1950 and 2000 was that the division of the subject into applied fields became institutionalized. Applied fields ceased to be simply convenient labels attached to courses offered to students but began to be reflected in the way in which the profession was organized. The most obvious sign of this was the proliferation of specialist journals and societies. Economists working within applied fields were able to talk to each other as much as to economists in general. The expansion of the literature meant that it became difficult to keep track of developments in multiple fields.

The histories of these applied fields are varied. Some fields are clearly linked to outside, political developments. In the era of the Cold War, 'comparative economic systems' had a clear role. It owed much to the earlier 'economics of socialism', a field whose history went back to the nineteenth century, but it was far from identical with it. With the collapse of the Soviet empire around 1990 and the extension of market activities in China, the capitalist system appeared, at least to most economists, to have won. Comparative economic systems, focusing on the choice between capitalism and socialism, had lost its raison d'être, even if there remained more subtle differences between different types of socialist and capitalist systems that remained to be understood. It gave way to the economics of transition and emerging markets. In contrast, the history of labour economics probably exhibited greater continuity, with problems such as wage determination and the organization of labour markets being of perennial concern. Other fields, such as health economics, urban economics, the economics of education and the economics of crime can be related to the increased concern with social problems in the 1960s and 1970s. A technical field such as econometrics no doubt emerged as a separate field because of the specialized range of mathematical techniques employed: a large investment is necessary to learn them.

Developments in information technology have had a profound effect on economics. The existence of high-speed computers and the internet made possible types of research that would previously have been impossible. For example, it became possible to obtain and analyse very high-frequency data on financial markets, observing prices continuously throughout the day, rather than simply observing prices at the close of business. It also became possible to obtain and process very large data sets on thousands, or even millions, of individuals. And it became possible to use statistical techniques that required a level of computation that would have been impossible a generation earlier.

A particularly important development was paying greater attention to research design, either using randomized control trials (RCTs) or finding some equivalent 'natural experiment'. Randomized control trials are a technique that has become standard in medicine, in which a group receiving some treatment is compared with a randomly chosen control group that does not receive the treatment. For example, suppose children start school in the first school year after their fifth birthday, and the school year begins on 1 September. A random sample of children born in August are effectively the same age as a sample born in September but will have a year's additional schooling; this makes it possible to distinguish the effect of schooling from age.

A particularly influential study promoting this technique was by David Card (1955–) and Alan Krueger (1960–2019), in 1993, on the effects of minimum wages on employment. Economists generally assume that an increase in the minimum wage must reduce employment, but although this is true in perfectly competitive markets, it is not necessarily true if competition is imperfect and employers have the power to set wages (a result shown by Joan Robinson in 1933). Card and Krueger tested this by comparing fast-food restaurants in New Jersey, where there was about to be an increase in the minimum wage, with equivalent ones across the border in Pennsylvania. Although it was consistent with earlier studies and therefore was not surprising, their finding that increasing the minimum wage from $4.25 to $5.05 per hour resulted in a very small *increase* in employment was widely noticed. The study received so much attention in part because their research design was so easily understood, and in part because some economists had strong ideological objections to such a result. For example, even though Robinson's theory was well understood, Buchanan claimed that Card and Krueger's results amounted to denying 'that there is even minimal scientific content in economics, and that in consequence economists can do nothing but write as advocates for ideological interests'.[2]

Another example of such methods, recognized by the award of the 2019 Nobel Memorial Prize to Abhijit Banerjee (1961–), Esther Duflo (1972–) and Michael Kremer (1964–) is the study of poverty, especially in Africa and India. The work of these three economists is at the opposite pole from the grand theories of development proposed in the 1950s. Instead of speculating on broad strategies for promoting development, they insist on breaking the problem of poverty down into much smaller, more manageable sub-problems, and then studying the choices of the people involved. Examples illustrating this include working out how to ensure that poor people in Indonesia received all the rice they were entitled to get under an anti-poverty programme and finding methods to increase the use of fertilizer by Kenyan farmers. Central to their work is the belief that simple solutions based on naive generalizations about the poor rarely work. For example, the reason people are malnourished may not be because they cannot afford to buy enough food: it may be that they want to eat tasty food or that they consider it important to save up to buy a television. Measures to increase the supply of food may therefore fail to reduce malnutrition.

However, though field experiments and the use of randomized controls are now very widely used, some economists have reservations about them. An example is Angus Deaton (1945–), awarded the 2015 Nobel Memorial Prize for showing, in the words of the Nobel authorities, 'how data on consumption can be used to analyse problems of welfare, poverty and economic development'.[3] He has questioned the usefulness of experimental methods when their results are often hard to generalize outside the very specific circumstances of the trials. He and Anne Case (1958–), a specialist in health economics, have identified what they call 'deaths of despair' – deaths from suicide, drug overdoses and alcoholism – as a major factor explaining why mortality is falling among college-educated Americans and among the less educated. Like Banerjee, Duflo and Kremer, Case and Deaton are trying to understand the situation of the poor, though they do it not through experiments but through analysing statistical trends. Their linking of this to the failure of both capitalism and the American political system to deliver prosperity for the working class was clearly controversial.

In the twenty-first century, economists had access to an increasing volume of real-world data, but they also wanted data generated in more controlled environments. To achieve this, many economists turned to laboratory experiments. This has a long history, for psychologists have always used experiments to establish and test theories about behaviour, and some economists followed suit. The modern literature on the subject dates from the 1930s and 1940s, and the early work addressed several types of problem. The earliest was the use of experiments to determine consumers' preferences. In 1931 L. L. Thurstone (1887–1955) did this by asking subjects, repeatedly, to say which of alternative bundles of goods they preferred. This was strongly criticized, for his subjects were not making real choices, but in the early 1950s other economists continued this type of study. A second type of work was the use of experiments to find out how markets operated. In 1948 Chamberlin constructed an experiment to find out whether a group of subjects would hit on the competitive-equilibrium price at which supply equalled demand.

Interest in both types of experiment increased significantly after the publication of von Neumann and Morgenstern's 1944 book on game theory. During the 1950s and 1960s, some influential results were discovered, such as that by Maurice Allais (1911–2010) that people frequently made choices inconsistent with the standard theory of utility maximization. However, although some economists began to pay systematic attention to questions of how experiments should be conducted, experimental economics remained small scale and in the 1960s it was still common to deny that economics could be an experimental science. For example, in his bestselling textbook, Samuelson wrote that economists 'cannot perform the controlled experiments of the chemist or the biologist. Like the astronomer, we must be content largely to "observe".'[4] However, in the 1970s experimental work attracted more funding, including support from the National Science Foundation in the USA, and it grew rapidly. By the end of the 1980s it had become a generally recognized (if still controversial) way to do research in economics, and by the end of the 1990s it had entered the mainstream, in that it was discussed in introductory textbooks. It had ceased to be an activity undertaken only by specialists. In 2002, experimental economics was recognized by the award of the Nobel Memorial Prize to Vernon Smith (1927–) for his use of laboratory experiments, which differed from early 'experiments' in that people were performing experiments for real money, to study how market mechanisms worked.

Smith shared the 2002 prize with Daniel Kahneman (1934–). Though Kahneman was also involved in experiments, as a psychologist his emphasis, in work with Amos Tversky (1937–96), was different. They focused on the cognitive biases that affect decision-making, suggesting that people do not behave according to the precepts of rational-choice theory (utility maximization) but are influenced by the way in which technically similar choices are presented to them. Further recognition of this approach came in 2017 when the Nobel Memorial Prize was awarded to Richard Thaler (1945–) for work that built on Kahneman's ideas. He showed that people are not completely rational, adopting rules that, through limiting their choices, prevent them from taking decisions they know they would later regret; they also value fairness, a concept that is absent from standard theory. Together with a legal scholar, Cass Sunstein (1954–), Thaler was responsible for popularizing 'nudge' theory, according to which people could be induced to make different decisions without constraining their choices. For example, people might be persuaded to improve their diet by having healthier food placed more prominently in supermarkets.

An important application of such ideas, known as 'behavioural' economics, was in the theory of finance. In the 1960s, Samuelson had formulated the theory of efficient markets – the theory that stock-market prices should reflect all available information, making them inherently difficult to predict – and there had developed a large literature applying mathematical models to finance. This literature was of great practical significance because it was used as the basis for the development of new financial products such as index funds, designed to track the performance of the market as a whole. According to the theory of efficient markets, this was the best that an investor could hope to achieve without access to information that was better than that available to other investors. This view of financial markets was challenged by behavioural finance. Robert Shiller (1945–), recognized by the Nobel committee in 2013, challenged efficient-market theory, arguing that fashion was as important in finance as in other walks of life. Fads, fashions and irrational enthusiasm among investors could, he argued, explain why stock-market prices were more volatile than efficient-market theory implied that they ought to be. Economists committed to both efficient-market theory and behavioural finance became involved with hedge funds, but there emerged no clear evidence that one was more successful than the other.

The background to these developments in applied economics is that, in the second half of the twentieth century, economic analysis had become more formal and economics had come to be dominated by modelling: by the construction of mathematical models, both theoretical and empirical. The result was the emergence of a much clearer 'core' of theoretical and empirical techniques that economists were expected to know. Theory came to be seen as fundamental to economics because, without a theory of individual behaviour, there was thought to be no explanation of what was happening. As Koopmans expressed it in 1947, when defending the Cowles Commission's methods, it was necessary to move from the 'Kepler' stage of scientific inquiry to the 'Newton' stage (Kepler had established that planets move in ellipses, but Newton had provided an explanation).

In contrast, by the twenty-first century, the situation had changed. Because controlled experiments, whether in the laboratory or in the field, and the analysis of large data sets made it possible to identify causes, applied work became more prestigious. Empirical work could stand on its own in the sense that it was taken seriously even if it was not based on a theory. In 2007, Deaton, reflecting on his experience at Princeton, one of the most prestigious universities in the world, wrote that, in contrast with the estimation of elaborate theoretical models using complicated statistical techniques typical of a doctoral thesis in the 1980s, 'the typical thesis of today uses little or no theory, much simpler econometrics, and hundreds of thousands of observations'.[5]

These changes in economics are often attributed to developments in information technology – to the internet and increasingly powerful computers. It is certainly true that improvements in information technology were crucial: they were a necessary condition for many new types of data analysis. However, it is wrong to argue that modern information technology explains what happened. The application of new techniques in economics requires software as well as hardware, and much of the necessary software was developed by, or in conjunction with, economists. The result is that software for analysing data, performing simulations and forecasts, and for conducting experiments reflects economists' choices. Also, it was not inevitable that developments in information technology had a much greater effect on statistical work than on economic theory. Computers can be used to automate the search for proofs of mathematical theorems, but few economists have adopted such methods even though they are used in mathematics.

The increased prestige of applied work and the weakening of the central theoretical core of the subject make it much harder to summarize what is going on in economics in the twenty-first century than was the case half a century earlier. Instead, this chapter now turns to a few of the most important issues to which economists have devoted attention. They are chosen not because they are representative of what most economists are doing. They are not. The enormous volume of economic literature would in any case make such generalization hazardous. They are chosen because, along with pandemics and war, they are widely recognized to be among the most serious economic issues facing societies today and, taken together with the examples discussed above (in this chapter and in Chapters 16 and 17), they illustrate some of the variety that exists in contemporary economics.

GLOBALIZATION AND INEQUALITY

The period since 1945, and especially since the 1980s, has widely been described as an age of globalization. During the 1930s, faced with a severe economic downturn, many countries turned to protection, raising tariff barriers, and the result was a collapse in world trade. After the Second World War, there was widespread agreement that this should not happen again, and institutions such as the IMF, the IBRD (later the World Bank) and GATT (later the World Trade Organization, WTO) were set up to ensure that it did not. However, for many years, international trade was subject to many restrictions. From the 1940s to the 1970s many European countries had restrictions on capital flows because, without them, they would have faced unmanageable balance-of-payments problems under the Bretton Woods system. In the centrally planned Communist world, from Eastern Europe to the USSR and China, trade flows were tightly controlled and the bloc's currencies were not convertible. And, excluding the areas of European settlement, there was widespread poverty in much of the rest of the world, notably in India and much of Africa. Economists debated whether the right strategy for poor countries was to be outward-looking, focused on expanding trade, or inward-looking, focused on developing domestic markets.

The changes to which the label 'globalization' is now attached gathered pace during the 1980s. Despite enormous efforts, many attempts to create development through promoting industry behind tariff barriers had failed. India's attempt to emulate Soviet five-year plans had not lifted the country out of poverty. Communist China under Mao remained extremely poor. The success stories were Japan, which grew extremely rapidly, albeit from a stronger starting point, and the 'Asian Tigers' – Hong Kong, Singapore, Korea and Taiwan – which had developed through strategies that focused on exports. A consensus developed among economists that a precondition for development was removing barriers and creating competition, including openness to trade and flows of capital from one country to another.

One stimulus to such reform came from the World Bank, which began 'adjustment lending' in 1980, and the IMF, which, during the 1980s, began to make its lending conditional on adopting structural adjustment programmes. The background to this was that during the 1970s many countries, notably in Latin America, had accumulated large debts and when interest rates rose in the early 1980s this led to a crisis.

Reflecting on this in 1989, John Williamson (1937–2021) coined the phrase 'the Washington consensus' to describe the ten policy measures that, in his view, most economists believed were appropriate in Latin America. These included reducing budget deficits to levels that could be financed without inflation; directing public spending to areas, such as primary education, with high economic returns and which might improve the distribution of income; privatization of state enterprises; openness to foreign direct investment; and the provision of secure property rights.[6] Williamson was concerned solely with policy in Latin America, but during the 1990s the term came to be used as a label for the conditions imposed by the World Bank and the IMF on their lending, which included institutional reforms and more comprehensive financial liberalization. It also came to be equated with 'neoliberalism': the view promoted by many organizations linked to the Mont Pelerin Society that prosperity was to be promoted by austerity, reducing the size of government and the removal of controls on private activity, a list of policies very different from those Williamson had advocated.

Events in Latin America were overshadowed in the early 1990s by the collapse of communist regimes in Eastern Europe and the break-up of the Soviet Union. Russia and Eastern European countries were eventually integrated into the world economy, but only at great cost. When China, still under the strict control of the Communist Party, changed its policy to one oriented to international trade, joining the WTO in 2001, the world economy was changed even more substantially.

Economists have largely been in favour of this move towards the removal of barriers to trade and restrictions on capital flows, seeing them as increasing overall prosperity. During the 1980s, the theory of international trade had been extended to take account of factors that up until then had been neglected: that many firms produce products that are different from those of their competitors (Volkwagen cars may perform the same function as Toyotas, but they are not identical and people may care which one they buy) and that businesses have some control over the prices they charge (competition is not perfect). In the 1990s economists developed these ideas further, as data made it clear that much trade was between countries selling similar products and that there were significant differences between firms selling in domestic markets and ones focused on exporting products. It was for such work that Paul Krugman (1953–), who later became prominent as a *New York Times* columnist, was awarded the Nobel Prize. New sources of data, including much firm-level data, made it possible to test theories more rigorously than previously. Particularly successful were so-called 'gravity' models in which the volume of trade was assumed to be related to the sizes of the trading partners, their proximity, and to the costs of selling abroad compared with the costs of selling goods in the domestic market.

It was during the 1990s that 'globalization' became an important political issue. Removing barriers to trade clearly produced losers as well as winners, notably workers in rich countries whose jobs disappeared as production moved to countries in which costs were lower. (Some of these concerns were similar to those raised by Ricardo in connection with the introduction of machinery two centuries earlier.) In addition, poor countries that should have benefited from offering cheap labour had not made progress. One economist calculated that the average growth rate in developing countries fell from 2½ per cent per annum in the 1960s and 1970s to zero in the 1980s and 1990s, even though the factors believed to favour growth, such as infrastructure, life expectancy and education had all improved.[7] In short, the 'Washington consensus' appeared to have failed. Just as important were the political objections to globalization: new laws and institutions appeared to be favouring large corporations, and national governments, even if they were democratically elected, were having their power reduced. During the twenty-first century the political consequences were also felt in developed countries where stagnating working-class and middle-class incomes contrasted with dramatic increases in the wealth of the top 1 per cent.

One economist who became critical of this process was Stiglitz, an academic economist who became involved in policy under the Clinton administration and subsequently in the World Bank and received the Nobel Prize in 2001 for his work on information. Remaining within the framework of economic arguments, he argued that although trade liberalization had the potential to improve well-being everywhere, it had been implemented in such a way that made poorer countries worse off. The United States and Europe insisted on free entry of their products to poor countries, while maintaining protection of the agricultural products that many poor countries were best placed to export. Freeing capital flows, a process that European countries had resisted until the 1970s, was a policy adopted by many developing countries even though, sometimes because of widespread corruption, their banking systems were too limited to handle it. Drawing on his earlier work on information, Stiglitz argued that the way the IMF had handled the East Asian financial crisis was counterproductive: the cutbacks in government spending, higher interest rates and other reforms required by the IMF reduced confidence and led to capital outflows, exacerbating the crisis.

It is fair to argue that there remains a wide, though not universal, consensus among economists that the reduction of barriers to international trade has the potential to make people better off. This is illustrated by the almost complete consensus among economists that Britain's exit from the European Union would be costly. However, there is also awareness that, unless the process is handled carefully, there will be losers as well as winners, and that more open markets can create problems such as increasing the degree of inequality.

Increasing concern with an increasingly unequal distribution of income and wealth was signalled when Thomas Piketty's *Capital in the 21st Century* (2014) topped the *New York Times* bestseller lists. Thomas Piketty (1971–) was one of a network of economists responsible for creating a comprehensive statistical picture of the way inequality had evolved since the beginning of the twentieth century. A key figure in this network was Anthony Atkinson, who was important in two ways. The first was that he invented a formula for measuring inequality (the Atkinson index). Taking up an idea found in a 1920 article by Hugh Dalton (1887–1962), an economist who later became a minister in the 1945 Labour government, Atkinson measured inequality by the loss of social welfare compared with what it would be if income were perfectly equally distributed. This leads to the paradoxical conclusion that, in order to measure inequality, it is necessary to make a normative judgement about how inequality affects social welfare.

The second reason for Atkinson's importance is that, motivated by a desire to establish the facts about inequality and poverty on which anti-poverty policies could be based, he was responsible for initiating the process of systematically compiling statistics on the distribution of income and wealth, notably from tax records, and on poverty. Piketty's *Capital in the 21st Century*, and his subsequent *Capital and*

Ideology (2020), which covered an even longer period, was based on his own research into French tax records and also on work with Atkinson on top incomes in many countries. In addition to suggesting mechanisms through which these developments came about, Piketty drew on the wealth of statistical data created since the 1970s to show that inequality had declined dramatically during the period between the First World War and the 1970s. For most of the nineteenth century, and after 1970, inequality was either very high or increasing. In the second of these books he probed behind the statistics into the social structures and ideologies that supported inequality; there is, he argues, no economic determinism that means we cannot change the level of inequality. The 'ownership society' that Piketty sees as justifying inequality today has much in common with the 'acquisitive society' criticized by Tawney a century earlier.

Another dimension of inequality is inequality between countries, creating problems for discussions of inequality at a global level. Global inequality between individuals depends on how incomes and wealth are distributed both between countries and within them. A major source of research on these problems was the World Bank. For example, Branko Milanovic (1953–), lead economist at the World Bank from 1991 to 2013, drew on a database of surveys of individual household incomes, compiled by the World Bank, to show that at a global level, most inequality was due to inequality between countries. This meant that trends in world inequality were largely dominated by what was happening in the most populous poor countries (China and India) relative to the richest countries (Western Europe and the United States).

Milanovic argued that, between the fall of the Berlin Wall and the Global Financial Crisis – the period of so-called 'globalization' – there had been a profound change in the world distribution of income. Those who had gained most were people on median world income or less (excluding the poorest 10 per cent of world population), and those in the top 1 per cent. Those near or just above median world income were predominantly in China, India and Indonesia, while the top 1 per cent were mostly in the United States and Western Europe. In between them was the Western middle class, which saw very low-income growth. The losers from globalization included the very poor (including many in Africa) and many workers in rich countries, a development with significant political implications.

FINANCIAL CRISIS

The globalization of capital markets was one reason why problems that emerged in the US home mortgage market could escalate into a global financial crisis. The other main reason was the development of trading in new types of financial asset – derivatives trading. This would not have been possible without developments in the theory of finance that go back to the 1960s and 1970s. A crucial result was the Black–Scholes theorem on the valuation of options, derived by Fischer Black (1938–95) and Myron Scholes (1941–) in the early 1970s. An option is the right to buy (a call option) or sell (a put option) something at a specified price either at or before a certain date. Markets for options on commodities (wheat, petroleum, cocoa, etc.) have a long history – they enable businesses to reduce the uncertainty arising from price fluctuations – but options on financial assets were more controversial. For example, in the United States, they were for a long time considered to amount to gambling and were not allowed.

The significance of the Black–Scholes formula was that it made it possible for markets in options to exist, because it provided a basis on which traders could calculate what options were worth. Options trading began in Chicago in 1973 and grew rapidly. The value of an option to purchase a stock obviously depends on the value of the underlying stock, though the relationship is complicated by the fact that the stock will have to be purchased only under specified circumstances. The significance of this is that it opened up the possibility of markets in 'derivatives' – financial assets the value of which depends on the value of other financial assets. With the deregulation of financial markets in the 1970s and 1980s, markets for derivatives mushroomed, and with them institutions focused on trading in such assets. The theory behind hedge funds was that by holding appropriate combinations of assets it was possible to increase returns without being exposed to excessive risk. In the 1990s, one of the most spectacular hedge funds was Long-term Capital Management, directors of which included Scholes and Robert Merton (1944–), who in 1997 received the Nobel Prize for their work on derivatives pricing. Large profits were made at first, but as other firms followed their example profits turned to losses, and in 1998, after Russia defaulted on some debt, the fund had to be bailed out.

Events such as this did not stop the growth of derivatives trading, which, by 2007, had extended to the housing market. Instead of mortgages being owned by the institutions that initially made the loans, banks packaged up mortgages and sold them to other institutions. These assets were, in turn, repackaged and sold on again. The theory behind the valuation of individual mortgages was sound: there was a risk that borrowers might default (someone gets ill or has an accident and cannot afford repayments), but for the theory to work these risks should not be correlated. What the theory had failed to allow for was the possibility that a downturn in the economy as a whole, or rising interest rates, would cause large numbers of borrowers to default simultaneously, which is what began to happen in 2007. The structure of the financial system meant that when this happened, instead of just the mortgage lenders failing, the entire financial system was threatened. Because of the way assets had been packaged and repackaged, banks and other institutions simply did not know the risks to which they were exposed.

The challenge to economics was that the crisis brought together two branches of economics which had become separated. One was finance, based on the analysis of individual financial assets but not taking into account the behaviour of the economy as a whole. The other was macroeconomics, which dealt with fluctuations in income, employment and prices but did not take account of the financial system. Not taking account of the risk of an economy-wide recession and rising interest rates, financial economists (and rating agencies, which attached grades to financial assets) were overconfident about the solvency of financial institutions. And, making the implicit assumption that the economy possessed a working financial system, macroeconomists did not realize the potential for a shock big enough to cause a serious depression. However, when the crisis did occur, the Federal Reserve chair was an economist, Ben Bernanke (p. 376). Having studied the Great Depression very closely, he was determined that mistakes made in the 1930s would not be repeated, so he took vigorous action, reducing interest rates and instituting a policy of quantitative easing (buying securities to increase the quantity of money in circulation).

The prospect of another Great Depression led to a resurgence of interest in Keynes. Emblematic of this was Richard Posner (pp. 357–8), who admitted that, because it was not relevant to his work in law, he had never previously read the *General Theory*, but when he did, he decided it was the best guide there was to the crisis. A spate of books appeared explaining the relevance of Keynes for the current situation. However, this enthusiasm for Keynes, at least in many governments, did not last, and concern with rising government deficits, caused by measures to combat depression, was used to justify a turn towards 'austerity'.

After the financial crisis, although economics, and especially macroeconomics, was severely criticized for not anticipating the crisis, economics generally continued along the lines established before 2007. Economists produced models that could explain the crisis but without changing the fundamentals of the way the economy as a whole was analysed.

When even zero interest rates could not stimulate the economy sufficiently to produce recovery from depression, there was renewed interest in Hansen's concept of secular (long-term) stagnation, developed in the late 1930s. One explanation of this came from Lawrence Summers (1954–), who argued, in Wicksellian terms, that the natural rate of interest had fallen below zero, with the result that the market interest rate (which was hard to push below zero because people had the option to hold cash) must be above it. This was radical in its implications, for it suggested that conventional monetary policy might not be able to promote full employment, even though the theoretical arguments on which it was based were well known. It turned out that, in the view of many economists, they had resources that could be used to explain the crisis. The problem that economists holding such views faced was overcoming politicians' fear of high government deficits. This was exactly the problem that Keynesian economists had faced in the 1940s.

THE ENVIRONMENT AND CLIMATE CHANGE

Economists have long been concerned with mankind's relationship to the environment. There were many economists in the eighteenth and nineteenth centuries who believed that growth might come to an end due to a shortage of natural resources. For much of the twentieth century such concerns faded into the background: during the 1920s and 1930s, though some economists, including Hotelling, analysed the use of natural resources, economic instability and depression were more urgent problems. In the mid-twentieth century there was an acceleration in human use of natural resources, causing some scientists to date the onset of an Anthropocene age to around 1950. However, after the Second World War there was a commitment to fostering economic growth, stimulated by the Cold War and increasing awareness of how poor many countries were. In the words of one environmental economist

> At the end of the Second World War, absolute poverty was endemic in much of Africa, Asia, and Latin America; and Europe needed reconstruction. It was natural to focus on the accumulation of produced capital (roads, machines, buildings, factories, and ports) and what we today call human capital (health and education). To introduce Nature, or natural capital, into economic models would have been to add unnecessary luggage to the exercise.[8]

Although some doubts about growth were raised earlier (Resources for the Future, an important think tank, was established in 1952 in response to concerns about limited supplies of natural resources), a significant change took place in the 1960s and 1970s. *The Costs of Economic Growth*, by Ezra Mishan (1917–2014), argued that economic growth came with unintended and undesirable side effects.

Boulding proposed the influential metaphor of 'spaceship earth', arguing for a move away from a 'cowboy economy' premised on the existence of unlimited resources that could be exploited. E. F. Schumacher (1911–77) popularized similar ideas in *Small is Beautiful* and Herman Daly (1938–), who later helped develop the Index of Sustainable Economic Welfare, questioned whether current rates of growth could continue indefinitely.

Such ideas were represented in a formal model in *World Dynamics* (1971), written by an MIT engineer, Jay Forrester, which presented a computer model showing that there might be barriers to permanent exponential growth. It was a revival of Malthusian ideas in that it saw a conflict between population growth and limited natural resources. The book received widespread attention, though less than a book it inspired, *The Limits to Growth*, produced by a group calling itself the Club of Rome, which appeared the following year. Resource shortages and economic disruption during the 1970s caused Club of Rome's message, like those of Boulding, Daly and others, to resonate with the public in a way that would not have been the case a decade earlier.

Forrester's team was made up of natural scientists, and in the 1970s and 1980s economists were generally not involved. However, the problem of environmental constraints on growth was fundamentally an economic problem, for decisions about climate-change policy involve issues of resource allocation and hence optimization. Forrester noted that some of the strongest criticisms of his model came from economists.[9]

One of the factors analysed in *World Dynamics* and *The Limits to Growth*, alongside population, natural resources and agricultural and industrial production, was pollution, a topic to which the environmental scientist Rachel Carson had drawn attention in her highly successful book *Silent Spring* (1962). *The Limits to Growth* mentioned both the accumulation of carbon dioxide (CO_2) and atmospheric warming from burning fossil fuels but, on this point, its tone was optimistic. The authors hoped that, if nuclear energy were eventually to replace burning fossil fuels, 'the rise in atmospheric CO_2 will eventually cease, one hopes before it has had any measurable ecological or climatological effect'.[10] However, during the 1970s scientists began to accumulate evidence that such hope was misplaced. The first World Climate Conference took place in 1979, bringing together scientific experts, and in 1988 the Intergovernmental Panel on Climate Change (IPCC) was established with the support of the United Nations. In 1990 this produced the first of a series of reports that would go on to present the dangers of climate change in stronger and stronger terms.

By the 1990s it became very clear that doing nothing was a recipe for disaster, and at the other extreme, immediate cessation of fossil-fuel use would cause economic collapse. It was necessary to balance the costs resulting from CO_2 emissions against the costs of reducing those emissions. Economists had developed some of the mathematical techniques necessary to analyse such problems. When it came to designing remedies, the problem is a classic externality problem of the type analysed by Samuelson: individuals bear the costs of changing the way they do things, but the effects are felt globally. The director of the Institute for International Economics, in Washington, described it as 'the quintessential international economic problem: it transcends national borders, involves irreversible change and the risk of major adverse surprise, confronts policymakers with the need to make decisions in the face of considerable uncertainty, and calls for a coordinated and multifaceted response by a large number of countries'.[11]

One of the first economists to address the problem was William Nordhaus (1941–). He first tackled the problem in 1976, but it was not until 1991, in an article titled 'To slow or not to slow', that he produced a model of the interaction of climate and economic activity from which he could estimate the optimal path of emission reduction.[12] Taking the parameters of his climate equations from the scientific literature and making assumptions about relevant economic variables, such as the rate of return on capital and the fraction of industry that would be affected by climate change, he calculated the effects of greenhouse warming on the GDP of the United States and the optimal rate at which emissions should be reduced. He reached extremely optimistic conclusions about the effects of climate change, concluding that even in the 'high damage case', the effect would be only 2 per cent of output.[13] In contrast, *The Economics of Global Warming* (1992), by William Cline (1941–), was much more pessimistic. He argued that there was a case for aggressive action to abate CO_2 emissions. Cline looked further ahead, when atmospheric CO_2 would have increased beyond the levels considered by Nordhaus, causing greater damage to the world economy, and he emphasized the need to reduce the risks of very bad outcomes even if those outcomes were far from certain. Their differences illustrate how, at this time, even though the scientific consensus was clear, economists were still trying to work out how to tackle the problem.

Over the following three decades, scientists' assessment of the urgency of the problem, as reflected in IPCC reports, increased and climate change became more prominent in the political agenda, with many countries making increasingly strong commitments to take action. Inevitably economists paid more attention to the problem but, beyond general agreement that the problem was serious, significant differences emerged on the optimal response. There were many reasons for this. Economists had to rely on climate scientists' models of how CO_2 emissions interacted with climate change, which had severe limitations. As one scientist put it, the climate models on which economists had to rely predicted 'The climate we get if we are very lucky'.[14] In addition to being faced with uncertainty in the scientific evidence, economists faced problems in analysing the economics – how climate change would affect economic activity and the consequences for human well-being. For example, if trends are worsening, extrapolation from past trends is hazardous. Societies are likely to adapt to climate change, but estimating what will happen is difficult: it is likely that drought will lead to harvest failures, famine and migration, but it is hard to estimate the magnitudes of the economic damage caused by climate change. It has been argued that uncertainties in both the scientific evidence and in economic responses to climate change mean that much economic modelling systematically underestimated the risk of catastrophic outcomes.

An economist who argued this very strongly was Martin Weitzman (1942–2019). His key point was that 'rare but catastrophic events may have unfathomable costs'.[15] The result was that, instead of seeing the goal of climate policy as being to reduce the most likely rise in global temperatures, we should see it as buying insurance against disastrous outcomes such as the earth becoming too hot for human life as we know it to continue. He argued that conventional analysis, such as that by Nordhaus, showing that a temperature rise of 3°C by the year 2100[16] represented the cost–benefit optimum, is not applicable under such circumstances.

Calculating an optimal climate policy also hinges critically on ethical assumptions, raising questions that neither science nor economics can answer. Working out an optimal policy involves balancing gains to future generations against costs incurred today: should those alive today sacrifice their consumption (and hence their well-being) for the benefit of generations that are not yet alive? Economists are used to discounting the future, typically using the market rate of interest. However, it can be argued that it is ethically unacceptable to discount the welfare of future generations compared with our own: the only ethically acceptable method is to value the well-being of future generations equally with our own. Nicholas Stern (1946–), responsible for a widely cited report commissioned by the British government, took this view.[17] Arguing that, on ethical grounds, the welfare of future generations should not be discounted, and the risks of catastrophic consequences should warming rise more than 1.5 to 2°C, he recommended policies to keep the stock of CO_2 in the atmosphere down to the level that would cause temperatures to stabilize at this level. He described the approach of setting a maximum permissible temperature increase as a 'guard-rail' approach, as justified by the immense uncertainties involved.[18] He also argued that, in addition to the public-good aspect of CO_2 emissions, the problem of emission reduction involved many other market failures, meaning that a wider range of policy interventions was needed than simply imposing an appropriate carbon tax.

The study of climate change is, of course, just one field within environmental economics. Others include the analysis of pollution, an example of which (control of sulphur dioxide emissions) was discussed in Chapter 16, and biodiversity loss. All of these fields illustrate the way economists have recently applied economic analysis to issues relating to the environment and possible solutions. Economics has become less a series of doctrines than, as Marshall advocated, an engine of analysis in which techniques, ranging from the theory of public goods and externalities, ideas about the role of property rights, negotiation, incentives and mechanism design, are used together with ideas from other disciplines to work out possible solutions to very difficult problems. In some cases taxes (often called Pigovian taxes) can be used to deal with externalities, whereas in other cases, such as sulphur dioxide emissions, defining property rights and creating a market is a more effective solution. In other cases, a mix of different policies is needed.

A good example of the way economics engages with other disciplines is a recent report on biodiversity and sustainable development by the economist Partha Dasgupta (1942–).[19] His interest in the subject was piqued by the observation that, in many parts of the world, extreme poverty and environmental degradation go alongside each other. *The Economics of Biodiversity: The Dasgupta Review* (2021) obviously relies heavily on scientific evidence about natural processes and, given that human decisions about fertility and consumption are central to the demand made by humanity on the ecosystem, the report turns to psychology. It thus goes beyond economics, but economic analysis is fundamental. The report begins by showing how the concept of capital, if it is expanded to include human capital (investment in human beings through education) and the value of natural resources as well as man-made physical capital, can be used as a framework within which to think systematically about the problem of sustainability and how it might be achieved.

Epilogue

The traditional core of the history of economic thought is an account of theories of value and distribution (of how prices are formed and how incomes are distributed between wages, profits and rent) and is dominated by a canon comprising Smith, Malthus, Ricardo, Marx and various economists seen as much closer to modern economics. Such a focus inevitably brings to the fore abstract theories about how markets work, which, in turn, can result in the subject appearing out of touch with reality. In contrast, I have paid more attention to the context in which economic inquiries have been undertaken and hence to the application of theoretical ideas. The rationale for this is that we cannot understand what economists were doing without knowing something about both the problems they were trying to tackle and the circumstances under which they worked. I hope this gives a more rounded picture of how the subject has evolved.

Economic ideas and economists' practices arise in specific institutional settings. Scholastic writers in the universities of the European Middle Ages wrote in a setting very different from that of seventeenth-century pamphleteers. Not only were the problems they faced different but so too were their modes of argumentation. Theological arguments that would have been persuasive to a medieval cleric would not have been relevant to an East India Company merchant or those he was trying to influence. In turn, the situation facing English merchants in the 1620 commercial crisis was very different from that facing the economists who discussed the problems facing France in the court of Louis XV or, still later, those who created the political economy that emerged during and immediately after the Napoleonic Wars.

There were, of course, continuities, for Adam Smith took important ideas from Quesnay and his circle and even from writers in Rome and ancient Greece, and the nineteenth-century political economists took much from Smith. But differences in circumstances mean that it would be surprising if economic ideas survived without modification.

Historians have often identified important transitions in the subject, sometimes considered sufficiently abrupt to merit the label 'revolution'. Such transitions have often been associated with significant changes in the institutional setting in which economists have worked. Quesnay's ability to collaborate – to create what one historian has called a 'writing workshop' – was clearly a significant development, as were the efflorescence of social inquiries in mid-eighteenth-century Scottish universities and the emergence of institutions that enabled political economy to establish an identity in nineteenth-century Britain. The changes often linked to a 'marginal revolution' at the end of the nineteenth century are closely linked to the emergence of economics as an academic discipline in which credentials as an economist were acquired not simply by reading and participation in public debate but by following a course of instruction and passing examinations. Similarly, mid-twentieth-century changes in economics can be linked to developments such as the rise to dominance of American research universities, the decimation of German economics in the 1930s, and changes in the patronage of economics (military and government and private funding). Throughout the twentieth and twenty-first centuries, though economic inquiries have been undertaken outside academia (notably in central banks and in international institutions such as the World Bank), universities have been central to the discipline.

To claim this is not to argue, in a Marxian vein, that institutions determine ideas. The ideas that emerge depend not only on the institutional setting but also on the problems confronting economists and the societies of which they are a part, and on the resources, both material and intellectual, that economists bring to the task. Here, it is important to note that economics has not evolved in isolation from other types of inquiry. For the scholastics, economic matters were considered as part of theology, the main questions concerning proper conduct. Smith's reference to the science of the legislator shows that, even in his day, politics and economics were not separated from each other in the way they are today. His *Wealth of Nations* was part of a much broader inquiry involving ethics, politics and jurisprudence, and failure to see this has contributed to his being misread as a modern economist in embryo. Even in the nineteenth century, when the notion of the science of political economy became accepted, its name should remind us that, although there were attempts to separate the two, economics and politics were not completely separate.

Finally, there is the crucial point, touched on already but which needs to be emphasized more strongly, that economic thinking has evolved in response to the problems facing the societies in which it emerged. There was a change when economics became a university discipline in that economists' agenda was increasingly shaped by problems that were internal to the discipline. The search for rigorous proofs of the existence and stability of general competitive equilibrium is the classic example. It has been defended on the ground that without such a proof we cannot know that the theory of supply and demand (of which general equilibrium is an instance) is coherent. However, the question has little, if any, significance outside economics. Other examples include demonstrating that the shares earned by wages, profits and rents in the marginal productivity theory of distribution add up to total national income; or working out rigorous microfoundations for macroeconomic theories. Such work has had a high profile in university curricula, mainly because it has been assumed that students need to understand the core theory (as well as empirical techniques) before they can apply it. However, it is probably safe to say that most economics has always been, in a very loose sense, applied economics in that it has typically been motivated by the need to solve problems facing society. (The qualification is inserted because before the early twentieth century the distinction between theory and application was much more blurred.)

The importance of applied work – of economic practices oriented towards understanding the real world and solving problems facing society – takes us back to the structure of the discipline and its institutions. In 1912, Schumpeter summarized the structure of economics in the following words:

The more we approach modern times the less possible it becomes to characterize briefly the wealth of currents and cross-currents and the more untrue, forced and misleading appears any systematic arrangement and grouping ... We must add that hand in hand with the progressing specialization resulting from the increase of the subject-matter and from the advances in analysis, which turned many of the best workers into laymen in all branches except their own special ones, a tendency established itself in most recent times to break down the barriers between the various specialized branches.[1]

Though written more than a century ago, these words sum up many of the themes discussed in the last few chapters of this book. Economics, especially since the middle of the twentieth century, has become much larger. The number of economists has increased, as has the range of fields covered by the discipline and the amount to be learned about each. In this book, order was imposed by picking out certain very broad themes, from the rise of mathematical economics and econometrics to the expanded role played by economists in advising governments. However, although a sometimes bewildering variety of ideas is discussed, even more has been left out. Schumpeter's judgement that as we approach modern times it becomes less possible to offer a brief characterization of the subject remains well justified.

Schumpeter had hoped that the 'non-scientific factors' behind the slogans of various groups would diminish, that economists would stop making excessive claims for their ideas. It seems safe to say that this has not happened. General-equilibrium theory and then game theory have both held out hopes of providing the organizing framework within which disputes might be clarified and resolved. However, while some disputes have been resolved, new ones have emerged, and old ones have re-emerged. Econometrics has made enormous advances, but its power to settle theoretical disputes arguably remains extremely controversial. The same is true of experimental methods. Schumpeter's hope of developing scientific economic techniques that would render economics uncontroversial remains a chimera. Reactions to Card and Krueger's minimum-wage study illustrate this very clearly. After the 1990s, Card stayed away from minimum-wage research because he felt that his work was misrepresented, both by those who want to raise the minimum wage and those opposed to it.[2] It will also be obvious that the conclusions reached by Piketty, Milanovic, Deaton and Case, some of which raise questions about the political system and about how well capitalism functions for those people who need to work in order to live, are not universally accepted. Similar remarks could be made concerning the role of vested interests in debates over globalization and climate change. Politics and ideology are never far away.

The structure of modern academia raises further issues. The increased competitiveness of the academic system and increased reliance on citation counts and other bibliometric indices provide people with an incentive to oversell their ideas – to claim excessive originality. To achieve tenure in an American university typically requires publication of half a dozen or more articles, and few economists can expect to have this many genuinely original ideas so early in their career. Once past this barrier, promotion and salary depend on regular publication, and reputations are made by claiming much, not by being modest. The founder of a controversial school will be rewarded by frequent citations of their work, and high citation counts are taken as a measure of prestige. Ending a controversy does not necessarily produce as many citations even though it may be a more significant achievement.

When we turn to Schumpeter's vision of the structure of the discipline, the picture is much more complicated. He wrote at a time when the institution of the academic school, based in a particular institution and often dominated by a single individual (Schmoller and Marshall being obvious examples) was at its zenith. Such groupings were, he argued, becoming less important:

> The slogans used to designate certain outstanding groups are much simpler than is warranted by the actual conditions. These slogans, moreover, are partly coloured by non-scientific factors ... [T]hey appear with a claim to universal validity, while in fact in every branch of the social sciences, and often with different problems in the same branch, conditions are different.[3]

In other words, the slogans about historical and theoretical methods were oversimplified. People had to use different methods alongside each other, with the result that barriers between different specializations were breaking down.

Since Schumpeter's time, the growth of the discipline has increased the barriers between fields (as he perceived was happening) because there is a limit to what a single person can read. It is difficult for a single economist to be familiar, in detail, with the latest developments in more than one or two fields. This effect has been reinforced by the emergence of specialized journals and conferences, which proliferated in the late twentieth century, making it much easier to be unaware of what is happening in other fields. On the other hand, the emergence, around the 1960s, of a common core of theoretical and empirical techniques changed the discipline by unifying fields. It became possible to be an expert in a particular set of techniques and to apply these to problems in a variety of fields. For example, a theorist who worked on models of imperfect competition could write articles applying such models to industrial organization, macroeconomics and international trade. Whereas, for previous generations, 'macro' and 'micro' were very separate fields, the barrier between them became much lower during the 1980s and 1990s when macroeconomic models were expected to be grounded in models of individual behaviour.

By the twenty-first century, the discipline had changed again, with applied work becoming much more prominent, as illustrated by the topics covered in Chapter 18. Economics in the twenty-first century is still concerned with the topics that have always defined the subject – markets, prices, the generation of wealth, unemployment and so on – but it is increasingly defined by its tools and techniques, notably experiments of various types, the analysis of 'big data' that were unknown to earlier generations and the development of statistical techniques that would have been inconceivable even fifty years ago because of the computing power required to implement them. Complementing this is a growing reliance on explanations drawn from behavioural economics. It still makes sense to talk of 'an economic approach' or 'thinking like an economist', where this involves optimization and the balancing of costs and benefits of alternative actions, the approach that could be said to have dominated the discipline for much of the twentieth century. Indeed, such methods remain pervasive. However, the most significant feature of economic analysis has arguably become not the development of grand theories but the application of theories and techniques to much more precisely defined problems.

A Note on the Literature

In one sense, the best suggestion for further reading is to read the original sources cited in the text, few of which are listed here. Many of these are as easy to read as modern commentaries. Smith and John Stuart Mill, for example, wrote for a wide audience, and it is tempting to say that no one's economic education is complete without having at least dipped into them. Smith even provides a very brief summary of what his *Wealth of Nations* is about. The suggestions offered here are almost entirely secondary sources. Listing them also serves as a way of acknowledging some of the works on which I drew in writing this book. Nevertheless, I should point out that this list does not indicate everything I read. There are many books that I found helpful but which are reflected in only a single sentence or even a short phrase. To list all these would stretch the patience of publisher and readers. In particular, I have cited only references that discuss economic ideas directly. General histories on which I relied for background information are, with a few exceptions, not mentioned here.

Readers should be warned that the dual function of this bibliography means that the technical level of the material listed varies considerably. Some of the readings cover material that is barely touched upon here, often because, even though it is fascinating and accessible to a wide audience, it would take us too far from the central story. The suggestions focus on books, though a few academic journal articles are mentioned, usually where I want to acknowledge an important source. A comprehensive list would make this list of suggested reading unacceptably long.

PRIMARY SOURCES

Since the first edition, the growth of the internet has transformed access to historical texts. Probably the most useful source for material from the 1920s and earlier is https://archive.org/, which contains facsimiles of thousands of works that are no longer in copyright. Facsimiles are valuable because you know you are looking at the original and because it is often possible to see first editions and works that are difficult to obtain in libraries. Texts are also made available by organizations with a political or ideological purpose, such as promoting Marxism or libertarian/free-market economics. Such sources need to be used with care but can be valuable sources of documentation. The Liberty Fund website, at https://oll.liberty-fund.org/, is particularly useful because it contains facsimiles of many important historical works, sometimes excellent scholarly editions, including texts by Smith (Edwin Cannan's edition), Ricardo (Royal Economic Society edition) and Mill ('Toronto' edition). The last two of these are multivolume editions that contain articles and correspondence as well as the major texts. Wikipedia is valuable for checking basic factual information such as dates, even if care has to be taken with the interpretations provided on controversial topics.

GENERAL READING

There exist many histories of economic thought, most written by economists. Perhaps the classic is

J. A. Schumpeter, *A History of Economic Analysis*, London: Allen and Unwin, 1954; Routledge, 1986.

Although some of Schumpeter's judgements have not stood up to more recent scholarship, and although his conception of the history of economics is one that few would now accept, this remains an outstanding book. Also useful is:

J. A. Schumpeter, *Ten Great Economists: From Marx to Keynes*, New York: Oxford University Press, 1951; London: Routledge, 1997.

For a more recent attempt to provide a history of economics on the same scale as Schumpeter's magnum opus, see

M. Perlman and C. R. McCann, *The Pillars of Economic Understanding*: Vol. 1, *Ideas and Traditions*; Vol. 2, *Factors and Markets*, Ann Arbor, MI: University of Michigan Press, 1998, 2000.

Among many textbooks, two stand out:

M. Blaug, *Economic Theory in Retrospect*, 5th edn, Cambridge: Cambridge University Press, 1997;

H. W. Spiegel, *The Growth of Economic Thought*, 3rd edn, Durham, NC: Duke University Press, 1991.

Blaug reviews economic ideas from the late eighteenth century to the present day from the point of view of modern economic theory in a manner likely to be accessible only to those trained in economics. Spiegel is wide-ranging and provides a particularly thorough coverage of early material. It is also worth mentioning two sets of lectures, both transcribed from tape recordings and students' notes:

W. C. Mitchell, *Types of Economic Theory: From Mercantilism to Institutionalism*, ed. J. Dorfman, 2 vols., New York: A. M. Kelley, 1967;

L. C. Robbins, *A History of Economic Thought: The LSE Lectures*, Princeton, NJ: Princeton University Press, 1998.

The above books are all very substantial works. Readers wanting something shorter and less comprehensive should try the following:

R. L. Heilbroner, *The Worldly Philosophers*, Harmondsworth: Penguin Books, 1973.

For readable essays on a selection of important twentieth-century economists, see

W. Breit and R. L. Ransom, *The Academic Scribblers*, 3rd edn, Princeton, NJ: Princeton University Press, 1998.

Although its focus on revolutions is different from the one adopted here, a book that still repays reading on topics ranging from Smith to Keynes, with particularly useful discussions of attitudes towards policy, is:

T. W. Hutchison, *On Revolutions and Progress in Economic Knowledge*, Cambridge: Cambridge University Press, 1978.

I also mention one of my own books. As history, I now consider it very limited, because it pays hardly any attention to the context in which economic ideas were developed, but it contains much evidence on which economists wrote what at different times in the twentieth century. When it was written, few books even tried to provide a systematic coverage of economics after the Second World War.

R. E. Backhouse, *A History of Modern Economic Analysis*, Oxford: Basil Blackwell, 1985.

Some of the most significant changes in the new edition of this book are based on ideas discussed in:

R. E. Backhouse and K. Tribe, *The History of Economics: A Course for Students and Teachers*, London: Agenda, 2018.

Each chapter is focused on a bibliography and chronology, followed by the outline of a lecture. It is thus useful as a source of reading. We have also written two chapters on the history of economics in Britain:

R. E. Backhouse and K. Tribe, 'Economic ideas and the emergence of political economy' and 'Economic thought and ideology in Britain, 1870–2010', in R. Floud, J. Humphries and P. Johnson (eds.), *The Cambridge Economic History of Modern Britain*: Vol. 1, *1700–1870*; Vol. 2, *1870 to the Present*, Cambridge: Cambridge University Press, 2014.

Useful reference books include

M. Blaug, *Great Economists before Keynes* and *Great Economists since Keynes*, Cheltenham: Edward Elgar, 1997, 1998;

M. Blaug, *Who's Who in Economics*, 3rd edn, Cheltenham: Edward Elgar, 1999;

S. Pressman, *Fifty Major Economists*, London: Routledge, 1999.

There are many other such collections of articles. The most valuable reference work, however, is

S. N. Durlauf and L. Blume (eds.), *The New Palgrave: A Dictionary of Economics*, 2nd edn, 8 vols., London: Macmillan, 2008. Online version, including new entries, at www.dictionaryofeconomics.com.

This contains numerous biographical entries as well as entries on important topics. It can be daunting finding the information required, but there is a lot of material there.

A 'coffee table' book, packed with illustrations but nonetheless a mine of reliable and useful information on an enormous variety of topics, is

S. G. Medema, *The Economics Book: From Xenophon to Cryptocurrency, 250 Milestones in the History of Economics*. New York: Sterling, 2019.

ANCIENT AND MEDIEVAL ECONOMICS

Of the textbooks mentioned above, Spiegel is particularly good on this period. A general survey is provided in

B. Gordon, *Economic Analysis before Adam Smith: Hesiod to Lessius*, London: Macmillan, 1975.

The work of writers from ancient Greece to sixteenth-century scholastics is discussed in

S. T. Lowry and B. Gordon (eds.), *Ancient and Medieval Economic Ideas and Concepts of Social Justice*, Leiden: E. J. Brill, 1998;

B. B. Price (ed.), *Ancient Economic Thought*, London: Routledge, 1997.

The most comprehensive account of ancient Greek ideas, focusing on the idea of an administrative order, is

S. T. Lowry, *The Archaeology of Economic Ideas: The Classical Greek Tradition*, Durham, NC: Duke University Press, 1987.

The outstanding writer on scholastic economics is Odd Langholm, who has written a series of books on the subject. The best starting points in his work are his article in the Lowry and Gordon collection cited above and

O. Langholm, *The Legacy of Scholasticism in Economic Thought: Antecedents of Choice and Power*, Cambridge: Cambridge University Press, 1998.

Focusing on the link between justice and compulsion, this book also offers valuable insights into ancient and particularly Roman thought, as well as some links to seventeenth-century and more recent economic thought.

EARLY MODERN ECONOMICS

A useful collection of primary texts (including translations from languages other than English) is

A. E. Monroe, *Early Economic Thought: Selections from Economic Literature Prior to Adam Smith*, Cambridge, MA: Harvard University Press, 1965.

Spanish writings are translated, with commentary, in

M. Grice Hutchison, *The School of Salamanca: Readings in Spanish Monetary Theory, 1544–1605*, Oxford: Clarendon Press, 1952.

For further essays on Spanish thought, see

M. Grice Hutchison, *Economic Thought in Spain*, ed. L. S. Moss and C. K. Ryan, Cheltenham: Edward Elgar, 1993.

On the reformation, see:

J. D. Singleton, '"Money is a sterile thing": Martin Luther on the immorality of usury reconsidered', *History of Political Economy* 43(4), 2011, pp. 683–98.

The literature on what is commonly described as 'mercantilism' goes beyond economic thought to economic policy and economic history. It is, however, worth mentioning what is probably the classic work on the subject:

E. Heckscher, *Mercantilism* (1935), 2 vols., London: Routledge, 1994.

A useful account, by an eminent economist, of how ideas about human motivations evolved from Machiavelli to Smith is found in

A. O. Hirschman, *The Passions and the Interests: Political Arguments for Capitalism before Its Triumph*, Princeton, NJ: Princeton University Press, 1977.

English writings are discussed in

J. O. Appleby, *Economic Thought and Ideology in Seventeenth-century England*, Princeton, NJ: Princeton University Press, 1978;
W. Letwin, *The Origins of Scientific Economics: English Economic Thought, 1660–1776*, London: Methuen, 1963;
B. E. Supple, *Commercial Crisis and Change in England, 1600–1642*, Cambridge: Cambridge University Press, 1959.

The best account of the English commercial crisis of the 1620s is

C. E. Suprinyak, 'Trade, money, and the grievances of the Commonwealth: economic debates in England during the commercial crisis of the early 1620s', *History of Economic Ideas* 24(1), 2016, pp. 27–55.

Turning to the early eighteenth century, a concise account of debates on luxury can be found in

I. Hont, 'The early Enlightenment debate on commerce and luxury', in M. Goldie and R. Wokler (eds.), *The Cambridge History of Eighteenth-century Political Thought*, Cambridge: Cambridge University Press, 2006, pp. 377–418.

For another treatment of overlapping issues, see the Introduction to

I. Hont, *Jealousy of Trade: International Competition and the Nation State in Historical Perspective*, Cambridge, MA: Harvard University Press, 2005.

This places economic discussions squarely in the context of political debates. The only comprehensive survey of eighteenth-century economic writing prior to Smith is

T. W. Hutchison, *Before Adam Smith: The Emergence of Political Economy, 1662–1776*, Oxford: Basil Blackwell, 1988.

Biographies of two of the period's most important writers are

A. Murphy, *John Law: Economic Theorist and Policy-Maker*, Oxford: Clarendon Press, 1997;

A. Murphy, *Richard Cantillon: Entrepreneur and Economist*, Oxford: Clarendon Press, 1986.

For another discussion of Cantillon's ideas, see

A. A. Brewer, *Richard Cantillon: Pioneer of Economic Theory*, London: Routledge, 1992.

THE EIGHTEENTH AND NINETEENTH CENTURIES

Once we reach the physiocrats, Adam Smith and classical economics, the volume of literature, both primary and secondary, expands dramatically. The following represents an even tinier proportion of what is available than is the case with previous periods. A useful short introduction is provided in

D. Winch, 'The emergence of economics as a science, 1750–1870', in C. M. Cipolla (ed.), *The Fontana Economic History of Europe*: Vol. 3, *The Industrial Revolution*, London: Fontana, 1973, Chapter 9.

A useful collection of eighteenth-century readings is contained in

R. L. Meek (ed.), *Precursors of Adam Smith, 1750–1775*, London: Dent, 1973.

On the physiocrats and Turgot, see

W. A. Eltis, *The Classical Theory of Economic Growth*, London: Macmillan, 1984;

P. D. Groenewegen, *The Economics of A. R. J. Turgot*, The Hague: Martinus Nijhoff, 1977.

As its title implies, the former also discusses classical economics. For an introduction to more recent work on Quesnay and the physiocrats, see

L. Charles and C. Théré, 'From Versailles to Paris: the creative communities of the physiocratic movement', *History of Political Economy* 43(1), 2011, pp. 25–58.

For an outstanding and concise survey of political economy in early-nineteenth-century Britain, see

D. P. O'Brien, *The Classical Economists Revisited*, Princeton, NJ: Princeton University Press, 2004.

This makes it clear that the term 'classical' is used to denote a community which held a wide range of views.

Because of his status (whether deserved or not) as a free-market icon and as the major figure in classical economics, one of the most intensively researched areas in the history of economic thought, the literature on Adam Smith is vast. The literature is surveyed in

V. Brown, "Mere inventions of the imagination": a survey of recent literature on Adam Smith', *Economics and Philosophy* 13(2), 1997, pp. 281–312;

K. Tribe, 'Adam Smith: critical theorist?', *Journal of Economic Literature* 37(2), 1999, pp. 609–32.

Mention has to be made of the work of Andrew Skinner, one of the editors of the 'Glasgow' edition of Smith's books:

A. S. Skinner, *A System of Social Science: Papers Relating to Adam Smith*, Oxford: Clarendon Press, 1979.

See also

D. D. Raphaoel, *Adam Smith*, Oxford: Clarendon Press, 1985;
I. Ross, *The Life of Adam Smith*, Oxford: Oxford University Press, 1995.

The transition to classical economics has been placed in its political context in

E. Rothschild, *Economic Sentiments: Adam Smith, Condorcet and the Enlightenment*, Cambridge, MA, and London: Harvard University Press, 2001;
G. Stedman Jones, *An End to Poverty? A Historical Debate*, New York: Columbia University Press, 2008;
D. Winch, *Riches and Poverty: An Intellectual History of Political Economy in Britain, 1750–1834*, Cambridge: Cambridge University Press, 1996.

The story of the ongoing contest between economists and their Romantic critics is taken forward through to 1914 in

D. Winch, *Wealth and Life: Essays on the Intellectual History of Political Economy in Britain, 1848–1914*, Cambridge: Cambridge University Press, 2009.

See also

D. Winch, *Malthus*, Oxford: Oxford University Press, 1987.

From the mass of literature on Ricardo, one of the best accounts is

T. Peach, *Interpreting Ricardo*, Cambridge: Cambridge University Press, 1993.

A more recent account is

R. Walter, *Before Method and Models: The Political Economy of Malthus and Ricardo*, Oxford: Oxford University Press, 2021.

Accessible editions of major works, with useful introductions, include

T. R. Malthus, *Essay on the Principle of Population*, ed. A. Flew, Harmondsworth: Penguin Books, 1970;

J. S. Mill, *Principles of Political Economy*, ed. D. Winch, Harmondsworth: Penguin Books, 1970;

D. Ricardo, *Principles of Political Economy and Taxation*, ed. R. M. Hartwell, Harmondsworth: Penguin Books, 1971;

A. Smith, *The Wealth of Nations*, ed. A. S. Skinner, Harmondsworth: Penguin Books, 1970.

Note, however, that Skinner's edition of *The Wealth of Nations* reproduces only part of the work. For an accessible edition of the whole work, see either the Cannan edition (available on the Liberty Fund website) or the definitive 'Glasgow' edition, included in the multivolume collected works (Oxford University Press).

The French engineering school is discussed in detail in

R. B. Ekelund and R. F. Hebert, *The Secret Origins of Modern Microeconomics: Dupuit and the Engineers*, Chicago: Chicago University Press, 1999.

Monetary economics is nicely covered in

A. Murphy, *The Genesis of Macroeconomics: New Ideas from Sir William Petty to Henry Thornton*, Oxford: Oxford University Press, 2009.

The literature on Marx is voluminous. A small selection of the most accessible items includes

A. A. Brewer, *A Guide to Marx's Capital*, Cambridge: Cambridge University Press, 1984;

G. Stedman Jones, *Karl Marx: Greatness and Illusion*, London: Penguin Books, 2017 (an intellectual biography);

D. McLennan, *The Thought of Karl Marx*, London: Macmillan, 1971.

For a discussion of German economics in relation to Menger's marginalism, see:

E. Streissler, 'The influence of German economics on the work of Menger and Marshall', in B. Caldwell (ed.), *Carl Menger and His Legacy in Economics*, Durham, NC: Duke University Press, 1990.

A book that can be strongly recommended for insights into Smith, Marx and Walras, is

K. Tribe, *Economy of the Word: Language, History, and Economics*, Oxford: Oxford University Press, 2015.

THE LATE NINETEENTH AND EARLY TWENTIETH CENTURIES

An old, though still extremely valuable, coverage of this period is provided by

T. W. Hutchison, *A Review of Economic Doctrines, 1870–1929*, Oxford: Oxford University Press, 1953;
B. B. Seligman, *Main Currents in Modern Economics*, New York: Free Press of Glencoe, 1962.

A useful collection of essays on the so-called 'marginal revolution' is

R. D. C. Black, A. W. Coats and C. D. W. Goodwin (eds.), *The Marginal Revolution in Economics*, Durham, NC: Duke University Press, 1972.

For an account of the emergence of economics as an academic discipline that pays attention to the way the subject was taught in different countries and explains the importance of Cambridge at the end of the nineteenth century and the subsequent position of American economics, see

K. Tribe, *Constructing Economic Science: The Invention of a Discipline, 1850–1950*. Oxford: Oxford University Press, 2022.

Several very useful essays on this period's economics in Britain and the United States are contained in Coats's collected papers:

A. W. Coats, *British and American Essays*: Vol. 1, *On the History of Economic Thought*; Vol. 2, *The Sociology and Professionalization of Economics*; Vol. 3, *The Historiography of Economics*, London: Routledge, 1992, 1993, 2014.

For more detailed discussion of Marshall and English historical economics see

P. D. Groenewegen, *A Soaring Eagle: Alfred Marshall, 1842–1924*, Cheltenham: Edward Elgar, 1995;

A. Kadish, *Historians, Economists and Economic History*, London: Routledge, 1989;

J. Maloney, *The Professionalization of Economics: Alfred Marshall and the Dominance of Orthodoxy*, New Brunswick, NJ: Transaction Publishers, 1991.

For more recent work on Marshall, see the large collection of essays in

T. Raffaelli, G. Becattini and M. Dardi (eds.), *The Elgar Companion to Alfred Marshall*, Cheltenham: Edward Elgar, 2009;

T. Raffaelli, *Marshall's Evolutionary Economics*, London: Routledge, 2003.

Marshall's one-time mentor, Sidgwick, is the subject of

B. Schultz, *Henry Sidgwick – Eye of the Universe: An Intellectual Biography*, Cambridge: Cambridge University Press, 2004.

This goes significantly beyond the history of economics but provides fascinating insights into an important Victorian intellectual.

Numerous essays on the history of welfare economics in the late nineteenth and twentieth centuries, from Sidgwick and Marshall to Arrow and Sen, are in

R. E. Backhouse and T. Nishizawa, *No Wealth but Life: Welfare Economics and the Welfare State in Britain, 1880–1945*, Cambridge: Cambridge University Press, 2010;

R. E. Backhouse, B. W. Bateman, T. Nishizawa and D. Plehwe (eds.), *Liberalism and the Welfare State: Economists and Arguments for the Welfare State*, Oxford: Oxford University Press, 2017;

R. E. Backhouse, A. Baujard and T. Nishizawa (eds.), *Welfare Theory, Public Action and Ethical Values: Revisiting the History of Welfare Economics*, Cambridge: Cambridge University Press, 2021.

American economics is comprehensively surveyed in the five volumes of

J. Dorfman, *The Economic Mind in American Civilization*, 5 vols., New York: Viking, 1946–59.

Volumes 3–5 are particularly useful for the material covered here. Earlier volumes cover topics I have omitted in order to keep the book to a manageable size.

The transformation of American economics in the first half of the twentieth century is covered in the many essays in

M. S. Morgan and M. Rutherford (eds.), *From Interwar Pluralism to Postwar Neoclassicism*, Durham, NC: Duke University Press, 1998 (supplement to *History of Political Economy*);

M. Rutherford, *The Institutionalist Movement in American Economics, 1918–1947: Science and Social Control*, Cambridge: Cambridge University Press, 2011.

The topics of eugenics and economists' attitudes towards race are ones on which only a limited amount of work has been done. The difficulties are that these are emotive issues and that understanding them requires a deeper exploration of the broader cultural history of the period, including Victorian Britain and post-bellum United States than is possible in this book. The best history of eugenics is

D. J. Kevles, *In the Name of Eugenics: Genetics and the Uses of Human Heredity*, Berkeley and Los Angeles: University of California Press, 1985.

Some recent works on race and eugenics are:

D. M. Levy, *How the Dismal Science Got Its Name*, Ann Arbor: University of Michigan Press, 2002;

S. Peart and D. M. Levy, *The 'Vanity of the Philosopher': From Equality to Hierarchy in Post-Classical Economics*, Ann Arbor: University of Michigan Press, 2005;

T. Leonard, *Illiberal Reformers: Race, Eugenics, and American Economics in the Progressive Era*, Princeton, NJ: Princeton University Press, 2016.

These are all useful for their coverage of material not generally found elsewhere, but it is worth reading them in conjunction with two reviews which provide different perspectives:

S. Zlotnik 'Contextualizing David Levy's "How the dismal science got its name"; or, revisiting the Victorian context of David Levy's "History of race and economics"', in D. Colander, R. E. Prasch and F. A. Sheth (eds.), *Race, Liberalism and Economics*, Ann Arbor: University of Michigan Press, 2004, pp. 85–99;

B. Bateman, 'T. Leonard, *Illiberal Reformers: Race, Eugenics, and American Economics in the Progressive Era*', *History of Political Economy* 49(4), 2017, pp. 717–21.

The period's monetary economics is brilliantly surveyed in

D. Laidler, *The Golden Age of the Quantity Theory*, Deddington: Philip Allan, 1991.

Also useful is

T. M. Humphrey, *Money, Banking and Inflation*, Cheltenham: Edward Elgar, 1993.

MICROECONOMICS AND MATHEMATICAL ECONOMICS IN THE TWENTIETH CENTURY

This is a topic on which widely divergent views can be found, ranging from accounts premissed on the assumption that the mathematization of economics has been a great success to ones that regard it as a total failure. From this large literature, a helpful starting point can be found in a symposium in *Daedalus*, 1997, especially in contributions by R. M. Solow and D. Kreps, two eminent economic theorists. Another excellent short account is

M. S. Morgan, 'The formation of "modern" economics: engineering and ideology', in T. H. Porter and D. Ross (eds.), *The Cambridge History of Science*: Vol. 7, *Modern Social and Behavioural Sciences*, Cambridge: Cambridge University Press, 2003.

For very critical views of these developments, focused on what happened between the 1940s and the 1980s, see

M. Blaug, 'The formalist revolution or what happened to orthodox economics after World War II?', in R. E. Backhouse and J. Creedy (eds.), *From Classical Economics to the Theory of the Firm: Essays in Honour of D. P. O'Brien*, Cheltenham: Edward Elgar, 1999;
T. W. Hutchison, *Changing Aims in Economics*, Oxford: Basil Blackwell, 1992.

The history of general-equilibrium theory has been tackled by several people (the following will provide references to other works by the same authors):

B. Ingrao and G. Israel, *The Invisible Hand: Economic Equilibrium in the History of Science*, Cambridge, MA: MIT Press, 1990;
E. R. Weintraub, *How Economics became a Mathematical Science*, Durham, NC: Duke University Press, 2002.

The following book provides a completely non-technical account of the human stories behind what was once considered one of the most important theorems in mathematical economics. As its title indicates, it shows that the story of who first reached a result can be very complicated.

T. Duppe and E. R. Weintraub, *Finding Equilibrium: Arrow, Debreu, McKenzie and the Problem of Scientific Credit*, Princeton, NJ: Princeton University Press, 2014.

For reprints and translations of some influential works, see

W. J. Baumol and S. M. Goldfield (eds.), *Precursors in Mathematical Economics: An Anthology. Series of Reprints of Scarce Works on Political Economy*, 19, London: London School of Economics, 1968.

On the origins of game theory, Leonard's book is crucial:

R. J. Leonard, *Von Neumann, Morgenstern and the Theory of Games: From Chess to Social Science, 1900–1960*, Cambridge: Cambridge University Press, 2010.

For an account of von Neumann's general equilibrium theory see

J. Carvajalino, 'Unlocking the mystery of the origins of John von Neumann's growth model', *History of Political Economy* 53(4), 2021, pp. 595–631.

A book focusing on operations research and the drive to provide a rational basis for policy is

W. Thomas, *Rational Action: The Sciences of Policy in Britain and America, 1940–1960*, Cambridge, MA: MIT Press, 2015.

The best account of how game theory was taken up after 1944 in economics and many other fields is

P. Erickson, *The World the Game Theorists Made*, Chicago: University of Chicago Press, 2015.

For a fascinating, partly overlapping, account of ideas about rational choice, also involving other social sciences as well as economics, see

P. Erickson et al., *How Reason Almost Lost Its Mind: The Strange Career of Cold War Rationality*, Chicago: University of Chicago Press, 2013.

Another book to place rationality in the context of the Cold War is

S. Amadae, *Rationalizing Capitalist Democracy: The Cold War Origins of Rational Choice Liberalism*, Chicago, University of Chicago Press, 2003.

See also

S. Nasar, *A Beautiful Mind*, London: Faber and Faber, 1999 (a biography of John Nash);
E. R. Weintraub (ed.), *Toward a History of Game Theory*, Durham, NC: Duke University Press, 1992. (Annual supplement to *History of Political Economy*).

One of the leading players in the rise of mathematical economics has given his own account of the genesis of his main work:

P. A. Samuelson, 'How "Foundations" came to be', *Journal of Economic Literature* 36(3), 1998, pp. 1375–86.

My own account of the origin of that book is provided, along with much else on this economist who was central to mid-twentieth-century economics, in

R. E. Backhouse, *Founder of Modern Economics: Paul A. Samuelson*: Vol. 1, *Becoming Samuelson, 1915–1948*, Oxford: Oxford University Press, 2017.

Some chapters reflect work done in preparing the as yet unfinished Volume 2.

The conceptions of competition in the socialist-calculation debate are discussed in

D. Lavoie, *Rivalry and Central Planning*, Cambridge: Cambridge University Press, 1985;

N. Cartwright, J. Cat, L. Fleck and T. E. Uebel, *Otto Neurath: Philosophy between Science and Politics*, Cambridge: Cambridge University Press, 1996;

K. Tribe, *Strategies of Economic Order: German Economic Discourse, 1750–1950*, Cambridge: Cambridge University Press, 1995.

The last of these is a wide-ranging discussion of economic thought in Germany.

On Hayek, in addition to the materials reprinted in the multivolume *Collected Works of F. A. Hayek* (Chicago: University of Chicago Press), see another book that appeared too late for me to take into account:

B. Caldwell and H. Klausinger, *Hayek: A Life, 1899–1950*, Chicago: University of Chicago Press, 2022.

Useful introductions to theories of imperfect competition and the theory of the firm are

D. P. O'Brien, 'Research programmes in competitive structure', *Journal of Economic Studies*, 1983, pp. 29–51, and 'The evolution of the theory of the firm', in F. H. Stephen (ed.), *Firms, Organization and Labour*, London: Macmillan, 1984. Both are reprinted in *Methodology, Money and the Firm: The Collected Essays of D. P. O'Brien*, 2 vols., Cheltenham: Edward Elgar, 1994;

A. Skinner, 'E. H. Chamberlin: the origins and development of monopolistic competition', *Journal of Economic Studies* 10, 1983, pp. 52–67.

QUANTITATIVE ECONOMICS

On the history of US national-income accounting, see

C. Carson, 'The history of the United States national income and product accounts: the development of an analytical tool', *Review of Income and Wealth* 21, 1975, pp. 153–81;

J. W. Duncan and W. C. Shelton, *Revolution in United States Government Statistics, 1926–1976*, Washington, DC: US Department of Commerce, 1978;

J. W. Kendrick, 'The historical development of national accounts', *History of Political Economy* 2, 1970, pp. 284–315;

M. Perlman, 'Political purpose and the national accounts', in *The Character of Economic Thought, Economic Characters and Economic Institutions: Selected Essays of Mark Perlman*, Ann Arbor, MI: University of Michigan Press, 1996.

Stone's contribution is discussed in

L. Johansen, 'Richard Stone's contributions to economics', *Scandinavian Journal of Economics* 87(1), 1985, pp. 4–32.

On the development of econometric techniques, see

M. S. Morgan, *A History of Econometric Ideas*, Cambridge: Cambridge University Press, 1990.

Edited versions of early articles on the subject are reprinted with substantial commentary in

D. F. Hendry and M. S. Morgan (eds.), *The Foundations of Econometric Analysis*, Cambridge: Cambridge University Press, 1995.

For a novel take on a key figure in the history of econometrics:

E. Dekker, *Jan Tinbergen (1903–1994) and the Rise of Economic Expertise*, Cambridge: Cambridge University Press, 2021.

There are several pieces on the history of the Cowles Commission, including

C. F. Christ, 'The Cowles Commission's contributions to econometrics at Chicago, 1939–55', *Journal of Economic Literature* 32(1), 1994, pp. 30–59;

C. F. Christ, 'History of the Cowles Commission 1932–1952', in Cowles Commission (ed.), *Economic Theory and Measurement*, Chicago: Cowles Commission, 1953.

An account of the history of macroeconometric modelling by practioners of the art is

R. G. Bodkin, L. R. Klein and K. Marwah (eds.), *A History of Macroeconometric Model-Building*, Cheltenham: Edward Elgar, 1991.

More recent historical discussions of the same topic can be found in a special issue of *History of Political Economy* 51(3), June 2019.

MACROECONOMICS AND FINANCE IN THE TWENTIETH CENTURY

By far the best source on interwar macroeconomics is

D. Laidler, *Fabricating the Keynesian Revolution: Studies in the Interwar Literature on Money, the Cycle and Unemployment*, Cambridge: Cambridge University Press, 1999.

This makes it very clear that there was much more to interwar economics than simply Keynes and his critics.

The literature on Keynes is vast. The biographies by Moggindge and Skidelsky are essential.

D. Moggridge, *Maynard Keynes: An Economist's Biography*, London: Routledge, 1992;

R. Skidelsky, *John Maynard Keynes*: Vol. 1, *Hopes Betrayed, 1883–1920*; Vol. 2, *The Economist as Saviour, 1920–1937*; Vol. 3, *Fighting for Britain, 1937–1946*; and *John Maynard Keynes: Economist, Philosopher, Statesman, 1883–1946*, London: Macmillan, 1983, 1992, 2000, 2003.

The last is an abridged version of the 3-volume biography. These authors have both also written much shorter biographies:

D. E. Moggridge, *Keynes*, London: Fontana, 1976;

R. Skidelsky, *Keynes*, Oxford: Oxford University Press, 1996.

A simpler account is offered in

M. Blaug, *John Maynard Keynes: Life, Ideas, Legacy*, London: Macmillan, 1990.

From the rest of the literature on Keynes, I list a volume that cover many aspects of his work and some short books that appeared as part of the revival of interest in Keynes after the 2007–8 crash, as well as my own recent attempt at a very simple account:

R. E. Backhouse and B. Bateman (eds.), *The Cambridge Companion to Keynes*, Cambridge: Cambridge University Press, 2006;

P. Clarke, *Keynes: The Twentieth Century's Most Influential Economist*, London: Bloomsbury, 2009;

P. Clarke, *The Locomotive of war: Money, Empire, power and Guilt*, London: Bloomsbury, 2017.

P. Clarke, *Keynes in Action: Truth and Expediency in Public Policy*, London: Bloomsbury, 2022;

R. Skidelsky, *Keynes: The Return of the Master*, London: Allen Lane, 2009;

R. E. Backhouse and B. Bateman, *Capitalist Revolutionary: John Maynard Keynes*, Cambridge, MA: Harvard University Press, 2011;

R. E. Backhouse, *Simply Keynes*, Simply Charly, 2022 (on Amazon Kindle).

An excellent biography of Frank Ramsey, which also gives an account of the environment in which Keynes worked, is

C. Misak, *Frank Ramsey: A Sheer Excess of Powers*, Oxford: Oxford University Press, 2020.

Macroeconomics since Keynes has not been comprehensively surveyed. Works that provide detailed coverage of particular themes include

W. Young, *Interpreting Mr Keynes: The IS–LM Enigma*, Cambridge: Polity Press, 1987.

This discusses the way in which the IS–LM model emerged from discussions of the General Theory.

P. G. Mehrling, *The Money Interest and the Public Interest: American Monetary Thought, 1920–1970*, Cambridge, MA, and London: Harvard University Press, 1997.

Three books on the modern theory of finance:

P. G. Mehrling, *Fischer Black and the Revolutionary Idea of Finance*, New York: Wiley, 2005;
D. MacKenzie, *An Engine Not a Camera: How Financial Models Shape Markets*, Cambridge, MA: MIT Press, 2008;
J. Fox, *The Myth of the Rational Market: A History of Risk, Reward, and Delusion on Wall Street*, New York: Harper, 2009.

A book with a self-explanatory title:

K. D. Hoover, *The New Classical Macroeconomics*, Oxford: Basil Blackwell, 1988.

Wider-ranging accounts of the history of modern macroeconomics that get into greater technicalities include

M. De Vroey, *A History of Macroeconomics from Keynes to Lucas and Beyond*, Cambridge: Cambridge University Press, 2016;

R. E. Backhouse and M. Boianovsky, *Transforming Modern Macroeconomics: Exploring Disequilibrium Microfoundations, 1956–2003*, Cambridge: Cambridge University Press, 2003.

The history of the Phillips curve is discussed in detail in

J. Forder, *Macroeconomics and the Phillips Curve Myth*, Oxford: Oxford University Press, 2014.

Finally, a revealing way into modern macroeconomics is to read some of the many interviews that have been conducted with leading economists:

A. Klamer, *The New Classical Macroeconomics: Conversations with New Classical Economists and Their Opponents*, Brighton: Wheatsheaf Books, 1987;

B. Snowdon and H. R. Vane (eds.), *Conversations with Leading Economists: Interpreting Modern Macroeconomics*, Cheltenham: Edward Elgar, 1999.

THEMES IN TWENTIETH-CENTURY ECONOMICS

Even in the modern academic world, economics does not exist in a vacuum, and a very useful interpretation of intellectual developments since the 1950s, in which economics plays a role but which ranges much more widely, is

D. T. Rodgers, *Age of Fracture*, Cambridge, MA: Harvard University Press, 2011.

The turn to free markets, covering the roles of Hayek and Friedman, is analysed in:

A. Burgin, *The Great Persuasion: Reinventing Free Markets since the Great Depression*, Cambridge, MA: Harvard University Press, 2012.

For a coverage of the spread of economic ideas in the US government, see

E. Popp Berman, *Thinking like an Economist: How Efficiency Replaced Equality in US Public Policy*, Princeton, NJ: Princeton University Press, 2022.

For an account of the Nobel Prize in Economics see

A. Offer and G. Söderberg, *The Nobel Factor: The Prize in Economics, Social Democracy, and the Market Turn*, Princeton, NJ: Princeton University Press, 2016.

The phenomenon of heterodoxy is discussed in a symposium in the *Journal of the History of Economic Thought* 22(2), June 2000, and in

M. Desai, 'The underworld of economics: heresy and heterodoxy in the history of economic thought', in G. K. Shaw (ed.), *Economics, Culture and Education: Essays in Honour of Mark Blaug*, Cheltenham: Edward Elgar, 1991.

The origins of modern Austrian economics are chronicled in

K. Vaughn, *Austrian Economics in America: The Migration of a Tradition*, Cambridge: Cambridge University Press, 1994.

A book that looks at contemporary economics, covering both heterodox economics and examples of applied work in a style aimed at non-economist readers is

R. E. Backhouse, *The Puzzle of Modern Economics*, Cambridge: Cambridge University Press, 2010.

Essays on applied economics – interpreted as referring both to applied fields and to the application of techniques – are brought together in

R. E. Backhouse and J. Biddle (eds.), *Toward a History of Applied Economics*, Durham, NC: Duke University Press, 2000. (Annual supplement to *History of Political Economy*);

R. E. Backhouse and B. Cherrier, *The Age of the Applied Economist*, Durham, NC: Duke University Press, 2017. (Annual supplement to *History of Political Economy*).

For an account of the role of information technology in recent developments, see two of the essays in this book:

R. E. Backhouse and B. Cherrier, '"It's computers, stupid!": the spread of computers' and 'The changing roles of theoretical and applied economics'.

Two collections of essays cover the relations between economics and other social sciences:

R. E. Backhouse and P. Fontaine (eds.), *The History of the Social Sciences since 1945*, Cambridge: Cambridge University Press, 2010;
R. E. Backhouse and P. Fontaine (eds.), *The Unsocial Social Science: Economics and Neighboring Disciplines since 1945*, Durham, NC: Duke University Press, 2010. (Annual supplement to *History of Political Economy*).

Soviet and Russian studies, a field that involved economists alongside other specialists, became important during the Cold War; its story is told in

D. C. Engerman, *Know Your Enemy: The Rise and Fall of America's Soviet Experts*, Oxford: Oxford University Press, 2009.

During the past two decades there have been many volumes of autobiographical essays published which give a picture of the burgeoning variety of approaches to economics, including

R. E. Backhouse and R. Middleton (eds.), *Exemplary Economists*: Vol. 1, *North America*; Vol. 2, *Europe, Asia and Australasia*, Cheltenham: Edward Elgar, 1999;
G. M. Meier and D. Seers (eds.), *Pioneers in Development*, and G. M. Meier (ed.), *Pioneers in Development*, Second Series, Oxford: Oxford University Press, 1984, 1987.

There are two excellent biographies of Hirschman, the former documenting his life, the latter explaining his ideas:

J. Adelman, *Worldly Philosopher: The Odyssey of Albert O. Hirschman*, Princeton, NJ: Princeton University Press, 2013;

M. Alacevich, *Albert O. Hirschman: An Intellectual Biography*, New York: Columbia University Press, 2023.

The international dimension of economic ideas is explored in

A. W. Coats (ed.), *The Development of Economics in Western Europe since 1945*, London: Routledge, 2000;

A. W. Coats (ed.), *The Post-1945 Internationalization of Economics*, Durham, NC: Duke University Press, 1996.

A useful and very readable reference that was published too late to be taken into account in this book is:

J. Burns *Milton Friedman: The Last Conservative*, New York, Farrar, Straus and Giroux, 2023.

Notes

PROLOGUE

1. L. C. Robbins, *An Essay on the Nature and Significance of Economic Science* (1932), 2nd edn, London: Macmillan, 1935, p. 16.
2. A. Marshall, *Principles of Economics* (1890), 8th edn, London: Macmillan, 1920, p. 1.
3. Paul A. Samuelson 'Out of the closet: a program for the Whig history of economic science', *History of Economics Society Bulletin* 9(1), 1987, pp. 51–60.

CHAPTER 1

1. Hesiod, *Theogony and Works and Days*, trans. M. L. West, Oxford: Oxford University Press, 1988, p. 39.
2. Ibid., p. 38.
3. B. F. Gordon, *Economic Analysis before Adam Smith: Hesiod to Lessius*, London: Macmillan, 1973, p. 11.
4. W. I. Matson, *A New History of Philosophy*, Vol. 1, London: Harcourt Brace Jovanovich, 1987, p. 67.
5. This term is taken from S. T. Lowry, *The Archaeology of Economic Ideas: The Classical Greek Tradition*, Durham, NC: Duke University Press, 1987.
6. Aristotle, *Nichomachean Ethics*, trans. David Ross, Oxford: Oxford University Press, 1980, p. 110.

CHAPTER 2

1. Genesis 1:28, 2:15.
2. Isaiah 2:6–8.

3. Amos 8:4–6.
4. Exodus 22:25–6.
5. Ecclesiastes 11:1–2.
6. J. J. Spengler, 'Economic thought of Islam: Ibn Khaldun', *Comparative Studies in Society and History* 6, April 1964, p. 290.
7. Quoted in O. Langholm, *Economics in the Medieval Schools*, Leiden: E. J. Brill, 1992, pp. 54–5.
8. *Summa Aurea,* quoted in Langholm, *Economics in the Medieval Schools*, p. 71.
9. Langholm, *Economics in the Medieval Schools*, p. 71.
10. Quoted in Langholm, *Economics in the Medieval Schools*, p. 187.
11. Luke 6:35.
12. Quoted in O. Langholm, *The Legacy of Scholasticism in Economic Thought: Antecedents of Choice and Power,* Cambridge: Cambridge University Press, 1998, p. 59.
13. Quoted in A. E. Monroe, *Early Economic Thought: Selections from Economic Literature Prior to Adam Smith*, Cambridge, MA: Harvard University Press, 1965, p. 101.

CHAPTER 3

1. Quoted in M. Grice Hutchison, *The School of Salamanca: Readings in Spanish Monetary Theory, 1544–1605*, Oxford: Clarendon Press, 1952, p. 94.
2. Ibid., p. 95.
3. It has also been attributed to John Hales (*d.*1571), a member of Parliament. For a detailed discussion, see D. Palliser, *The Age of Elizabeth: England under the Later Tudors 1547–1603*, London: Longman, 1983, Appendix 2.
4. M. Dewar (ed.), *A Discourse of the Common Weal of This Realm of England*, Charlottesville: University Press of Virginia, 1959, p. 59.
5. Ibid., p. 54.

CHAPTER 4

1. C. Suprinyak 'Trade, money and the grievances of the Commonwealth: economic debates in England during the commercial crisis of the early 1620s', *History of Economic Ideas* 24(1), 2016, p. 45.

2. T. Mun, *England's Treasure by Forraign Trade* (1664), quoted in A. E. Monroe, *Early Economic Thought: Selections from Economic Literature Prior to Adam Smith*, Cambridge, MA: Harvard University Press, 1965, p. 180.

3. Quoted in A. O. Hirschman, *The Passions and the Interests: Arguments for Capitalism before its Triumph*, Princeton, NJ: Princeton University Press, 1977, p. 39.

4. Quoted in Hirschman, *The Passions and the Interests*, pp. 25-6.

5. W. Petty, *The Economic Writings of Sir William Petty*, Vol. I, ed. C. H. Hull, Cambridge: Cambridge University Press, 1899, p. 244.

6. Ibid., pp. 244-5.

7. Ibid., p. 304.

8. W. Letwin, *The Origins of Scientific Economics: English Economic Thought, 1660–1776*, London: Methuen, 1963, p. 3.

9. J. Child, *Brief Observations Concerning Trade and Interest of Money* (1668), at https://socialsciences.mcmaster.ca/econ/ugcm/3ll3/child/trade.txt, accessed 14 July 2023.

10. J. Locke, *Locke on Money*, Vol. I, ed. P. H. Kelly, Oxford: Clarendon Press, 1991, p. 216.

11. Ibid., pp. 235-6.

12. J. R. McCulloch (ed.), *Early English Tracts on Commerce*, London: Political Economy Club, 1856; reprinted Cambridge: Economic History Society, 1952, p. 510.

13. Ibid., p. 516.

14. Ibid., p. 525.

15. Ibid., pp. 529-30.

16. Ibid., p. 528.

17. Ibid., pp. 513-14.

CHAPTER 5

1. Istvan Hont, 'The early Enlightenment debate on commerce and luxury', in M. Goldie and R. Wokler (eds.), *The Cambridge History of Eighteenth-century Political Thought*, Cambridge: Cambridge University Press, 2008, p. 385, on which much of this section draws.

2. Quoted in T. W. Hutchison, *Before Adam Smith: The Emergence of Political Economy, 1662–1776*, Oxford: Basil Blackwell, 1988, p. 111.

3. R. Cantillon, *Essai sur la nature du commerce en générale* (1755), trans. and ed. H. Higgs, London: Macmillan, 1931, p. 3.

4. Ibid., p. 59.
5. Ibid., pp. 61–3.
6. Ibid., p. 65.
7. Ibid., p. 161.
8. Ibid, p. 185.
9. Ibid, p. 189.
10. Quoted in P. D. Groenewegen, *The Economics of A. R. J. Turgot*, The Hague: Martinus Nijhoff, 1977, p. 26.
11. Ibid., p. 29.
12. Ibid., p. 84.
13. Ibid., p. 141.

CHAPTER 6

1. Quoted in A. S. Skinner, *A System of Social Science: Papers Relating to Adam Smith*, Oxford: Clarendon Press, 1979, p. 1.
2. Ibid., p. 5.
3. A. Ferguson, *Principles of Moral and Political Science*, Vol. I, Edinburgh, 1792, p. 47.
4. D. Hume, *Writings on Economics*, ed. E. Rotwein, Edinburgh: Nelson, 1955, p. 5.
5. Ibid., p. 11.
6. Ibid., pp. 11–12.
7. Ibid., p. 33.
8. Ibid., p. 37.
9. Hobbes, *Leviathan*, quoted in I. Hont, *Jealousy of Trade*, Cambridge, MA: Harvard University Press, 2005, p. 2.
10. Hume, 'Of civil liberty', quoted in Hont, *Jealousy of Trade*, p. 8.
11. J. Steuart, *An Inquiry into the Principles of Political Economy* (1767), ed. A. S. Skinner, Edinburgh: Oliver and Boyd, 1966, p. 153.
12. Ibid., p. 5.
13. Ibid., p. 12.
14. Ibid., pp. 40, 41.
15. Ibid., p. 195.
16. Ibid., p. 198.
17. Ibid., p. 339.
18. Ibid., p. 345.
19. Ibid., pp. 142–3.
20. A. Smith, *The Theory of Moral Sentiments (1759–90)*, ed. D. D. Raphael and A. L. MacFie, Oxford: Oxford University Press, 1976, p. 3.

21. Ibid., p. 86.
22. Ibid.
23. A. Smith, *An Inquiry into the Nature and Causes of the Wealth of Nations* (1776), ed. R. H. Campbell, A. S. Skinner and W. B. Todd, Oxford: Oxford University Press, 1976, p. 25.
24. Ibid., p. 75.
25. Smith, *Theory of Moral Sentiments*, pp. 184-5.
26. Smith, *Wealth of Nations*, p. 456.
27. Ibid., p. 330.
28. Ibid., p. 337.
29. Ibid., pp. 337-8.
30. This is the title of *Wealth of Nations*, Book II, Chapter I.
31. *Wealth of Nations*, I, p. 113.
32. Smith, *Theory of Moral Sentiments*, p. 234.
33. Ibid., pp. 163-4.
34. Ibid., p. 723.
35. *Wealth of Nations*, II, pp. 674.

CHAPTER 7

1. T. R. Malthus, *An Essay on the Principle of Population* (1798), ed. A. Flew, Harmondsworth: Penguin Books, 1970, p. 100.
2. G. Garnier 'View of the doctrine of Smith compared with that of the French economists; with a method of facilitating the study of his works', in A. Smith *An Inquiry into the Nature and Causes of the Wealth of Nations*, Vol.1, Edinburgh: 1811, p. xxi.
3. Ibid., p. xxiv.
4. J. Marcet, *Conversations on Political Economy*, 5th edn., 1824, p. iv.
5. D. P. O'Brien, *The Classical Economists*, Oxford: Oxford University Press, 1973, p. 45.
6. S. Bailey, *A Critical Dissertation on the Nature, Measure and Causes of Value* (1825), London: LSE Reprints, 1925, p. 1.

CHAPTER 8

1. K. Marx, *Capital*, Vol. 1, trans. S. Moore and E. Aveling, Moscow: Progress Publishers, Chapter 1, fn. 33. Reproduced at https://www.marxists.org/archive/marx/works/1867-c1/index.htm.

2. J. S. Mill, *Principles of Political Economy and Some of their Applications to Social Philosophy* (1848), London: Longmans, 1873, 'Preliminary remarks', p. 13.

3. Ibid., pp. 13–14.

4. Ibid., Book V, Chapter 9, Section 16, p. 590.

5. K. Marx, *Capital*, Vol. 1 (1867), Afterword to the second German edition, trans. S. Moore and E. Aveling, Delhi: Macmillan of India, p. 16. Online at: https://archive.org/details/in.ernet.dli.2015.124620, accessed 9 June 2022.

6. K. Marx, *Capital*, Vol. 2 (1885), London: Lawrence and Wishart, 1974, p. 189.

7. Ibid., Vol. 1, p. 763.

8. Ibid.

9. Ibid.

10. The diagram is taken from Fig. 6 in A. A. Cournot, *Recherches sur les principes mathématiques de la théorie des richesses*, Paris: Hachette, 1838 (unnumbered fold-out page), at archive.org.

CHAPTER 9

1. W. S. Jevons, *The Theory of Political Economy* (1871), ed. R. D. C. Black, Harmondsworth: Penguin Books, 1970, p. 187.

2. C. Menger, *Principles of Economics* (1871), trans. J. Dingwall and B. F. Hoselitz, Grove City, PA: Libertarian Press, 1994, p. 52.

3. Ibid., p. 164.

4. Ibid., p. 217.

5. Ibid., p. 97.

6. A. Marshall, *Principles of Economics* (1890), 8th edn, London: Macmillan, 1920, p. 315.

CHAPTER 10

1. J. B. Clark, *The Philosophy of Wealth* (1886), 2nd edn, Boston, 1987, p. 151.

2. J. B. Clark, *The Distribution of Wealth* (1899), 2nd edn, New York: Macmillan, 1902, pp. 401–2.

3. I. Fisher, *The Purchasing Power of Money*, New York: Macmillan, 1911, p. 23.

4. Ibid., p. 119.

5. T. B. Veblen, *Theory of Business Enterprise*, New York: Scribners, 1904, p. 67.

6. Ibid., p. 66.

7. T. B. Veblen, *The Engineers and the Price System* (1921), New York: A. M. Kelley, 1965, pp. 81–2.

8. T. B. Veblen, 'The preconceptions of economic science II', *Quarterly Journal of Economics* 13, 1899, p. 422.

9. W. C. Mitchell, 'Quantitative analysis in economic theory', *American Economic Review* 15, 1925, p. 5.

10. F. H. Knight, *Risk, Uncertainty, and Profit* (1921), London: LSE Reprints, 1933, p. vii.

11. Ibid., pp. 52–3.

12. F. H. Knight, *The Ethics of Competition* (1935), New Brunswick, NJ: Transaction Publishers, 1997, p. 87.

13. E. H. Chamberlin, *The Theory of Monopolistic Competition*, Cambridge, MA: Harvard University Press, 1933, p. 10.

CHAPTER 11

1. A. Marshall and M. P. Marshall, *The Economics of Industry* (1879), Bristol: Thoemmes Press, 1994, pp. 154–5.

2. J. M. Keynes, *The Collected Writings of John Maynard Keynes*: Vol. 4, *A Tract on Monetary Reform* (1923), London: Macmillan, 1971, p. 65.

3. Ibid., p. 138.

4. D. Laidler, *Fabricating the Keynesian Revolution: Studies of the Inter-War Literature on Money, the Cycle and Unemployment*, Cambridge: Cambridge University Press, 1999, p. 243.

5. Quoted in Laidler, *Fabricating the Keynesian Revolution*, p. 215.

6. J. M. Keynes, *The Collected Writings of John Maynard Keynes*: Vol. 7, *The General Theory of Employment, Interest and Money* (1936), London: Macmillan, 1971, pp. 149–50.

7. Ibid., p. 152.

8. Ibid., p. 3.

9. This way of putting it is due to Laidler, *Fabricating the Keynesian Revolution*.

CHAPTER 12

1. R. Stone, 'The accounts of society', *American Economic Review* 87(6), 1997, p. 20.
2. Quoted in R. Frisch, 'Editorial', *Econometrica* 1, 1933, p. 1.
3. T. Haavelmo, 'The probability approach in econometrics', *Econometrica* 12 (supplement), 1944, p. iii. (Italics have been removed from the original.)
4. T. Haavelmo, 'The statistical implications of a system of simultaneous equations', *Econometrica* 11, 1943, p. 1.
5. M. S. Morgan, *A History of Econometric Ideas*, Cambridge: Cambridge University Press, 1990, p. 264.

CHAPTER 13

1. F. Taussig, 'Alfred Marshall', *Quarterly Journal of Economics* 39(1), 1924, p. 1.
2. P. A. Samuelson, *Foundations of Economic Analysis*, Cambridge, MA: Harvard University Press, 1947, pp. 3, 4. ('Hypothesis' has been changed to plural.)
3. Ibid., p. 6.
4. P. A. Samuelson, 'How "Foundations" came to be,' *Journal of Economic Literature* 36(3), 1998, p. 1382.
5. G. Debreu, *Theory of Value: An Axiomatic Theory of Economic Equilibrium*, New Haven, CN: Yale University Press, 1959, p. x.
6. J. von Neumann and O. Morgenstern, *The Theory of Games and Economic Behaviour*, Princeton, NJ: Princeton University Press, 1944, p. 38.

CHAPTER 14

1. W. S. Jevons, *The State in Relation to Labour* (1882), 3rd edn, London, 1894, p. 14.
2. H. Sidgwick, *The Principles of Political Economy* (1883), 2nd edn, London: Macmillan, 1887, p. 71.
3. A. Marshall, *Principles of Economics* (1890), 8th edn, London: Macmillan, 1920, p. 108.
4. A. C. Pigou, *The Economics of Welfare*, London: Macmillan, 1920, p. 10.
5. Ibid., p. 11.

6. A. C. Pigou, *Wealth and Welfare*, London: Macmillan, 1912, p. 248.

7. A. C. Pigou, *Economics in Practice: Six Lectures on Current Issues*, London: Macmillan, 1935, p. 124.

8. Pigou, *Wealth and Welfare*, p. 3.

9. R. H. Tawney *R. H. Tawney's Commonplace Book*, eds. J. M. Winter and D. M. Joslin, Cambridge: Cambridge University Press, 2006, p. 30.

10. V. Pareto, *Manual of Political Economy* (1906), trans. A. S. Schwier, New York: A. M. Kelley, 1971, p. 155.

11. Ibid., p. 268.

12. Ibid., p. 261.

13. Neurath speech, 25 January 1919, quoted in K. Tribe, *Strategies of Economic Order*, Cambridge: Cambridge University Press, 1995, p. 155 (italics in original).

14. M. Weber, *Economy and Society*, trans. K. Tribe, Cambridge, MA: Harvard University Press, 2019, p. 172.

15. Ibid.

16. F. A. Hayek, *The Road to Serfdom*, London: Routledge, 1944, p. 3.

17. Ibid., p. 79.

18. E. F. M. Durbin, *Problems of Economic Planning*, London: Routledge and Kegan Paul, 1949, p. 96.

19. Ibid., p. 98.

20. J. E. Meade, *Planning and the Price Mechanism*, London: George Allen and Unwin, 1948, p. 11.

21. A. P. Lerner, *The Economics of Control*, New York: Macmillan, 1944, p. viii.

22. A. Bergson, 'Socialist economics', in H. S. Ellis (ed.), *A Survey of Contemporary Economics*, Vol. 1, Homewood, IL: Richard D. Irwin, 1948, p. 412.

23. William Loucks, quoted in M. L. Balisciano, 'Hope for America: American notions of economic planning between pluralism and neoclassicism', *History of Political Economy* 30 (supplement), 1998, p. 153.

24. Ibid., 158.

CHAPTER 15

1. Kantorovich's memory of a remark by Boris Yastremskii, quoted in I. Boldyrev and T. Düppe, 'Programming the USSR: Leonid V. Kantorovich in context', *British Journal for the History of Science* 53(2), 2020, p. 263.

2. I. Boldyrev and O. Kirtchik 'The cultures of mathematical economics in the postwar Soviet Union: more than a method, less than a discipline', *Studies in History and Philosophy of Science* 63, 2017.

3. R. Huret, 'Poverty in Cold War America', *History of Political Economy* 42 (supplement), 2010, p. 99.

4. A. O. Hirschman, *Essays in Trespassing: Economics to Politics and Beyond*, Cambridge: Cambridge University Press, 1981; *Crossing Boundaries: Selected Writings*, New York: Zone Books, 1998.

CHAPTER 16

1. Samuelson, *Foundations*, p. 221.

2. J. de V. Graaf, *Theoretical Welfare Economics*, Cambridge: Cambridge University Press, 1957, p. 169.

3. I. Little, *A Critique of Welfare Economics*, Oxford: Clarendon Press, 1957, p. 279.

4. A. K. Sen, *Inequality Reexamined*, Oxford: Oxford University Press, 1995, pp. 109–10.

5. M. Gilardone, 'The influence of Sen's applied economics on his non-welfarist approach to justice', in R. E. Backhouse, A. Baujard and T. Nishizawa (eds.), *Welfare Theory, Public Action and Ethical Values*, Cambridge: Cambridge University Press, 2021, p. 299, quoting Sen.

6. A. Liptak, 'An exit interview with Richard Posner, judicial provocateur', *New York Times*, 11 Sept. 2017.

7. J. Niehans, 'Transactions costs', in J. Eatwell, M. Milgate and P. Newman (eds.), *The New Palgrave: A Dictionary of Economics*, London: Macmillan, 1987, Vol. 4, p. 676.

CHAPTER 17

1. K. Boulding, 'Economic analysis and agricultural policy', *Canadian Journal of Economics and Political Science* 13(3), 1947, p. 437.

2. P. A. Samuelson, *Economics: An Introductory Analysis*, New York: McGraw Hill, 1948, p. 253.

3. P. A. Samuelson and R. M. Solow, 'Analytical aspects of anti-inflation policy', *American Economic Review* 50(2), 1960, p. 192.

4. Ibid., p. 189.

5. Ibid., p. 181.

6. M. Friedman 'The role of monetary policy', *American Economic Review* 58(1), 1968, p. 8.

CHAPTER 18

1. J. A. Schumpeter, *A History of Economic Analysis*, London: Allen and Unwin, 1954, p. 23.
2. J. Buchanan, *Wall Street Journal*, 25 April 1996, quoted in https://youtu.be/wD48p6m8U-8.
3. https://www.nobelprize.org/prizes/economic-sciences/2015/deaton/facts/; accessed 8 June 2022.
4. P. A. Samuelson, *Economics*, New York: McGraw Hill, 1967, p. 6. Similar comments were made in the first twelve editions of the book.
5. Angus Deaton, quoted in R. E. Backhouse and B. Cherrier, 'The age of the applied economist: the transformation of economics since the 1970s', *History of Political Economy* 49 (supplement), 2017, p. 1.
6. J. Williamson 'The strange history of the Washington Consensus', *Journal of Post Keynesian Economics* 27(2), 2004, p. 196.
7. W. Easterly, 'The lost decades: developing countries' stagnation in spite of policy reform 1980–1999', *Journal of Economic Growth* 6(2), 2001, p. 135.
8. P. Dasgupta, *The Economics of Biodiversity: The Dasgupta Review, Abridged Version*, London: HM Treasury, 2021, p. 3; online at https://assets.publishing.service.gov.uk/government/uploads/system/uploads/attachment_data/file/957292/Dasgupta_Review_-_Abridged_Version.pdf.
9. J. Forrester, *World Dynamics*, 2nd edn, Cambridge, MA: Wright-Allen Press, p. vii.
10. D. H. Meadows, D. L. Meadows, J. Randers and W. W. Behrens, *The Limits to Growth*, New York: Universe Books, 1972, p. 73.
11. Preface by F. Bergsten in W. R. Cline, *The Economics of Global Warming*, Washington, DC: Institute of International Economics, 1992, p. ix.
12. D. Nordhaus, 'To slow or not to slow: the economics of the greenhouse effect,' *Economic Journal* 101(407), 1991.
13. Ibid., p. 936.
14. Brian Hoskins, quoted in N. Stern, 'The structure of economic modeling of the potential impacts of climate change: grafting gross underestimation of risk on to narrow science models', *Journal of Economic Literature* 51(3), 2013, p. 842.

15. M. Weitzman, 'Insurance for a warming planet', *Nature* 467, 4 Oct. 2010, p. 785.
16. https://www.nobelprize.org/uploads/2018/10/nordhaus-lecture.pdf, p. 452.
17. N. Stern, *The Economics of Climate Change*, Cambridge: Cambridge University Press, 2007.
18. N. Stern, 'A time for action on climate change and a time for change in economics', *Economic Journal* 132(644), 2022, p. 1262.
19. The full report is at https://www.gov.uk/government/publications/final-report-the-economics-of-biodiversity-the-dasgupta-review.

EPILOGUE

1. J. A. Schumpeter, *Economic Doctrine and Method* (1912), trans. R. Aris, London: Allen and Unwin, 1934, p. 132.
2. https://www.minneapolisfed.org/article/2006/interview-with-david-card.
3. Ibid.

Index

Abelard, Peter, 43
acid rain, 366
Aftalion, Albert, 204
Akerlof, George, 362–3
Albert the Great, 45–6
Alembert, Jean le Rond d', 107
Alexander the Great, 26–7
Allais, Maurice, 395
Allen, Roy, 286
American Economic Association, 209, 223, 369
American Institutionalism, 223–5, 342–3
American treasure (16th century), 60–2
Anaximander, 15
Anderson, Benjamin, 251
Anglo-Dutch naval wars, 69
Aquinas, Thomas, 45–7, 49
Aristotle, 22–7, 30, 38–9, 43, 45, 46
Arrow, Kenneth: and general equilibrium, 290–2, 351; health economics, 362; *Social Choice and Individual Values* (1951), 349
Arrow-Debreu model, 291–2, 349–50
Ashley, William James, 199

Athens, economy of, 16–18
Atkinson, Anthony, 351, 402–3
auctions, for resources, 366–7
Augustine of Hippo, 36
Austrian economics, 182, 198, 241–2, 251, 344
Averroes (Ibn Rushd), 38–9, 43

Bacon, Francis, 67–8, 74, 77
Bailey, Samuel, 156
balance of trade, 64, 71–3, 87, 90, 104
Banerjee, Abhijit, 393
Bank of England: foundation of, 96; and paper currency, 105, 144, 160–2
banking system, 105–6, 160–2
Barbon, Nicholas, 90
Barone, Enrico, 309, 312, 318
Bator, Francis, 355
Becker, Gary, 339, 340, 345
behavioural economics, 396–7
Benanke, Ben, 376, 406
Bentham, Jeremy, 148–9, 189
Bergson, Abram, 316, 317, 348
Berle, Adolf, 230
Beveridge, William, 347
biodiversity, 412

Black, Duncan, 349
Black, Fischer, 404
Black Death, 43, 49
Black-Scholes theorem, 404
Bland-Allison Silver Act (1878), 213
Bodin, Jean, 62, 63
Böhm-Bawerk, Eugen von, 177, 204, 235
Boisguilbert, Pierre de, 93, 97–9
Boulding, Kenneth, 325, 369, 408
Bourbaki group, 291
Bowley, A. L., 268
Boyle, Robert, 77
Brady, Dorothy, 338
Brahe, Tycho, 55
Bretton Woods system, 385, 399
Brexit, 402
Bridgman, Percy, 287
British Association for the Advancement of Science, 157
Brookings model, 372
Brunner, Karl, 386
Buchanan, James, 339, 340, 393

Calabresi, Guido, 356–7
Calvin, Jean, 57
Cambridge welfare economics, 303–4, 315
Cameralism, 60
Cantillon, Richard, 101–6
Card, David, 393, 416–17
Carlyle, Thomas, 147
Carmichael, Gershom, 121
Carson, Rachel, Silent Spring (1962), 408
Case, Anne, 394
Cassel, Gustav, 285, 318
Catchings, Waddil, 251–2

Chamberlin, Edward, 225, 228–9, 282, 395
Champernowne, David, 259, 261
Charlemagne, 42, 57
Charles I of England, 70, 73
Charles Martel, 37, 41–2
Chicago Law School, 357
Child, Sir Josiah, 82–3
China, 400
Christianity, influence of, 31–2, 35–6
city states, decline of, 59
Clark, Colin, National Income and Outlay (1937), 270–1, 329
Clark, John Bates, 210–12, 214, 224
Clark, John Maurice, 224, 225, 227–8
classical economics, 12, 257–9
climate change, and economic growth, 407–12
Cline, William, The Economics of Global Warming (1992), 410
Coase, Ronald, 355–8, 360, 361
'Coase theorem', 357
Colbert, Jean-Baptiste, 93–4
Cold War, 334–5, 392
Coleridge, Samuel Taylor, 147
Combination Laws, repeal of (1824), 159
common-property resources, 355, 359–60
Commons, John R., 221–3, 360
computers, and modelling, 371–2
Condillac, Etienne Bonnot de, 107, 193
Condorcet, Marquis de, 144, 145, 178, 187
Constantinople, fall of (1453), 53
consumer demand, 88, 241, 256, 275, 286, 288–9, 299

Copernicus, 54–5
Corn Laws, 158
corvée, 95
Cournot, Antoine Augustin, 178–9, 187, 265
Cowles, Alfred, 273–4
Cowles Commission, 233, 274, 278–80, 290, 295, 375, 397
Cromwell, Oliver, 73, 77
Crusades, 42
'cumulative process', 235–8
Cunningham, William, 199, 203
currency, debasement of, 49–50, 63, 69
Currie, Laughlin, 252, 253, 270, 324
Cynicism, 28

Dalton, Hugh, 402
Daly, Herman, 408
Dantzig, George, 322–3
Darwin, Charles, *Origin of Species* (1859), 186
Dasgupta, Partha, 412
Davenant, Charles, 81
Deaton, Angus, 394, 397
debasement of currency, 49–50, 63, 69
Debreu, Gerard, 291–2, 349
  see also Arrow-Debreu model
demand analysis, 275
deregulation, 367
derivatives trading, 404–5
Descartes, René, 55, 67–8
development economics, 329–32, 335–7
Diamond, Douglas, 376
Dickinson, H. D., 312
Diderot, Denis, *Encyclopédie*, 106–7, 108

Diogenes of Sinope, 28
Director, Aaron, 357
Discourse of the Common Weal (16th century) *see* Smith, Sir Thomas
division of labour, 133–4
Domestic Credit Expansion (DCE), 386
Douglas, Paul, 253
Downs, Anthony, 339
DSGE (Dynamic Stochastic General Equilibrium), 384
Du Pont de Nemours, 107
Duflo, Esther, 393
Dupuit, Jules, 180–1
Durbin, Evan, 314
Dybvig, Philip, 376

East India Company, 87
Econometric Society, 273–4, 280, 297
econometrics, 273–6, 284, 297–8
economic growth, and the environment, 407–12
economics: 16th century, 64–5; 17th century England, 90–1; 18th century, 141–2; 19th century, 163, 183–4; 19th century USA, 207–9; 20th century USA, 232–3; Americanization of, 346; applied fields, 391–2; definitions, 4–6, 283–4; mathematization of, 265–7, 296–9; 'new economics', 369–73; origins of word, 18; professionalization of, 185–7
  see also political economy
economists: 19th century, 157–9; expanding role of, 324–7; role during second world war, 321–4, 327–9

Edgeworth, Francis Ysidro, 205, 266
Edinburgh Review, 157
efficient-market theory, 396–7
Eichner, Alfred, 343
Eisenhower, Dwight D., 328, 347
Ely, R. T., 221
enclosures, 63–4
Engels, Friedrich, 170–1, 176
Enlightenment: French, 106–7;
    Scottish, 119–21
environmental issues, 407–12
eugenics, 186–7
European Union, 365, 402
exchange value, 116
experimental economics, 366,
    394–8

Factory Acts, 159
feminist economics, 344
Fénélon, François, 95–7, 150
Ferguson, Adam, 120
Fetter, Frank Albert, 214
feudalism, 41–3
First World War: migration to USA,
    230; post-war economics, 238–9
Fisher, Irving: and bank reserves,
    253–4; Econometric Society,
    273–4; and eugenics, 187;
    quantity theory of money,
    215–16, 250, 274; use of
    mathematics, 213–15, 224, 266;
    Mathematical Investigations,
    213–15; *The Purchasing Power
    of Money*, 215–17
FMP model, 372
Forrester, Jay, *World Dynamics*,
    408
Foster, William Truffant, 251–2
Foxwell, H. S., 203

France: 18th century economic
    thinking, 93–5; civil engineering
    projects and theories of value,
    178–81; Ecole des Ponts et
    Chaussées, 178–9, 181, 186,
    188; economic reform, 117;
    Enlightenment, 106–7;
    physiocracy, 107–12
free trade, 84–6, 145, 158, 163,
    208–9
free-market policies, 348
French Revolution, 144–5
Friedman, Milton: endorses
    Marshall's *Principles*, 300; and
    free market economics, 345, 364;
    and inflation, 380, 385–7;
    monetary economics, 254,
    261–2, 388–9; quantity theory of
    money, 373–5; at the University
    of Chicago, 225; *A Monetary
    History of the United States,
    1867–1960* (1963), 373–5
Friedman, Rose, 364
Frisch, Ragnar, 261, 273, 274,
    276–7, 300

Galbraith, John Kenneth, *The
    Affluent Society* (1958), 342–3
Galiani, Ferdinando, 116–17
Galileo, 55
Galton, Francis, 186, 266
game theory, 293–6, 323–4, 366,
    395
Garnier, Germain, 147–8
General Agreement on Tariffs and
    Trade (GATT), 326, 398
general-equilibrium theory, 284–92,
    299
George, Henry, 205

Germany: Cameralism, 185; debates over socialism in, 309-11; early marginalism in, 188; economics taught in universities, 185; emigration from, 230, 297, 346; historical movement in economics, 193-8; hyperinflation, 239-41; influence on American economics, 209-10; interwar problems, 238-41; national income estimates, 268; supply and demand theories in, 129-30, 181

Gibbs, Willard, 213, 287
Gilbert, Martin, 272, 329
global financial crisis (2008), 404-7
globalization, 398-404
Godwin, William, 145
gold standard, 89, 236-7, 247-8
Goodhart, Charles, 387
Gournay, Vincent de, 112-13
government, role of, 347-8, 358-60
Graaf, Jan, 350
Graunt, John, 81
Great Moderation, 389
Gresham's Law, 89
gross national product (GNP), 270
Grossman, Sanford, 363
Grotius, Hugo, 116

Haavelmo, Trygve, 279
Haberler, Gottfried, 251, 326
Hadley, Arthur T., 214
Hansen, Alvin, 251, 262-3, 370, 406; A Guide to Keynes, 371
Haq, Mahbub ul, 353
Hardin, Garrett, 355, 359
Harrington, Michael, 339

Harvard University, 209
Hawtrey, Ralph, 244-5, 252
Hayek, Freidrich: Austrian economics, 241-2; critique of market-socialism, 312-14, 363; disagreement with Keynes, 249; and laissez-faire economics, 204, 319, 344; and the Mont Pelerin Society, 347-8; and political philosophy, 261; The Road to Serfdom, 313-14, 347, 357
health economics, 362
Heckscher, Eli, 318
hedge funds, 404-5
Hegel, Georg Wilhelm Friedrich, 170
Heller, Walter, 328
Hermann, Friedrich, 181, 200
Hesiod, Works and Days, 14-15
heterodox economics, 341-5
Hicks, John, 259, 261, 272, 286-9, 315
Hilbert, David, 290
Hilferding, Rudolf, 177
Hirschman, Albert, 331, 341
Hobbes, Thomas, 74-6, 77, 88, 91, 125
Hobson, J. A., 252, 307
Homer, Iliad and Odyssey, 13-14
Hooke, Robert, 77
Hotelling, Harold, 290, 407
human development index (HDI), 353-4
Humboldt University of Berlin, 185
Hume, David, 74, 119-20, 122-5
Hurwicz, Leonid, 363-4, 365
Hutcheson, Francis, 121-2

Ibn Khaldun, 39-41
Ibn Rushd, see Averroes

indifference curves, 286
industrial economics, 342
inequality, and globalization, 401–4
inflation, 377–80
information, availability and
    processing of, 361–3
information technology, effect on
    economics, 371–2, 392–3, 397–8
Institute of Economic Affairs, 348
interest rates: 17th century, 69,
    82–6; American, 371; Austrian
    school, 241–2; Calvin on, 57;
    and global financial crisis, 405–7;
    Keynes on, 249; Marshall on,
    244; monetary economics, 373,
    375–6; Stockholm School,
    242–3; 'Taylor rule', 388;
    Thomas Tooke on, 162
Intergovernmental Panel on Climate
    Change (IPCC), 409, 410
International Monetary Fund
    (IMF), 326, 386, 398, 399–400,
    402
intrinsic value, 102
Islam, and economic development,
    37–41
IS-LM model, 261, 369–70, 371
Italy, economic dominance
    (17th century), 69

Jacobs, Jane, 365
James I of England, 70, 73
James II of England, 73, 97
Jevons, William Stanley, 188–93,
    196–7, 200, 266, 302
Johnson, Harry, 386
Johnson, Lyndon, 332, 338
Jones, Richard, 198
journals, economics, 185, 209

Judaism, 33–4
jurisprudence, 28–9

Kahn, Richard, 254, 255
Kahneman, Daniel, 396
Kaldor, Nicholas, 315
Kantorovich, Leonid, 323, 333–4
Kautsky, Karl, 308
Kennedy, John F., 328, 384
Kepler, 55
Keynes, John Maynard: critique
    of Clark's static theory, 211;
    editor of Economic Journal,
    246; and Marshallian
    economics, 244, 246–7;
    monetary economics, 247–9;
    The Economic Consequences of
    the Peace, 247; General Theory
    of Employment, Interest and
    Money (1936), 254–60, 262–3,
    327, 369–70, 388, 406; How to
    Pay for the War (1940), 271,
    328; Treatise on Money,
    247–8
Keynesian economics, 257–63,
    327–32, 343, 369–71, 373,
    384–5, 388
Khrushchev, Nikita, 334
King, Gregory, 81
King, Willford I., The Wealth and
    Income of the People of the
    United States (1915), 268
Klein, Lawrence, 279–80, 370,
    371–2
Knies, Karl, 210, 221
Knight, Frank, 224, 225–7, 361
Koopmans, Tjalling, 322–3, 334,
    397
Koran, and economic thinking, 37

Kregel, Jan, 343
Kremer, Michael, 393
Krueger, Alan, 393
Krueger, Anne, 358–9
Krugman, Paul, 400
Kuhn, Thomas, 332–3
Kuznets, Simon, 232, 269, 271–2, 328–9
Kydland, Fynn, 383

La Follette, Robert, 269
labour theory of value, 133–5, 142, 153–4, 156, 171, 174, 176, 181, 196
laissez-faire economics, 98, 117, 138–41, 169, 304
Lampman, Robert, 338–9
Lancaster, Kelvin, 350
land, as source of wealth, 101–3
Lange, Oskar, 312, 315, 363
Latin America, 399–400
Laughlin, James Laurence, 225
Lavoisier, Antoine, 114
Law, John, 99–100
League of Nations, 272, 277, 326
Leontief, Wassily, 117, 230–1, 323
Lerner, Abba, 315, 316–17
Leslie, Thomas Edward Cliffe, 198–9
Lewis, Arthur, 331
Lindhal, Erik, 242
linear programming, 322–3, 333–4
Lipsey, Richard, 350, 378–9
Little, Ian, 336–7, 349, 351
Locke, John, 77, 83–4, 87, 89–90, 103, 106
Lombard, Peter, 45

London, population growth, 16th century, 59
London School of Economics (LSE), 203–4
Longfield, Mountifort, 157
Louis XIV of France, 93–5, 106
Lucas, Robert, 345, 381–3, 388
Luddites, 155
Lundberg, Erik, 242
Luther, Martin, 56–7

Machiavelli, Niccolò, 74, 76
macroeconomics: definition, 300; and Keynesian economics, 327–32; and policy, 369–73, 384–8; post-war, 260–3; and rational expectations, 381–4
Malthus, Thomas Robert, 145–7, 151–3, 158–9, 187
Malynes, Gerard de, 3, 71, 87
management science, 340
Mandeville, Bernard, 96–7
Mangoldt, Hans von, 181–2
Marcet, Jane, Conversations on Political Economy, 150
marginal utility, 156, 165, 188, 189, 193, 196, 203, 210
marginalism, 302–3
market failure, 354–60
markets, role of, 363–8
Marschak, Jacob, 278, 360
Marshall, Alfred: challenges to, 281; consumers' surplus, 304–5; definition of economics, 4; economic ideas, 199–203; money and the business cycle, 243–5; 'neoclassical' economics, 221; on state intervention, 302; support for free trade, 205; The

Economics of Industry, 243–4;
Industry and Trade (1919), 361;
Principles of Economics (1890),
166, 199, 202–3, 299–300
Marshall, Mary Paley, 244
Martineau, Harriet, *Illustrations
of Political Economy*, 150–1
Marx, Karl, 12, 147, 155, 165,
169–77, 176–7, 190
Marxist economics, 169–77, 342,
345
Maskin, Eric, 365
Mason, Edward, 364
Massachusetts Institute of
Technology (MIT), 345
mathematics, used in economics,
187–8, 212–17, 265–7, 288–90,
296–9, 333–4
McCarthy, Joseph, 338
McCulloch, John Ramsay, 156,
157, 158, 266
McKenzie, Lionel, 291
McNamara, Robert, 326–7, 364
Meade, James, 271–2, 314
Means, Gardiner, 230
Menger, Carl, 195–8, 344
Menger, Karl, 284–5, 294, 297
Mercado, Thomas de, 61–2
mercantilism, 11–12, 64, 80, 90,
105, 124, 138–41, 158
Merchant Adventurers, 70, 71
Mercier de la Rivière, Pierre-Paul le, 107
Merriam, Ida, 338
Merton, Robert, 405
microeconomics, 300, 336
Milanovic, Branko, 403
Milgrom, Paul, 365
military problems, and economics,
321–4

Mill, James, 149, 150, 151
Mill, John Stuart, 149–50, 166–9,
183
Minard, Joseph, 180
Mirabeau, Victor Riqueti, Marquis
de, 93, 107, 108
Mirrlees, James, 336–7
Mises, Ludwig von, 241–2,
310–12, 317, 344
Mishan, Ezra, *The Costs of
Economic Growth*, 407–8
Misselden, Edward, 71–2, 90
Mitchell, Wesley Clair, 224–5,
252–3, 261, 269, 274, 275
modelling, 267, 267–80, 371–3
Modigliani, Franco, 371
monasticism, 41–2
Monchretien, Antoyne, 126
monetarism, 373–7, 386–8
money: and balance of payments,
386; circulation, 97–100, 103–6,
108–12; David Hume on, 123–4;
development of monetary policy,
160–2; quantity theory, 213,
215–16, 247, 250, 373–5;
supply, 103–5
Mont Pelerin Society, 348, 400
Montesquieu, 106–7, 119–20
Moore, Henry Ludwell, 274–5
Morgenstern, Oskar, 293–5, 395
Mun, Thomas, 3, 71–3, 87, 90
Mushkin, Selma, 362
Myrdal, Gunnar, 242, 318, 325
Myserson, Roger, 366

Nader, Ralph, 365
NAIRU (Non-accelerating Inflation
Rate of Unemployment), 380
Nash, John, 295

Nathan, Robert, 269, 271–2, 328–9

National Bureau of Economic Research, 225, 233, 269, 274

national income accounting, 267–72, 328–9

Navarrus (Martin de Azpilcueta Navarro), 60–1

Navier, Claude-Louis Marie Henri, 179–80

neoclassical economics, 12, 223–5

Netherlands, commercial dominance (17th century), 69–70

Neumann, John von, 285, 289, 290, 293–5, 395

Neurath, Otto, 309–10

'new economics', 369–73

New World, European trade with, 59, 60–2

Newcomb, Simon, 212–13

Newmarch, William, 266

Newton, Isaac, 55, 77, 90, 106, 186

Nordhaus, William, 409–10

North, Dudley, 84–6, 87

North, Roger, 84, 86

'nudge' theory, 396

Nurkse, Ragnar, 330

Nussbaum, Martha, 352

Ohlin, Bertil, 242, 318

oil crisis (1970s), 332, 382, 385

Old Testament, and economic thinking, 33–4

Olson, Mancur, 339

Oresme, Nicole, *Treatise on the Origin of Money*, 50–2

Organization for Economic Cooperation and Development (OECD), 326, 330, 336, 337

Organization of Petroleum Exporting Countries (OPEC), 385

Orshansky, Mollie, 338

Ostrom, Elinor, 359

Overstone, Lord, 162

Owen, Robert, 150, 163

Paine, Thomas, 144–5

paper money, 98–100, 124, 160–2

paradigm shifts, 332–3

Pareto, Vilfredo, 203, 308–9; Pareto criterion, 315–16, 348, 349–50

Paris university, 43

Patinkin, Don, 371

Pearson, Karl, 266

Pepys, Samuel, 77

Periclean Age, 17

Persons, Warren, 274

Petrarch, 53–4

Petty, William, 77–81, 87

Phelps, Edmund, 379–80, 381, 384

Phillips, A. W., 377–8

Phillips curve, 377–80, 385

Philosophic Radicals, 149–50, 157–8

physiocracy, 107–12

Pierson, Nicholaas, 308

Pigou, A. C., 203, 205, 244, 245–6, 305–7, 355

Piketty, Thomas, 402–3

Plato, 16, 17–18, 20–1, 25, 30, 54

Polak, Jacques, 326, 386

political economy, 126, 157, 163, 165

Political Economy Club, 157

Poor Law, 59, 158–9

Posner, Richard, 357–8, 406

poverty, research into, 393–4
Prebisch, Raul, 326, 330–1
Prescott, Edward, 383
price-specie-flow mechanism, 105
printing, invention of, 56
privatization, 367
Protagoras (Greek sophist), 17
Proudhon, Pierre-Joseph, 190
public-choice theory, 339–40, 345
Pufendorf, Samuel, 76, 91, 116, 121
Pythagoras, 15

quantitative easing, 406
quantity theory of money, 213,
    215–16, 247, 250, 373
quantum mechanics, 290
Quarterly Journal of Economics, 209
Quarterly Review, 157
Quesnay, François, 107–12, 130,
    173, 265, 414

Ramsey, Frank, 246
RAND Corporation (Project
    RAND), 323–4
randomized control trials (RCTs),
    393–4
rational-choice theory, 340–1, 342,
    396
Rau, Karl Heinrich, 181, 200
Rawls, John, *A Theory of Justice*,
    351–2
Reagan, Ronald, 332
real-business-cycle theory, 383–4
recoinage crisis (1690s), 86–90
Reform Acts, 183
Reformation, Protestant, 56–8
Renaissance: 12th century, 43–9;
    15th century, 53–6
Resources for the Future, 407

Ricardo, David: bullionist view,
    161; influence on Stuart Mill and
    Marx, 165–6; and Malthus, 150;
    Philosophic Radicals, 149;
    Ricardian economics, 151–7,
    158; use of mathematics, 265
Robbins, Lionel: definition of
    economics, 4, 283–4, 300; and
    economic theory, 289; at the
    LSE, 204, 285; *The Nature and
    Significance of Economic Science*,
    283, 315
Robertson, Dennis, 244, 245
Robinson, Austin, 254
Robinson, Joan, 254, 261, 281–3,
    297, 299, 343, 393
Rogers, J. E. Thorold, 199
Roman Empire, 27–9, 33
Roos, Charles, 273, 274
Roosevelt, Franklin D., 327
Roscher, Wilhelm, 181, 193–4
Rosenstein-Rodan, Paul, 329, 330
Roth, Alvin, 366
Royal Society, 77, 157
Royal Statistical Society, 157, 198
Ruskin, John, 147, 184

Saint-Simonians, 167
Sakharov, Andrei, 334
Salamanca, school of, 60–2
Samuelson, Paul: and inflation,
    379; and Keynesian economics,
    258, 263; theory of efficient
    markets, 396; theory of public
    goods, 354–5; *Economics: An
    Introductory Analysis*, 370–1,
    395; *Foundations of Economic
    Analysis*, 287–9, 299, 316, 348
'satisficing', 362

Say, Jean-Baptiste, 117, 148, 156–7, 181

Schelling, Thomas, 323–4

Schlesiger, Karl, 284–5

Schmoller, Gustav, 193, 194, 197–8

scholasticism, 11, 43–9, 52, 60

Scholes, Myron, 404, 405

Schultz, Henry, 275

Schumacher, E. F., *Small is Beautiful*, 408

Schumpeter, Elizabeth Boody, 232

Schumpeter, Joseph Alois: and applied fields, 391; career and writings, 231–3; and the Great Depression, 251; at Harvard, 230, 287; structure of economics, 415–16, 417; *The Theory of Economic Development* (1912), 204, 231

Schwartz, Anna J., *A Monetary History of the United States, 1867–1960* (1963), 373–5

Scientific Revolution, 54–6

Scitovsky, Tibor, 316

Scotland, Enlightenment, 119–21

Second World War: national income accounting, 271–2; role of economists, 321–4, 327–9

Sen, Amartya, 352–3

Senior, Nassau, 156, 158, 159, 184

Seville, Atlantic trade (17th century), 69

Shiller, Robert, 396

Shubik, Martin, 295–6

Sidgwick, Henry, 303–4

Simon, Herbert, 325, 362

Simons, Henry, 253–4

Slutsky, Eugen, 276

Smith, Adam: on capitalist systems, 365; influence of French economic thinking, 117; and mercantilism, 11, 90, 140; moral philosopher, 3, 130; scepticism over Petty's *Political Arithmetick*, 81; *Theory of Moral Sentiments*, 130–2, 135–6; *Wealth of Nations*, 132–42, 144, 146, 147–8, 156, 163, 183, 414–15

Smith, Sir Thomas, *A Discourse of the Common Weal* (16th century), 62–4

Smith, Vernon, 395

social-choice theory, 349–53

socialism, 166, 183, 301–3, 308–12, 317–19

Socrates, 17–18

Solon, 16

Solow, Robert, 324, 379

Southey, Robert, 147

Soviet Union: Cold War, 334–5; collapse of, 337, 365, 392, 400; five-year plans, 329–30; mathematical economics, 333–4

Speenhamland System (1790s), 144

Spence, Michael, 363

Spencer, Herbert, 186

Spiethoff, Arthur, 204

Sraffa, Piero, 281

Stable Money League (*later* Association), 217, 250

Stackelberg, Heinrich von, 282

'stagflation', 298, 385

Stalin, Josef, 329–30

static theories, 211–12

statistical modelling, 276

Stern, Nicholas, 411
Steuart, Sir James, 125-30, 181
Stigler, George, 225, 345, 357, 361
Stiglitz, Joseph, 324, 363, 384, 401-2
Stockholm School, 242-3
Stoicism, 28
Stone, Richard, 271-2
Summers, Lawrence, 406
Sunstein, Cass, 396
supply and demand, 201, 299
Swedish school of economics, 242-3
Swift, Jonathan, 77, 80
systems analysis, 324

Taussig, Frank, 224, 281
Tawney, Richard, 307-8
Taylor, Fred M., 312
Taylor, Harriet, 166
Taylor, John, 388
Thaler, Richard, 396
Thales (Greek philosopher), 15
Thatcher, Margaret, 332, 387
Thirty Years War, 69-70, 75
Thomas of Chobham, 3, 44, 48-9
Thornton, Henry, *Paper Credit*, 160-2
Thünen, Johann Heinrich von, 182, 200, 265
Thurstone, L. L., 395
Tinbergen, Jan, 261, 276-8, 326, 370
Tobin, James, 324, 375-6, 389
Tooke, Thomas, 162, 266
Torrens, Robert, 151, 157
Toynbee, Arnold, 155, 199
transaction costs, 360-1
Tucker, Josiah, 113
Tudor England, 62-4

Tugan-Baranovsky, Mikhail Ivanovich, 177, 204
Tugwell, Rexford, 327
Tullock, Gordon, 339, 340
Turgot, Anne Robert Jacques, 107, 112-17
Tversky, Amos, 396

UN Industrial Development Organization (UNIDO), 337
Union of Radical Political Economy (URPE), 343
United Nations, 326, 329-30; *Human Development Report*, 353-4
United States of America: Civil Rights Act (1964), 332; Cold War, 334-5; development of economic thought, 207-9, 232-3; Equal Pay Act (1963), 332; Great Depression, 239-40, 251, 374, 376; influence of universities, 345, 346; monetary economics, 249-54; national income accounting, 269-70; New Deal, 327, 328; post-war growth, 238; War on Poverty, 332, 338-9
universities, establishment of, 43
usury, 25, 44, 48, 57, 61
Utilitarianism, 148-51, 188-9

value, theories of, 116
Veblen, Thorstein, 12, 217-21, 223
Venice, 69
Vienna Circle, 284
Vietnam war, 323-4, 332, 340, 384
Viner, Jacob, 5, 224, 225

Wald, Abraham, 284-5, 289, 290

Walras, Auguste, 190
Walras, Leon: and general
    equilibrium theory, 284; and
    mathematical economics, 188,
    189–93, 196–7, 200; and
    socialism, 302–3
Warburton, Clark, 270
Warming, Jens, 255
Washington consensus, 337,
    399–400, 401
wealth acquisition, 25–7, 33–6, 47
Webb, Beatrice and Sidney, 204
Weber, Max, 310, 311
Weitzman, Martin, 410–11
welfare economics, 315–17, 348–54
West, Edward, 151, 157
Westminster Review, 157
Wharton model, 372
Whewell, William, 186
Wicksell, Knut, 203, 235–8, 242–3,
    388, 389
Wieser, Friedrich von, 204
William of Auxerre, 45
William of Ockham, 56
William of Orange, 73
Williamson, John, 399–400

Williamson, Oliver, 360–1
Wilson, E. B., 287
Wollstonecraft, Mary, 144
women, in the history of
    economics, 12
    see also feminist economics
Woodford, Michael, *Interest and
    Prices* (2003), 384, 388
World Bank, 326–7, 330, 337, 398,
    399–400, 403
World Trade Organization (WTO),
    398, 400

Xenophon, 16, 18–20, 23, 25
*Economics of Biodiversity: The
    Dasgupta Review* (2021), 412
The Limits to Growth (Club of
    Rome; 1972), 408

Yellen, Janet, 384
Yom Kippur War, 332, 385
Young, Allyn, 224, 252, 254
Yule, George Udny, 275–6

Zeuthen, Frederik, 282